The Daily Telegraph

YACHTSMAN'S GUIDE
TO THE
CHANNEL HARBOURS
OF ENGLAND & FRANCE

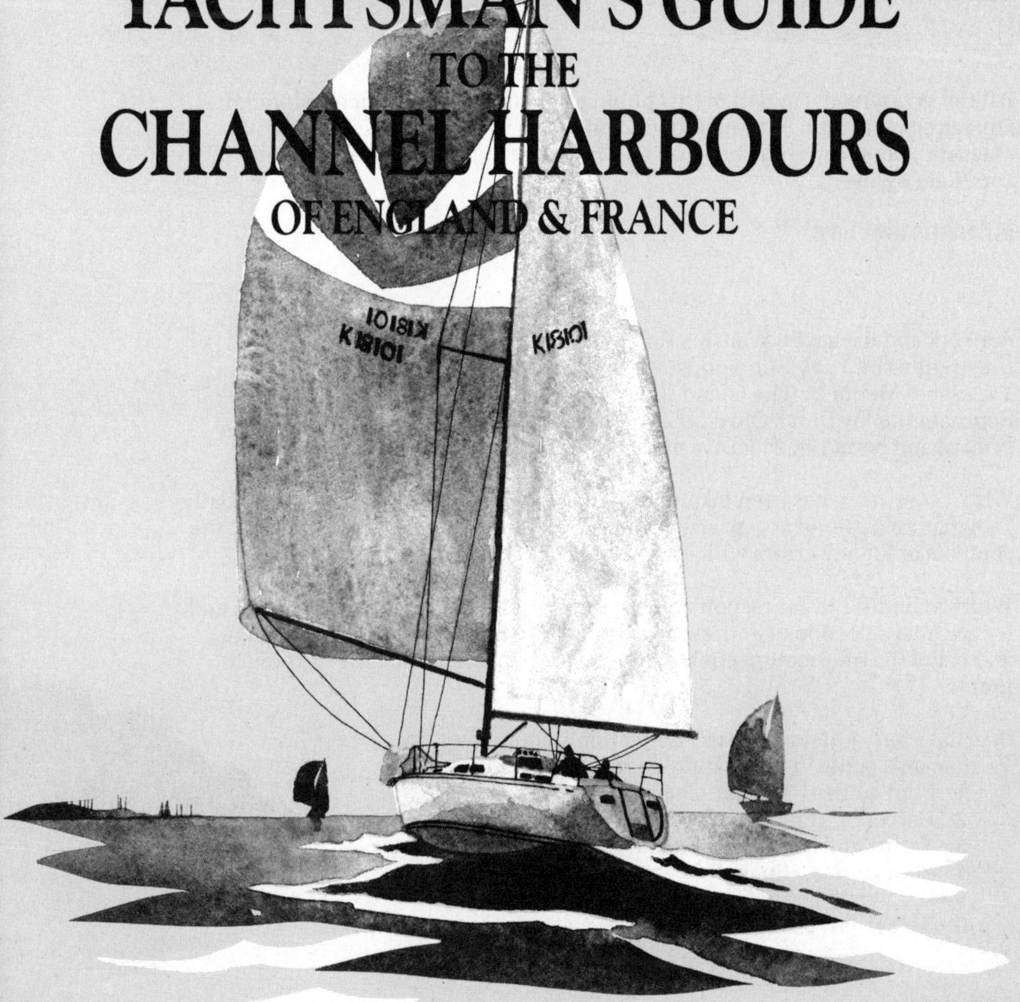

Copyright © 1987 White's Guides Ltd.
Published by White's Guides Ltd.
Island House
Moor Road
Chesham
Bucks HP5 1NZ.

Jointly with

Telegraph Publications
135 Fleet Street
London EC4P 4BL.

ISBN 0 86367 188 8

Artwork and design by Wensley Bown, Chesham Bucks.
Illustrations by Tony Simmonds, Amersham Bucks.
Typeset in Melior by The Island Graphics Company, Chesham Bucks.
Reproduction by Derek Croxson Ltd, Chesham Bucks.
Printed and bound by Mackays of Chatham Ltd.

British Library Cataloguing in Publication Data.
Yachtsman's guide to the channel harbours.
    1. Pilot guides – English Channel
    2. Harbours – England
    3. Yachts and Yachting – England
    4. Pilot guides – English Channel
    5. Harbours – France
    6. Yachts and yachting – France

I. Knox-Johnston, Robin
387.' 09422   VK841

The Daily Telegraph

YACHTSMAN'S GUIDE
TO THE
CHANNEL HARBOURS
OF ENGLAND & FRANCE

Edited by Robin Knox-Johnston

CONTENTS

GEOGRAPHIC PAGE LOCATION

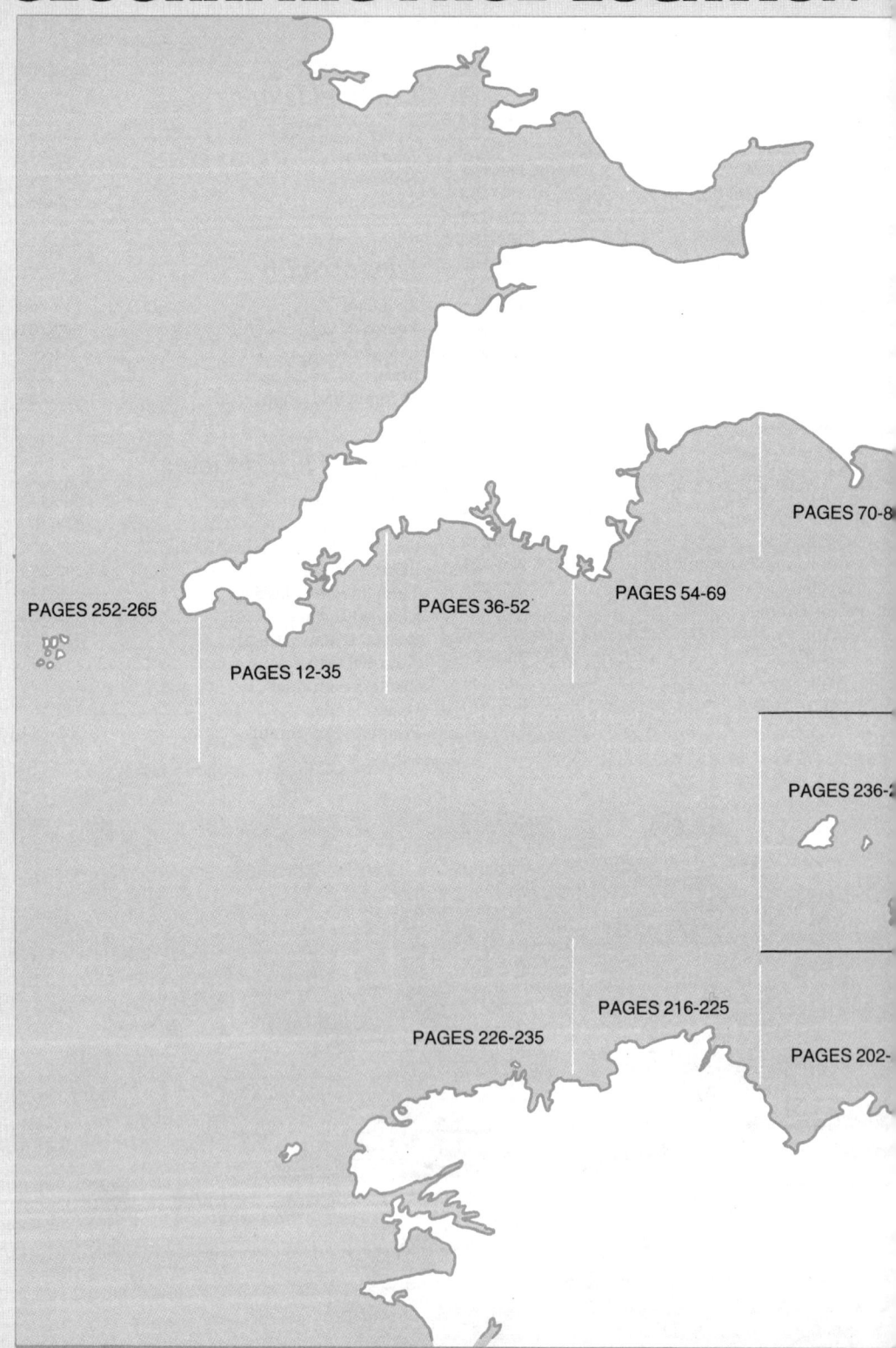

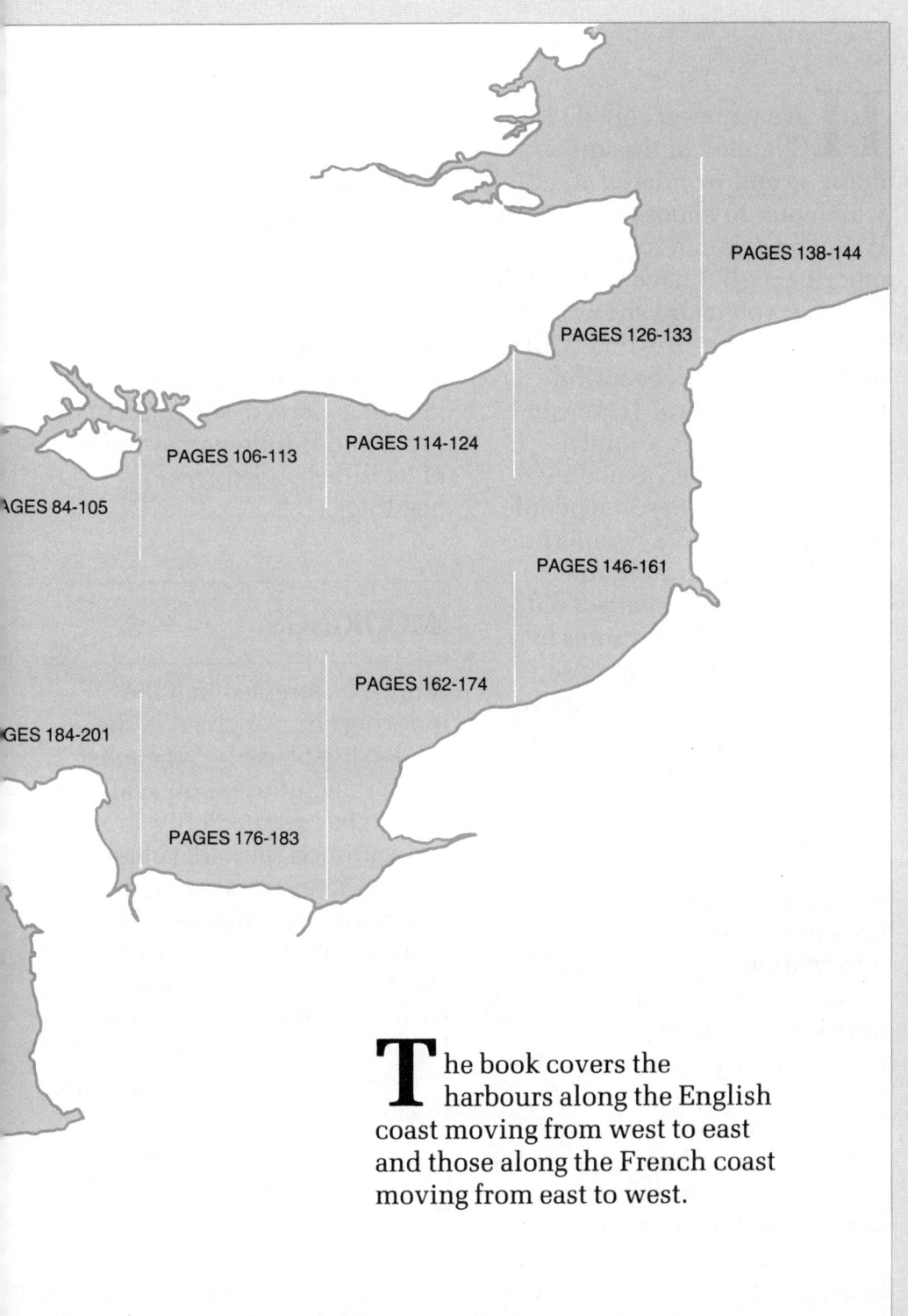

PAGES 138-144

PAGES 126-133

PAGES 106-113

PAGES 114-124

AGES 84-105

PAGES 146-161

PAGES 162-174

GES 184-201

PAGES 176-183

The book covers the harbours along the English coast moving from west to east and those along the French coast moving from east to west.

INTRODUCTION

Have you ever sailed in the Channel, or dreamt of doing so and wondered about which port to choose to moor in? Will it be difficult to find a mooring: will it have water and fuel; can you take a shower there; will it be crowded with tourists, peaceful, beautiful historic or modern? Have you ever visited a port, found a restaurant and had a mediocre meal, only to meet some people who tell you of this wonderful little place just around the corner? Have you ever got onto a mooring with five minutes to spare before the banks close, only to arrive just after they've shut since you could not find the way?

This guide has been produced to answer these questions and many more. The objective has been to provide as much information as possible about the shore facilities of harbours in the Channel, and to give the first-time visitor a general feel of the place and its main points of interest. The book covers the harbours along the English coast moving from west to east and those along the French coast moving from east to west. Each harbour is treated the same way.

The map on pages six and seven show the locations and for many of the harbours there are detailed maps showing the street layout with a numbered key showing places mentioned in the text.

Each harbour is treated in the same way. The introductory text gives a general description of the place and is followed by details of facilities under various headings.

MOORINGS

It must be stressed that the mooring charges given in the book whilst based on the most up-to-date information available, should be regarded only as an indication as they are subject to change. In most cases the charges quoted are based on a 35 foot monohull, but there are several instances where a harbour cannot accommodate a boat of this length. In these instances the charges shown and the length of boat that can use the mooring are specified. Charges are always shown in local currency.

RESTAURANTS

The restaurant guide has been compiled on the basis of personal visits and recommendations. The opinions are those of the inspectors, and in no instance was a restaurant aware that it was being inspected. It must be said that there are some harbours that simply do not have a restaurant you would choose to go to, and some where the best available would not merit an entry in any guide. In France the problem is rather different. Here, there are many average to good restaurants and quite a number of extremely good ones. In most cases this guide suggests the restaurant that in the inspectors' opinion was the best available. To help with the interpretation of French menus the publishers are indebted to Richard Binns, the best-selling author of several French travel books: his latest title is French Leave Favourites (Chiltern House Publishers).

PUBS

These have generally been chosen because of the warmth of their welcome and their atmosphere. An absence of fruit machines, pool tables and juke boxes was considered a definite plus.

Restaurants, pubs and the other facilities listed have all been chosen partly because of their convenience to the harbour. Wherever possible the criteria used has been 'within easy walking distance'. This has meant that some restaurants have not been included which in other circumstances would have been. Conversely, certain moorings are some distance away from the nearest town – Saltern's Marina, for example, is well away from Poole Quay and only the most determined would walk to the Poole Quay area from there. To help find the facilities listed, some of the entries are accompanied by street maps.

All the information is, to the best of our knowledge, correct at the time of writing. Inevitably there will have been some changes with time and we can only apologise if you find some information out of date or inaccurate.

At the back of the book are some pages where we invite your comments and any suggestions you may have. Please do use these pages as we would very much welcome your views.

It has taken well over a year to compile this guide and whilst it has been hard work it has also been very gratifying and enjoyable. If you find the result useful and your sailing trips the more enjoyable because of it, then it has all been worthwhile.

Patrick White
WHITE'S GUIDES LTD.

FOREWORD

One of the nicest things about cruising in a yacht is the opportunity that it provides to drop into port and relax for an evening – or longer. Most of the time the port will pick itself because of its convenience to the boat's position, or be chosen because a friend has recommended it.

Whilst this rather haphazard approach can provide some delightful surprises, it can lead to some disappointments as well.

Hence this guide, designed to take the chance out of a port visit. With it we hope you will be able to plan a more interesting voyage, and hopefully, find a few new places to visit that will make the cruise memorable.

Robin Knox-Johnston C.B.E., R.D.

MOUSEHOLE

This picture-postcard old Cornish fishing village with its neat tiered cottages and narrow winding alleys attracts many visitors in the summer months and is well worth visiting for its rugged beauty. The very small harbour dries out and the fishing boats make mooring in it even more limited. Visiting yachts can, however, anchor up outside the harbour when the conditions are right but it is advisable to contact the Harbour Master on arrival as there are some rocky outcrops close by.

Mousehole was a major fishing port until the development of Newlyn towards the end of the last century. It was from near here that the Spanish Armada was first sighted and a few years later Mousehole was sacked by troops from Spanish ships of the line. More recently the people of Mousehole suffered a major tragedy when in December 1981 the lifeboat *Solomon Browne* was lost when trying to rescue the crew of the *Union Star*. All eight lifeboatmen lost their lives and the coxswain was posthumously awarded the Gold Medal.

MOORINGS

Harbour Master. (0736) 731511
£3.00 per day.   £17.00 per week.

RESTAURANTS

The Lobster Pot:
South Cliff. (0736) 731251.
Overlooking the harbour, opposite its entrance, this little hotel converted from fishermen's cottages is a must for visitors in search of an outstanding meal in traditional surroundings. As it is small and during the summer the hotel is almost always full, booking is essential.
Credit Cards: Access, Amex, Visa.

PUBS

The Ship Inn:
A granite building on the quayside houses this fine old inn which dates back to the early 17th century. It was a favourite haunt of Dylan Thomas, who was living in Mousehole just before the Second World War. Many a seafaring yarn has been told in the flagstone bar, where you can get a wide variety of good bar food. Whilst it is unlikely that many yachtsmen will visit Mousehole in winter, if you happen to be there on 23 December try the famous local speciality of 'Starry Gazey Pie' which is served each year on that day.

HARBOUR SERVICES (YACHTS)

SERVICES AVAILABLE

● Petrol		● Water
● Diesel		☐ Slipway
☐ Calor Gas		☐ Chandlery
☐ Camping Gas		

HARBOUR SERVICES (PERSONAL)

Post Office: North Street.

POLICE: (0736) 62395

NEWLYN

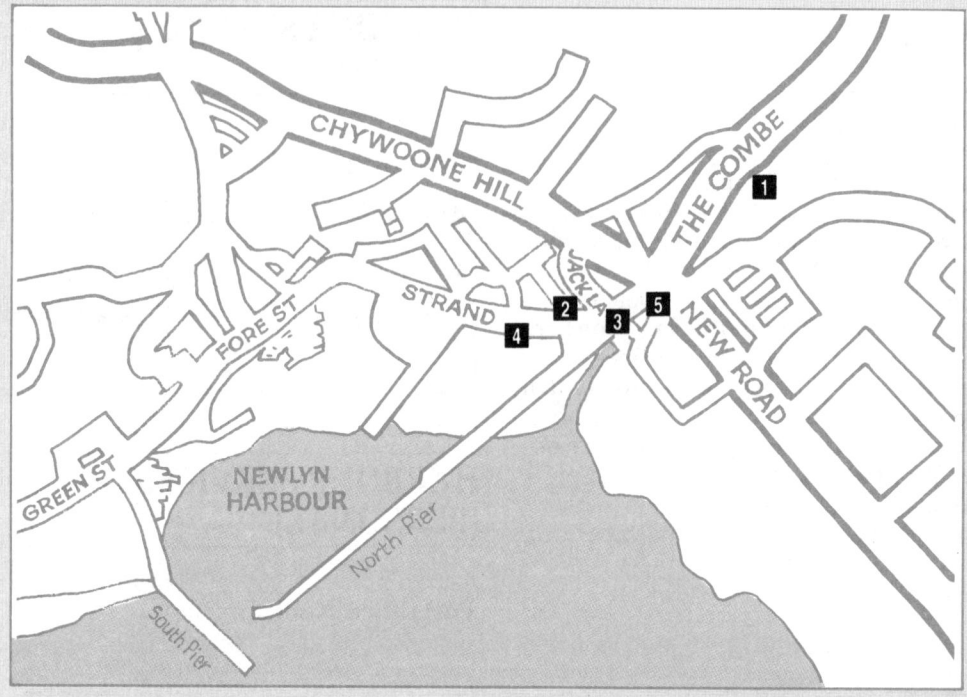

HARBOUR MASTER: (0736) 62523 or radio VHF Ch 16

T he fourth largest fishing port in the UK, Newlyn is the home base of upwards of 150 fishing boats. Its harbour is very busy and as a result there are no long-term moorings. Overnight moorings only are available and since these are limited, it is as well to contact the Harbour Master before arrival.

Fishing has always played a major role in the history of Newlyn so it might come as something of a surprise to find that at the turn of the century the town became a centre for artists,

later known as the Newlyn School. Works of theirs and more contemporary painters can be seen in the Newlyn Orion Gallery.

Newlyn can hardly be described as an attractive town from a

visitor's standpoint since it is very much a working port and there is a constant bustle of activity around the harbour. However it does provide a sheltered port accessible at all stages of the tide and is a good jumping-off point for the Scilly Isles and southern Ireland.

MOORINGS

Harbour Master. (0736) 62523
£3.22 per day.   £16.10 per week.

RESTAURANTS

1 The Meadery:
The Coombe. (0736) 65375.
This is a slightly bizarre restaurant which serves, in addition to the expected selection of drinks, a variety of meads. The atmosphere is Olde England, so 'Chicken in the Basket' becomes 'Chicken in the Rough'. A good place for a hearty evening.
No Credit Cards.

PUBS

2 The Swordfish:
The Strand (Foundry Lane and Orchard Place)
A long pub with several bars, popular with fishermen and visitors alike, it serves a range of bar food and a good selection of real ales.

HARBOUR SERVICES (YACHTS)

Mechanical Engineers:
C.K.Jones, North Pier. (0736) 63095.

Electronic Engineers:
Kernow Marine Electronics, 3 Duke Street. (0736) 68606.

Boat Builders & Repairers:
C.K.Jones, North Pier. (0736) 63095.

SERVICES AVAILABLE

- ● Petrol
- ● Diesel
- ☐ Calor Gas
- ☐ Camping Gas
- ● Water
- ● Slipway
- ☐ Chandlery

HARBOUR SERVICES (PERSONAL)

3 Post Office:
North Pier.

Laundry:
Newlyn Laundry, 4 New Road.

Taxi & Cars:
Stones Taxi (0736) 63400.
Dee Bee Car Hire (0736) 69100.

CHEMISTS AND MEDICAL SERVICES

Medical:
West Cornwall Hospital, St Clare Street. (0726) 62382.

BANKS

4 Barclays Bank: The Strand.

5 Lloyds: The Strand.

COASTGUARD: (0736) 87351
POLICE: (0736) 62395

PENZANCE

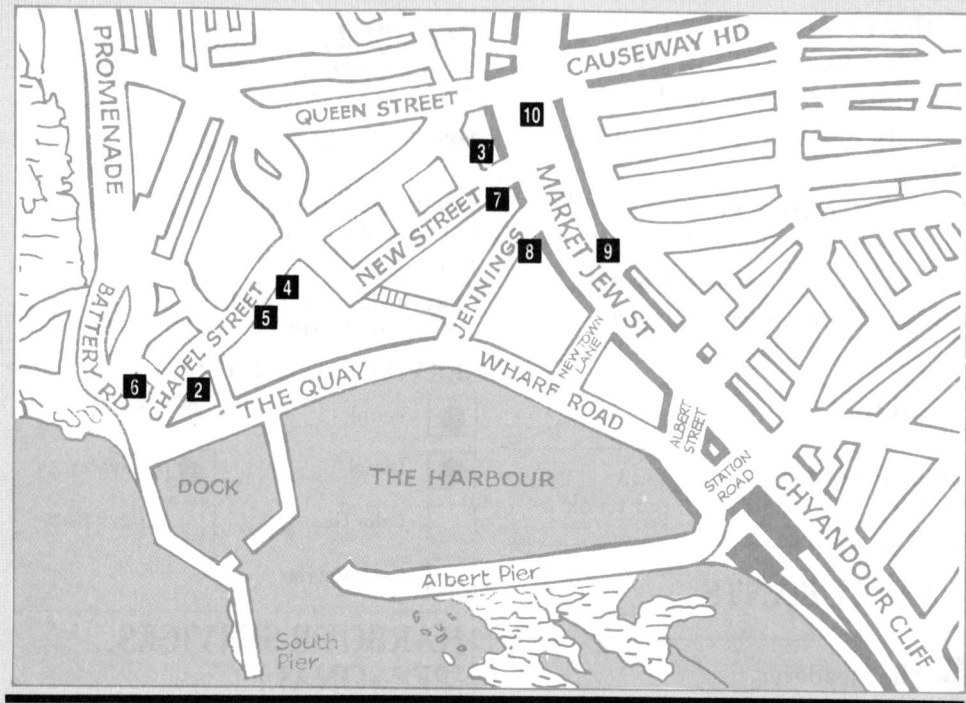

HARBOUR MASTER: (0736) 66113 or radio VHF Ch 16/12

This is a very busy market town and popular holiday resort. Blessed with a 'Mediterranean' climate, there is an abundance of palms in subtropical gardens, which with the close proximity of sheltered beaches attract many visitors.

Before the advent of the train in the mid-19th century, Penzance was a major centre for fishing and the tin trade. A walk along Market Jew Street will take you to the town hall, in front of which stands a statue of Sir Humphrey Davey whose name is synonomous with the miner's lamp. The most picturesque street is Chapel Street, where you will find a wide variety of architecture from small fishermen's cottages to the ornate Egyptian House. Here too you will find the Roland Morris Maritime Museum with many interesting treasures saved from the wrecks that abound along the Cornish coast.

Penzance is the westernmost harbour to offer shelter in all conditions and its suitability as a staging port for those on their way to Ireland or the Scilly Isles makes it very popular. As usual it is advisable to contact the Harbour Master even if anchoring outside the dock as Penzance is a busy port with many fishing boats and a daily ferry service to the Scilly Isles. Moorings are available in the dock at the direction of the Berthing Master and, if not scenically attractive, they are extremely convenient for the town centre.

MOORINGS

Harbour Master.
(0736) 661133
£5.23 per day.   £26.15 per week.

RESTAURANTS

1 The Baytree Restaurant:
Off Causeway Head. (0736) 68383.
A tiny alleyway leads up to this small wholefood restaurant. A terrace provides for outdoor eating in the summer and a large picture window gives the interior a spacious, airy feel. If you want quiche and salad, then this place will suit admirably.
Credit Cards: Access, Visa.

2 The Bosun's Locker:
Dock Lane. (0736) 66746.
A major attraction of this place for yachtsmen is its convenience. It faces the quay and is only a minute away from the visitors' moorings. The menu is extensive with many of the standard dishes you would expect and for a cheerful evening out with not far to go afterwards it has a great deal to recommend it.
Credit Cards: Access, Visa.

3 Harris's:
46 New Street. (0736) 64408.
It is essential to book here to avoid disappointment. Awarded two knives and forks by Michelin, this small, well-run restaurant provides simple but very well-prepared food. The menu changes frequently according to the availability of produce.
Credit Cards: Access, Amex, Diners, Visa.

PENZANCE Continued

4 Lally's:
Old Bakehouse Lane, off Chapel Street.
(0736) 63446.
The setting for this happy bistro is one
of its strong points. A little mews
almost opposite the famous Egyptian
House has been tastefully converted
and is now home to a number of bijou
businesses as well as Lally's. Friendly,
informal and not too expensive.
No Credit Cards.

PUBS

5 The Admiral Benbow:
Chapel Street. (0736) 63448.
This unique free house could easily fall
into the restaurant category since, as
well as a variety of bars, there are a
number of restaurants. Don't think that
this is a huge pub: imagine instead a
17th-century inn with a maze of rooms
and staircases, a great deal of
atmosphere, even a ghost, and you will
be close to the mark. The Great Cabin
restaurant is worth eating in if only for
the atmosphere, but add the fact that
the food is good and you can be certain
of a memorable meal. If time does not
allow, go for a drink and a sandwich,
but don't miss it.

6 The Dolphin Tavern: The Quay.
This old pub used to be on the seafront
until the land where the road runs was
reclaimed in the 19th century. A terrace
in the front for summer drinking and
granite floors in the bars help make this
a very popular watering hole for
visitors and locals alike. It is part of the
Dolphin's legend that the first tobacco
in England was smoked here when Sir
Walter Raleigh lit up on his return from
North America. On a more sinister
note, 'Bloody' Judge Jeffreys held court
in the pub.

HARBOUR SERVICES (YACHTS)

General: Penzance Chandlers, The Old
Smithy, Holmans Wharf, Rossbridge.
(0736) 66406.

Mechanical Engineers:
Albert Pier Engineering, Albert Pier.
(0736) 63566.

Electronic Engineers:
Kernow Marine Electronics, Newlyn.
(0736) 68606.

Sailmakers:
A.Mathews, Sail Loft, New Street.
(0736) 4008.

Boat Builders & Repairers:
Marine Sevices, Bread Street. (0736)
61995.

SERVICES AVAILABLE

● Petrol		● Water	
● Diesel		● Slipway	
● Calor Gas		● Chandlery	
● Camping Gas			

HARBOUR SERVICES (PERSONAL)

7 Post Office:
Market Jew Street.

Telephone:
Post Office.

Laundry:
Polyclean, 4 East Terrace.

Taxi & Cars:
Cares Taxis (0736) 67433.
Godfrey Davis (0736) 68338.

CHEMISTS AND MEDICAL SERVICES

8 **Chemists:**
Boots. 100-102 Market Jew Street.

Medical:
West Cornwall Hospital, St Clare Street. (0736) 62382.

BANKS

9 **Barclays:**
8-9 Market Jew Street.

10 **Lloyds:**
Market House, Market Jew Street.

Midland: 1 Green Market.

National Westminster:
31a Alverton Street.

TSB: 5 Green Market.
All have cash dispensers.

COASTGUARD: (0736) 87351
POLICE: (0736) 62395

ST MICHAEL'S MOUNT

It must be visited for its romance and drama but maybe from another harbour since not only does the harbour here dry out, it has no facilities for fuel. The Mount, which stands about 90 metres above sea level, is accessible at low water across a causeway from Marazion.

The tiny island with its castle has a long history dating back to Roman times, when it was known as Ictis. Edward the Confessor gave the Mount to Benedictine monks from Mont St Michel, who were thrown out when Henry IV decided to fortify the monastery. It remained a fortress till three quarters of the way through the 17th century when it was acquired by the St Aubyn family and it remained in the hands of successive generations until given to the National Trust some 30 years ago.

PORTHLEVEN

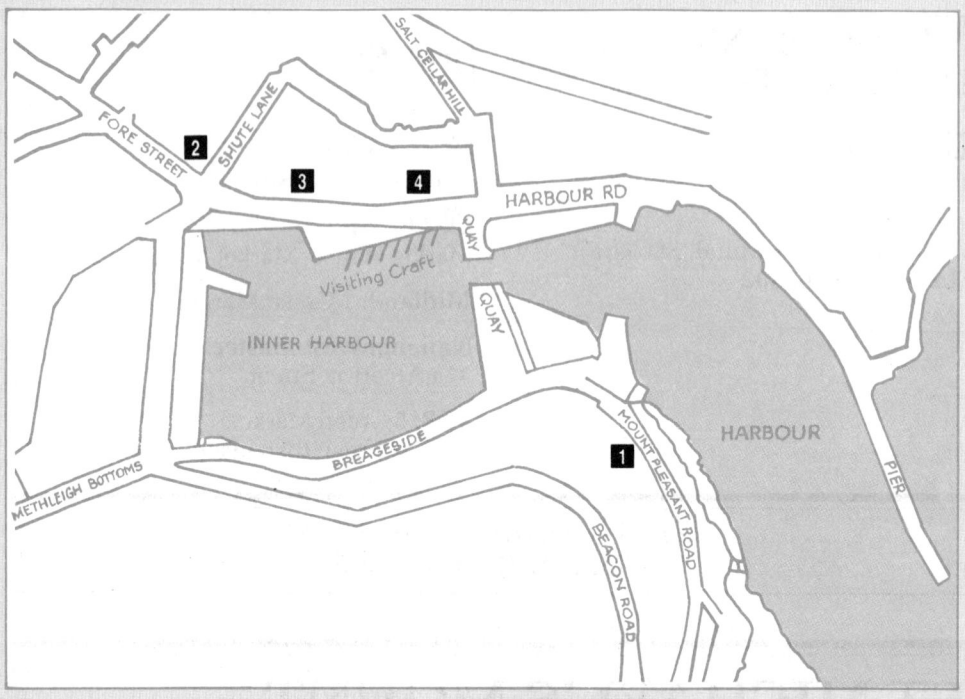

HARBOUR MASTER: (0326) 563042

The harbour here can be very tricky as it is exposed to the south and west. In rough weather the inner harbour is closed off and you might find your stay involuntarily extended. To further complicate matters the harbour dries out at low tide.

Porthleven is still a commercial port though not of the consequence it was at the beginning of the century. Originally built to import mining machinery and to export tin and copper, Porthleven today is an interesting reminder of that period. The Wesleyan Chapel is worth seeing as it typifies the ornate style of architecture so beloved by the Victorians.

MOORINGS

Contact Harbour Master.
(0326) 563042
£1.72 per day.   £9.00 per week.

PUBS

1 The Ship Inn:
This fine pub stands on the quayside by the outer harbour. From the public bar it is possible to enjoy the views out to sea and over the little port. Lots of traditional atmosphere, a warm welcome and good bar food, what more do you need? It is believed that this is the oldest building in the village and that it was standing here before the harbour was built.

HARBOUR SERVICES (YACHTS)

General: Porthleven Chandlery, Commercial Road.

Boat Builders & Repairers: Curnow Shipping.

SERVICES AVAILABLE

- ● Petrol
- ● Diesel
- ☐ Calor Gas
- ☐ Camping Gas
- ● Water
- ☐ Slipway
- ● Chandlery

CHEMISTS AND MEDICAL SERVICES

2 Chemists:
L. Rodgers, Fore Street.

BANKS

3 Barclays: Commercial Road.
4 Lloyds: Commercial Road.

POLICE: (0326) 562220

HELFORD RIVER

HARBOUR MASTER: (0326) 280422 or radio VHF Ch M

One of the most beautiful harbours in the south-west, Helford is understandably very popular with visitors from both sides of the Channel. The shelter is good except when the wind is from the east. As you enter the Helford River, the first mooring you come to is at Durgan, on the north bank. It is not perhaps a place to overnight at as there are few facilities but it is gorgeous to anchor off, take the dinghy to the beach and visit the tiny hamlet of Durgan. Walk up to the Glendurgan estate, now owned by the National Trust, and visit the gardens, which apart from the many tropical plants contain a maze.

Continuing upriver you come to Helford village on the south bank and Helford Passage on the north, which are connected by a foot-passenger ferry. Moorings here are under the control of the Helford boatyard on the southern shore and the Ferry Boat Inn on the northern. Beyond Helford Passage, to the west, lies Porth Navas on the edge of Porth Navas creek. This is the centre of the Duchy of Cornwall's oyster fisheries, where oysters have been farmed since Roman times. Further along the south bank and a little further west you come to Frenchman's Creek, made famous by Daphne du Maurier's novel of the same name.

Many of the creeks and the river's upper reaches are best visited by dinghy and they are worth taking the time to see. Yachtsmen often come here for a long stay and those who stop only overnight almost certainly plan to return for longer.

MOORINGS

Helford River Moorings.
Contact (0326) 280422.
£3.00 per day.   £18.00 per week.

Ferry Boat Inn. (0326) 250116.
£3.00 per day.   £18.00 per week.

Gweek Quay. (0326) 22657.
£7.00 per day.   £18.00 per week.

RESTAURANTS

Riverside:
(0326) 23443.
Arguably the West Country's and England's answer to the Roux brothers; in this instance the team is George Perry-Smith, Heather Crosbie and Joyce Molyneux, owners of the equally prestigious Carved Angel at Dartmouth. Abigail Iversen must not be left out as she and George Perry-Smith are responsible for the delights that emerge from the kitchen. The setting of the hotel must be one of the finest on the south coast and the thought of a pre-dinner drink overlooking the dreamy village and calm water of the Helford River on a warm summmer's evening is a pleasure indeed. The standard of the food and service has been recognised by the award of two knives and forks by Michelin. Clearly a must for anyone who takes eating seriously but booking is absolutely essential – and for this level of restaurant you must be prepared to pay. Open evenings only.

PUBS

The Shipwrights Arms:
(0326) 23235.
This is a very old pub dating back to the Middle Ages, superbly located and well worth a visit. Lunch and dinner are available during the summer months (lunch daily and dinner Thursday-Saturday during the winter). Good news for those intent on drinking real ale.

The Ferry Boat Inn:
Helford Passage.
A pub offering many amenities to yachtsmen, from moorings to showers and a launderette. Equally welcoming to those wanting a snack or a full meal in the restaurant.

HARBOUR SERVICES (YACHTS)

General: Quay Shop, Helford Boatyard.

Mechanical Engineers:
Helford Boatyard. (0326) 23232.

Boat Builders & Repairers:
Helford Boatyard. (0326) 23232.

SERVICES AVAILABLE

●	Petrol	●	Water
●	Diesel	●	Slipway
☐	Calor Gas	●	Chandlery
☐	Camping Gas		

HARBOUR SERVICES (PERSONAL)

Showers: Ferry Boat Inn.

Post Office: Helford Post Office and Stores.

Telephone: Post Office. Ferry Boat Inn.

Laundry: Ferry Boat Inn.

Taxi & Cars: OTS. (0326) 40703.

Yacht Clubs: Helford River Sailing Club. (0326) 23583.

COASTGUARD: (0326) 280221
POLICE: (0326) 72231

FALMOUTH

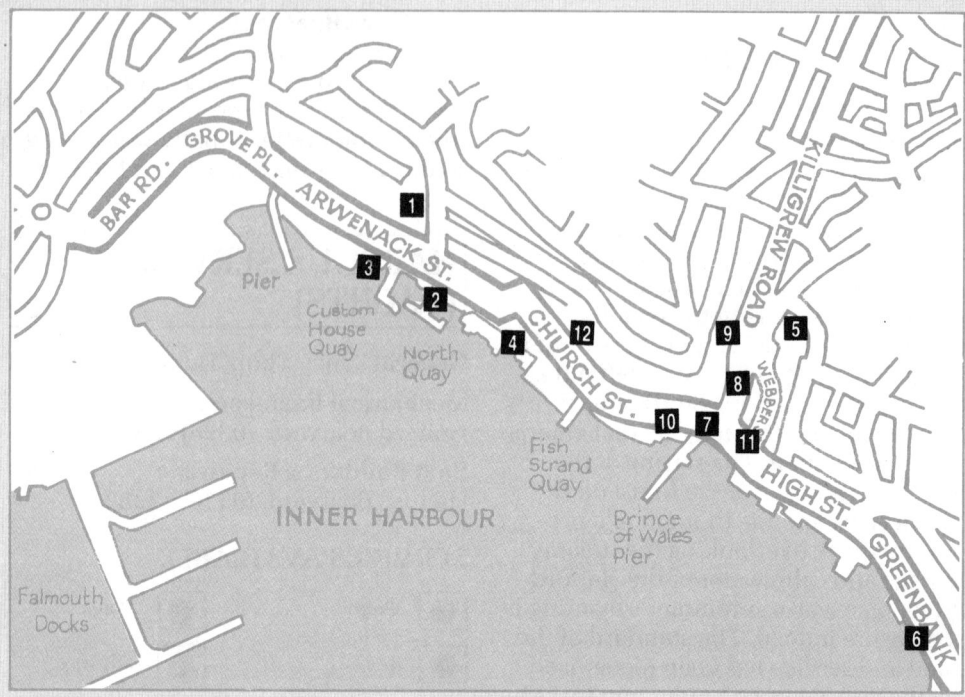

HARBOUR MASTER: (0326) 312285 or radio VHF Ch16/14

O ne of the finest natural harbours in the world, Carrick Roads provides everything a visiting yachtsman could require. It is completely sheltered from the elements, so you can sail on the extensive waters of the Roads even when there is a gale blowing outside. Also there is an abundance of choice for the visitor.

Falmouth itself is a large town of just under 20,000 inhabitants, beautifully situated on the south-west of Carrick Roads and

enjoying a warm climate, which make it very popular as a holiday resort. It owes its prosperity largely to Sir Walter Raleigh, who recognised the potential of Carrick Roads to provide shelter for his ships. His plan was put into action by a colleague, Sir Peter Killigrew, and Falmouth flourished as a port. For centuries it served as the base for packet ships, fast armed boats of about 200 tons, which under charter to the Royal Mail carried letters and post to Europe and across the Atlantic. With the advent of steam, the packets lost their contract to carry the mail, and this business was transferred to Southampton. Fortunately, by this time Falmouth was connected to London by rail and soon rose in popularity as a tourist resort. It remains the busiest port in Cornwall and takes some very large ships. In June 1968 Robin Knox-Johnston set sail in *Suhaili* from here to start his historic circumnavigation of the world. Three hundred and thirteen days later he returned to Falmouth stepping ashore at the Royal Cornwall Yacht Club jetty, the first man ever to have sailed non-stop around the world single-handed. This achievement is marked on the jetty with a small plaque on the spot he first set foot.

MOORINGS

Falmouth Harbour Commissioners.
(0326) 312285 VHF Ch 16, 14, 13, 12
£4.00 per day.   £20.00 per week.

Falmouth Yacht Marina.
(0326) 316620 VHF Ch M (37)
£9.00 per day.   £45.00 per week.

Royal Cornwall Yacht Club, Harbourside.
(0326) 311105
£4.00 per day.   £20.00 per week.

RESTAURANTS

1 Hannan:
Arwenack Street.
A friendly, comfortable, tandoori restaurant with a take-away service but it is worth saving the effort and eating on the premises.
Credit Cards: Access, Amex, Diners, Visa.

2 The Seafood Bar:
Quay Hill. (0326) 315129.
Falmouth does not possess a wide selection of really good restaurants, so it is a special pleasure to find one where the ambiance and food are really worth recommending. Hidden away down a side street off Arwenack Street, this tiny restaurant offers an interesting range of fish dishes as well as some standard steaks for those not interested in fish. Very relaxed yet attentive service makes this a must for those lucky enough to secure a table: moral – book.

FALMOUTH Continued

PUBS

4 **The Chain Locker:**
Custom House Quay.
Maybe the answer to some people's dreams of what a seamen's pub should be: a stone floor, bay windows overlooking the harbour and a mass of maritime artefacts. This is a very busy place during the season, though the terrace on the quayside provides additional space in summer.

5 **The Grapes Inn:**
Church Street.
A well-modernised pub with plenty of seating. Real ale, good bar food and a pleasant atmosphere. Worth a visit.

HARBOUR SERVICES (YACHTS)

General: West Country Chandlers, 39 High Street.

Mechanical Engineers:
Robin Curnow, Commercial Road, Penryn. (0326) 73438.

Electronic Engineers:
Western Electronic Services. (0326) 317728.

Sailmakers:
Penrose Sailmakers Ltd, 50 Church Street. (0326) 312705.

Boat Builders & Repairers:
Falmouth Boat Construction Ltd, Flushing. (0326) 74309.

SERVICES AVAILABLE

- ● Petrol
- ● Diesel
- ● Calor Gas
- ● Camping Gas
- ● Water
- ● Slipway
- ● Chandlery

HARBOUR SERVICES (PERSONAL)

Showers: Visitors Yacht Haven. Falmouth Marina. R.C.Y.C.

6 **Post Office:**
Main Post Office, The Moor.

Telephone: Post Office.
Royal Cornwall Yacht Club.
Falmouth Marina.

Laundry:
Cornish Linen Services, 47 Church Street.

Taxi & Cars:
A.1 Cabs (0326) 312404.
Godfrey Davis (0326) 312192.

7 **Yacht Clubs:**
Royal Cornwall Yacht Club. (0326) 312126.

CHEMISTS AND MEDICAL SERVICES

Chemists:
Boots. 47-49 Market Street.

Inns and Taylor. 115 Killigrew Street.

Medical:
Falmouth Hospital, Trescobeas Road. (0326) 311841.

BANKS

8 **Barclays:** 6 Killigrew Street.

9 **Lloyds:** 11-12 Killigrew Street.

10 **Midland:** 46 Market Street.

11 **National Westminster:**
4 Killigrew Street.

12 **TSB:** Church Street.

COASTGUARD: (0326) 317575 or radio VHF Ch 16/67
POLICE: (0326) 72231

MYLOR

Going up the estuary of the Penryn River you come to Mylor yacht harbour on the western side. Previously a Royal Navy dockyard, it was used during the Second World War as a base for Free French Resistance operations and for the building of D-Day landing craft. Nearby are the villages of Mylor Bridge, accessible at high water by dinghy, and Mylor Churchtown, where St Mylor's Church is well worth a visit. Saint Melor is reputed to be buried by the cross after his martyrdom in the 5th century.

Also accessible at high water is Restronguet, where quite large boats can anchor off or moor up to the pontoon by the Pandora Inn for two hours at high tide.

MOORINGS

Mylor Yacht Harbour.
(0326) 72121
£4.60 per day.   £23.00 per week.

Restronguet Creek, Pandora Inn.
(patrons at high tide only).

RESTAURANTS

The Ganges:
(0326) 74320.
Right by the yacht harbour, this lively restaurant enjoys panoramic views over the water and its location makes it extremely convenient for yachtsmen. Perhaps needless to say, fish is the speciality of the house and lemon sole in particular.

PUBS

The Pandora Inn:
Restronguet Creek. (0326) 72678.
This wonderful thatched waterside inn, part of which dates back to the 13th century, should be visited by anyone on Carrick Roads for the first time. Once you have come here, the chances are that you will return. There are several bars downstairs and a restaurant on the first floor, all enjoying splendid views over the Roads. The pub got its name from *HMS Pandora*, whose master, Captain Edwards, took

over the inn on his dismissal from the service after he ill advisedly put the ship on a reef. It was *HMS Pandora* under the command of Edwards which was sent to rescue the 'loyal' crew of the *Bounty*.

Although it is possible to moor up to the pontoon at high water, a trip here in the dinghy is probably a better idea since you will be able to stay longer. Care should be taken when mooring as the beach around the inn is private property and oysters are farmed in the vicinity, so the owners rightly object to dinghies being left on or dragged over their land.

HARBOUR SERVICES (YACHTS)

General: Mylor Yacht Harbour has all facilities.

SERVICES AVAILABLE

- ● Petrol
- ● Diesel
- ● Calor Gas
- ● Camping Gas
- ● Water
- ● Slipway
- ● Chandlery

HARBOUR SERVICES (PERSONAL)

Showers: Mylor Yacht Harbour.

Post Office: P.O. Box at the Yacht Harbour.

Telephone: At the Yacht Harbour.

Laundry: At the Yacht Harbour.

Taxi & Cars:
A.1 Cabs (0326) 311841.
Godfrey Davis (0326) 312192.

Yacht Clubs:
Mylor Yacht Club. (0326) 74391.

CHEMISTS AND MEDICAL SERVICES

Chemists:
Boots. 47-49 Market Street, Falmouth.
Inns and Taylor. 115 Killigrew Street. Falmouth.

Medical:
Falmouth Hospital, Trescobeas Road (0326) 311841

POLICE: (0326) 72231

ST JUST-IN-ROSELAND

For those wanting to be away from it all St Just must be the ideal mooring. This creek is situated on the eastern side of the River Fal and provides some deepwater moorings. The church of St Just, fringed by subtropical trees, is regarded by many as the most beautiful in England and it would be a shame not to seize the chance to visit it. If going by water, it is probably best visited by dinghy.

POLICE: 0326 788420

ST MAWES

Reputed to be the warmest place in the United Kingdom, St Mawes has long enjoyed a reputation as an up-market holiday resort. This situation has changed somewhat; one of the major hotels is now run for package holiday-makers and there is a slightly tarnished air about the place. But it remains a quite un-commercial town compared to its neighbour Falmouth across the estuary.

There are records of a settlement existing at St Mawes for many hundreds of years but until Henry VIII built the castle here it was too susceptible to enemy attack to flourish. Once the castle was built, St Mawes enjoyed a period of some prosperity under Queen Elizabeth I and it acquired a royal charter and two Members of Parliament. After the Civil War St Mawes maintained its position for some years but with the development of Falmouth it started to slip into commercial obscurity, only to re-emerge as the holiday resort and retirement centre that it is today.

MOORINGS

Harbour Master.
(0326) 270553
£3.00 per day.   £21.00 per week.

Freshwater Boatyard.
(0326) 270443
£4.00 per day.   £28.00 per week.

St Mawes Sailing Club.
(0326) 270686
£3.00 per day.   £21.00 per week.

RESTAURANTS

Idle Rocks Hotel:
Tredeham Road. (0326) 270771.
It is impossible to miss this superbly located hotel which faces directly on to the sea and has an attractive terrace that provides an ideal setting for a pre-meal drink. Because of its popularity it is usually full during the season, so booking is advisable.
Credit Cards: Access, Amex, Diners, Visa.

The Rising Sun Inn:
The Quay. (0326) 270233.
This is a traditional, privately run hotel whose owner knows her clientèle and they repay her by returning year after year. The comfortable bar to the right as you enter has the sort of cocktail party atmosphere you might expect in a place full of local regulars, with plenty of sailing club ties in evidence. Bar snacks are available for those not wishing to make use of the small dining room where you will be served traditional, unfussy food from a small menu at reasonable prices.
Credit Cards: Access, Amex, Diners, Visa.

PUBS

The Victory:
Situated just off the quay, this is a charming traditional pub with a relatively small bar that is comfortable and warm. Bar snacks are available.

HARBOUR SERVICES (YACHTS)

General: Top Sail, 4 The Arcade.

Mechanical Engineers:
Freshwater Boatyard. (0326) 270443.

Boat Builders & Repairers:
Freshwater Boatyard. (0326) 270443.

SERVICES AVAILABLE

☐ Petrol		● Water	
● Diesel		● Slipway	
● Calor Gas		● Chandlery	
● Camping Gas			

HARBOUR SERVICES (PERSONAL)

Showers: St Mawes Sailing Club.
Post Office: St Mawes Post Office.
Telephone: St Mawes Post Office.

CHEMISTS AND MEDICAL SERVICES

Chemists:
G.S. and E.M. Heath. 3 Marine Parade.

BANKS

Barclays: 4-5 Marine Parade.
Lloyds: 3 The Quay.
National Westminster:
Castle Cottage, The Quay.

POLICE: (0326) 270222

MEVAGISSEY

I t is extremely difficult for a visiting yachtsman to find a berth here so a call to the Harbour Master is strongly recommended. The lack of moorings is a shame as this little fishing village would otherwise undoubtedly attract a great number of yachtsmen. As it is, Mevagissey attracts more than its fair share of land-based visitors during the summer and its traditional activity of pilchard fishing has given way to bijou shops catering to the tourists. None of this can take away the charm of the village, among the most photographed in the country.

RESTAURANTS

Mr Bistro:
East Quay. (0726) 842432.
There is a beautiful view over the harbour from this small fish restaurant, which has succeeded in avoiding the temptation to go 'simple' with fish and chips and provides a well-chosen selection of fresh fish and shellfish, interestingly prepared and pleasantly served.
Credit Cards: Access, Amex, Diners, Visa.

MOORINGS

Contact Harbour Master.
(0726) 843305
£3.00 per day.   £21.00 per week.

Wit's End:
1 Polkirt Hill. (0726) 842174.
An interesting menu awaits anyone visiting this pleasantly decorated restaurant. Dishes like Walnut and Mustard Steak and Burgundy Lamb are among the more interesting and if you are fed up with the sight of water it is perfectly located, close to the quay but out of sight of the harbour.

PUBS

The King's Arms:
Fore Street.
A very comfortable, large pub refurbished in traditional style and serving a wide variety of bar snacks and, for those wanting more, steaks and sea food. It is very attractive and worth a visit, but it gets very busy during the summer.

HARBOUR SERVICES (YACHTS)

General: G. Mitchell and Sons, Port Mellon. (0726) 842407.

Boat Builders & Repairers:
G. Mitchell and Sons, Port Mellon. (0726) 84207.

SERVICES AVAILABLE

- ● Petrol
- ● Diesel
- ● Calor Gas
- ● Camping Gas
- ● Water
- ● Slipway
- ● Chandlery

CHEMISTS AND MEDICAL SERVICES

Chemists:
D.J. Boyle, 3 Fore Street.

BANKS

Barclays: Fore Street.

Lloyds: Fore Street.

Midland: Market Square.

COASTGUARD: (0726) 842353
POLICE: (0726) 842262

FOWEY

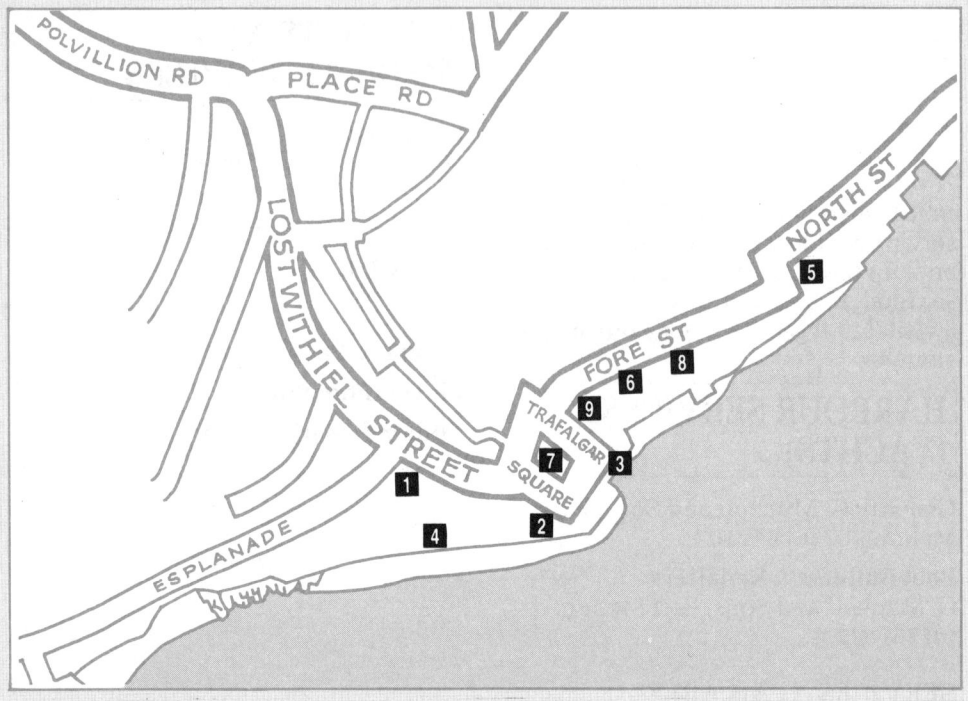

HARBOUR MASTER: (072 683) 2471 or radio VHF Ch16/12

A warm welcome is extended to visiting yachtsmen here. The moorings are sheltered except when the wind is from the south and if the swell becomes too strong, you will be given a chance to move upstream into more sheltered water. All the moorings are offshore but there is a dinghy park by Albert Quay and a water taxi (VHF Ch 16) is available to those who prefer being chauffeur-driven. Fowey itself is a very attractive town and whilst popular with visitors, it has

somehow succeeded in maintaining its charm. No modern eyesores here. It is a delightful place, and a good base from which to sail the west country.

The marvellous facility of the deepwater harbour has meant that Fowey has always been commercially involved with the sea. Even in mediaeval times there are records of tin being shipped from here to France. Around this period the 'Fowey Gallants' came into being, men who sailed the seas with apparent immunity, combining trade, piracy and the ferrying of pilgrims to the shrine of St James in Spain with equal equanimity. In later centuries Fowey became more law-abiding as its trade and military significance developed, and it received royal charters from Elizabeth I, James II, and William and Mary. After the Napoleonic Wars the military importance of Fowey declined but fortunately trade in china clay started to prosper and today this is the single most important export from the port. Consequently, ships of considerable size come into Fowey to berth at the commercial jetties just to the north of the town. There is a swing area for these ships almost opposite Albert Quay so care needs to be taken when mooring. However, you will probably be met at the entrance and helped to a mooring.

Generally, you will moor on the Polruan side of the estuary and whilst Fowey is the attraction for most people, Polruan itself is worth a visit. It does not have the shopping and banking facilities of Fowey but there are some pleasant pubs and one particularly apt restaurant for yachtsmen.

MOORINGS

Fowey Harbour Contact Harbour Master.
(072 683) 2471.
£5.00 per day.   £22.00 per week.

Alan Toms. (072 687) 232.
£1.00 per day.   £7.00 per week.

RESTAURANTS

1 Cordon Bleu:
3 The Esplanade. (072 683) 2359.
The mood is created with pre-dinner drinks in a Victorian style sitting-room before sitting down for an excellent meal in their period dining-room. The menu provides something for everybody at a reasonable price. Credit Cards: Access, Amex, Diners, Visa.

FOWEY Continued

2 **Food for Thought:**
4 Town Quay. (072 683) 2221.
Booking is essential at this quayside
restaurant, which has been awarded
two knives and forks by Michelin,
perhaps worth it for the location alone.
The small cane-furnished bar that
greets you on entering looks most
attractive, although the cane seats can
get uncomfortable if you stay any
length of time before going to your
table. However, the meal that awaits
you will soon make up for this rather
minor inadequacy. A relatively small
menu provides a selection that will suit
the most discerning palate and the food
is charmingly served in a quiet,
efficient way. Very well worth visiting.
Credit Cards: Access, Visa.

The Waterfront Bistro and Wine Bar:
West Street, Polruan. (072 687) 428.
Hidden away down a flight of stone
stairs but easily located from the
estuary, this very friendly large bistro is
the answer to many a yachtsman's
dreams. It must possess the finest
location in the area and has a large
waterside terrace with beautiful views
over to Fowey and, if the weather lets
you down, the restaurant and bar have
large picture windows so your
enjoyment of the situation is
unimpaired. You can moor your dinghy
at the restaurant's own dinghy park and
the owners understand and accept
yachtsmen tend to come ashore in
oilies and wellies. Last and not least,
there is a menu that enables you to give
children a hamburger whilst you eat
freshly caught scallops cooked in a
light wine sauce. Add the fact that you
do not have to rush off to a cashpoint
and you have one of the best general
restaurants on the south coast.

PUBS

3 **The King of Prussia:**
Town Quay.
This large 200-year-old pub dominates
the Town Quay and serves real ale and
bar food. Very busy during the season.

The Lugger Inn:
The Quay, Polruan.
This very small, traditional old pub is a
must if you want a pint of bitter with
the locals. Certainly in no way is it
pretentious.

The Russell Inn:
West Street, Polruan.
Just up a flight of stairs from the
quayside, this is another genuine
locals' pub where most of the people in
the bar seem to earn their living from a
connection with the sea.

HARBOUR SERVICES (YACHTS)

General: Upper Deck Marine, Albert
Quay.
Troy Chandlers, 10 Lostwithiel Street.
(072 683) 3265.
Ship Shape, Fore Street, Polruan. (072
687) 473.
Mechanical Engineers:
C.Toms Boatyard, Toms Yard, East
Street. (072 687) 232.
Boat Builders & Repairers:
C.Toms Boatyard, Toms Yard, East
Street. (072 687) 232.

SERVICES AVAILABLE

Petrol		Water	
● Diesel		● Slipway	
● Calor Gas		● Chandlery	
● Camping Gas			

HARBOUR SERVICES (PERSONAL)

4 **Showers:** Royal Fowey Yacht Club.

5 **Post Office:** Fore Street.

Telephone:
Post Office. Royal Fowey Yacht Club.

Laundry:
Dhobi Room, 10 Passage Street.

Taxi & Cars:
C.A. Baseley. (072 683) 3385.

4 **Yacht Clubs:**
Royal Fowey Yacht Club, Whitford Yard. (072 683) 3573.

CHEMISTS AND MEDICAL SERVICES

6 **Chemists:**
John W. Howlett, 18 Fore Street.

Medical:
Fowey Hospital, Green Lane. (072 683) 2241.

BANKS

7 **Barclays:** Trafalgar Square.

8 **Lloyds:** Fore Street.

9 **Midland:** Fore Street.

COASTGUARD: (072 687) 228
POLICE: (072 683) 3438

POLPERRO

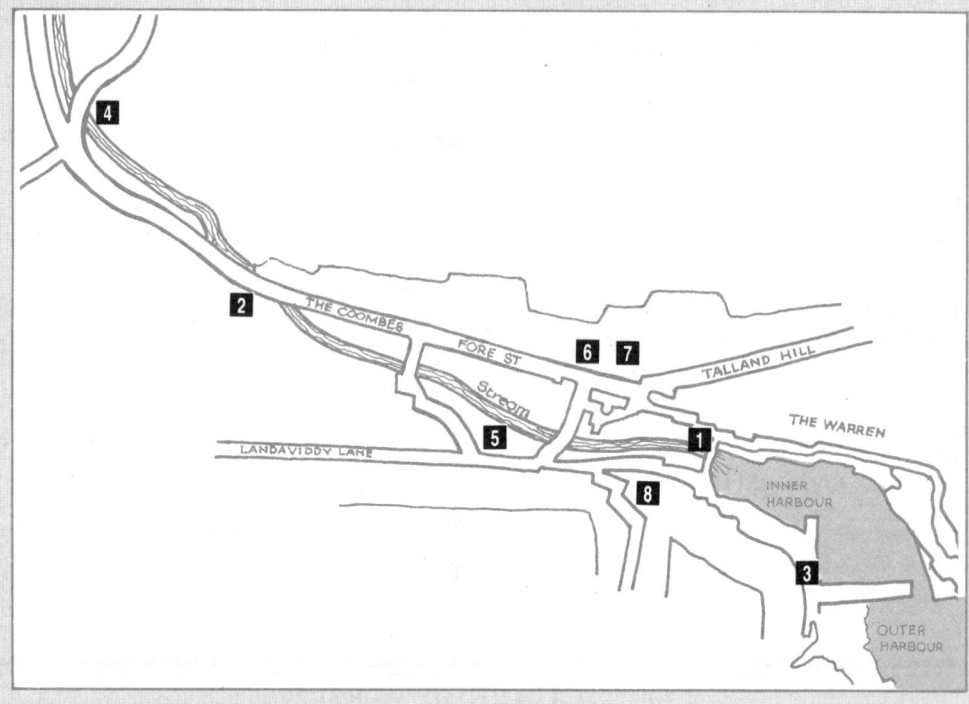

I t is difficult to know what to say about this old Cornish fishing village. If – and for a yachtsman this is most unlikely – you were to come here in December you would see a village of breathtaking beauty. Little streets wind their way to the small harbour flanked by whitewashed cottages, whilst at the harbour itself a few fishermen may be seen quietly attending to their boats. In summer this tranquillity is lost as thousands of holiday visitors arrive, cramming the little streets as they walk down from the vast car-park that stands at the entrance to the village. The result is that everywhere is busy, the pubs and restaurants full to overflowing.

The harbour here dries out, so visiting yachtsmen have to anchor outside if the weather permits. Because Polperro does not set itself up to cater for yachtsmen, you have to decide if the intrinsic beauty of the place is worth the hassle you will have on arrival.

RESTAURANTS

1 The House on Props:
Talland Street. (0503) 72310.
Architects and historians will love this beautiful restaurant built partially over the stream that flows into the harbour, the supporting wooden props giving it its name. The menu is one you will find replicated all over the country, which may be appropriate if you are attracting visitors from everywhere but can also be rather boring.
Credit Cards: Access, Visa.

2 The Kitchen:
The Coombes. (0503) 72780.
A very small restaurant, with pine tables and chairs and an earnest approach. Anyone taking the trouble to walk up the hill is unlikely to be disappointed by the food. Reservations are essential.
Credit Cards: Access, Amex, Diners, Visa.

PUBS

3 Blue Peter Inn:
By Fish Quay.
Apparently this is the smallest pub in Polperro, which given the number of visitors that Polperro attracts may or may not be a good thing. If you can catch it in a quiet moment, you will find a delightful old pub, with a pleasant bar and plenty of atmosphere.

4 The Crumplehorn Inn:
The Coombes.
A brisk 10-minute walk from the harbour brings you to this fine pub at the top of the town. A very attractive bar with a small restaurant leading off it provides a warm welcome to all visitors. Bar food and full meals are available.

5 Noughts and Crosses:
Lansallos Street.
Many years ago this was a bakery. Its name derives from the custom of one of its owners who noted the supply of a small loaf with a small nought, a large one with a large nought and payment for them with a cross. Today it is a charming pub which, even though quite large, gets very crowded in the season.

HARBOUR SERVICES (PERSONAL)

6 Post Office: Fore Street.

BANKS

7 Barclays: Fore Street.

8 Midland: Lansallos Street.

LOOE

It is doubtful if people living here at the turn of the century would recognise the town today. What used to be a quiet fishing village typical of Cornwall has given way to a brash holiday resort. The old streets are now filled with cafes, amusement arcades and fast food bars.

Looe, divided in two by the River Looe, has long been an important fishing port and whilst fishing now takes second place to tourism, it remains significant to the town's economy. West Looe, which is where visitors' moorings are to be found, is the smaller of the two parts. Most of the action is in East Looe and a walk into the little streets behind the jetty here gives a glimpse of the town as it was, although you may ask yourself if it was really worth it.

HARBOUR SERVICES (YACHTS)

General: Jack Bray and Son, The Quay. (050 36) 2504.

SERVICES AVAILABLE

●	Petrol	●	Water
●	Diesel	☐	Slipway
●	Calor Gas	●	Chandlery
●	Camping Gas		

MOORINGS

Harbour Master. (050 36) 2839
£8.85 per day.   £35.45 per week.

HARBOUR SERVICES (PERSONAL)

Showers:
Looe Sailing Club, Buller Street, East Looe.

Post Office:
Fore Street, East Looe.

Telephone:
Looe Sailing Club.

Taxi & Cars:
Looe Taxis. (050 36) 2405.

Yacht Clubs:
Looe Sailing Club. (050 36) 2559.

CHEMISTS AND MEDICAL SERVICES

Chemists:
Boots. Fore Street, East Looe.

BANKS

Barclays: Fore Street, East Looe.

Lloyds: Fore Street, East Looe.

Midland: Higher Market Street, East Looe.

**COASTGUARD: (050 36) 2138
POLICE: (050 36) 2233**

PLYMOUTH

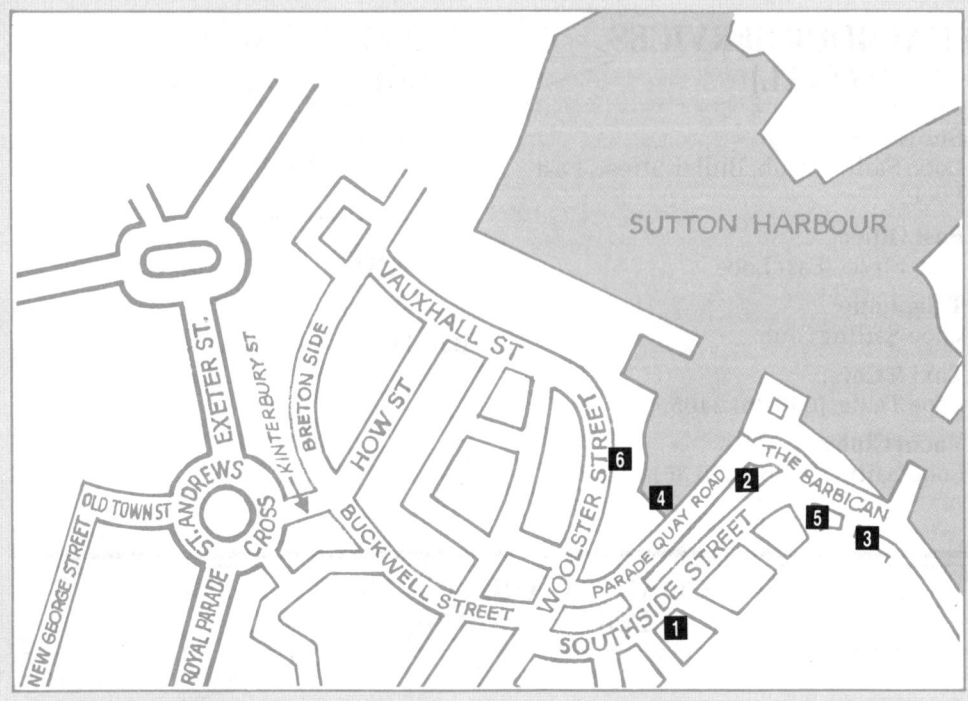

HARBOUR MASTER: (0752) 663225 or radio VHF 16

Plymouth, incorporating Stonehouse, Devonport, Plymstock and Plympton, is the largest city west of Bristol. For centuries it has been a major naval port, associated with many famous sea voyages and personalities. It was the base for the seafaring exploits and journeys of discovery of the great Elizabethan sea captains, Drake, Raleigh, Hawkins and Frobisher, and from here Drake set sail in 1588 to defeat the Spanish Armada. A little later, in 1620, the Pilgrim Fathers embarked for the New World from the steps which can still be seen at the Barbican. More recently, Plymouth saw the departure and return of the late Sir Francis Chichester when he made his solo circumnavigation of the world. More recently still Operation Corporate, the Falkland's task force, assembled and sailed from Plymouth.

Surprisingly, given the heavy bombing Plymouth suffered during the Second World War, there are still many fine old buildings to see. The Merchant's House in St Andrew's Street is a splendid example; built by a privateer, William Parker, during the 16th century it has been restored to its former glory and is now a museum of Plymouth History. A few yards from the Merchant's House is 15th-century Prysten House, which is now also a museum, with exhibits relating to the *Mayflower*.

The whole district around Sutton Harbour known as the Barbican has been kept in its true character. This was once the main port area and whilst the cobbled streets no longer hum with commercial traffic, you can still find the fish market on the quayside though all around are restaurants, bistros, wine bars and pubs. Those mooring at Sutton Marina have all of this on their doorstep and the main city centre just a five-minute walk away.

MOORINGS

Mayflower Marina. (0752) 556633
£11.00 per day.   £55.00 per week.

Sutton Marina, Sutton Harbour.
(0752) 664186 VHF Ch 16,37.
£9.00 per day.   £36.00 per week.

Queen Anne's Battery. (0752) 671142
£10.06 per day.   £50.31 per week.

RESTAURANTS

1 **Hosteria Romana:**
58 Southside Street, The Barbican.
(0752) 668827.
An Italian restaurant where you find a nearby table occupied by visiting Italian businessmen must have a lot to be said for it. Situated at the back of a small courtyard by Blackfriars Distillery, the home of Plymouth Gin, it has a massive interior and the high ceiling provides space for a further, balconied dining area. Every conceiveable type of pasta, a wide range of veal and other meat dishes and inevitably magnificent ice cream are served in substantial amounts by a professional and friendly staff. If you lost your provisions overboard, this is the right place to come to catch up on your eating and if you just want a good Italian meal with good wine, it will be hard to beat. No matter that this is a large restaurant, it also gets very full, so do book.
Credit Cards: Access, Amex, Diners, Visa.

2 **Piermasters:**
33 Southside Street, The Barbican.
(0752) 229345.
This is a charming, informal, fishy
bistro, where the atmosphere is
perhaps enhanced by the fact that no
space has been missed when setting up
the tables. Two floors help
accommodate the many people who
want to eat here but booking is
essential.
Credit Cards: Access, Amex, Visa.

3 **Platters:**
The Barbican.
Plastic tables range down both walls,
with the deep fat-frier at the far end, in
this restaurant-cum-cafe that makes no
pretence to be other than a fast,
efficient eatery. A glance at the menu
might deter people looking for a
'proper' restaurant meal but a closer
look shows that besides the chipolatas,
eggs, beans, burgers and chips there is
bouillabaisse, lobster, red mullet and
skate among many other fish dishes.
Not for those looking for comfort but if
you have a young family and want to
satisfy all tastes or are in a hurry, you
could do a great deal worse.

PUBS

4 **The Barbican Wine Lodge:**
Parade Quay Road.
A fun, bouncy wine bar with friendly
staff and upstairs a good restaurant
with an attractive view over the inner
harbour. Its atmosphere is helped by
the uneven timbered floor. The menu is
very extensive but not all dishes are
always available as they are bought
according to market availability. Quite
probably if you call in for a drink you
will finish up spending the evening
here and it is equally probable that you
will have a good time.

5 **The Dolphin:**
The Barbican.
As basic a pub as you are likely to find,
with cracked leatherette benches and
the occasional chair, but those who
love beer straight from the barrel will
not mind these minor discomforts.

6 **The Three Crowns:**
Vauxhall Quay.
A stylish, well-refurbished quayside
pub serving real ales and bar food, with
a restaurant upstairs.

HARBOUR SERVICES (YACHTS)

General: All marinas have all facilities.

SERVICES AVAILABLE

●	Petrol	●	Water
●	Diesel	●	Slipway
●	Calor Gas	●	Chandlery
●	Camping Gas		

HARBOUR SERVICES (PERSONAL)

Showers:
All marinas have shower facilities.

Post Office: Drake Circus.

Telephone: Both marinas.

Laundry:
All marinas have launderettes.

Taxi & Cars:
Pilgrim Cabs. (0752) 669000.

Yacht Clubs:
Royal Plymouth Corinthian Yacht Club, Madeira Road, The Hoe. (0752) 664327.
The Royal Western, 9 Grand Parade. (0752) 660077.

CHEMISTS AND MEDICAL SERVICES

Chemists:
D. Toy. 12 Southside Street.

Medical:
Plymouth General, Freedom Fields. (0752) 668080.

BANKS

Barclays: 19 Princess Street.

Lloyds: 8 Royal Parade.

Midland: 4 Old Town Street.

National Westminster:
16 Old Town Street.

COASTGUARD: (0752) 822239
POLICE: (0752) 701188

NEWTON FERRERS

This favourite mooring at the mouth of the River Yealm is quiet, very beautiful and well-sheltered. The land falls steeply on both sides of the estuary and remains unspoilt by buildings and other developments. Mooring can be difficult due to the popularity of the Yealm and visiting yachtsmen should always contact the Harbour Master as most of the moorings are private and their use by visitors depends on the movements of the owner. A narrow high street runs from the quay upwards, with a few shops on either side.

MOORINGS

Harbour Master.
(0752) 872533
£4.00 per day.   £20.00 per week.

RESTAURANTS

The Court House:
Court Road. (0752) 872354.

The River Yealm Hotel:
(0752) 872419.
This large rambling building overlooks the River Yealm between Warren Point and Madge Point. Coming ashore by dinghy, there is a footpath leading up to the hotel from the road that skirts the east side of the river. The restaurant offers spectacular views and simple fare.

PUBS

The Dolphin:
A very popular riverside pub, with a sunny outdoor terrace giving fine views over the Yealm. Excellent bar food, real ales and a friendly atmosphere.

CHEMISTS AND MEDICAL SERVICES

Chemists:
D.A. Tubb Ltd. Newton Hill.

Medical:
Plymouth General, Freedom Fields.
(0752) 668080.

BANKS

Barclays: Newton Hill.

**COASTGUARD: (0752) 822239
POLICE: (0752) 701188**

SHIPS LYING OFF THE EDDYSTONE LIGHTHOUSE.

SALCOMBE

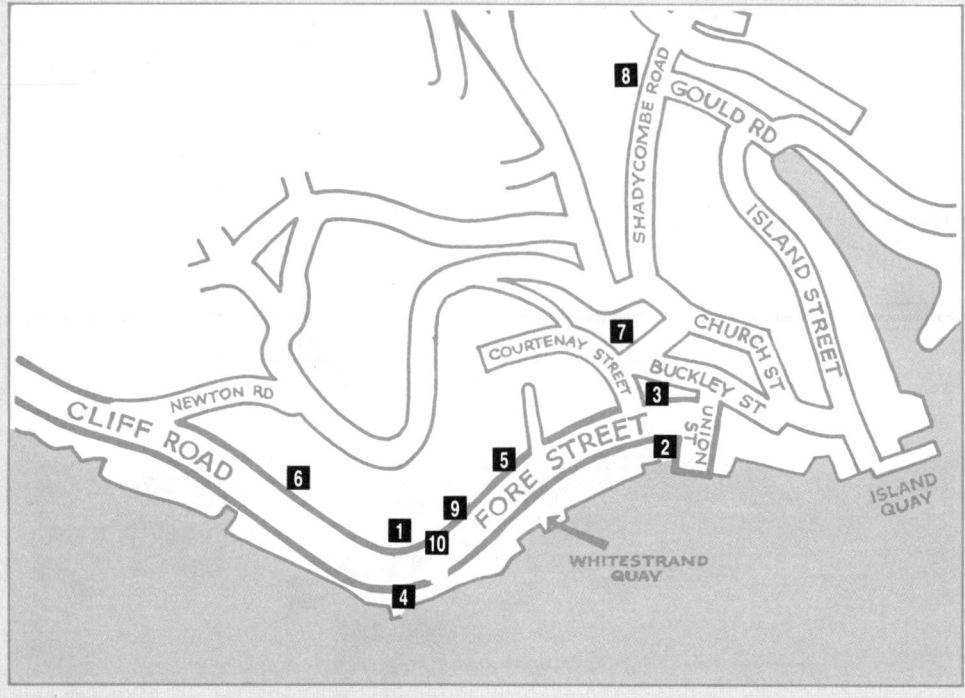

HARBOUR MASTER: (054 884) 3791 or radio VHF Ch 16/14

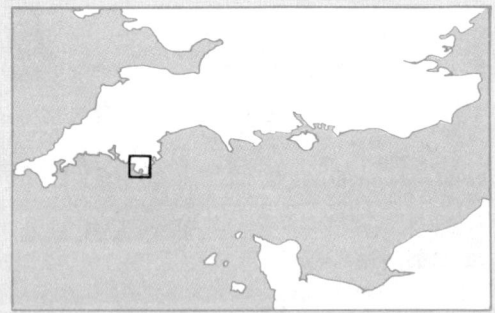

Salcombe lives up to its reputation as a Mecca for yachtsmen. In summer months the little streets are packed with visitors, most of them wearing yellow wellies. Do not let this put you off as Salcombe really does deserve its popularity. The estuary provides sheltered mooring in delightful surroundings and if the mood takes you for a day on the beach, moor off Sunny Cove or take the dinghy to Mill Bay where you will find all the sand and safe swimming you could wish for.

Today tourism is the main source of income but this was not always so. In the 19th century Salcombe was an important commercial port, particularly known for the fruit clippers that sailed from the estuary and were built on her shores. It is hard to believe that the little village lying opposite on the eastern bank, East Portlemouth, was once more important and that ships and men were sent from here to help Edward III at Crécy.

MOORINGS

Contact Harbour Master. Whitestrand. (054 884) 3791 VHF Ch 16/14
£6.85 per day.   £38.24 per week.

RESTAURANTS

1 Dusters:
50 Fore Street. (054 884) 2634.
Almost an institution in Salcombe, this cheerful, friendly bistro which opens evenings only is always full, so booking is essential. The food is eclectic and generally very good. In terms of value for money this is the place.

2 The Galley:
5 Fore Street. (054 884) 2828.
A long thin restaurant with a superb view over the estuary for those lucky enough to secure a seat near the window. Drinking in the bar can be like having a drink in a corridor of the Euston/Glasgow express, but do not be dismayed. The staff are friendly, the food is simple but good, and you will certainly not leave feeling hungry. An added attraction is the children's menu served during the early part of the evening.
Credit Cards: Access, Amex, Visa.

3 Wellingtons:
84 Fore Street. (054 884) 3385.
The only restaurant in Salcombe to attract a mention in Michelin, which awards it a knife and fork. It may not be noticeably better than the other places mentioned, although it is possibly not so formal as the Galley and not so informal as Dusters, but it is definitely worth a visit.
Credit Cards: Access, Amex, Diners, Visa.

PUBS

4 The Ferry:
Fore Street.
As its name suggests, this pub is situated right on the waterfront overlooking the foot-passenger ferry that runs between Salcombe and East Portlemouth. On sunny days the terrace is packed. It serves a selection of real ales, expensive locally caught crab sandwiches which can take so long coming that you almost believe they are being caught especially for you, plus a whole variety of snacks. There are two bars: the terrace bar which is loud and gives the impression of being full of juke-boxes, pool tables and fruit machines, and an upstairs bar which is in complete contrast – quiet, restrained, with a superb view over the estuary. There used to be a middle-level bar but this has now been converted into a fish restaurant.

5 The Victoria:
Fore Street.
If you like Bass straight out of the barrel, then head for this small pub right opposite Whitestrand, with one splendidly traditional bar and another cocktailish bar where they also serve some extremely good snacks.

SALCOMBE Continued

HARBOUR SERVICES (YACHTS)

General: Salcombe Chandlery, Fore Street.

Mechanical Engineers:
E.S.J. Engineering, Island Street. (054 884) 2680.

Electronic Engineers:
Burwin Marine Electronics, Island Street. (054 884) 3321.

Sailmakers:
Jon Alsop, The Sail Loft, Croft Road. (054 884)3702.

Boat Builders & Repairers:
Tideway Boat Construction Ltd., Island Street. (054 884) 2987.

SERVICES AVAILABLE

 Petrol   Water

 Diesel   Slipway

 Calor Gas   Chandlery

 Camping Gas

HARBOUR SERVICES (PERSONAL)

6 Showers:
Salcombe Yacht Club, Cliff Road.

7 Post Office: Market Street.

Telephone:
Post Office. Whitestrand Car Park.

Taxi & Cars:
H. Duderstadt. (054 884) 2739.

6 Yacht Clubs:
Salcombe Yacht Club, Cliff Road. (054 884) 2872.

CHEMISTS AND MEDICAL SERVICES

Chemists:
T.C. Beare. 25 Fore Street.
Mavis Lawrence. 53a Fore Street.

8 Medical:
Redfern Health Centre, Shadycombe Road. (054 884) 2284.

BANKS

9 Lloyds: Fore Street.
10 Midland: Fore Street.

DARTMOUTH

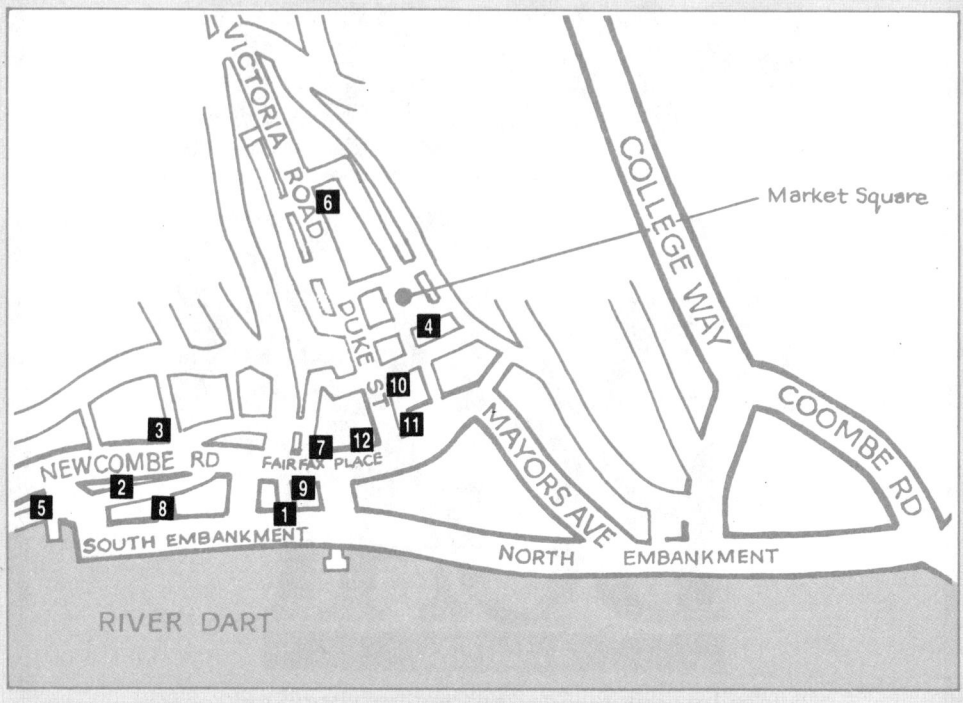

Market Square

HARBOUR MASTER: (080 43) 2337 or radio VHF Ch11

A splendidly sheltered location has meant that for centuries Dartmouth has been a port of great significance. The surrounding hills provide a fortress-like defence and with the building of the two castles at the mouth of the River Dart in the late 15th century the town became virtually impregnable. Men departed from here to fight in the Crusades, the Pilgrim Fathers landed here to effect repairs and from here many expeditions were fitted out before sailing on voyages of

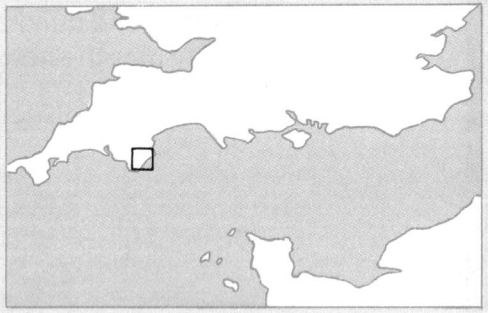

discovery around the globe. It is little wonder that a town with such a magnificent maritime heritage should be home to the Britannia Royal Naval College, which since 1905 has been housed in a building overlooking the town, replacing the two ships moored in the Dart that previously served as its base.

The town itself is most attractive, with small winding streets running down to the quay. The famous Butterwalk, built in the 17th century, and Bayards Cove are two strikingly beautiful parts, both of which have featured in several films, not least in the television series *The Onedin Line*. Apart from being a major tourist attraction, the town is still very much a working port and it is not unusual to see factory ships from the Soviet Union, France and Spain moored in the shelter of the Dart.

Many yachtsmen feel that a visit to Dartmouth is an expensive exercise and the welcome there 'discerning'. Maybe Dartmouth takes the attitude that it is a privilege to share in its great maritime history. But to shun visiting it would be a shame, for the town itself has much to offer.

MOORINGS

Dart Harbour and Navigation Authority.
(080 43) 2337 VHF Ch11
£3.15 per day.   £22.05 per week.

Darthaven Marina. (080 425) 545
£10.46 per day.   £62.76 per week.

Dart Marina. (080 43) 3351
£8.86 per day.   £61.99 per week.

Kingswear Marina. (080 43) 3351
£8.45 per day.   £59.15 per week.

RESTAURANTS

1 The Carved Angel:
2 South Embankment. (080 43) 2465. The only restaurant on the south coast to be awarded a rosette by Michelin, it is set on the Embankment and is wonderfully convenient for yachtsmen who want nothing but the very best. The dining room is not over-large, with well-spaced tables, and you do eat in comfort. The small, imaginative menu reflects the seasons and market availablity. Expensive? Where there is any doubt about value for money, then a place can be said to be expensive. In this case the care that is taken in the selection, preparation and service of your meal fully justifies the amount that you will be charged. Booking is essential.

DARTMOUTH Continued

2 **Bistro 33:**
33 Lower Street. (080 43) 2882.
This recently opened bistro is a real
find. The chef was previously at the
Carved Angel and his time there was
not wasted. The highly imaginative
menu is in the prix fixe format and the
wine is well-selected and reasonably
priced. It is not as formal as the Carved
Angel, but there is little space so you
will need to book, particularly as its
reputation grows.

PUBS

3 **The Cherub:**
Higher Street.
The oldest building in Dartmouth, this
former merchant's house believed to
have been built in 1380 is a Grade 1
listed building and worth visiting for
this reason alone. You will probably
find that most of the other people in the
pub are there for the same reason but,
having popped in for a quick drink and
a good look, you may well be tempted
to stay for a meal in the restaurant
where such seafood as shark steak is
served. Or you can pick from a wide
selection of bar snacks.

4 **The Old Country House:**
Market Street.
This 'Victorian' pub full of atmosphere
and comfort is a bit of a walk up Duke
Street, but anyone visiting the market at
lunchtime would be well advised to
call in.

5 **The Dartmouth Arms:**
Lower Street (just before Bayards
Cove).
A friendly traditional pub with a good
atmosphere and possibly the first place
a fisherman will look if short of crew,
so be careful not to be press-ganged into
a sea trip you did not intend. During
the filming of *The Onedin Line* this
became the regular , as is shown by the
many photographs on the walls.

HARBOUR SERVICES (YACHTS)

General: All marinas have full
chandlery services.

Sailmakers:
Dart Sails, 26 Foss Street.

Boat Builders & Repairers:
All marinas have complete services
available.

SERVICES AVAILABLE

●	Petrol	●	Water
●	Diesel	●	Slipway
●	Calor Gas	●	Chandlery
●	Camping Gas		

HARBOUR SERVICES (PERSONAL)

Showers: All marinas.

6 Post Office:
20-22 Victoria Road.

Telephone:
Post Office. Both marinas.

Laundry:
Monogram Launderette, 2 Market Street.

Taxi & Cars:
Devon Taxis. (080 43) 3778.

Yacht Clubs:
Royal Dart Yacht Club, Kingswear. (080 425) 272.

CHEMISTS AND MEDICAL SERVICES

7 Chemists:
Boots. 6 The Quay.

8 Medical:
Dartmouth and Kingswear Hospital, Hauley Road. (080 43) 2255.

BANKS

9 Lloyds: 2 Spithead.

10 Midland: Duke Street.

11 National Westminster:
2 Duke Street.

12 TSB: 9 The Quay.

COASTGUARD: (080 45) 58292
POLICE: (080 43) 2288

DARTMOUTH MID 19TH CENTURY.

BRIXHAM

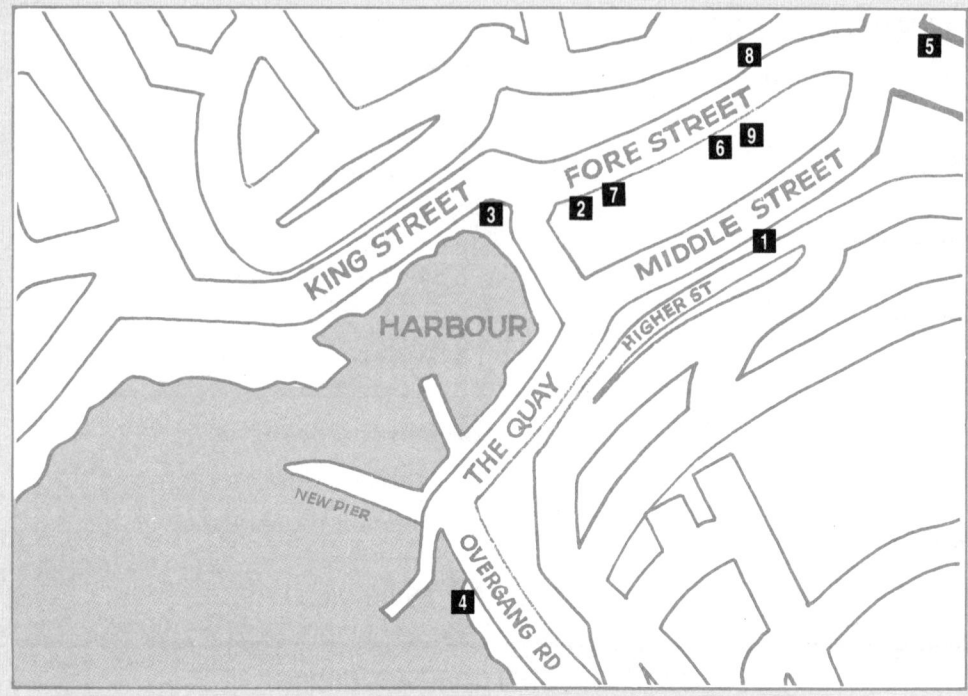

HARBOUR MASTER: (080 45) 3321 or radio VHF Ch 14

When William of Orange landed here in 1688 saying 'The liberties of England and the Protestant religion I will maintain', he could little have dreamt of the changes that would take place. Nor would Napoleon, gazing out from his imprisonment on the *Bellerophon*, moored just outside Brixham before taking him to exile on St Helena, be able to recognise the town. Even up to the First World War Brixham was an important port and the daily life of the town revolved around fish. Today, although there is still some fishing activity, the emphasis is on tourism and there are many quayside activities to amuse and interest the visitor, not the least of which is a replica of the

Golden Hind.

The harbour itself is large and provides sheltered mooring in most conditions. The exception is when the wind is from the north. It also offers all the facilities a visiting yachtsman might require but, given the choice, you may prefer to go to Dartmouth.

MOORINGS

Harbour Master. (080 45) 3321.
£5.64 per day.   £39.45 per week.

Brixham Yacht Club. (080 45) 3332.
£0.00 per day.   £0.00 per week.

RESTAURANTS

1 The Elizabethan:
8 Middle Street. (080 45) 3722.
This is a solid restaurant with a solid decor. The menu is not adventurous – it too might even be described as solid – but you might do a lot worse.
Credit Cards: Amex, Diners.

2 La Table du Capitaine:
64b Fore Street. (080 45) 3983.
This ornate *fin de siècle* restaurant has clearly been designed to give its patrons what is considered to be a French evening out: Frog's legs and escargots or Grenouilles and snails. But the staff make a big effort and unless you are trying to recreate magical moments in France an evening here will be not be found wanting.
Credit Card: Access, Amex, Diners, Visa.

PUBS

3 Hole in The Wall:
King Street.
This pub in an old world setting has a great atmosphere and can get very busy during the summer, deservedly so.

HARBOUR SERVICES (YACHTS)

General: The Boat Shop, Uphams Yard. Brixham Yacht Supplies, 72 Middle Street
Mechanical Engineers:
Brixham Boating Centre, Higher Furzeham Road. (080 45) 51888.
Boat Builders & Repairers:
Brixham Bunkering and Devon Marine Ltd, Breakwater Quarry. (080 45) 2250.

SERVICES AVAILABLE

● Petrol	● Water	
● Diesel	● Slipway	
● Calor Gas	● Chandlery	
● Camping Gas		

HARBOUR SERVICES (PERSONAL)

4 Showers: Brixham Yacht Club.

5 Post Office: New Road.

Telephone: Post Office.

Laundry: 15 Bolton Street.

Taxi & Cars:
Brixham Radio Taxis (080 45) 4600.

4 Yacht Clubs:
Brixham Yacht Club, Overgang. (080 45) 3332.

BRIXHAM Continued

CHEMISTS AND MEDICAL SERVICES

Chemists:
Boots. 5 Bolton Street.

Medical:
Brixham Hospital, Greenwood Road.
(080 45) 2153.

BANKS

6 **Barclays:** Fore Street.

7 **Lloyds:** Fore Street.

8 **Midland:** 19 Fore Street.

9 **National Westminster:** Fore Street.

10 **TSB:** 51 Fore Street.

COASTGUARD: (080 45) 58292 or radio VHF Ch 16/10
POLICE: (080 45) 2231

If you think BOATS SHOULD BE BOATS

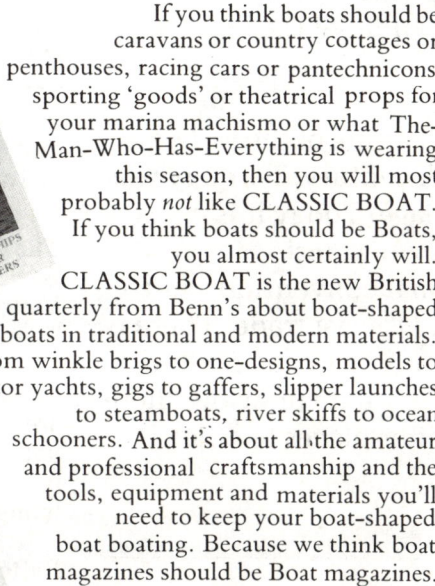

If you think boats should be caravans or country cottages or penthouses, racing cars or pantechnicons, sporting 'goods' or theatrical props for your marina machismo or what The-Man-Who-Has-Everything is wearing this season, then you will most probably *not* like CLASSIC BOAT. If you think boats should be Boats, you almost certainly will. CLASSIC BOAT is the new British quarterly from Benn's about boat-shaped boats in traditional and modern materials. From winkle brigs to one-designs, models to motor yachts, gigs to gaffers, slipper launches to steamboats, river skiffs to ocean schooners. And it's about all the amateur and professional craftsmanship and the tools, equipment and materials you'll need to keep your boat-shaped boat boating. Because we think boat magazines should be Boat magazines.

Benn Consumer Publications,
Schweppes House, Grosvenor Road, St. Albans,
Herts AL1 3TN. Tel. 0727 59166.

TORQUAY

The town of Torquay, regarded by some as England's premier resort, looks rather like a wedding cake with its tall hotels and apartment buildings which rise in tiers on the hills surrounding the town centre. There is certainly a Mediterranean feel to the place, which supports Torquay's claim to be the capital of the English Riviera.

Until the coming of the railway in the 19th century, Torquay was a little village. Today it is a modern town, catering for international conventions and a year-round tourist trade. There is therefore plenty to do and if night-life is what you want, there are few better places to enjoy it than here.

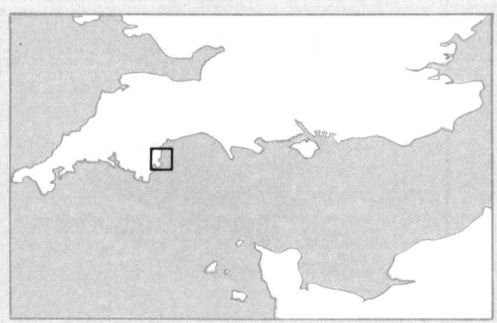

MOORINGS

Harbour Master. (0803) 22429.
£5.64 per day.   £39.45 per week.

Torquay Marina. (0803) 214624.
£12.10 per day.   £72.45 per week.

RESTAURANTS

For such a lively town, it is interesting that there is no restaurant in the whole of Torquay that merits a mention in Michelin.

The Carvery Restaurant and Madisons Bar:
Victoria Parade.
There is a pleasing modern decor in this bright building overlooking the old harbour, where beef, lamb, turkey, etc., are carved for you and you help yourself to the rest. Not *haute cuisine* by any means but good value for money.

Rafters:
22 Victoria Parade. (0803) 26416.
This tastefully decorated wholefood restaurant – the owner was previously an interior designer – serves good, imaginative food and whilst not a place for a hearty evening, fine for a genteel escape from the rigours of life afloat.
Closed Tuesdays and Sundays.
Credit Cards: Access, Amex, Visa.

The Tudor Rose:
Victoria Parade.
A tea-room-cum-restaurant which is a must for nostalgia lovers. Wicker chairs, a fine selection of cream cakes, light meals of the quiche variety; if there were space, a palm court band would surely be playing in the corner.

HARBOUR SERVICES (YACHTS)

General: Torquay Marina has all facilities.

Mechanical Engineers:
Torquay Marina.

Electronic Engineers:
Torquay Marina.

Sailmakers:
Torquay Marina.

Boat Builders & Repairers:
Torquay Marina.

SERVICES AVAILABLE

 Petrol   Water

Diesel   Slipway

Calor Gas   Chandlery

 Camping Gas

HARBOUR SERVICES (PERSONAL)

Showers: Torquay Marina.

Post Office: Fleet Street.

Telephone: Torquay Marina.

Laundry:
Collections can be made from the marina.

Taxi & Cars:
Star Taxi (0803) 38511.
Plainmore Self-Drive Car Hire (0803) 35069.

Yacht Clubs:
Royal Torbay Yacht Club, Beacon Hill. (0803) 22006.

CHEMISTS AND MEDICAL SERVICES

Chemists:
Boots. 46-48 Fleet Street.

Medical:
Torbay Hospital. (0803) 64567.

BANKS

Barclays: 39-40 Fleet Street.

Lloyds: 45 Union Street.

Midland: 4 The Strand.

National Westminster: 15 The Strand.

TSB: 6 Fleet Street.

COASTGUARD: (080 45) 58292
POLICE: (0803) 214491

TEIGNMOUTH

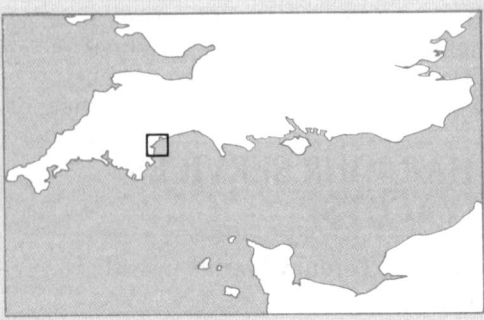

An attractive holiday resort but one that poses problems for the yachtsman since entering can be hazardous without local knowledge. The town dates back to Saxon times and has survived many attacks from the sea, notably at the hands of the French, who succeeded in burning it to the ground on one occasion. It became popular as a holiday resort in the early 19th century, when one of its visitors was John Keats who whilst here wrote Endymion – A thing of beauty is a joy for ever . The place has a timeless quality and shares with its neighbours a climate noticeably warmer than the rest of the United Kingdom.

MOORINGS

Harbour Master. (062 67) 3165
£5.75 per day.   £40.25 per week.

HARBOUR SERVICES (YACHTS)

General: Mariner's Weigh, 15 Fore Street, Shaldon. (0626 87) 3698.

Electronic Engineers:
Mariner's Weigh, 15 Fore Street, Shaldon. (0626 87) 3698.

Boat Builders & Repairers:
Mariner's Weigh, 15 Fore Street, Shaldon. (0626 87) 3698.

SERVICES AVAILABLE

- ● Petrol
- ● Diesel
- ● Calor Gas
- ● Camping Gas
- ● Water
- ● Slipway
- ● Chandlery

HARBOUR SERVICES (PERSONAL)

Post Office: Den Road.

Telephone: Post Office.

Laundry:
Jax Wash, 36 Brunswick Street.

Taxi & Cars:
Roma Taxi (062 67) 3130.
B&M Car Hire (062 67) 6886.

CHEMISTS AND MEDICAL SERVICES

Chemists:
Boots. 5 Wellington Street.

Medical:
Hospital, Mill Lane. (062 67) 2161.

BANKS

Barclays: Wellington Street.

Lloyds: Regent Street.

Midland: Wellington Street.

National Westminster: Den Road.

TSB: Wellington Street.

**COASTGUARD: (080 45) 58292
POLICE: (062 67) 2433**

EXMOUTH

This town was the first of the Devon holiday resorts, however before this it was an important port, and, apart from trade with European countries, it was the home port for many voyages of discovery. Sir Walter Raleigh set sail on some of his historic journeys from this town.

In the nineteenth century this changed and the popularity of the magnificent sandy beaches that lie to the east of the town helped make it a favoured holiday town. Bathers should beware of the strong currents that flow near the mouth of the River Exe, and these also are a problem for yachtsmen.

HARBOUR SERVICES (YACHTS)

General: Rowsell and Morrison, 24 Camperdown Terrace. (0395) 263911.

Electronic Engineers: Rowsell and Morrison, 24 Camperdown Terrace. (0395) 263911.

Sailmakers: Rowsell and Morrison, 24 Camperdown Terrace. (0395) 263911.

Boat Builders & Repairers: Dixon and Son, 1 Dock Road. (0395) 263063.

SERVICES AVAILABLE

- ● Petrol
- ● Diesel
- ☐ Calor Gas
- ☐ Camping Gas
- ● Water
- ☐ Slipway
- ☐ Chandlery

HARBOUR SERVICES (PERSONAL)

Post Office: 4 Chapel Street.

Telephone: Post Office.

Laundry:
Exmouth Launderette, 6 High Street.

Taxi & Cars:
Allied Cabs (0395) 264188.
Mike's Private Hire (0395) 275500.

CHEMISTS AND MEDICAL SERVICES

Chemists:
Boots. 21 Chapel Street.

Medical:
Claremount Grove Hospital. (0395) 279684.

BANKS

Barclays: Fore Street.

Lloyds: 22 The Strand.

Midland: 1 Rolle Street.

National Westminster:
11 Rolle Street.

TSB: 9 Rolle Street.

COASTGUARD: (0395) 263232
POLICE: (0395) 264651

LYME REGIS

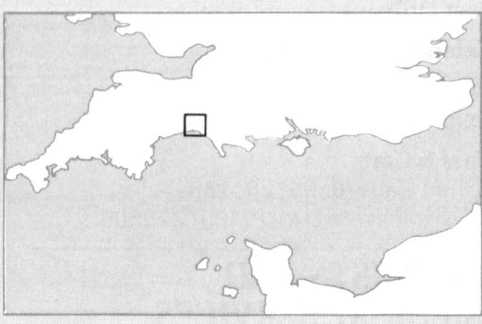

If the trip across Lyme Bay is too daunting to take in one go and the weather is kind, try to secure a berth here. There are a few visitors' moorings alongside the quay but it is advisable to contact the Harbour Master first. Most of the harbour dries out at low water.

Lyme Regis dates back to Saxon times and by 1284, when it was given its royal charter by Edward I, it had become a port of some significance. Probably its most notable moment in history was the landing here of the Duke of Monmouth in 1685 in his ill-fated attempt to overthrow James II. The beach to the west of Lyme Regis is still known as Monmouth beach. Today, Lyme Regis is a small holiday resort of great charm with many interesting places to visit. The Cobb was built in the 14th century and for those intersted in prehistory there is a fine collection of fossils on display in the local museum.

RESTAURANTS

Drakes:
14-15 Monmouth Street. (029 74) 2079.
Credit Cards: Access, Amex, Visa.

HARBOUR SERVICES (YACHTS)

General: Sails Marine and Sports Centre, 62 Broad Street. (029 74) 2420.

Electronic Engineers:
Sails Marine and Sports Centre, 62 Broad Street. (029 74) 2420.

SERVICES AVAILABLE

- ● Petrol
- ● Diesel
- ● Calor Gas
- ● Camping Gas
- ● Water
- ● Slipway
- ● Chandlery

MOORINGS

Harbour Master. (029 74) 2137.
£6.00 per day.   £42.00 per week.

HARBOUR SERVICES (PERSONAL)

Taxi & Cars:
Tolman's Taxi (029 74) 3181.
E.C.Turner (029 74) 2930.

CHEMISTS AND MEDICAL SERVICES

Chemists:
Boots. 45 Broad Street.

Medical:
Hospital, Pound Road. (02974) 2254.

BANKS

Lloyds: 54 Broad Street.
Midland: 25 Broad Street.
National Westminster: 22 Broad Street.

COASTGUARD: (0297) 21814
POLICE: (029 74) 2603

WEYMOUTH

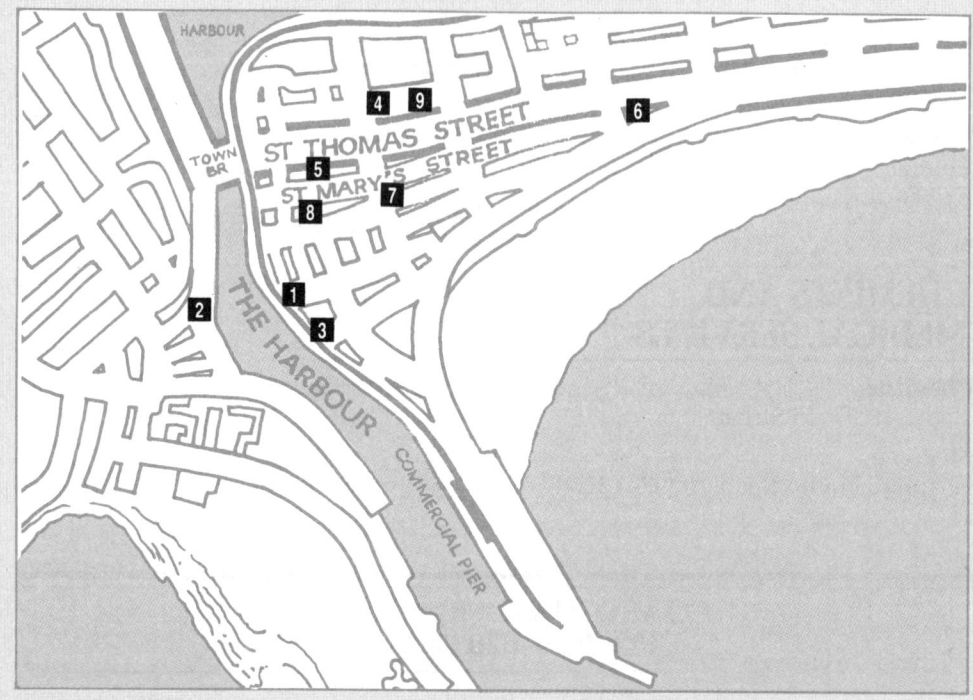

HARBOUR MASTER: (0305) 761222 or radio VHF Ch 16

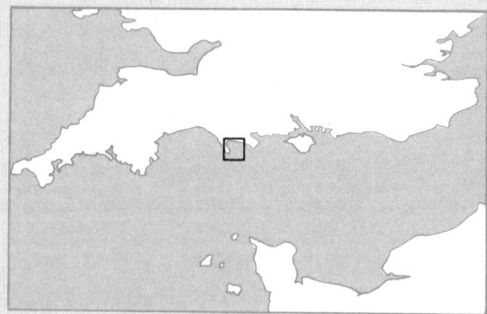

Weymouth was a port of local importance for centuries before King George III visited the town, liked it, and started spending his summers there. This royal patronage had the inevitable effect of making Weymouth very fashionable, the results of which can still be seen today in the tall Georgian houses that line the seafront. Here also stands a statue of George III, erected by the town's grateful inhabitants. Before 1571 Weymouth was in fact two towns, Weymouth and Melcombe Regis, whose main source of income was from the port and its associated activities, but these had gone into decline when the timely arrival of George III occurred. Weymouth continues to attract many holiday-makers and it is also a busy ferry terminal.

For the yachtsman Weymouth makes an excellent stopover if you are going east or west and the port is always the scene of much activity. There is also plenty to do in the town itself. The museum includes George III's bathing machine, in which he was towed out to sea and, having removed his clothes, would plunge from its steps naked into the water, well away from prying eyes and to the distant accompaniment of his band. Theatres, restaurants and nightclubs cater for the many visitors and on hot sunny days the beach in front of the Esplanade gets packed with people taking advantage of the safe bathing here. Certainly Weymouth is not for those wanting to be away from it all but if you enjoy bustle and the sight of the English on holiday, then you cannot lose.

MOORINGS

Harbour Master. (0305) 761222.
£5.25 per day.   £36.75 per week.

RESTAURANTS

1 Sea Cow Bistro:
7 Custom House Quay. (0305) 783524. This cheerful, busy quayside bistro is popular with holiday-makers and visiting yachtsmen alike. You sit at scrubbed wooden tables and enjoy a menu that features 'local' specialities and both seafood and steak.

PUBS

2 The King's Arms:
15 Trinity Road.
Since most yachts moor on the south side of the quay, this little southern quayside pub is even more convenient. You will also have to pass by it when going into the town, or even when going for a shower at the Yacht Club, so there is every excuse to try it - and you should find it pleasant enough.

WEYMOUTH Continued

HARBOUR SERVICES (YACHTS)

General: Weymouth Chandlers, 10a Custom House Quay.

Mechanical Engineers:
Barretts Marine Service, Commercial Road. (0305) 779550.

Electronic Engineers:
Marine Radio, 6 St Edmunds Street. (0305) 779297.

Sailmakers:
Blue Peter Sails, 11 Nothe Parade. (0305) 779629.

Boat Builders & Repairers:
Briggs Boats, Lower Edmund Street. (0305) 775744.

SERVICES AVAILABLE

- ● Petrol
- ● Diesel
- ● Calor Gas
- ● Camping Gas
- ● Water
- ● Slipway
- ● Chandlery

HARBOUR SERVICES (PERSONAL)

3 Showers:
Royal Dorset Yacht Club, Custom House Quay.
Harbour Commission, Custom House Quay.

4 Post Office:
67 St Thomas Street.

3 Telephone:
Royal Dorset Yacht Club.
Telephone kiosks: Town Bridge/ St Thomas Street.

Laundry:
Lodmore Launderette, 64 Dorchester Road.

Taxi & Cars:
Fleetline Taxis. (0305) 784252.

Yacht Clubs:
Royal Dorset Yacht Club, 11 Custom House Quay. (0305) 771155.

CHEMISTS AND MEDICAL SERVICES

5 Chemists:
Boots. 81 St Mary Street.

Medical:
Sandsfoot Day Unit, 34 Buxton Road. (0305) 782086.
Weymouth and District Hospital, Melcome Avenue. (0305) 772211.

BANKS

6 Barclays: 2 St Mary Street.

7 Lloyds: 92 St Mary Street.

8 Midland: 18 St Mary Street.

9 National Westminster:
76 St Thomas Street.

COASTGUARD: (0305) 820400
POLICE: (0305) 63011

Mount Gay is not
the most-advertised rum in the
world and not everyone has
heard of it. But ask anyone in
the trade who knows about
rums and liqueurs, and they'll
tell you that Mount Gay is
certainly the oldest, and
probably the best rum on the
market today.

It comes from a distillery
that has been refining since
1663 and it is often called
'the yachtsman's rum' because
yachtsmen from all over the
world call at Barbados and take
a supply home.

The most popular is Mount
Gay Eclipse Barbados Rum
which is soft and mellow on its
own, but has enough body and
stamina to make an excellent
base for cocktails.

You can get your supplies
from Atkinson Baldwin & Co.
Ltd. who will be pleased to tell
you about Eclipse Barbados
Rum and the other Mount Gay
Rums: Liqueur, Sugar Cane and
Special White Rum.

Atkinson Baldwin & Co Ltd
Mary's House 42 Vicarage Crescent London SW11 3LB
Telephone: 01-223 7634

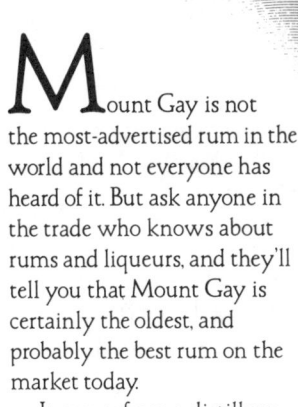

LULWORTH COVE

Much-loved by geography teachers, this circular bay provides a fair anchorage in a spectacular setting. It can be difficult to enter because of the flukey winds around the entrance and should not be attempted when there is a strong southerly wind blowing. Although Lulworth Cove would seem to be the perfect anchorage for those wishing for a sheltered mooring, a meal on board and a quiet time away from everyone else, there are many other yachtsmen with the same idea and the natural beauty of the place draws many visitors in good weather.

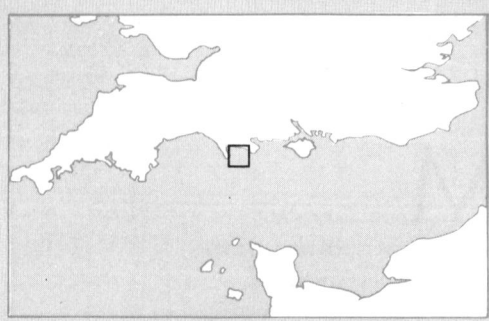

Lulworth (West Lulworth) is about one mile away and whilst it is impossible to claim that there are many facilities for yachtsmen, in emergencies basics like water can always be found.

Much of the area around Lulworth is an army-firing range and the many good walks in the surrounding countryside are restricted to times when the ranges are not in use. Sometimes firing takes place out to sea, so be sure to keep an eye out for the warning flags that are flown on these occasions. The country is worth exploring and anyone particularly interested in geology will find Lulworth fascinating as there are fossils to be found along the shore and nearby there is a petrified forest.

RESTAURANTS

The Castle:
West Lulworth. (092 941) 311. Situated just under a mile away from Lulworth Cove, this seemingly small, old thatched pub is worth the walk up the hill. A cosy saloon bar with pewter-hung beams, a larger general bar and a fine restaurant all make for a pleasant visit. Inevitably the place gets very busy in the summer but there is a large beer garden behind which takes much of the pressure off the interior accommodation and where you can buy freshly cooked food off the barbecue. It is necessary to book for the restaurant.
Credit Cards: Access, Amex, Diners, Visa.

The Mill House:
(092 941) 404.
Conveniently located a few yards from
the Cove, this licensed restaurant has a
small but varied menu with locally
caught crab and lobster as house
specialities.

POLICE: (09295) 2222

THE SUN DISPELLING A MIST, WITH SMUGGLERS LANDING THEIR CARGO.

SWANAGE

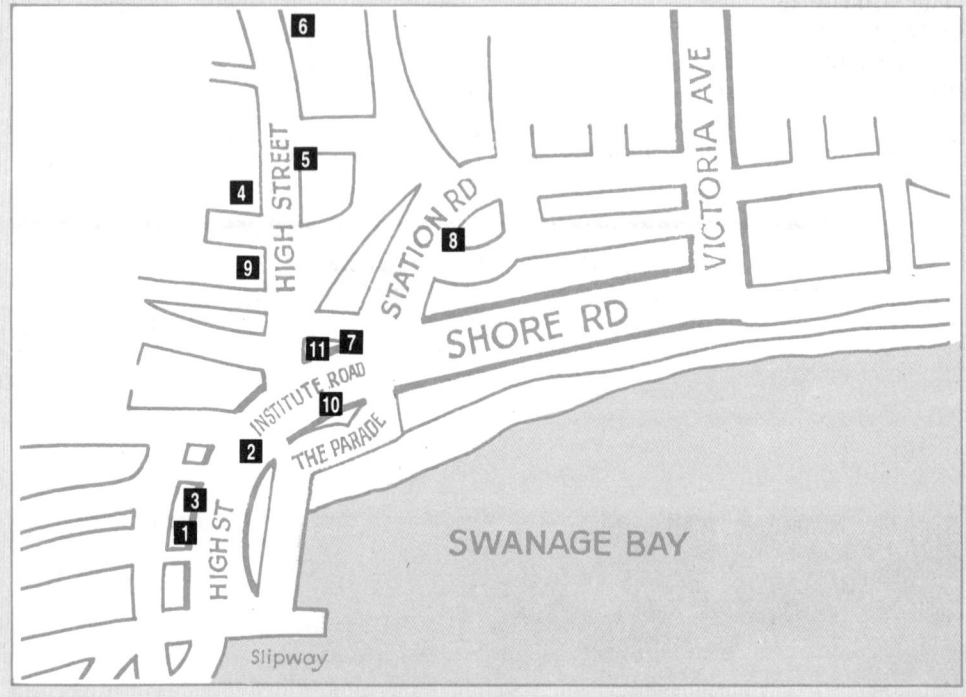

The mooring here is deepwater but there are plans to build a marina. Most people anchor near the pier but if the weather is good, most of the pier side of the bay is suitable.

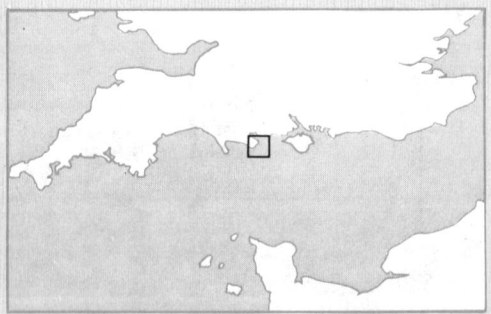

Swanage is a minor holiday resort and can be full of visitors in the summer. The town has a long history stretching back to Saxon times and it was in the bay that King Alfred defeated the Danes in AD 877. Much of the present town dates from the 19th century when the railway made it accessible, but if you take the time to explore the part beyond the front, you will find some unspoilt old streets and houses. Bathing is safe away from Peveril Point on the western side.

RESTAURANTS

1 **J's Cauldron:**
5 High Street. (0929) 422671.
A cheap cheerful, friendly bistro where they try hard and you should have a fun evening.

2 **La Trattoria:**
12 High Street. (0929) 423784.
Many Italian restaurants are interchangeable both in decor and menu, and this is no exception. It is also rather expensive.
Credit Cards: Access, Amex, Diners, Visa.

PUBS

3 **The White Horse Inn:**
High Street.
A pleasant pub with a very good selection of bar food.

4 **The Red Lion:**
High Street.
A small pub in traditional style, a bit of a walk up the High Street.

5 **Tawny's:**
50 High Street.
A rather spartan interior does not detract from this friendly, unassuming wine bar where they serve a good selection of wines and an interesting, reasonably priced selection of bar food.

HARBOUR SERVICES (PERSONAL)

6 **Post Office:**
Kings Road.

Telephone: Post Office.

Laundry:
Town and Country Launderette, 59 King's Road.

Taxi & Cars:
Swanage Taxi Hire. (0929) 423737.

CHEMISTS AND MEDICAL SERVICES

7 **Chemists:**
Boots. 1 Station Road.

Medical:
Swanage Hospital, Queens Road. (0929) 422282.

BANKS

8 **Barclays:** 22 Station Road.

9 **Lloyds:** 41 High Street.

10 **Midland:** 19 Institute Road.

11 **National Westminster:**
2 Institute Road.

COASTGUARD: (0929) 422596
POLICE: (0929) 422004

STUDLAND

Studland is a pleasant anchorage in good weather. Sheltered to the south by Ballard Down, it is a very popular place for yachtsmen and in the right conditions there can be a fleet of yachts moored up here. Mooring is all deepwater and there are no special facilities for boats.

Studland itself is a tiny village surrounded by a nature reserve. The beach runs towards Poole Harbour and whilst it is very popular with holiday-makers, it is more than big enough to give everybody plenty of space. The nature reserve stretches towards Wareham and there are miles and miles of walks for those anxious to regain their land-legs.

PUBS

The Bankes Arms:
This popular pub is five minutes at the most off the beach. Opposite the main entrance is a beer garden, which can get packed in the summer. Bar snacks and restaurant food are available, there is a good atmosphere and it's all very friendly.

Headway
make sails
make
headway

POOLE

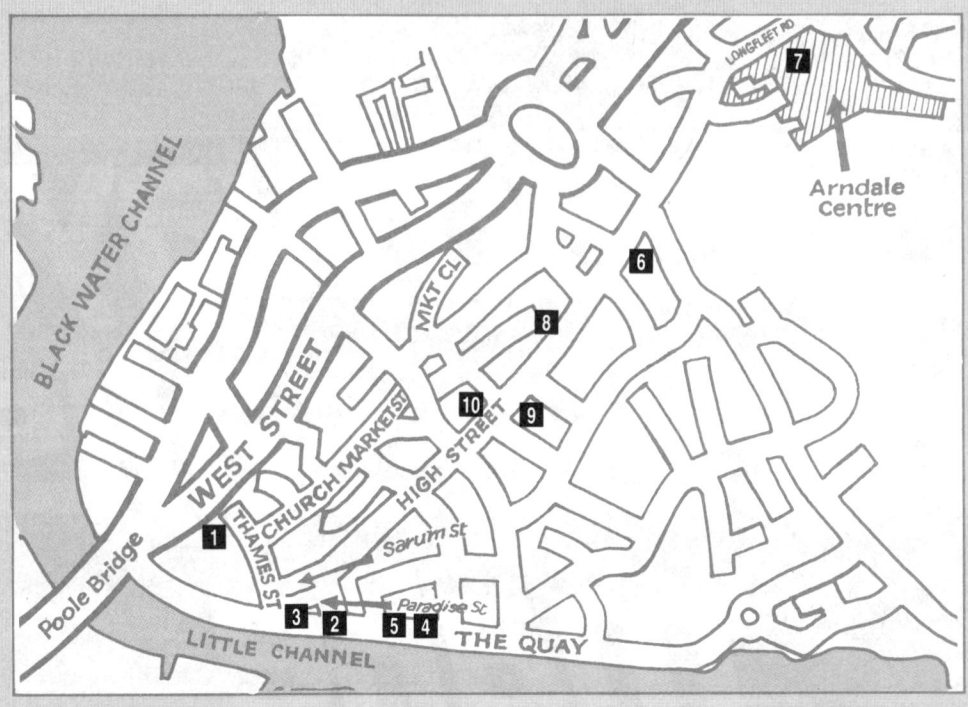

HARBOUR MASTER: (0202) 685261 or radio VHF 16/14

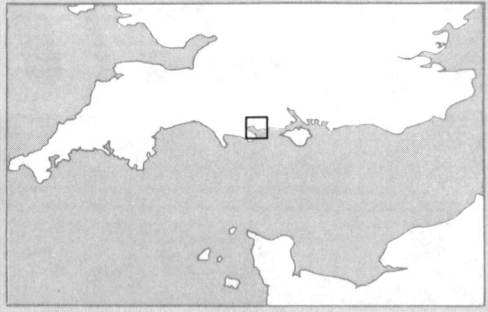

The natural harbour and a double high tide have long made this area important in maritime terms. Formerly Wareham was the pre-eminent port but as the River Frome silted up, Poole came to the fore. By the time of Queen Elizabeth I the town was sufficiently significant for it to be granted the title in 1568 of 'a County incorporate, separate and distinct from the County of Dorset'. Subsequently Poole grew in prosperity due to trade with Newfoundland, and fine Georgian houses still stand in the little streets behind the quay.

Today Poole is a centre of business with many new high-rise buildings but it remains an important port, with one of the largest roll-on roll-off docking systems in the country as well as ferry traffic. It is to the credit of the planning authorities that they have managed to retain many of the buildings and therefore the charm and atmosphere of the old town while developing the new. Take a walk around the streets that lead off the quay and you are part of history; a few hundred yards farther on and you are in the modern Arndale shopping centre and very much part of the 20th century.

This is a great place to visit not only because it has all the amenities but also because the wide expanse of water provides plenty of good sailing and many opportunities to explore with the dinghy where the water is too shallow for big boats. Take the time to visit the Maritime Museum on the quay which houses many exhibits of interest to sea-going people.

MOORINGS

Poole Harbour Yacht Club.
Salterns Marina, 40 Salterns Way.
(0202) 707321 VHF Ch M
£12.00 per day.   £60.00 per week.

Cobbs Quay.
Hamworthy (0202) 674299 VHF Ch M
£7.00 per day.   £34.50 per week.

Poole Quay.
Contact the Harbour Master.
(0202) 685261 VHF CH 16/14
£14.46 per day.   £101.22 per week.

RESTAURANTS

1 The Mansion House:
Thames Street. (0202) 685666.
In this beautiful Georgian building just off the quay is a luxurious restaurant/club. If you are not a member or a resident in the hotel, a cover charge will be added to your bill but if that does not deter you, you will find the food very good, well-prepared from fresh materials. The price is understandably on the high side, even without the supplement. Closed Saturday lunch.
Credit Cards: Access, Amex, Diners, Visa.

2 Corkers Wine Bar and Restaurant:
1 High Street. (0202) 681393.
Downstairs is a busy wine bar, upstairs a pleasant restaurant with views over the harbour. It's very relaxed and friendly, with a menu that gives you the opportunity of enjoying yourself for little money or, if you are feeling more expansive, there are plenty of dishes to satisfy the discerning palate.
Credit Cards: Access, Amex, Diners, Visa.

POOLE Continued

3 **The Warehouse:**
The Quay. (0202) 677238.
Just opposite Corkers, this comfortable, welcoming restaurant also has a first-floor dining room with views over the harbour. Fish plays a main role on the menu and is usually very good. If fish is not for you, don't be put off as the menu caters to all tastes and you are sure to find something to enjoy. Closed Saturday lunch and all day Sunday. Credit Cards: Access, Amex, Diners, Visa.

PUBS

4 **Poole Arms:**
The Quay.
It would be impossible to miss this pub as it has a bright green facade. Inside it is warm and friendly. Real ales and bar food.

5 **Portsmouth Hoy:**
The Quay.
This will be of particular interest to anyone fascinated with mechanical memorabilia. The walls are crowded with brass housed ships engine room gauges. There is also a considerable collection of ship's crests. The pub itself has recently been redecorated and is a pleasant if impersonal place to unwind.

HARBOUR SERVICES (YACHTS)

General: Salterns Marina. (0202) 707321.
Cobbs Quay Chandlers. (0202) 682095.

Mechanical Engineers:
As above and Poole Marine Services. (0202) 679577.

Electronic Engineers:
Danlea Electronics. (0202) 673880.

Sailmakers:
Crusader Sails. (0202) 670580.

Boat Builders & Repairers:
As above.

SERVICES AVAILABLE

- ● Petrol
- ● Diesel
- ● Calor Gas
- ● Camping Gas
- ● Water
- ● Slipway
- ● Chandlery

HARBOUR SERVICES (PERSONAL)

Showers:
Salterns Marina. Cobbs Quay. The Viking Club.

6 **Post Office:**
141 High Street.

Telephone:
All marinas. The Post Office.

Laundry:
Salterns Marina.

Taxi & Cars:
Hertz (0202) 680069.
Newports (0202) 674187.
Ariel Taxi (0202) 672251.
British Car Rental (0202) 677511.

CHEMISTS AND MEDICAL SERVICES

7 **Chemists:**
Boots. Arndale Centre.

Medical:
Poole General Hospital, Longfleet Road. (0202) 675100.

BANKS

8 **Barclays:** 100 High Street.

9 **Lloyds:** 85 High Street.

10 **National Westminster:** 243 High Street.

COASTGUARD: (0202) 670776
POLICE: (0202) 22099

CHRISTCHURCH

The biggest problem is getting over the bar but once in the harbour Christchurch has much to offer. Moorings are limited so an advance call to the mooring superintendent is a good idea.

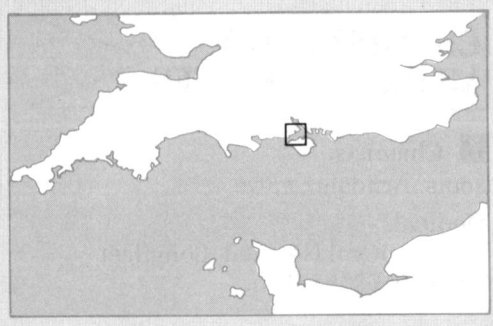

Christchurch dates back to Saxon times when it was known as Twynham, the town between waters, these being the Stour and the Avon. The dominant feature is the Priory, which has claims to be the longest church in England and includes two ancient bells in its tower. The town has a refined feel to it and you can imagine people here drinking cups of China tea with their little fingers extended.

HARBOUR SERVICES (YACHTS)

General: Rossiter Yachts Ltd. (0202) 483250.

Mechanical Engineers: Rossiter Yachts Ltd. (0202) 483250.

Electronic Engineers: Rossiter Yachts Ltd. (0202) 483250.

Boat Builders & Repairers: Rossiter Yachts Ltd. (0202) 483250.

SERVICES AVAILABLE

- ● Petrol
- ● Diesel
- ● Calor Gas
- ● Camping Gas
- ● Water
- ● Slipway
- ● Chandlery

MOORINGS

Rossiter Yachts Ltd.
(0202) 483250
£5.00 per day.   £28.60 per week.

CHEMISTS AND MEDICAL SERVICES

Chemists:
B.D. Nickels. 131 Purewell.

BANKS

Barclays: 22 High Street.

Lloyds: 4 Castle Street.

Midland: 15 High Street.

National Westminster:
57 High Street.

COASTGUARD: (0202) 425204
POLICE: (0202) 486333

NEEDLES 19TH CENTURY.

LYMINGTON

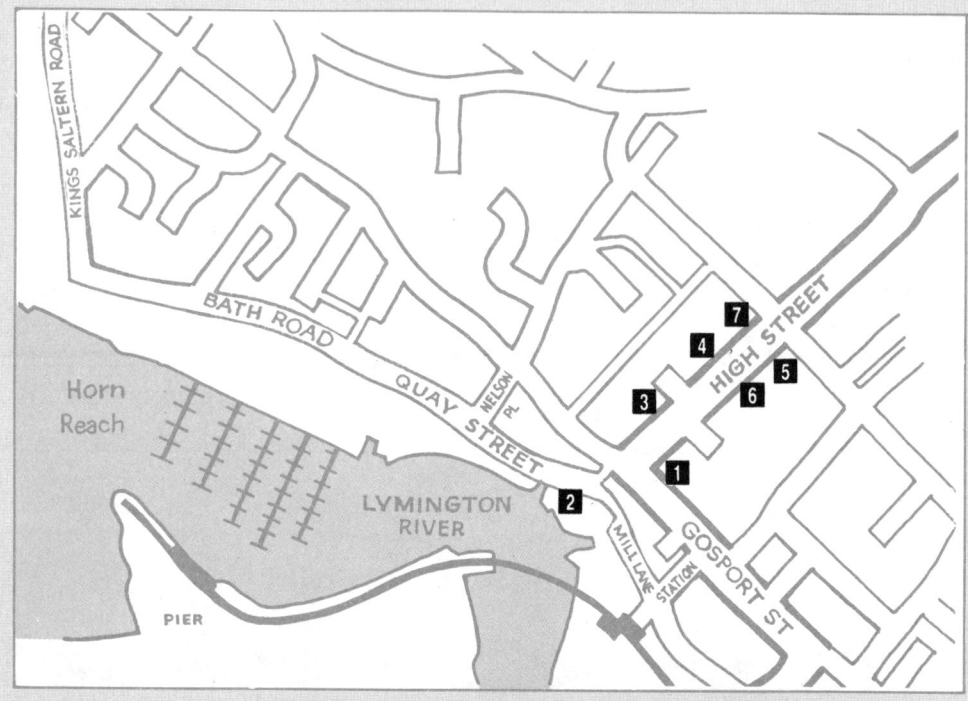

HARBOUR MASTER: (0590) 72014

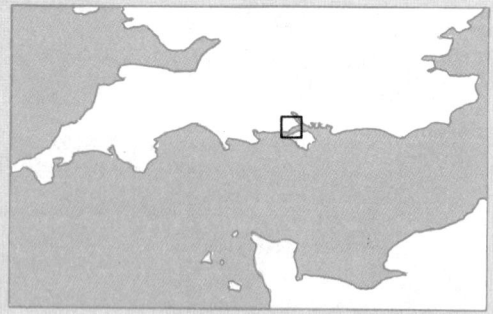

This is a major home port for many yachtsmen and is very well provided for in terms of all facilities. It also serves as a ferry terminal for boats going to the Isle of Wight.

Lymington first received a royal charter in the 13th century and became prosperous as a centre for the refining of salt. It is an attractive town, particularly around Quay Hill, and is awash with visitors during the summer. A market is held on Saturdays and the High Street gets very busy. Yarmouth is a short sail away, and Christchurch Bay readily accessible.

MOORINGS

Lymington Marina.
(0590) 75444
£9.80 per day.　　£49.00 per week.

Lymington Yacht Haven.
(0590) 77073
£12.00 per day.　　£60.40 per week.

Harbour Master.
(0590) 72014
£6.00 per day.　　£42.00 per week.

RESTAURANTS

1 Fagins:
135 High Street. (0590) 73074.
Timbered booths reminiscent of a London steak house, engravings from Dickens on the walls and fine food at reasonable prices help explain the continuing popularity of this very pleasant restaurant. Booking is essential close to the weekend; if you are a party of more than four, try to secure the round table in the corner. Credit Cards: Access, Amex, Diners, Visa.

2 New Flounders:
5 Quay Street. (0590) 77364.
Whilst her husband runs Fagins, his wife masterminds this very pleasant fish restaurant just off the quay. It is small and cosy, serves adventurous fish dishes and plenty of people agree it's fun, so booking is essential. Credit Cards: Access, Amex, Diners, Visa.

HARBOUR SERVICES (YACHTS)

General: Lymington Yacht Haven.
(0590) 77073.

Mechanical Engineers:
Berthon Boat Company. (0590) 73312.

Electronic Engineers:
Regis Marine Electronics. (0590) 79251.

SERVICES AVAILABLE

●	Petrol	●	Water
●	Diesel	●	Slipway
●	Calor Gas	●	Chandlery
●	Camping Gas		

HARBOUR SERVICES (PERSONAL)

Showers: Both marinas.

3 Post Office: 54 High Street.

Telephone: Both marinas.
The Post Office.

Laundry:
Lymington Launderette, ll New Street.

Taxi & Cars:
Ken Cars (0590) 73372.
Pennington Cross Car Hire. (0590) 73227.

CHEMISTS AND MEDICAL SERVICES

Chemists:
C.D. Smith. 72 High Street.

Medical:
Lymington Hospital. (0590) 77011.

BANKS

4 **Barclays:** 21 High Street.

5 **LLoyds:** 39 High Street.

6 **Midland:** 102 High Street.

7 **National Westminster:**
38 High Street.

POLICE: (0590) 75411

THE SAILING MATCH.

YARMOUTH, ISLE OF WIGHT

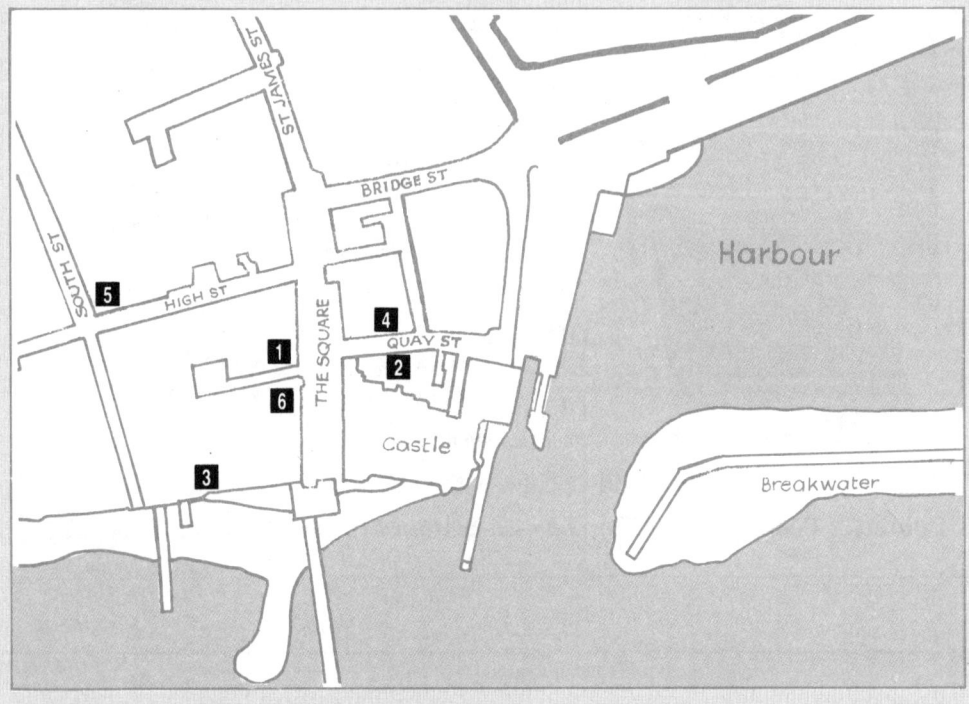

HARBOUR MASTER: (0983) 760300

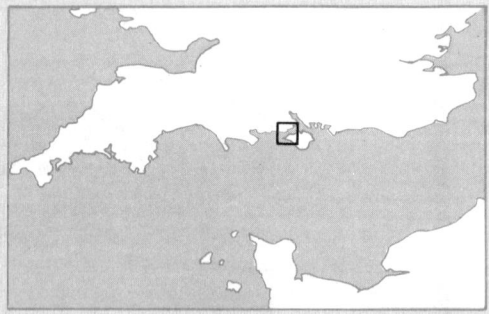

T his is a very popular port, ideally situated for those wishing to catch the tide past the Needles to go west or across the Channel, and it often gets very full. Boats come and go at all times so you are quite likely to find your sleep disturbed as neighbouring yachts try to extricate themselves. It is all very friendly and the harbour staff are helpful in seeking out a mooring for you. However they sometimes simply cannot accommodate everybody and the harbour has to be closed.

Yarmouth was the main port on the Isle of Wight as long ago as the 12th century; it received a royal charter and remained a borough till 1891. A ferry service runs between it and Lymington on the mainland opposite. The town itself is small and picturesque, with narrow streets that run from the harbour and the remains of a castle built by Henry VIII. Everything is close to the quayside.

For those interested in seafood a visit to Puffins Fisheries on the banks of the Yar will prove most rewarding. By dinghy go under the bridge up the Yar for about 200 yards and look for the River Yar Boatyard situated up a creek on the starboard side. From there Puffins is clearly visible. The sheds contain tanks of live crabs and lobsters, and you can pick which you want and have them cooked on the premises. There are few more pleasant experiences than to sit in the cockpit of the boat on a sunny lunchtime with a glass of cold white wine, eating a freshly cooked lobster, watching all the activity in the harbour.

MOORINGS

Contact The Harbourmaster.
(0983) 760300
£4.50 per day.

RESTAURANTS

1 The Bugle:
This old hotel in the main square facing down the High Street has several bars and a small courtyard where there is a barbecue. While not providing *haute cuisine*, the food is reasonable and the service attentive and willing.

2 The George:
The facade of this hotel is unprepossessing but the interior is comfortable, with a pleasant bar, newly refurbished with a nautical flavour, and a large garden to the rear where you can sit out and watch the yachts on the Solent.
The dining room is large and elegant, and no one is going to be dissappointed with the food providing they are not expecting west end standards.

HARBOUR SERVICES (YACHTS)

General: Harwood's Ltd, The Square.

Mechanical Engineers:
Buzzard Engineering, Saltern Wood Quay. (0983) 760065.

Sailmakers:
Saltern Sail Company, Saltern Wood Quay. (0983) 760120.

Boat Builders & Repairers:
Harold Hayles. (0983) 760373.

SERVICES AVAILABLE

● Petrol		● Water	
● Diesel		● Slipway	
● Calor Gas		● Chandlery	
● Camping Gas			

HARBOUR SERVICES (PERSONAL)

3 **Showers:** Royal Solent Yacht Club.

4 **Post Office:** Quay Street.

Telephone: Post Office.
Royal Solent Yacht Club.

Taxi & Cars:
Yarmouth Cab and Car Hire. (0983)
761176.

3 **Yacht Clubs:**
Royal Solent Yacht Club, The Square.
(0983) 760239.

CHEMISTS AND MEDICAL SERVICES

5 **Chemists:**
Dorringtons. High Street.

Medical:
The Surgery, Station Road. (0983)
760434.

BANKS

6 **Lloyds:** The Square.

COASTGUARD: (0705) 552100
POLICE: (0983) 528000

BEAULIEU RIVER

Probably the most picturesque of all the Solent anchorages, the Beaulieu estuary is accessible in all states of the tide and the marina at Bucklers Hard provides a quiet sheltered mooring in beautiful surroundings. After the motorway of the Solent, this tranquil backlane offers a real escape.

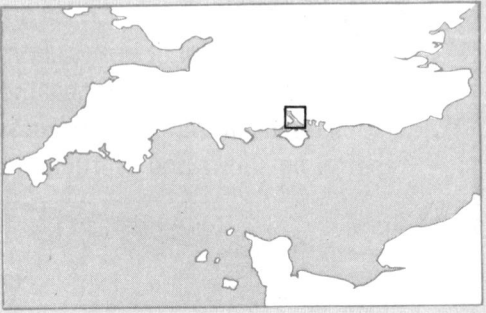

A short walk alongside the river takes you to the village of Bucklers Hard, where two rows of 18th-century cottages face each other across a broad green swathe. It is part of the Montagu estate - Beaulieu Palace House lies six miles north - and was originally conceived as a port for the importing of sugar from the West Indies but became a shipbuilding community when the sugar islands were captured by the French. Two of Nelson's fleet, the *Euryalus* and the *Agamemnon*, were built here. The village has been restored to its former glory and today's visitors seem slightly misplaced in these gracious surroundings. The hotel and restaurant, The Master Builder, was originally the home of Henry Adams, the master shipbuilder of Buckler's Hard. Next door to it is the tiny chapel of St Mary, a very popular church for weddings.

MOORINGS

Bucklers Hard Yacht Harbour.
(0590) 63234
River £6.00 per day.   £27.70 per week.

Bucklers Hard Yacht Harbour.
(0590) 63234
Marina £11.20 per day.   £56.00 per week.

RESTAURANTS

The Master Builder:
Bucklers Hard. (0590) 253.
Now a large hotel, this inn has not lost any of its charm. Try to secure a table by the windows and watch the sunset over the river. The food is fairly standard English *à la carte* but after a day on the Solent you probably won't worry too much, and the position and friendly service make everything seem rather better than it is.
Credit Cards: Access, Amex, Diners, Visa.

PUBS

The Master Builder:
Bucklers Hard.
Not only a hotel and restaurant but a very pleasant pub as well. Traditional beers and a wide selection of snacks make it very popular with tourists and the yachting fraternity. One of those places where you are almost bound to bump into somebody you know.

HARBOUR SERVICES (YACHTS)

General: Bucklers Hard Boat Builders at the harbour provide all facilities.

SERVICES AVAILABLE

 Petrol   Water

Diesel Slipway

Calor Gas Chandlery

Camping Gas

HARBOUR SERVICES (PERSONAL)

Showers: Bucklers Hard Yacht Harbour.

Telephone: Bucklers Hard Yacht Harbour.

Laundry: None.

Taxi & Cars:
Maurice Badland. (0590) 612267.

CHEMISTS AND MEDICAL SERVICES

Medical:
Lymington General Hospital. (0590) 77011.

COASTGUARD: (0703) 893574

COWES

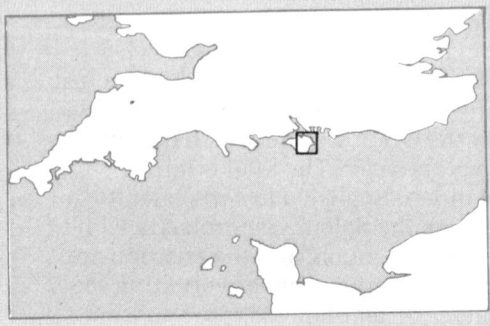

Cowes is likely to be something of a disappointment on first approach. The English think of it as the yachting capital of the world, and certainly it does have a worldwide reputation, but this leaves the visitor unprepared for the drab industrial atmosphere that surrounds the harbour. However, that is soon over and the persuading feature of Cowes is that almost everybody there has the same interest, sailing. It is of course home of the Royal Yacht Squadron, which was formed in 1815 as the Yacht Club, became the Royal Yacht Club in 1820 and the Royal Yacht Squadron in 1833.

The only surviving part of the castle now forms a platform on the promenade mounted with 21 brass cannons which are fitted to start the many yacht races that take place during the season. Cowes week, the first in August, attracts many visitors from all over the world and the Round the Island race enables everyone to have a go at 'ocean racing'. It was from Cowes that the first America's Cup took place on 22 August 1851, when Commodore George Stevens beat 14 English boats in a race around the island. At this time Cowes was beginning to develop in stature as a yachting centre but it was not until the Prince of Wales, later Edward VII, started racing yachts from here in the 1890s that it became a really fashionable resort and the reputed yachting capital of the world.

MOORINGS

Ancasta Marine.
£11.55 per day.   £80.85 per week.

RESTAURANTS

The Capri:
Princess Building, Bath Road. (0983) 295137.
An authentic, family-run Italian restaurant where the food is of a good standard and the service most attentive. Cowes has long been deprived of a

selection of places to eat and this is a most welcome addition.
Credit Cards: Access, Visa.

The Holmwood Hotel:
Egypt Point. (0983) 292508.
The hotel is quite a walk from the centre of town but the effort is rewarded. Its Flying Dutchman restaurant is comfortable and well-appointed. When sitting in the bar there is no doubt about its yachting connections, for the doors are covered with the signatures of many of the crews that have stayed at the hotel and it can be fun trying to decipher the names. The food is of a reasonable standard and the views from the dining room magnificent.
Credit Cards: Access, Amex, Diners, Visa.

HARBOUR SERVICES (YACHTS)

General: Ancasta Marine has all facilities.

SERVICES AVAILABLE

 Petrol   Water

 Diesel   Slipway

Calor Gas   Chandlery

 Camping Gas

HARBOUR SERVICES (PERSONAL)

Showers: Ancasta Marine.

Post Office: High Street.

Telephone: Ancasta Marine.

Laundry: Ancasta Marine.

Taxi & Cars: Rank. (0983) 297024.

Yacht Clubs:
Royal Yacht Squadron. (0983) 292191.
The Royal Corinthian. (0983) 292608.
The Royal London. (0983) 292949.
The Island Sailing Club. (0983) 293061.

CHEMISTS AND MEDICAL SERVICES

Medical:
Frank James Hospital, Adelaide Square.
(0983) 296504.

BANKS

Barclays: 57 High Street.

Lloyds: 71 High Street.

Midland: 86 High Street.

National Westminster:
104 High Street. Cowes harbour.

POLICE: (0983) 528000

SOUTHAMPTON

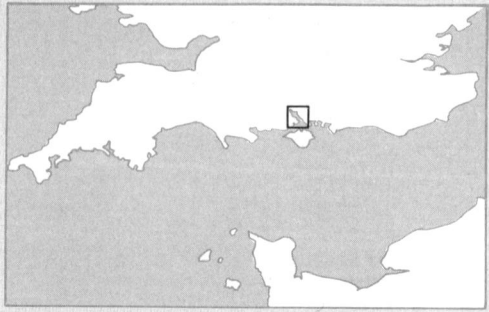

From a yachtsman's point of view Southampton has one significant disadvantage: from the Solent you are faced with a trek of about an hour to one of the available moorings. For people looking for a permanent mooring Southampton has much to offer, but for visitors the long haul through waters crowded with ferries and hydrofoils as well as other commercial and naval shipping should be seriously considered before deciding to take advantage of the newly developed marinas.

Southampton has had a long and important history. There was a Roman settlement on the banks of the Itchen and by Saxon times it was one of the largest towns of Europe. Following the Norman invasion, William the Conqueror developed the town and it became one of his foremost supply ports. It underwent a decline in fortunes during Tudor and Stuart times, only to find importance during the 18th and 19th centuries as a health resort. The building of the docks in the middle of the 19th century saw the start of Southampton's golden period. During the time of the great ocean liners the port became synonymous with luxury travel and people seeking fame and fortune in far off countries.

Southampton was heavily bombed during the last war but many historic buildings remain, among them the Tudor House Museum in Bugle Street and nearby the Wool House Museum, which is situated in a mediaeval warehouse and is devoted to maritime history. Of more recent interest is the Southampton Hall of Aviation, also known as the R.J. Mitchell Museum after the designer of the Spitfire.

The three new marina developments, Hythe, Ocean Village and Shamrock Quay, are all sited some way from the city centre but all provide excellent facilities for yachtsmen, along with restaurants, bars and boutiques. They have the advantage of being self-contained and the visitor will find all services on site.

MOORINGS

Hythe Marina.
(0703) 849263)
£7.00 per day.   £35.00 per week.

Ocean Village Marina.
(0703) 228353
£7.00 per day.   £35.00 per week.

Shamrock Quay.
(0703) 229461
£5.25 per day.   £26.25 per week.

HARBOUR SERVICES (YACHTS)

General: All marinas have all facilities.

SERVICES AVAILABLE

- ● Petrol
- ● Diesel
- ● Calor Gas
- ● Camping Gas
- ● Water
- ● Slipway
- ● Chandlery

HARBOUR SERVICES (PERSONAL)

Showers: All marinas.

Post Office: 59 High Street.

Telephone: All marinas.

Laundry: All marinas.

Taxi & Cars:
Associated Taxi Service. (0703) 223450.

CHEMISTS AND MEDICAL SERVICES

Chemists:
Boots. 19 Above Bar Street.

Medical:
Southampton General, Tremona Road, Shirley. (0703) 777222.

BANKS

Barclays: 171 High Street.

Lloyds: 125 Above Bar.

Midland: 165 High Street.

National Westminster:
129 High Street.

POLICE: (0703) 26222

HAMBLE RIVER

This estuary probably has more boats to the square metre than any other in the UK. Plastic yachties, Hooray Henries and the genuine article rub shoulders with seeming equanimity. The river's popularity with visitors means that coming in and going out can be a bit of a procession since the channel is narrow due to all the boats moored up to pontoons in the middle.

Hamble was a fishing port up to the First World War and also famous for its oysters. All this has changed and the whole village is devoted to yachting. It is a most attractive place, with little streets meandering down to the quayside. There is no shortage of inns, but they all become crowded during the summer.

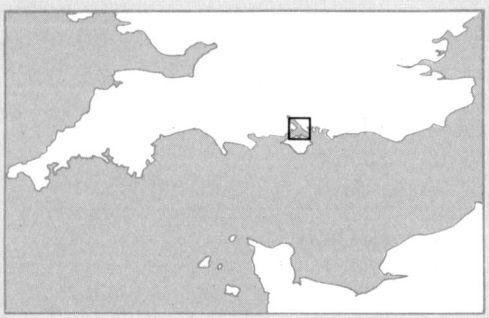

RESTAURANTS

Beth's:
The Quay. (0703) 454314.
By far the best reason to visit Hamble is this splendid restaurant. A large drawing room style bar on the ground floor provides a quiet comfortable atmosphere to recover from the day's activities and to ponder on the delights of the menu. As with most of the better restaurants the emphasis is on a small number of dishes that reflect the availability of fresh produce. The dining room upstairs is quite small so to avoid disappointment you should book. A really pleasant place well deserving of its two knives and forks rating from Michelin. Closed Sundays. Credit Cards: Access, Amex, Diners, Visa.

MOORINGS

Harbour Master.
(04895) 6387
£2.00 per day.   £12.00 per week.

Hamble Point Marina.
(0703) 452464
£8.50 per day.   £44.27 per week.

PUBS

The Bugle:
High Street.
An extremely large and popular Inn. There is a restaurant that overlooks the river.

The King and Queen:
High Street.
A wide selection of pies and other bar food make this friendly pub busy most of the year and pretty frantic in the season.

HARBOUR SERVICES (YACHTS)

General: Hamble Point Marina. (0703) 452464.
Compass Point Chandlery, The Quay.

Mechanical Engineers:
Hamble Point Marina.

Sailmakers:
Williams Sails, Satchel Lane.

Boat Builders & Repairers:
Hamble Point Marina.

SERVICES AVAILABLE

- ● Petrol
- ● Diesel
- ● Calor Gas
- ● Camping Gas
- ● Water
- ● Slipway
- ● Chandlery

BANKS

Barclays:
St Andrew's Building, High Street.

Lloyds: High Street.

National Westminster:
4 High Street.

COASTGUARD: (0705) 552100

BURSLEDON

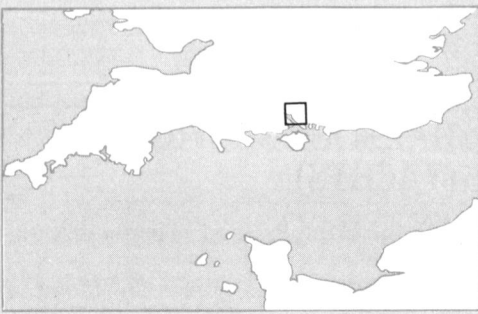

This village on the River Hamble has gained notoriety as Tarrant in the BBC television series *Howards Way*. Addicts of the programme will recognise the Jolly Sailor and the Elephant Boatyard. You can even take a guided cruise on the river where all the places featured in the series are pointed out, though you probably will not stay long enough to ascertain if life is as frenetic and seamy as shown on television.

The great disadvantage to Bursledon is the trek down the Hamble but if you do undertake it, a mooring at Moody's Marina and a quick run across to the Jolly Sailor in the dinghy can be quite rewarding. The village is in two parts, one straggling along the main A3024, the other secluded on the hillside overlooking the river. It has long been a centre for boatbuilding; Nelson's flagship *Elephant*, from which he commanded the fleet at the Battle of Copenhagen, was built here. Today most boatbuilding is of leisure craft and there is an industrial air to the buildings that surround the river.

MOORINGS

Moody Marina, Swanwick.
(0489) 885000
£9.66 per day.   £60.38 per week.

PUBS

The Jolly Sailor:
Bursledon.
A charming 18th-century pub right on the water's edge, with small beamed bars which get very crowded in the summer and good snacks ranging from sandwiches to basket meals. There is a terrace and jetty where you can drink and eat in good weather.

HARBOUR SERVICES (YACHTS)

General: Moody Marina, Swanwick. (0489) 885000.

Mechanical Engineers:
Moody Marina, Swanwick. (0489) 885000.

Electronic Engineers:
Moody Marina, Swanwick. (0489) 88500.

Sailmakers:
Bruce Banks. (0489) 82444.

Boat Builders & Repairers:
The Elephant Boatyard, Landsend Road. (042 121) 3268.
Moody Marina, Swanwick. (0489) 885000.

SERVICES AVAILABLE

●	Petrol	●	Water
●	Diesel	●	Slipway
●	Calor Gas	●	Chandlery
●	Camping Gas		

HARBOUR SERVICES (PERSONAL)

Showers: Moody Marina.

Telephone: Moody Marina.

CHEMISTS AND MEDICAL SERVICES

Chemists:
Instore Pharmacy.
Tesco Store.
Bursledon Towers.

COASTGUARD: (0705) 552100

PORTSMOUTH

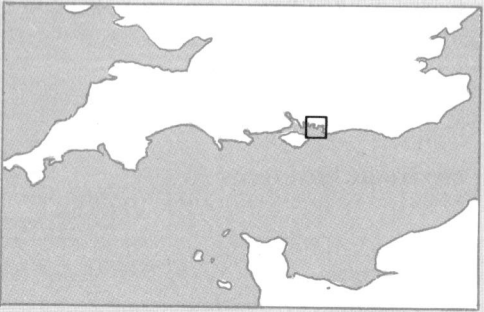

From the time of Henry VII Portsmouth has been first and foremost a naval town. While today there is some commercial and ferry traffic, it remains primarily a naval port. It developed from a village whose prime activity was ship repair work, and it is believed that the first dry dock was constructed here towards the end of the 14th century.

It is difficult to miss the Round Tower when entering the harbour. This was built by Henry V to protect the harbour from attack and chains were hauled across from it to another tower at the other side to prohibit the entrance of enemy vessels. During the Napoleonic Wars Portsmouth became the senior British naval port, renowned for its association with *HMS Victory*, Nelson's flagship during the Battle of Trafalgar. Although she is now a museum open to the public, she is still a serving ship. In the dockyards close by is the *Mary Rose*, a warship of Henry VIII's that was only recently raised from the seabed.

Not all of Portsmouth's claims to fame are naval. In 1812 Charles Dickens was born here at 393 Commercial Road. The house has been restored and is now a museum dedicated to his life and work.

Whilst Portsmouth offers splendid facilities for someone looking for permanent moorings, it lacks some of the charm that many cruising yachtsmen may be seeking.

MOORINGS

Camper and Nicholson Marina.
(0705) 524811.
£10.50 per day.   £52.50 per week.

HARBOUR SERVICES (PERSONAL)

General: Camper and Nicholson have all services.

Mechanical Engineers:
Camper and Nicholson have all services.

Electronic Engineers:
Camper and Nicholson have all services

Sailmakers:
Camper and Nicholson.

Boat Builders & Repairers:
Camper and Nicholson have all services.

SERVICES AVAILABLE

 Petrol   Water

 Diesel   Slipway

 Calor Gas   Chandlery

 Camping Gas

HARBOUR SERVICES (YACHTS)

Showers: Camper and Nicholson.

Post Office: 136 High Street.

Telephone: Camper and Nicholson.

Laundry: Camper and Nicholson.

Taxi & Cars:
Associated Taxi (0705) 522552.
Southern Self Drive Hire Service (0705) 525325.

CHEMISTS AND MEDICAL SERVICES

Chemists:
Boots. 109 High Street.

Medical:
Gosport War Memorial Hospital. (0705) 524611.

BANKS

Barclays: 43-44 High Street.

Lloyds: 24 High Street.

Midland: 26-27 High Street.

National Westminster:
5 High Street.

TSB: 18 High Street.

COASTGUARD: (0705) 552100
POLICE: (0705) 321111

CHICHESTER

HARBOUR MASTER: (0243) 512301 or radio VHF Ch 14

Chichester Harbour provides many alternative mooring facilities. The whole harbour is sheltered and is home for almost 7,000 yachts. The main moorings are at Hayling Island, Emsworth, Bosham and Birdham.

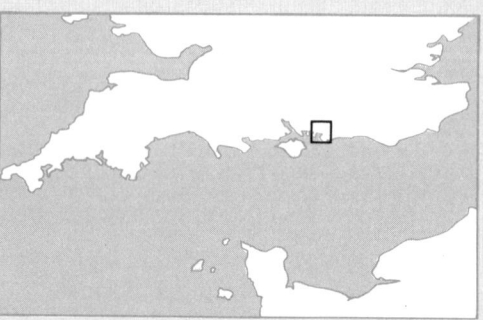

The cathedral city of Chichester lies to the north-east of the harbour, about three miles from Birdham, though the graceful spire of the cathedral can be seen for miles. The place has a long and proud history. A Roman camp from AD43, when it was known as Noviomagus, it developed in importance when the Normans built the cathedral and during the Middle Ages it became a centre of learning and the wool trade. There are few more attractive cities in the UK and this is enhanced by the traffic-free town centre. It is very much worth taking the time to visit, particularly as there are some notable restaurants to enjoy.

Chichester Yacht Basin is about two and a half miles south, with enough facilities for the visitor not to need to leave the site.

Bosham, pronounced Bozzum, a delightfully unspoilt village with a long history. The Roman Emperor Vespasian is reputed to have lived there and King Canute also had some association with the once-important port. A scene in the Bayeux Tapestry depicts King Harold entering Bosham Church, which still stands though altered over the centuries.

MOORINGS

Birdham Pool.
(0243) 512310
£8.05 per day.   £28.17 per week.

Chichester Yacht Basin, Birdham.
(0243) 512731
£8.28 per day.

RESTAURANTS

The Millstream:
Bosham Lane, Bosham. (0243) 573234.
This is a large, imposing hotel, part of the Best Western chain, situated a few hundred metres from the quay. You are unlikely to be welcomed with open arms if you turn up in dripping foul weather gear as it is a plushly furnished and decorated establishment. The dining room is spacious and restfully appointed but by comparison the food may be something of a disappointment. The cold buffet is good value.

PUBS

Anchor Bleu:
High Street, Bosham.
This is a most delightful small pub that has one major disadvantage. It is so popular that it is sometimes very difficult to get in at all. In good weather this problem is alleviated somewhat as it is possible to drink outside.

HARBOUR SERVICES (YACHTS)

General: Chichester Yacht Basin has all facilities.

SERVICES AVAILABLE

- ● Petrol
- ● Diesel
- ● Calor Gas
- ● Camping Gas
- ● Water
- ● Slipway
- ● Chandlery

HARBOUR SERVICES (PERSONAL)

Showers: Chichester Yacht Basin.

Post Office: 10 West Street.

Telephone: Chichester Yacht Basin.

Laundry:
Chichester Yacht Basin. Laundromat, Eastgate Square.

Taxi & Cars:
Blue Line Taxi (0243) 774279.
Whyke Auto-Rent (0243) 775538.

Yacht Clubs:
Chichester Yacht Club, Chichester Yacht Basin. (0243) 512918.

CHEMISTS AND MEDICAL SERVICES

Chemists:
Boots. 89 East Street.

Medical:
Royal West Sussex Hospital, Broyle Road. (0243) 781411.

BANKS

Barclays: 74/75 East Street.

Lloyds: 10 East Street.

Midland: 94 East Street.

National Westminster:
5 East Street.

TSB: Ambassador House, 5/7 Crane Street.

COASTGUARD: (0705) 4095
POLICE: (0243) 784433

HAYLING ISLAND

This island is very popular with holiday-makers during the summer and some of the associated paraphernalia has not helped its natural beauty. A bridge, usually crowded with fishermen, joins the island to the mainland. The Island itself is very flat – the highest point is only 8 metres above sea level – and as a result it has been subject to frequent flooding. There are two villages, North Hayling and South Hayling, the second of which has an interesting architectural oddity in the Crescent. This was built well over 100 years ago to rival the great crescents of Bath but was never completed so that only the eastern part exists.

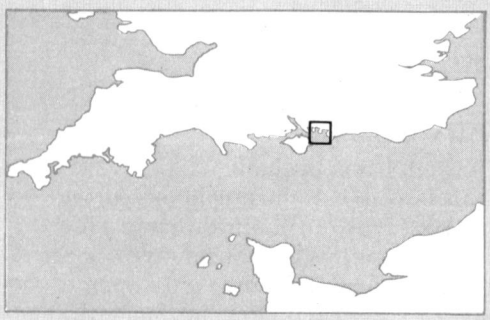

HARBOUR SERVICES (YACHTS)

General: The marinas have all facilities.

Mechanical Engineers: The marinas have all facilities.

Boat Builders & Repairers: The marinas have all facilities.

SERVICES AVAILABLE

- ● Petrol
- ● Diesel
- ● Calor Gas
- ● Camping Gas
- ● Water
- ● Slipway
- ● Chandlery

MOORINGS

Hayling Island Yacht Co.
(0705) 463592.
£3.50 per day.   £12.00 per week.

Northney Marina.
(0705) 466321.
£10.00 per day.   £56.00 per week.

Sparkes Boat Yard.
(0705) 463572.
£10.00 per day.   £56.00 per week.

HARBOUR SERVICES (PERSONAL)

Showers: Hayling Island Yacht Co.
Northney Marina.
Sparkes Yacht Harbour.

Post Office: St Mary's Road.

Telephone: Northney Marina.
Sparkes Yacht Harbour.

Laundry:
Hayling Island Launderette, 9 Elm Grove.

Taxi & Cars:
Summerfield Cars (0705) 467381.
Hayden Self Drive (0705) 462660.

Yacht Clubs:
Hayling Island Sailing Club, Sandy Point. (0705) 463768.

CHEMISTS AND MEDICAL SERVICES

Chemists:
Savory and Moore. 42 Elm Grove.

Medical:
The War Memorial Hospital, Havant.
(0705) 484256.

BANKS

Barclays:
67 Beach Road, South Hayling.

Lloyds: 23 Elm Grove.

National Westminster:
22 Mengham Road.

COASTGUARD: (0705) 4095
POLICE: (0705) 321111

EMSWORTH

msworth is a picturesque little town located at the far end of the Emsworth Channel. It was once the most important port of Chichester Harbour and had a reputation as a smugglers' haunt. Until the beginning of the century it was also a major oyster fishery but sadly the beds were polluted and this industry went into decline. South Street is a charming reminder of how Emsworth must have looked in times gone by and, quite apart from the pubs and restaurants to be found there, is worth visiting.

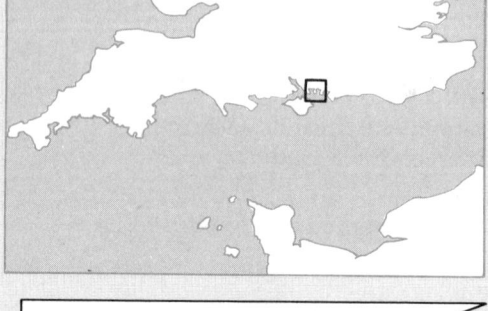

RESTAURANTS

Inn on the Quay:
47 South Street. (0243) 372257.
As it's name suggests this is a waterfront restaurant. You enter through a small bar which can get a little crowded. The restaurant itself is very spacious and the views over the harbour very charming. The menu has some American overtones like Surf and Turf for fillet steak with scallops. In terms of price this is not for the faint hearted.
Credit Cards: Access, Amex, Diners, Visa.

Julie's:
30 South Street. (0243) 377914.
A charming small restaurant close to the quay. The menu has been carefully thought out and the results are pleasant and imaginative. Book to avoid any disappointment.
Credit Cards: Access, Diners, Visa.

MOORINGS

Emsworth Yacht Harbour.
(0243) 375211. VHF Ch 37.
(Max size possible ca.30').
£6.00 per day.   £30.00 per week.

PUBS

The Coal Exchange:
South Street.
A traditional pub that makes few concessions to the passage of time and is probably much the better for it. Very conveniently located if you are making for either of the two restaurants recommended.

HARBOUR SERVICES (PERSONAL)

Showers: Emsworth Yacht Harbour.

Post Office: North Street.

Telephone: Emsworth Yacht Harbour.

Laundry: Coinwash, Victoria Road.

Taxi & Cars:
Pennicutts Taxi (0243) 372078.
C.J.W. Wilshire (0243) 373195.

Yacht Clubs:
Emsworth Sailing Club, 55 Bath Road.
(024 34) 3065.

CHEMISTS AND MEDICAL SERVICES

Chemists:
John Preddy. 38 High Street.

Medical:
Victoria Cottage Hospital. (0243) 372394.

BANKS

Barclays: 10-12 High Street.

Lloyds: 30 High Street.

National Westminster:
15 High Street.

COASTGUARD: (0705) 4095
POLICE: (0705) 321111

LITTLEHAMPTON

HARBOUR MASTER: (0903) 721215 or radio VHF Ch 16

Littlehampton is a small town with a thriving tourist trade and a busy commercial harbour. The facilities for yachtsmen are sparse, though the Harbour Board are contemplating the building of a shower block. It has a loyal following of annual visitors, particularly from Holland. Care has to be taken entering the harbour as there is a bar and the tides can be very fierce.

To the west side of the Arun there is a wide stretch of sandy beach backed by dunes which offer some protection from the wind. To the east side of the river is the main part of the town, dominated by a huge amusement arcade, a far cry from the days when writers such as Byron and Galsworthy came here for quiet relaxation.

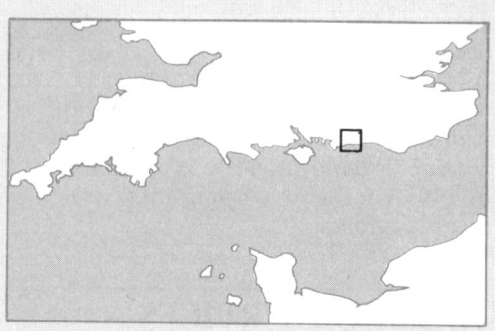

MOORINGS

Arun Yacht Club.
(0903) 714553. (32' max).
£4.60 per day.   £23.00 per week.

Littlehampton Harbour Board.
(0903) 721215
£3.00 per day.

HARBOUR SERVICES (YACHTS)

General: Britannia Watersports, Fishermans Quay.
Littlehampton Marina.

Mechanical Engineers:
Viking Marine Services, 129 Clun Road. (0903) 724873.

Electronic Engineers:
Viking Marine Services, 129 Clun Road. (0903) 724873.

Boat Builders & Repairers:
Viking Marine Services, 129 Clun Road. (0903) 724873.

SERVICES AVAILABLE

●	Petrol	●	Water
●	Diesel	●	Slipway
●	Calor Gas	●	Chandlery
●	Camping Gas		

HARBOUR SERVICES (PERSONAL)

Showers: Arun Yacht Club.

Post Office: The Arcade.

Telephone: Arun Yacht Club. Post Office.

Laundry: The Launderette, Norfolk Road.

Taxi & Cars: Arun Taxis. (0903) 717200.

Yacht Clubs: Arun Yacht Club, Riverside West. (0903) 714533.

CHEMISTS AND MEDICAL SERVICES

Chemists: Boots. High Street.

Medical: Health Centre, Fitzallen Road. (0903) 714113.

BANKS

Barclays: East Street.

Lloyds: Beech Road.

Midland: High Street.

National Westminster: High Street.

COASTGUARD: (0903) 715512
POLICE: (0903) 716161

BRIGHTON 19TH CENTURY.

BRIGHTON

HARBOUR MASTER: (0273) 693636

The Brighton marina is situated about two miles from the Palace Pier, so anyone putting into the marina with a view to visiting the town itself should bear this in mind. Taxis are easy to come by and there is an electric railway that runs from close by the marina to near the pier.

The development of the marina has been a long hard project, but when it was taken over by the Brent Walker group it began to take on a new momentum.

Before long, apart from all the yachting associated activities, there will be the Harbour Village, a giant Gateway superstore, a hotel and leisure complex all built with the aim to make Brighton marina as good as

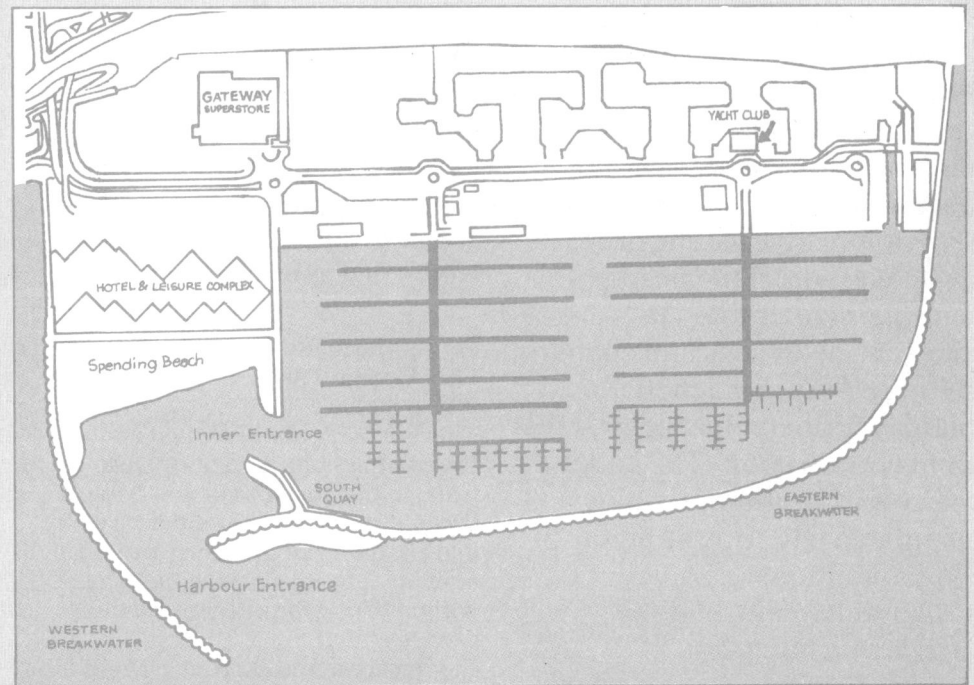

Map labels: GATEWAY SUPERSTORE · YACHT CLUB · HOTEL & LEISURE COMPLEX · Spending Beach · Inner Entrance · SOUTH QUAY · EASTERN BREAKWATER · Harbour Entrance · WESTERN BREAKWATER

any. The plans are exciting and it will be interesting to see how they develop.

Brighton is like a many seasoned showgirl who still manages to pack in the paying customers. It was once an insignificant seaside village, known as Brightelmstone, which came to prominence after a Doctor Russell published a book extolling the virtues of living by the coast in the mid-18th century. The idea caught on with the fashionable, who were soon coming to the seaside in their droves. The seal was set when the Prince Regent, later George IV, visited the village in 1783 and decided to build a summerhouse there. This was to become the Royal Pavilion, which began as an elegant country house and over the years grew increasingly elaborate as the fantasies of the Prince were embodied in the design. It stands just behind the seafront, a dashing monument to incongruity. Having found such favour in the eyes of the Prince Regent, the village became enormously popular with the nobility, wealthy and fashionable and soon Brightelmstone was no more and the Regency resort of Brighton had taken its place.

As with many seaside resorts, there is plenty to do and Brighton can certainly claim to cater to all tastes. Wide promenades with rows of deckchairs pointing towards the sea conjure up a feeling of nostalgia, whilst the nearby buildings are devoted to amusement arcades and shops selling all the usual modern holiday frippery. Just behind the front you will find The Lanes , a maze of little alleyways now populated with tiny antique shops, boutiques and restaurants, a must for the jackdaws among you.

Brighton succeeds in accommodating comfortably the brash and gaudy with the refined and sophisticated.

MOORINGS

Brighton Marina.
(0273) 693636
£10.56 per day.   £48.40 per week.

RESTAURANTS

The new Brighton marina project encompasses the construction of a village in which a selection of pubs and restaurants are envisaged, so as the development proceeds these facilities will become available.

1 La Marinade:
77 St George's Road, Kemp Town.
(0273) 600992.
This is a particularly elegant and welcoming small restaurant, reached through the upstairs bar and down a flight of stairs. You should dine well here, but it is not a place to go to in oilskins. The food is imaginative without being forcedly so and the service attentive.
Credit cards: Access, Amex, Diners, Visa.

2 The Laughing Onion:
80 St George's Road, Kemp Town.
(0273) 696555.
£17.25 might seem a lot of money to pay for dinner, but when that allows for choosing the most expensive dishes off the menu as starter, main course and dessert, a bottle of wine and a brandy, then it becomes very good value. The menu is excitingly different in French bistro style and Jean-Jacques Jordane has certainly produced a formula that appeals.
Credit Cards: Access, Amex, Diners, Visa.

PUBS

3 The Burlington:
St Georges Road Kemptown.
Remodelled to a regency theme. Large, remote but comfortable and only a brisk ten minutes from the marina.

4 The Golden Cannon:
St Georges Road Kemptown.
More traditional than The Burlington and a fraction closer.

HARBOUR SERVICES (YACHTS)

General: All facilities are available at the marina.

Mechanical Engineers:
Felton Marine Engineer. (0273) 601779.

SERVICES AVAILABLE

- ● Petrol
- ● Diesel
- ● Calor Gas
- ● Camping Gas
- ● Water
- ● Slipway
- ● Chandlery

HARBOUR SERVICES (PERSONAL)

Showers: Brighton Marina.

Post Office: Ship Street.

Telephone: Brighton Marina.

Laundry: Brighton Marina.
The Laundromat, 5 Powis Road.

Taxi & Cars:
Brighton and Hove Radio Cars (0273) 24245.
Avis Rent a Car (0273) 773233.

CHEMISTS AND MEDICAL SERVICES

5 Chemist.
St Georges Road, Kemptown.

Medical:
Brighton General Hospital, Elm Grove. (0273) 696011.

BANKS

6 Barclays:
St Georges Road, Kemptown.

7 Lloyds:
10-11 St Georges Road, Kemptown.

Midland: 153 North Street.

National Westminster:
137 North Street.

TSB: 16 New Road.

COASTGUARD: (0705) 552100
POLICE: (0273) 606744

NEWHAVEN

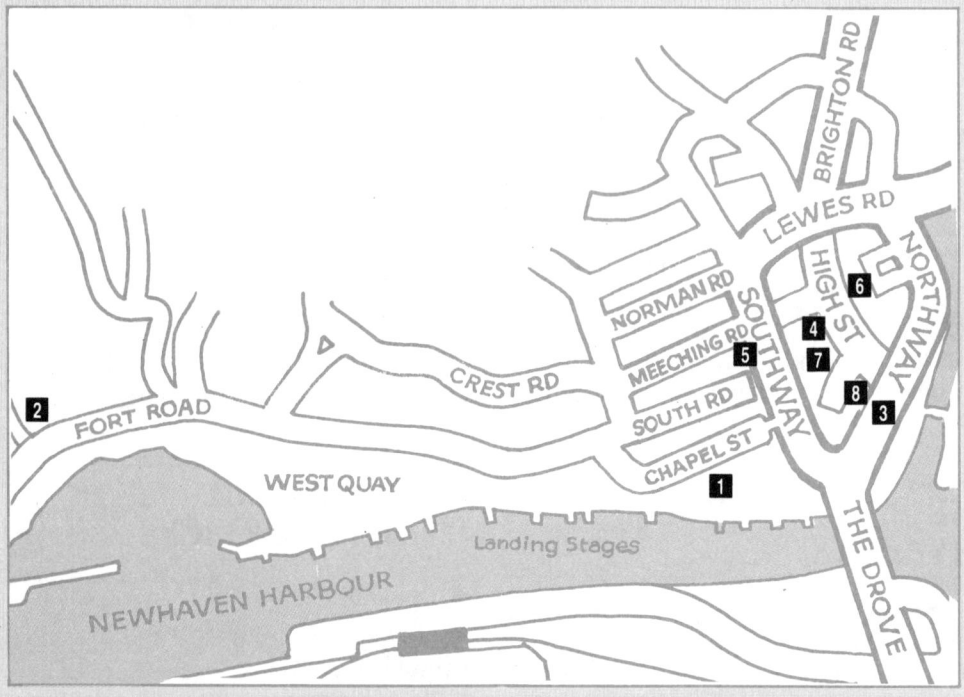

HARBOUR MASTER: (0273) 514131 or radio VHF Ch 16

Whilst it is easy to understand boat-owners keeping their craft at the marina here, it is very difficult to imagine anyone choosing to visit this port. It is a major ferry terminal and recently the commercial activities of the port have increased.

The River Ouse used to run into the Channel at Seaford but a freak tempest in the 16th century caused it to change course so that it flowed out further west near a village called Meeching.

This became Newhaven and as the port developed the main traffic was cross-Channel. Indeed it was to Newhaven that King Louis-Philippe of France fled during the revolution of 1848.

MOORINGS

Newhaven Marina Ltd.
(0273) 513881
£10.00 per day.   £50.00 per week.

Harbour Authority.
Contact The Harbourmaster (0273)
514131
£7.33 per day.   £105.77 per week.

RESTAURANTS

1 Buttimers:
16-18 Chapel Street. (0273) 514632.
A strange name for a restaurant with a
strong Spanish influence. Buttimers is
comfortable and expensive but then
with little competition you can
probably charge what you like.

PUBS

2 The Shenfield Arms:
Fort Road.
An imposing pub right by the marina
entrance and though not maybe a place
you would seek out, its very
convenience makes up for a great deal.
Salads, steaks and roast beef are
available for those looking for a bit
more than a drink.

3 The Bridge Hotel:
High Street.

time to visit this slightly dilapidated
pub where King Louis Philippe of
France fled after the 1848 revolution.

HARBOUR SERVICES (YACHTS)

General: Newhaven Marina. (0273)
513881.

Mechanical Engineers:
Leonard Marine, The Workshops,
Newhaven Marina.

Electronic Engineers:
Simpson Russel Marine Ltd. (0323)
3458.

SERVICES AVAILABLE

● Petrol   ● Water

● Diesel   ● Slipway

● Calor Gas   ● Chandlery

● Camping Gas

HARBOUR SERVICES (PERSONAL)

Showers: Newhaven Marina.

Post Office: 62 High Street.

Telephone: Newhaven Marina.

Laundry: By Marina.

Taxi & Cars:
Horace Taxi. (0273) 514764.

CHEMISTS AND MEDICAL SERVICES

4 Chemists:
Boots. 23 High Street.

Medical:
Newhaven Downs Hospital, Church
Hill. (0273) 513441.
For accidents and emergencies (0273)
609411.

BANKS

5 **Barclays:** 1 Newhaven Square.

6 **Lloyds:** 48 High Street.

7 **Midland:** 21 High Street.

8 **National Westminster:**
52 High Street.

COASTGUARD: (0273) 514008
POLICE: (0273) 514131

NEWHAVEN SIGNAL STATION 19TH CENTURY.

RYE

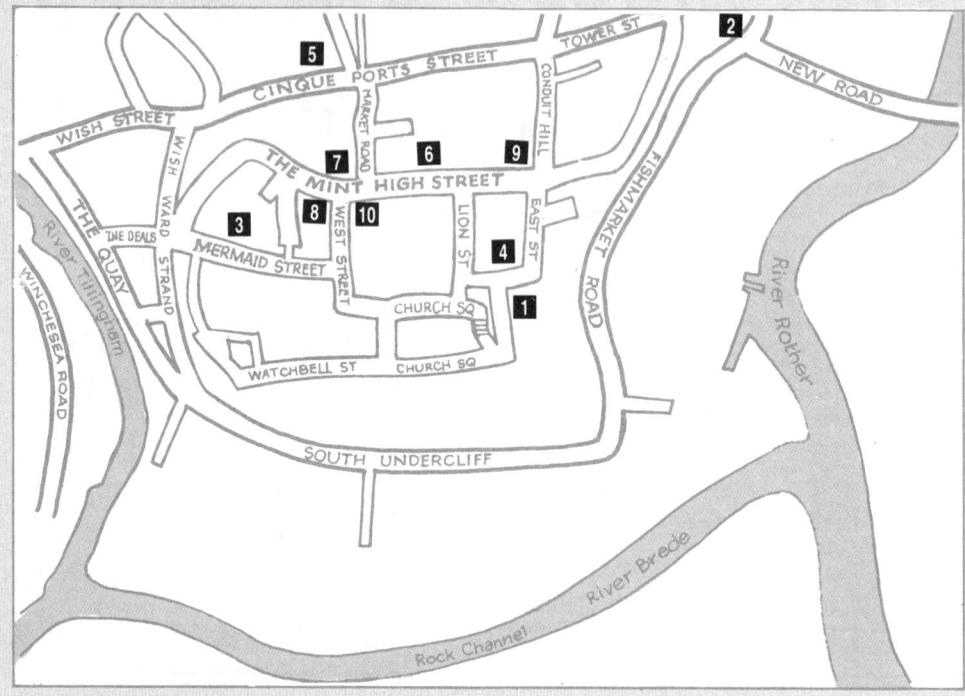

HARBOUR MASTER: (0797) 225225 or radio VHF Ch 16

One of the great historical towns of the south of England, Rye became a major port as early as the 14th century after a change in the course of the River Rother denied future development of New Romney and made Rye the senior of the Confederation of Cinque ports. The town is now some two miles from the sea and visiting yachtsmen should be prepared for a brisk walk to get there. The nearest mooring to the town is Rye Yachting Centre; Rye Harbour is closer to the sea. Both

dry out and can get very crowded, and although there is talk of building a marina, this has yet to materialise.

Rye is worth the walk. It remains a fascinating town, and though the mediaeval walls have long since ceased to fully surround it there is still an enclosed feel to the place. Narrow cobbled streets and gabled houses testify to the time when wealthy merchants lived and worked here and even the hordes of visitors have not brought the usual trappings of tourism in their wake to detract from the charm. Rye was a great haunt of smugglers - the Mermaid Inn played host to most of them - and interconnecting attics of the old houses enabled them to move freely and undetected about the town.

MOORINGS

Harbour Master.
(0797) 225225
£8.00 per day.   £50.00 per week.

Rye Yacht Centre.
(0797) 223336
£0.00 per day.   £0.00 per week.

Rye Harbour Marine.
(0797) 223152
£0.00 per day.   £0.00 per week.

Sandrock Auto Marine Ltd.
(0797) 222679
£5.00 per day.   £35.00 per week.

RESTAURANTS

1 Flushing Inn:
Market Street. (0797) 223292.
This is a heavyweight restaurant where the food is taken very seriously. From time to time special menus are created, reflecting a national style of cuisine with wines to match.
The building, which dates from the 15th century, stands on the site of another inn that was destroyed along with many other buildings by a fire in 1377. One of the main features of the restaurant is a 16th century wall painting. Certainly a welcome experience, but not for yachtsmen who have forgotten to pack at least a tie and better still a jacket as well.
Credit Cards: Access, Amex, Diners, Visa.

2 Landgate Bistro:
5-6 Landgate. (0797) 222829.
Do not be fooled by the term bistro. This is an ambitious restaurant where great care is taken in the preparation and serving of mainly local produce. Sauces and herbs play a major part in the style of cooking and there is a particular emphasis on fish.
Credit Cards: Access, Amex, Diners, Visa.

PUBS

3 The Mermaid:
Mermaid Street.
A popular tourist attraction, this famous Inn was once the haunt of smugglers.
Plenty of wood and armour add to the atmosphere.

4 The Union:
East Street.
A most attractive pub just off the High Street, which gets very crowded as many of the clientele come for the excellent food.

HARBOUR SERVICES (YACHTS)

General: Rye Yacht Centre.(0797) 223336.

Mechanical Engineers:
Sandrock Marine.(0797) 222679.

Boat Builders & Repairers:
Marine Traders, The Point.(0797) 224846.

SERVICES AVAILABLE

- ● Petrol
- ● Diesel
- ● Calor Gas
- ● Camping Gas
- ● Water
- ☐ Slipway
- ● Chandlery

HARBOUR SERVICES (PERSONAL)

5 Post Office: Cinque Port Streets.

Taxi & Cars:
Taxi-Time (0797) 224016.
Davies Limited (0797) 222329.

CHEMISTS AND MEDICAL SERVICES

6 Chemists:
Boots. 25 High Street.
Horrells. 17 High Street.

Medical:
Rye Memorial Hospital, Rye Hill.
(0797) 222109.

BANKS

7 Barclays: High Street.

8 Lloyds: High Street.

9 Midland: High Street.

10 National Westminster:
High Street.

COASTGUARD: (0797) 813171
POLICE: (0797) 222112

FOLKESTONE

Until the arrival of the railway, Folkestone was a small fishing port. With the trains came visitors from the towns and it became a popular holiday centre, unusual in that there is no seafront promenade. Later, the port became a ferry terminal and today Folkestone is a mixture of fishing port, tourist resort and ferry terminal.

The Stade provides a beautiful backdrop to anyone mooring here and gives an idea of what Folkestone must have been like when Charles Dickens wrote very favourably about the town. The Old High Street could be very attractive, but it has now been largely taken over by fish and chip cafes, junky tourist shops and amusement arcades.

As in many commercial ports, yachtsmen are only welcomed, or tolerated, on a temporary basis. The inner harbour dries out and the outer harbour is very exposed to the weather. There is also a great deal of traffic. So, unless you have a very specific reason to come here, you would be better advised to moor up at Rye.

MOORINGS

Harbour Master.
(0303) 54947
£5.00 per day.   £35.00 per week.

Folkestone Y & M.B. Club.
(0303) 51574

HARBOUR SERVICES (YACHTS)

General: Forepeak. (0303) 55752.

HARBOUR SERVICES (PERSONAL)

Showers: Yacht Club.

Post Office: 7 Bouverie Place.

Telephone: Post Office.

Taxi & Cars:
Taxi service (0303) 77777 (24-hour service).
Peacocks (Godfrey Davies) (0303) 58830.

Yacht Clubs:
Folkestone Yacht and Motor Boat Club,
North Street. (0303) 51574.

CHEMISTS AND MEDICAL SERVICES

Chemists:
Boots. 24 Sandgate Road.

Medical:
Royal Victoria Hospital. (0303) 57311.

BANKS

Barclays: 67 Sandgate Road.

LLoyds: 43 Sandgate Road.

Midland: 41 Sandgate Road

National Westminster:
Cheriton, 48 High Street.

TSB: 110 Sandgate Road.

POLICE: (0303) 53128

FOLKESTONE LATE 19TH CENTURY.

DOVER

Dover is the busiest ferry terminal in the UK and as a result visiting yachts are limited to a maximum stay of two weeks. Any visitor should look out for signals from the harbour authorities since there is a great deal of shipping movement here as well as frequent hovercraft flights.

Dover has been the gateway to England for centuries. The famous white cliffs were written about by Caesar and after the Roman conquest the port of Dubris was established here. Among the reminders of this period are the Roman Painted House, still with its wall paintings and under-floor heating, and the Pharos, a lighthouse built to guide ships across the Channel and which was probably about 12.5 metres high, although today only the lower stages remain.

The town was always strongly fortified, but it was William the Conqueror who started the massive development of Dover Castle which overlooks the town. In the following centuries it continued to be strengthened and a warren of underground defences was built during the Napoleonic Wars, which are open to the public. But although there are pockets that speak of its history, Dover almost inevitably has an air of transience about it and there is no overall feel to the place.

MOORINGS

Harbour Master.
(0304) 206560
£6.60 per day.   £46.20 per week.

HARBOUR SERVICES (YACHTS)

General: Dover Marine Supplies. (0304) 201677.

Mechanical Engineers:
Dover Yacht Company. (0304) 201073.

SERVICES AVAILABLE

- ● Petrol
- ● Diesel
- ● Calor Gas
- ● Camping Gas
- ● Water
- ● Slipway
- ● Chandlery

CHEMISTS AND MEDICAL SERVICES

Chemists:
Boots. 19 Biggin Street.

Medical:
Royal Victoria Hospital. (0304) 204508.

HARBOUR SERVICES (PERSONAL)

Post Office: 65 Biggin Street.

Taxi & Cars:
Dover Taxi (0304) 201915.
Hire Service/Port Service Centre (0304) 203655.

BANKS

Barclays: Market Square.

Lloyds: Market Square.

Midland: Biggin Street.

National Westminster: 25 Market Square.

TSB: 71 Castle Street.

COASTGUARD: (0304) 210008
POLICE: (0304) 201010

SANDWICH

I t is a pity that this fine historic town presents so many problems for visiting yachtsmen. The Stour is very narrow and difficult. Sandwich marina can offer berths only when the owners are away and is some distance from the town, while the quayside berths are very few and you will take the bottom at low tide.

Sandwich, one of the Cinque Ports, was once important. It provided a safe anchorage and was close to the continent. As such it was frequently attacked by the French, the bloodiest raid taking place in 1457 when some 4,000 French, mainly from Honfleur, took the town and put many of its leading inhabitants to the sword, including the mayor. To this day the mayor of Sandwich wears a black robe in memory of the event.

The importance of the port declined as the river silted up but its economy continued to thrive as weavers from the Netherlands took up residence in the town and many of Rye's fine houses date from this period. It is difficult to recommend Sandwich as a port to visit by yacht but if you are in Ramsgate it makes a very pleasant outing by car.

MOORINGS

Sandwich Quay.
(0304) 613283 (Quaymaster)
£4.50 per day.

RESTAURANTS

The Bell:
The interior is much more attractive than the exterior would lead you to believe, with well-appointed public rooms and a largish restaurant where the service is very good. You will certainly eat in comfort, although at probably more cost than you feel is justified.
Credit Cards: Access, Amex, Diners, Visa.

HARBOUR SERVICES (YACHTS)

General: Highway Marine, Pillory Gate Wharf. (0304) 613925.

Sailmakers:
Highway Marine, Pillory Gate Wharf. (0304) 613925.

Boat Builders & Repairers:
Highway Marine, Pillory Gate Wharf. (0304) 613925.

SERVICES AVAILABLE

- ● Petrol
- ● Diesel
- ● Calor Gas
- ● Camping Gas
- ● Water
- ☐ Slipway
- ● Chandlery

HARBOUR SERVICES (PERSONAL)

Post Office: 34 King Street.

Telephone: The Post Office.

Taxi & Cars:
Brians Cars. (0304) 612852.

CHEMISTS AND MEDICAL SERVICES

Chemists:
Satterleys. Cattle Market.

Medical:
Eastry Hospital. (0304) 614110.

BANKS

Barclays: 2 Cattle Market.

Lloyds: 12 Market Street.

Midland: 10 Cattle Market.

National Westminster:
Eastry, 1 The Parade.

POLICE: (0304) 362167

RAMSGATE

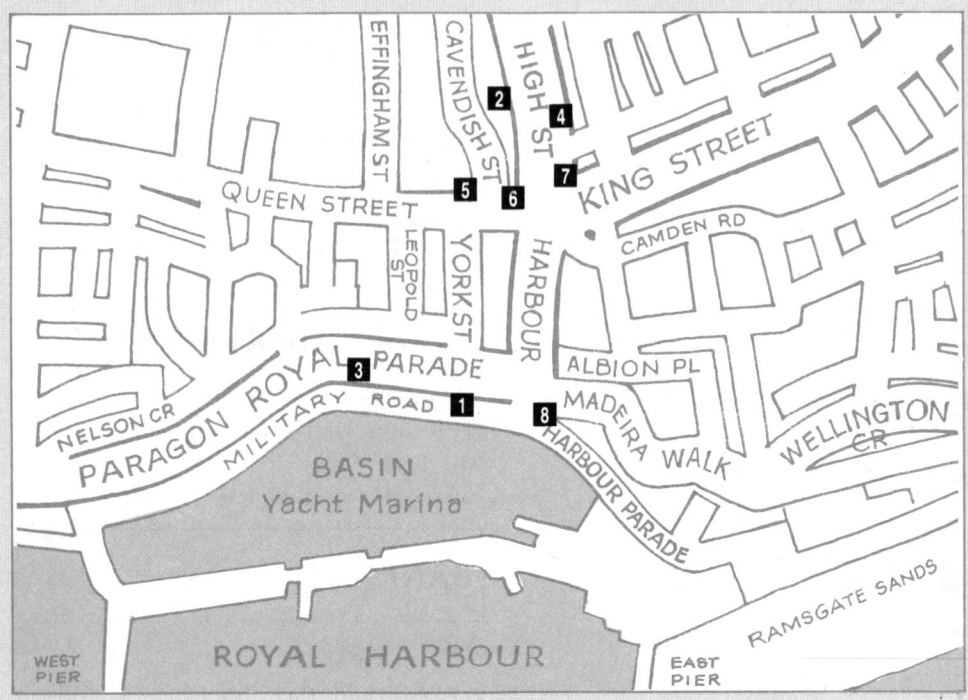

HARBOUR MASTER: (0843) 592277 or radio VHF 16/14

This port is a good jumping-off place for those planning a trip across the North Sea or to Belgium and the eastern French Channel ports. Visitors are welcomed but because Ramsgate is a busy ferry terminal care should be taken both when approaching and once in the harbour. The yacht harbour is very sheltered and conveniently located near the town's main shopping centre.

There is a slightly schizophrenic atmosphere to Ramsgate, which does not seem to know whether to be staid and respectable like Broadstairs or gaudy and rumbustious like Margate. The result is rather pleasant and those coming here for the first time may be agreeably surprised.

It was a quiet fishing port till George IV spent a holiday here in the early 19th century and, as with Brighton, this was sufficient to turn a village into a holiday resort. In fact most of the development took place after the King's death and there is a Victorian rather than Georgian feel to the streets that spread out from the harbour.

MOORINGS

Ramsgate Yacht Harbour.
(0843) 592277 VHF Ch 16/14
£7.00 per day.   £32.00 per week.

RESTAURANTS

1 Harvey's Crab and Oyster Bar: Harbour Parade. (0843) 591110. Plenty of wood gives this restaurant a good atmosphere. The helpings are generous and the service attentive and friendly. As its name suggests fish and shellfish are the house specialities but there are other dishes for those wanting them. It is most conveniently located to the marina and you can also use it as a pub.
Credit cards: Access, Visa.

HARBOUR SERVICES (YACHTS)

General: The Bosun's Locker, Military Road, Royal Harbour.
Ramsgate Yacht Harbour. (0843) 592277.

Mechanical Engineers: Ramsgate Yacht Harbour.

Electronic Engineers: Ramsgate Yacht Harbour.

Boat Builders & Repairers: Ramsgate Yacht Harbour.

SERVICES AVAILABLE

●	Petrol	●	Water
●	Diesel	●	Slipway
●	Calor Gas	●	Chandlery
●	Camping Gas		

HARBOUR SERVICES (PERSONAL)

Showers: Ramsgate Yacht Harbour.

2 Post Office: High Street.

Telephone: Post Office.
Ramsgate Yacht Harbour.

Laundry:
Prices Launderette, 112 Hearson Road.

Taxi & Cars:
Broadstairs Taxi. (0843) 585585.

3 Yacht Clubs:
Royal Temple Yacht Club, Keelhaul.
(0843) 52737.

RAMSGATE Continued

CHEMISTS AND MEDICAL SERVICES

4 **Chemists:**
Boots. High Street.

Medical:
Ramsgate Hospital, Westcliff Road.
(0843) 581441.

BANKS

5 **Barclays:** 11-13 Queen Street.

6 **Lloyds:** 3 Queen Street.

7 **Midland:** 1 High Street.

8 **National Westminster:**
Harbour Parade.

COASTGUARD: (0304) 210008
POLICE: (0843) 581724

HOLIDAY MAKERS AT RAMSGATE LATE 19TH CENTURY (NOTE: BATHING MACHINES).

RABIES
PREVENTION

NEVER SAIL ABROAD WITH ANIMALS ON BOARD

Sailing overseas? If you're travelling to any place outside territorial waters, always leave pets at home and never bring back any animals. The reason, in a word, is rabies.

A horrifying disease, rabies is invariably fatal in humans, once symptoms develop. It is usually caused by the bite of a pet that has been infected by a wild or stray animal. With the sea as a natural barrier, Britain has been free of the disease for over 60 years. But this situation can only be maintained by the observance of strict animal import and quarantine controls. In other words, the care and common-sense of us all.

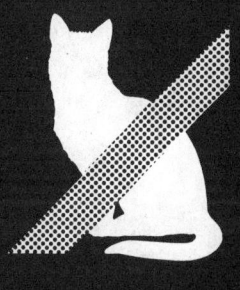

Any animal shipped overseas is automatically liable to quarantine regulations, whether or not it has stepped ashore. So you should consider, before deciding to take pets abroad, the expense and separation of six-months quarantine on return.

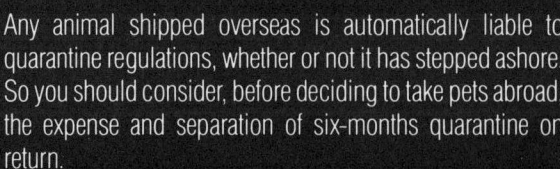

Moreover, the penalties for evading regulations are severe. So-called 'pet-lovers' attempting to break the rules face an unlimited fine or up to a year's imprisonment. In addition, the animal may be destroyed, and at best will have to undergo the full six-months quarantine.

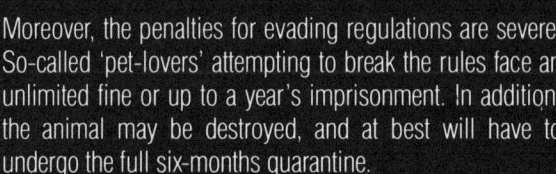

Just one infected animal would endanger humans and animals throughout Britain.

IT'S JUST NOT WORTH THE RISK.

THE CHAMPAGNE MUMM ADMIRAL'S CUP.

NO EXCUSE TO GO OVERBOARD WITH THE BUBBLY.

MUMM CORDON ROUGE. THE CHAMPAGNE THAT'S TOO GOOD TO WASTE.

FRENCH CHANNEL PORTS INTRODUCTION

The development of yachting facilities on the French Channel coast has been far more extensive than in England. In most cases the Ports des Plaisances are modern and purpose built, which makes cruising on the French Channel coast a great pleasure. Another factor that adds to the enjoyment of sailing in these waters is the attitude of the Port Captains. During the preparation of this guide there were many meetings with Port Captains and it was striking that they all were very aware of the need to market the facility for which they were responsible and to be aware of and provide for the yachtsman's needs.

The lack of customs formality is still another benefit that greets the visiting yachtsman. Providing that the items onboard are the personal belongings of the crew and such goods as would attract duty are within the duty free allowance, and provided there are no materials on board the possession of which contravenes the law of France, then there is no need to report to customs on arriving in French waters.

Of course the great joy of sailing to France is the opportunity it provides to partake of their fine cooking. As with all great cuisines the style has evolved through the combination of the needs of the people, the availability of produce and the flair of the cook. After the harbour guide there is a section on the local specialities.

DUNKERQUE

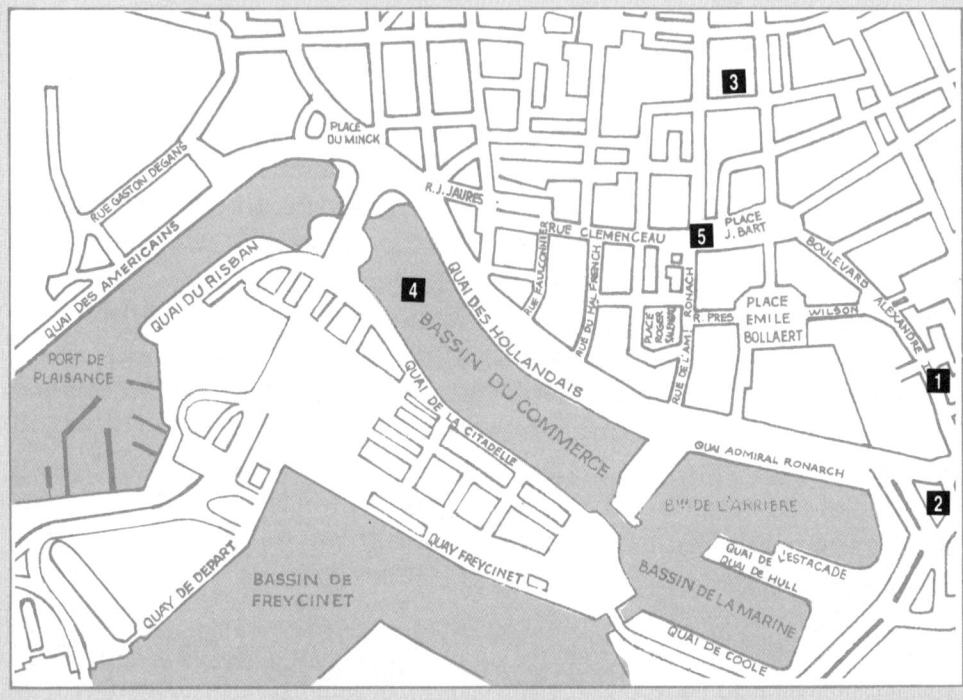

HARBOUR MASTER: (28) 65 99 22 or radio VHF 16/12

Dunkerque came into being some 900 years ago, built on land that had previously been under the sea, and consisted then of a few fishermen's houses and a church – hence its name Dunkerque, or church in the dunes. The town was often involved in war, particularly as it was so close to the French border, but it managed to retain an identity. At one stage it was ruled by Jean Bart, a native of Dunkerque whose fleet of privateers were feared around the oceans of the world in the late 17th century. The evacuation of the British army from Dunkerque in 1940 made the town part of world history. During the war most of the old buildings were destroyed and today you find a modern, vibrant industrial town whose port is the third largest in France. It is also a major ferry terminal.

There have been some endeavours recently to attract visitors to industrial towns, in the belief that many people will find the spectre of industry of great interest. Dunkerque is the perfect place for any yachtsman with similar inclinations.

MOORINGS

Yacht Club de la Mer du Nord.
(28) 66 79 90
FF65.00 per day.   FF455.00 per week.

RESTAURANTS

1 **Le Sourbise:**
2 Rue de Lion d'Or. (28) 63 88 55. There are not many old buildings in Dunkerque and this restaurant situated in the cellar of one of the few adds greatly to its charm. It is quite a walk from the yacht basin, but well worth it. You will find well-spaced tables and quiet, efficient service from staff who expect you to leave happy with the food you have had and try hard to ensure this is the case. Closed Sunday evening and all day Monday.
Credit Cards: Amex, Carte Bleu, Diners, Visa.

2 **Le Richelieu:**
In main railway station. (28) 66 52 13. Those familiar with the railway buffets of the main line termini in London should prepare themselves for a shock on entering this French equivalent. Strong Regency surroundings provide the setting for what is to some the best restaurant in Dunkerque. Lobster is a speciality of the house but there are plenty of meat dishes for those not wanting fish or shellfish. Closed Sunday evening.
Credit Cards: Amex, Carte Bleu.

HARBOUR SERVICES (YACHTS)

General: Bleu Marine, 12 Rue L'Hermite. (28) 63 93 33.

Mechanical Engineers:
Ets Bomy. (28) 66 58 14.

Electronic Engineers:
Ets Bomy. (28) 66 58 14.

SERVICES AVAILABLE

● Petrol	● Water
● Diesel	● Slipway
● Calor Gas	● Chandlery
● Camping Gas	

DUNKERQUE Continued

HARBOUR SERVICES (PERSONAL)

Showers: Port de Plaisance.

3 Post Office:
Rue du President Poincaré.

Telephone: Port de Plaisance.

Taxi & Cars:
Taxi station, Place Jean-Bart.

Yacht Clubs:
Yacht Club de la Mer du Nord, Quai des Monitors. (28) 66 79 90.

CHEMISTS AND MEDICAL SERVICES

4 Chemists:
Pharmacie du Port. Quai des Hollandais.

Medical: Hôpital. (28) 63 34 00.

BANKS

5 Société Generale:
Place Jean-Bart.

COASTGUARD: (28) 63 23 60
POLICE: (28) 64 51 09

CALAIS

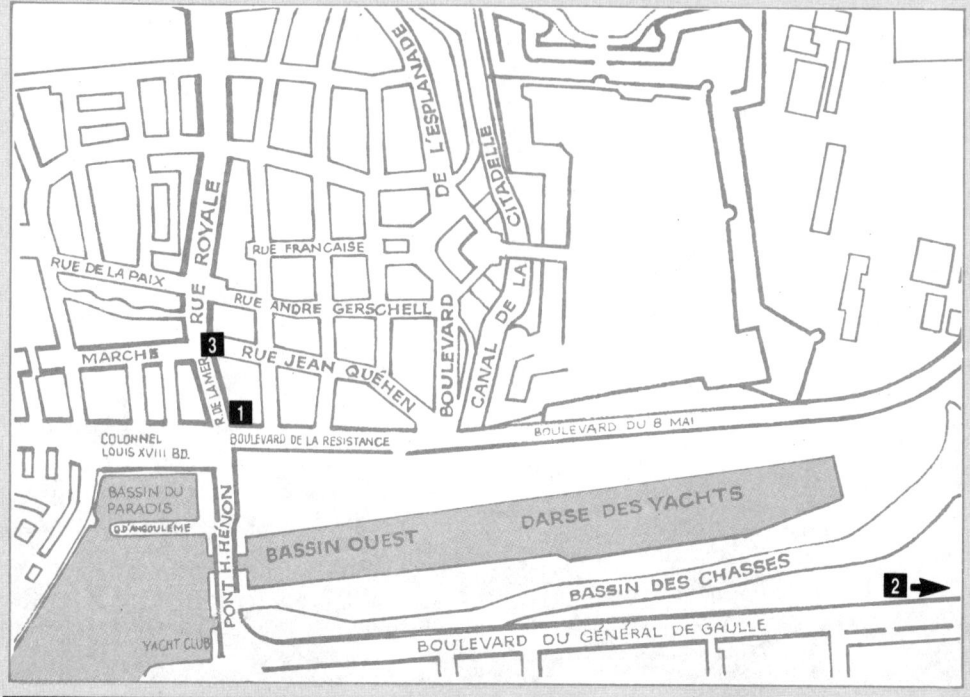

HARBOUR MASTER: (21) 34 55 23 or radio VHF 12

More English people have their first experience of foreign soil in this busy cross-Channel ferry port than anywhere else. Once the very mention of Calais would conjure up feelings of disquiet in the English breast. People there ate strange food, drove on the wrong side of the road and, *sacre bleu*, spoke another language. Fortunately such feelings have now almost disappeared, even if Mary Tudor is still blamed for losing Calais to the French in 1558 after over two centuries of English rule. It had taken an eight-month siege in 1347 to capture it and one legacy from that time is the manufacture of lace, introduced by lace-makers from Nottingham, which has been a main activity in Calais over the years.

Much of historic Calais was destroyed in World War II and whilst it cannot be said to have been lovingly rebuilt, it deserves more than the brief attention paid to it by the majority of visitors as they dash to the autoroutes.

The yachting harbour, Port de Plaisance, is found in the Bassin Ouest and involves going through a lock. Times of the opening of the lock gates are posted in the Yacht Club du Nord.

MOORINGS

Port de Plaisance.
FF45.00 per day.

RESTAURANTS

1 Le Channel:
3 Boulevard de la Resistance. (21) 34 42 30.
A solid restaurant, Le Channel has been popular for many years. It serves very good fish and the food generally is of a slightly higher order than the service. It is situated extremely close to the yacht basin, which is an obvious advantage, but you get the feeling that meals are served according to the ferry timetable. You will certainly not be the only English present. Closed on Sunday. Credit Cards: Amex, Diners, Visa.

2 Hotel des Dunes:
(Blériot Plage). (21) 34 54 30.
Just under a mile from the yacht basin and worth every step, this restaurant boasts a comfortable dining room, excellent food and friendly service. It recently changed ownership and there is a definite attempt to build on the reputation for good cooking. As you might expect, fish plays a starring role on the menu and the *plateau de fruits de mer* is outstanding. There is a small bar where you can enjoy a pre-meal drink and extend the pleasure of the occasion.

HARBOUR SERVICES (YACHTS)

General: La Marinerie, 6 Quai de la Colonne. (21) 34 47 83.

Mechanical Engineers:
Godin Moteurs, 208 Boulevard Gambetta. (21) 96 29 97.

SERVICES AVAILABLE

● Petrol	● Water	
● Diesel	● Slipway	
● Calor Gas	● Chandlery	
● Camping Gas		

HARBOUR SERVICES (PERSONAL)

Showers: Yacht Club du Nord.

Telephone: Yacht Club du Nord.

Laundry: Yacht Club du Nord.

Yacht Clubs:
Yacht Club du Nord, Bassin Ouest. (21) 34 55 23.

CALAIS Continued

CHEMISTS AND MEDICAL SERVICES

3 **Chemists:**
Pharmacie de la Mer. Rue Jean Quehen.
Quehen.

Medical: Hôpital, (21) 97 99 60.

BANKS

BNP: Place d'Armes.

COASTGUARD: (21) 34 50 32
POLICE: (21) 96 74 17

SAILING IN A CROSS CHANNEL SAILING RACE.

THE HOUSE OF
SANDEMAN

SHIPPERS OF FINE PORT SINCE 1790

BOULOGNE

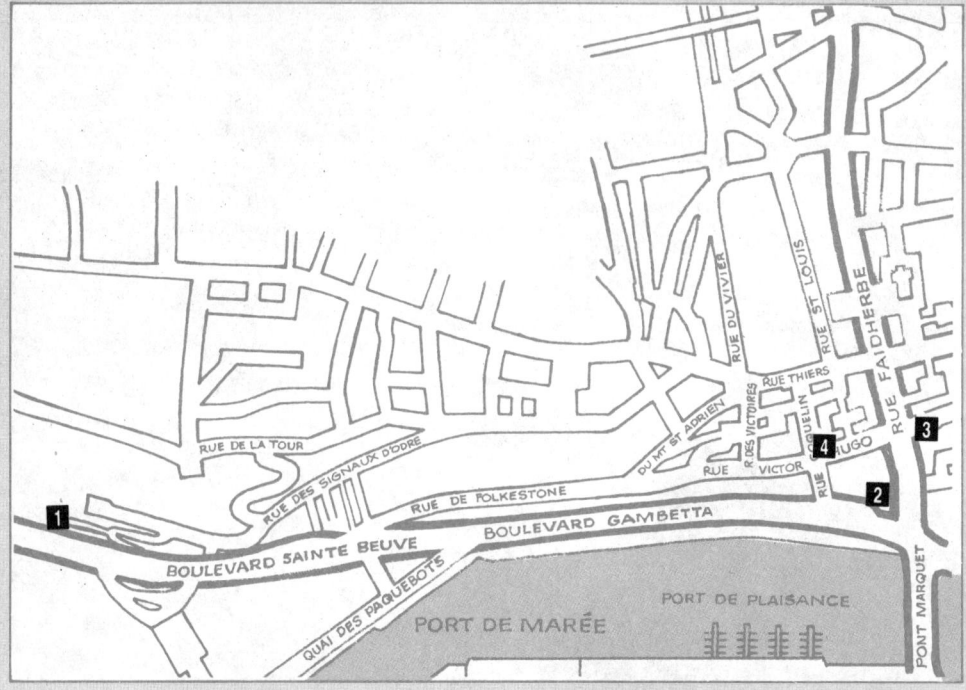

HARBOUR MASTER: (21) 30 10 00 or radio VHF 12

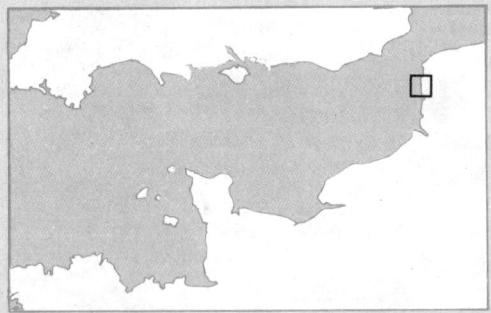

Like Calais, Boulogne is a major ferry terminal and fishing port. It has become popular with English day-trippers who flock across on shopping expeditions, which has left an obvious mark on the town. The yacht basin is conveniently situated by the Quai Gambetta and anything you are likely to require is readily accessible.

From the cliffs nearby, Caesar, Napoleon and Hitler all gazed across the Channel pondering how to invade the island in the distance; only Caesar succeeded and it is an interesting experience to go to Cap Gris-Nez and imagine the thoughts that must have crossed their minds.

Over the centuries Boulogne developed as a fishing port and today is the major fishing port of France. Sadly there is little left of its past charm and given some very pleasant alternatives close by, you may prefer to go elsewhere.

RESTAURANTS

1 La Matelote:
80 Boulevard Sainte Beuve. (21) 30 17 97.
Tony Lestienne's restaurant is one reason to be tempted to come to Boulogne. It is almost immediately opposite the casino, and sitting at the tables here will almost certainly be less expensive and a great deal more satisfying than in the rather ugly new casino. The standards vary only upwards and, as time passes, La Matelote's place as one of the great restaurants of northern France becomes more firmly established. The cooking is individual and there are many simple dishes where the cooking transforms the ordinary to the superb. Closed Sunday evening and Tuesday. Credit Cards: Carte Bleu, Visa.

2 Hamiot:
1 Rue Faidherbe. (21) 31 44 20.
This has a very busy downstairs bar which is functional rather than attractive and an equally busy upstairs dining room where the accent is again on practicality. Probably its most attractive feature is the price, as you certainly can eat very cheaply. Against this is the fact that some of the food is pre-prepared, then microwaved and it is not unknown for it to arrive still with the chill of the deep freeze.

HARBOUR SERVICES (YACHTS)

General: Ets Angelo, 83 Rue du Port-d'Etain. (21) 31 37 61.

Mechanical Engineers:
Mécanique Plaisance. (21) 30 36 19.

SERVICES AVAILABLE

● Petrol		● Water
● Diesel		● Slipway
● Calor Gas		● Chandlery
● Camping Gas		

HARBOUR SERVICES (PERSONAL)

Showers: Port de Plaisance.

Post Office: Place Frederic-Sauvage.

Telephone: Port de Plaisance.

Yacht Clubs:
Yacht Club Boulonnais, 234 Boulevard Sainte-Beuve. (21) 31 80 67.

BOULOGNE Continued

CHEMISTS AND MEDICAL SERVICES

3 **Chemists:**
Pharmacie Sagot. Rue Victor Hugo.

Medical: Hôpital. (21) 33 92 13.

BANKS

4 **Société Generale:**
60 Rue Victor Hugo.

COASTGUARD: (21) 31 42 58
POLICE: (21) 31 75 17

OFF BOULOGNE.

Pouring your first Chivas can be an unnerving experience.

ETAPLES/LE TOUQUET

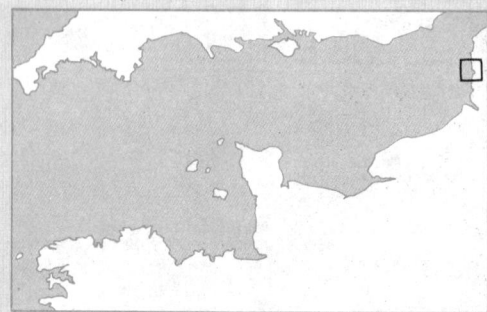

Getting down the River Canche to Étaples or mooring off Le Touquet can be an interesting experience particularly at low water. You will almost certainly take the bottom off Le Touquet, and Étaples is only accessible at high water.

Étaples is a small, dreamy market town with a very small marina just below the bridge that takes the road between Étaples and Le Touquet across the Canche. Apart from agriculture, fishing is a major activity.

Le Touquet is as different as it is possible to be. A playground for wealthy Parisians and also much favoured by their English counterparts, it contains beautiful summer residences, with many weekend homes found in the surrounding woods. Smart shops and restaurants abound in the town and there are always the two casinos to amuse yourself in or two golf courses to play round. All of this is splendid and Le Touquet could easily be one of the most popular harbours of the Channel if only mooring was a bit easier, or even possible.

MOORINGS

Port de Plaisance, Étaples.
FF50.00 per day.

RESTAURANTS

Flavio:
1-2 avenue de Verger. (21) 05 10 22.
One of the pleasant features of this long-established restaurant, arguably Le Touquet's premier restaurant, is its situation on the edge of the Forest of Touquet, close by the golf course. The menu is fish-orientated with certain favourites like *Le waterzoi de homard* which people travel some distance to enjoy. Given the problems associated with mooring here, Flavio is not really suited for those watching the tide but splendid for those who disembark with their golf clubs whilst the crew make off and await further instructions.
Credit Cards: Amex, Carte Bleu, Diners.

Perrard:
67 Rue de Metz. (21) 05 13 33.
This is a restaurant of particular
interest to those who like fish soup. Not
only does Serge Perrard do a roaring
trade serving meals here but he also
sells the fish soup from the 'factory',
open to the public, next door. It is good
value for money with many *prix fixe*
menus to choose from and to suit most
pockets.

HARBOUR SERVICES (YACHTS)

General: Jean Lefevre Construction
Navales. (21) 94 72 77.

Mechanical Engineers:
Perrault. (21) 94 62 66.

SERVICES AVAILABLE

● Petrol	● Water
● Diesel	● Slipway
● Calor Gas	● Chandlery
● Camping Gas	

HARBOUR SERVICES (PERSONAL)

Showers: Capitainerie.

Post Office: 9, Rue du General-Obert.

Telephone: Capitainerie.

Yacht Clubs:
Cercle Nautique du Touquet. (21) 05 12
77.

CHEMISTS AND MEDICAL SERVICES

Chemists:
Pharmacie Leloir. Place du General de
Gaulle.

POLICE: 21 94 60 17

LE CROTOY

L e Crotoy is a small village situated on the north side of the Somme estuary. The Port de Plaisance has most facilities for yachtsmen and though rather less professional than most other ports, it all seems to add to the atmosphere. It is only accessible for a few hours around high water and the channels through the flats change, so considerable care needs to be taken. The expanse of the estuary is desolate indeed at low water but it takes on a different aspect at high tide. However there is a new casino and at the right state of the tide a superb south-facing beach.

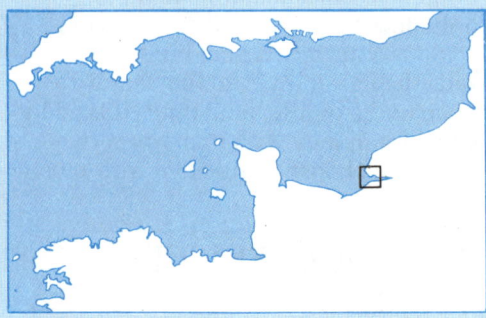

MOORINGS

Port de Plaisance.
FF60.00 per day.   FF300.00 per week.

RESTAURANTS

Chez Mado (Hotel de la Baie): Quai Leonard. (22) 27 81 22. However much the channels change, however difficult the tides, there will always be yachtsmen who will overcome all to have the pleasure of a meal here. Built at the turn of the century, the restaurant seems to have changed little from that time. On entering you will be amazed at the amount of plants, ornaments and bric-a-brac that greet you. Cats and parrots seem to exist in perfect harmony. The glassed-in verandah provides great views over the estuary and if all this is not enough the food is excellent. The owner is the legendary bejewelled Madame Mado who still keeps a strict eye on everything that is happening. Not suprisingly it is a most popular restaurant and booking is essential.

HARBOUR SERVICES (YACHTS)

General: Baie Nautique, Avenue des Ecluses.

SERVICES AVAILABLE

- ● Petrol
- ● Diesel
- ☐ Calor Gas
- ☐ Camping Gas
- ● Water
- ☐ Slipway
- ● Chandlery

HARBOUR SERVICES (PERSONAL)

Showers: Port de Plaisance.

Telephone: Port de Plaisance.

COASTGUARD: (22) 27 80 24

ST VALERY-SUR-SOMME

St Valery-sur-Somme is a very attractive mooring, particularly as the Port de Plaisance has been rebuilt and now provides most facilities. There is a timeless feel to the small town, which you can reach from the port by walking along the quayside. William Duke of Normandy embarked some of his army here prior to the invasion of England, and this is reflected in some of the street names. More recently St Valery was a major supply port for the British Army during the First World War.

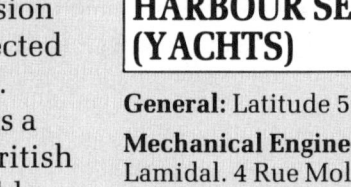

HARBOUR SERVICES (YACHTS)

General: Latitude 50. (22) 26 82 06.

Mechanical Engineers: Lamidal. 4 Rue Mollenel.

Electronic Engineers: Latitude 50. (22) 26 82 06.

Boat Builders & Repairers: Latitude 50. (22) 26 82 06.

SERVICES AVAILABLE

- ● Petrol
- ● Diesel
- ● Calor Gas
- ● Camping Gas
- ● Water
- ● Slipway
- ● Chandlery

MOORINGS

Port de Plaisance.
FF44.00 per day.

RESTAURANTS

Hotel des Pilotes.
Quai Perée.
An honest French auberge with a first floor dining room offering splendid views across the mouth of the Somme.

HARBOUR SERVICES (PERSONAL)

Showers: Port de Plaisance.

Post Office:
45 metres up from Place Guillaume le Conquerant.

Telephone: Port de Plaisance.

Laundry: Port de Plaisance.

CHEMISTS AND MEDICAL SERVICES

Chemists:
Pharmacie, just up from Place Guillaume le Conquerant.

BANKS

Exchange: 180 yards on left from Port de Plaisance.

COASTGUARD: (21) 92 86 66
POLICE: (22) 60 82 08

FISHING FOR MACKEREL

LE TRÉPORT

HARBOUR MASTER: (35) 86 17 91 or radio VHF 16/12

As the River Bresle silted up, the significance of Le Tréport as a fishing village diminished. Before this time it was a port of some importance and was burnt to the ground on several occasions by the British during the One Hundred Years War. It is only two hours from Paris and tourism, particularly of the long weekend type, now plays an important role in the town's economy. The quayside is lined with small restaurants and gift shops, and a broad promenade, Digue Promenade, runs the length of the beach, with a large casino and swimming pool at the port end. Another feature of Le Tréport are the white cliffs that rise behind it and stretch as far as Le Havre. From these cliffs is derived the name Alabaster coast.

Sadly the yacht harbour is found in the least attractive part of the town, although the facilities here are very good. Weather permitting, it is possible to moor up in the outer port but this does dry out and can be dangerous in other than settled weather.

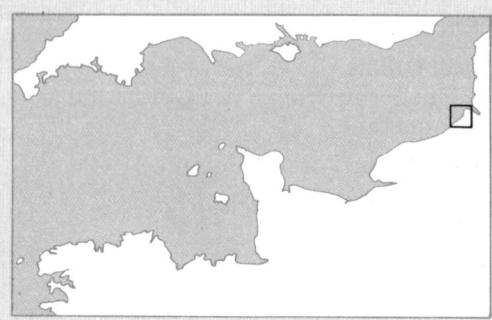

RESTAURANTS

La Marée:
34 Quai François 1er. (35) 86 01 13. This modern restaurant is very conveniently situated by the port. A wide variety of fish and shellfish make up most of the menu and are all fresh and well prepared.
Credit Cards: Amex, Carte Bleu, Diners.

HARBOUR SERVICES (YACHTS)

General: Société Française de Nautisme. (35) 86 60 52.

SERVICES AVAILABLE

● Petrol		● Water
● Diesel		● Slipway
● Calor Gas		● Chandlery
● Camping Gas		

HARBOUR SERVICES (PERSONAL)

Showers: Yacht Club de Bresle.

Post Office: Rue Abbe-Vincheneux.

Telephone: Yacht Club de Bresle.

Yacht Clubs:
Yacht Club de Bresle. (35) 86 14 93.

CHEMISTS AND MEDICAL SERVICES

Medical: Hôpital. (35) 86 04 33.

BANKS

Société Générale: 2 Quai Francois 1e.

COASTGUARD: (35) 86 33 71
POLICE: (35) 86 08 88

DIEPPE

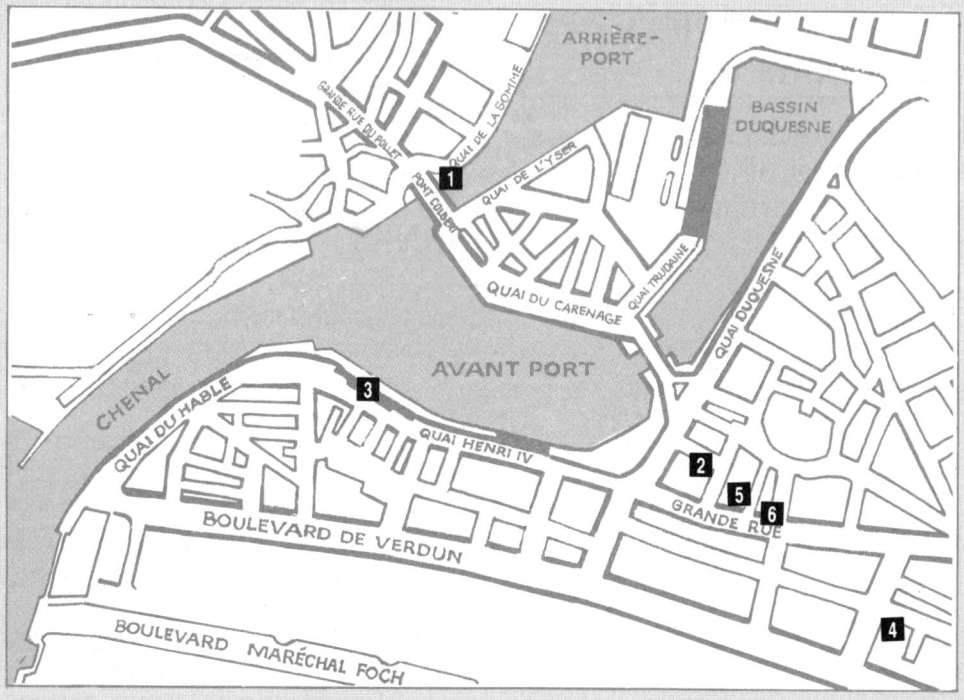

HARBOUR MASTER: (35) 84 22 99

This bustling port has managed to retain a charm and intimacy that make it a very popular place to visit for yachtsmen and tourists alike. As a major ferry terminal it is also a good port for leaving a yacht or for crew changeovers.

Dieppe was first colonised by the Vikings and the depth of the water here assured its future and prosperity. The Dukes of Normandy introduced shipbuilding to the town and one 16th-century shipbuilder, Jehan Ango, was so successful that he lent money to King Francis I and was also able to wage an independent war against Portugal.

Because of its importance, Dieppe has had a violent past and in 1695 it was reduced to ruins as a result of a naval bombardment by the British. Most of the surviving old town consequently dates from the 18th century. More recently Dieppe suffered much damage in August 1942 when it was shelled prior to Operation Jubilee, when a 7,000 strong commando force made up largely of Canadians landed. Their bravery and the terrible losses inflicted on them are now part of history but walking around Dieppe the visitor is reminded of the awful occasion by the memorials to the many dead and the Canadian flags flying.

Dieppe has survived and provides the visitor with a cameo French port. Small bars and restaurants line the quaysides and many people seem happy to spend the day watching the movements of the ships in the port. As well as the cross-Channel ferries, ships carrying bananas and citrus fruits are plentiful, for Dieppe is France's largest port for such fruits, and all these vessels mingle with the large fishing fleet.

Just by the yacht harbour is the fish market, which is well worth visiting, and across on the Quai Duquesne are the bars and restaurants. Walking towards the Quai Henri IV you will find the beginning of the Grande Rue, which is primarily a pedestrian thoroughfare but the occasional delivery van and the odd crossroads can give the unwary walker something of a shock.

Like most ferry terminals there is no shortage of tourists and businesses catering to them. Some restaurants are unnecessarily expensive but with a little care you can thoroughly enjoy a visit to this fascinating port.

MOORINGS

Port de Plaisance.
FF50.00 per day.

DIEPPE Continued

RESTAURANTS

1 La Mélie:
2 Grande-Rue-du-Pollet. (35) 84 21 19.
Guy Brachais recently opened this
restaurant in the old fishing quarter of
Dieppe and in the short time it has been
open he has achieved an enviable
reputation for fine food.
It is a serious restaurant with well-
spaced tables in a quiet ambiance, not a
place to go if you want a busy bistro-
like atmosphere. An increasing number
of regulars come to enjoy the well-
prepared food and since the restaurant
seats only about 30, booking is
essential. Some people consider that La
Melie is destined to become one of the
best restaurants in this region, and now
may well be the time to try it.
Credit Cards: Amex, Carte Bleu, Diners.

2 La Marmite:
Dieppoise 8 Rue St-Jean. (35) 84 24 26.
This restaurant found hidden away just
off the Quai Duquesne is a very genuine
place with a mainly fish menu that
includes 'Marmite Dieppoise', a type of
fish stew and absolutely delicious. Not
a place that will break the bank.
Credit Cards: Visa.

3 Le Port:
99 Quai Henri IV. (35) 84 36 64.
A simple, busy bistro, full of life and
atmosphere, where again most of the
specialities are fish. The dishes are well
prepared and served, and the prices
reasonable. Don't be put off by the
walk: it is one of those places that you
think you must have passed and turn
back to find it, but it is well past the
Gare Maritime.

PUBS

4 Cambridge Arms Pub:
2 Rue de l'Épée.
Run by a young couple, the husband is
French and the wife Scottish, who
together have created an ambiance that
puts many English pubs to shame. Do
not be put off by the fact that the door is
only opened once they have checked
you out. This is to keep the standards
up and should be welcomed. A very
pleasant place and warmly
recommended.

HARBOUR SERVICES (YACHTS)

General: Dieppe Nautic, 9 Rue Ancien
Port. Thalassa Dieppe, 2 Quai de la
Cale.

Mechanical Engineers:
Dieppe Nautic, 9 Rue Ancien Port.

SERVICES AVAILABLE

●	Petrol	●	Water
●	Diesel	●	Slipway
●	Calor Gas	●	Chandlery
●	Camping Gas		

HARBOUR SERVICES (PERSONAL)

Showers: Cercle de Voile de Dieppe.

Post Office: Quai Duquesne.

Telephone: By the club house.

Taxi & Cars: By the club house.

Yacht Clubs:
Cercle de Voile de Dieppe. (35) 84 22 29.

CHEMISTS AND MEDICAL SERVICES

5 **Chemists:**
Pharmacie, Grande Rue and Place Nationale.

Medical: Hôpital. (35) 82 20 75.

BANKS

6 **Crédit Lyonnais:**
66 Grande Rue.

COASTGUARD: (35) 84 30 76
POLICE: (35) 82 04 35

ST VALERY-EN-CAUX

On the high cliff, La Falaise d'Amont, by the town stands a monument to the 51st Highland Division which in 1940 fought a desperate rearguard action at St Valéry-en-Caux after the collapse of the front on the Somme. During the course of this action the town was virtually destroyed and it has been rebuilt with great care, so that it is difficult to imagine that the Henri IV house standing on the quayside is in fact a loving restoration.

Fishing and tourism are the town's main activities and good facilities exist for any visiting yachtsmen.

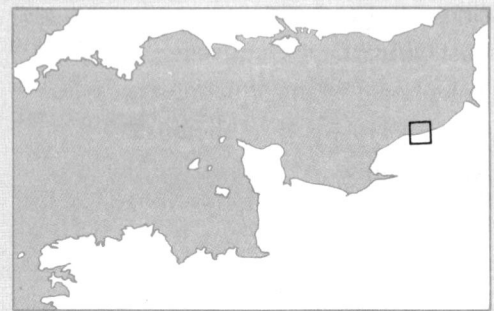

RESTAURANTS

Le Port:
18 Quai d'Amont. (35) 97 08 93. Marc Tellier will cook you a memorable meal in his restaurant overlooking the outer harbour and across from the maison Henri IV. The turbot with langouste tails and salmon eggs is really outstanding.
Credit Cards: Carte Bleu.

MOORINGS

Port de Plaisance.
FF78.00 per day.

HARBOUR SERVICES (YACHTS)

General: Boudois SA, Quai du Havre.

SERVICES AVAILABLE

● Petrol	● Water
● Diesel	■● Slipway
● Calor Gas	● Chandlery
● Camping Gas	

HARBOUR SERVICES (PERSONAL)

Showers: Club house.

Post Office: Rue de la Poste.

Telephone: Club house.

Yacht Clubs:
Club Nautique Valeriquais. (35) 97 10 88.

CHEMISTS AND MEDICAL SERVICES

Medical:
Hôpital. (35) 97 00 11.

BANKS

Société Générale:
17 Place de la Chapelle.

COASTGUARD: (35) 97 05 27
POLICE: (35) 97 05 27

FÉCAMP

If the name Alexandre le Grand means anything to you, you will probably want to pay a visit to this port. One of Fécamp's main claims to fame is that a monk named Vincelli is reputed to have first distilled Benedictine here. The recipe was lost for many years but rediscovered by Alexandre le Grand, whose name can be found on every bottle. It is possible to visit the distillery, although it is some way from the yacht harbour.

Fécamp, a sizeable town of about 21,000 inhabitants, is the fourth largest fishing port of France, most of the catches being cod, and as in most French ports the quaysides are full of small restaurants specialising in fish.

The town developed around the site of a Benedictine monastery which, according to historical legend, was founded after part of a fig tree was washed ashore in the 7th century and discovered to have a phial inside containing drops of blood from the body of Christ.

These bits of information may have whetted your appetite for a visit, but there is an industrial rather than charming historical air to the harbour and there are certainly many more attractive places to visit.

MOORINGS

Port de Plaisance.
FF76.00 per day.

RESTAURANTS

Le Maritime:
2 Place Nicolas Selles. (35) 28 21 71.
Conveniently situated by the Port de Plaisance, this restaurant has had much care taken over its interior design, to produce two dining rooms and two styles of decor, both informal. Local fish cooked in the local way provides the main part of the menu and there are several *prix fixe* menus to choose from. It makes a good place for an evening out, with not too far to walk back to your mooring afterwards.
Credit Cards: Amex, Carte Bleu.

Le Viking:
63 Albert 1er. (35) 29 22 92.
Under the same ownership as Le Maritime, this place provides the perfect answer to those crews where there is split in interest when it comes to eating out. Whilst the building has all the charm of an airport lounge there are several different restaurants under the one roof, including a pizza bar downstairs for those not prepared to tackle the full menu of Le Viking upstairs. It is a good place to accommodate the whole family, the food is of a high standard and from upstairs there are panoramic views over the sea. The plastic decor is the only criticism.
Credit Cards: Amex, Carte Bleu, Diners.

HARBOUR SERVICES (YACHTS)

General: L'Hélice, 39 Quai Bérigny.

Mechanical Engineers:
Chantiers C. Moré, Quai de Verdun.

SERVICES AVAILABLE

 Petrol   Water

 Diesel   Slipway

Calor Gas   Chandlery

 Camping Gas

HARBOUR SERVICES (PERSONAL)

Showers: Port de Plaisance.

Post Office: Place Bellet.

Telephone: Port de Plaisance.

Yacht Clubs:
Société des Régates de Fécamp. (35) 28 08 44.

CHEMISTS AND MEDICAL SERVICES

Chemists:
Pharmacie du Port, Place Nicolas Selles.

Medical: Hôpital. (35) 28 05 13.

BANKS

Société Générale:
23 Place Général Charles de Gaulle.

COASTGUARD: (35) 28 28 15
POLICE: (35) 28 16 69

LE HAVRE

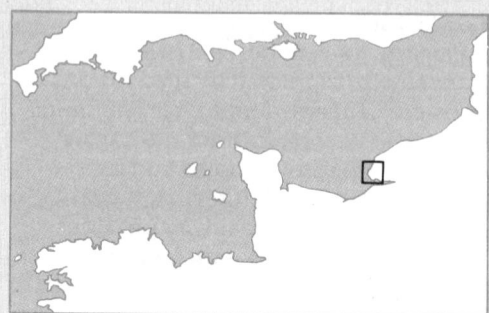

This is a port where obvious disadvantages can in certain circumstances be made up for by its very convenience. It is the second largest port of France after Marseilles and consequently always busy. Any trace of its history was destroyed by Allied bombing during the Second World War, when the devastation was such that it took over two years to clear away the rubble. The modern city that has been built in its place is thought by many to be drab and uniform, very untypical for France.

Although there cannot be many yachtsmen who would choose to visit Le Havre other than for necessity, the facilities are very good and there are ferries to and from England that make this a good place to leave your boat or to change crew. Also, because of its size, if you have something very serious the matter with your boat there are plenty of people with the expertise to help you.

From the yacht harbour you look across the Boulevard Clemenceau, which is lined with high-rise buildings and fronted by a considerable highway, but you will probably have a mooring far enough away from this road not to be disturbed by the traffic. Yachtsmen intending to take their boats down through France by way of the Seine will need to come here and it makes a good resting point after a cross-Channel sail.

MOORINGS

Port de Plaisance.
FF69.00 per day.   FF371.00 per week.

RESTAURANTS

La Manche:
18 Boulevard Albert 1er. (35) 41 20 13.
Amongst the serried ranks of grey
buildings it is something of a relief to
find this attractive restaurant
overlooking the sea, which is also not
too far from the Port de Plaisance.
Pierre Pimmel has created an elegant
dining room seating about 35 people
where you can enjoy the best oysters in
Le Havre. For those tired of fish there
are a number of dishes like *Magret de
canard* and pigeon to satisfy the need
for a change.
Credit Cards: Amex, Carte Bleu, Diners.

Guimbarde:
61 Rue Louis-Brindeau. (35) 42 15 36.
A small bistro just off the Boulevard
Francois 1er which offers good value
for money and is popular with the
English who want to grab their last
meal in France before the ferry home. It
is advisable to book.
Credit cards: Visa.

HARBOUR SERVICES (YACHTS)

General: Manche Yachting. (35) 21 08
06.

Mechanical Engineers:
Manche Yachting. (35) 21 08 06.

SERVICES AVAILABLE

 Petrol   Water

Diesel Slipway

Calor Gas Chandlery

 Camping Gas

HARBOUR SERVICES (PERSONAL)

Showers: Port de Plaisance.

Post Office: Place J. Ferry.

Telephone: Port de Plaisance.

Taxi & Cars: (35) 25 81 81.

Yacht Clubs:
Société des Régates du Havre. (35) 42
41 21.

CHEMISTS AND MEDICAL SERVICES

Chemists:
Pharmacie, Rue de Paris.

Medical: Hôpital, (35) 22 81 23.

BANKS

Crédit Lyonnais:
106 Boulevard de Strasbourg.

COASTGUARD: (35) 22 41 03
POLICE: (35) 42 40 65

HONFLEUR

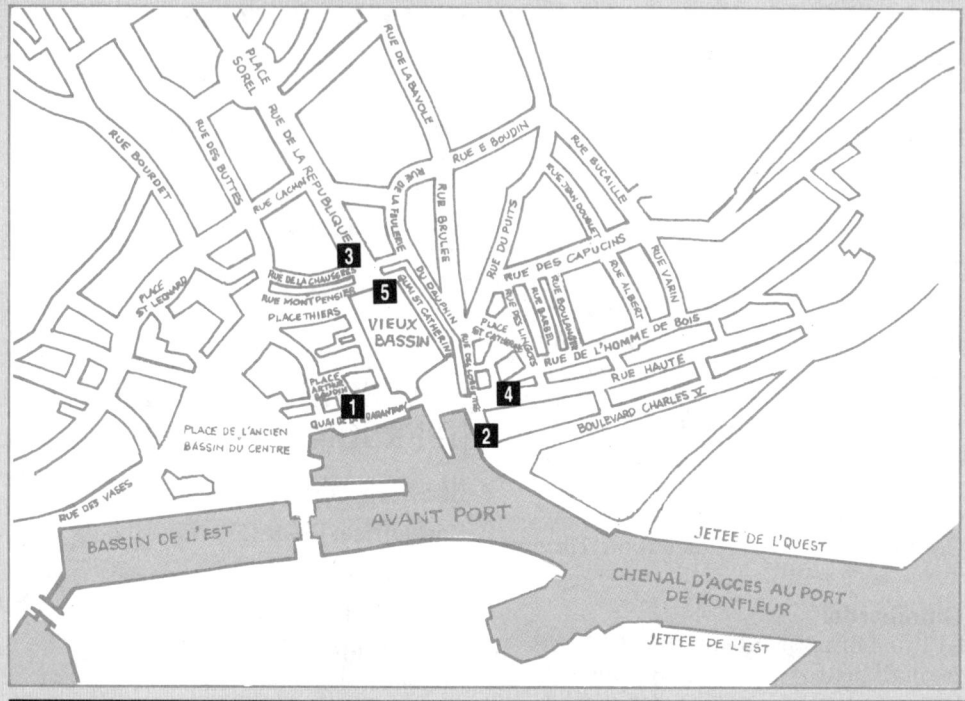

HARBOUR MASTER: (31) 89 20 02

onfleur must be one of the most picturesque ports of the Channel, if not *the* most. The harbour is situated in the middle of the old part of the town, with cobbled quaysides and tall old buildings with pitched roofs that seem to drop to the streets below. Quaint, charming, the St Tropez of the north coast, are all descriptions accorded this delightful town. Inevitably this means tourists in their thousands, but the town remains itself despite all and even in the busiest of the season anyone

visiting Honfleur will not be able to resist its inherent beauty.

Its many interesting old buildings include the Capitainerie, the former home of the Governor of Honfleur, situated in what was part of the town fortifications. Just behind the harbour is the Place Sainte Cathérine with its famous wooden church, constructed by the town's shipbuilders in the 15th century to give thanks for the departure of the British. The seamen of Honfleur have an enviable tradition. They discovered Brazil and in 1608 de Champlain, who sailed from here, founded the city of Quebec.

The Vieux Bassin was built in the 17th century and fishing remained one of the major activities till the 19th century. At that time a thriving artists' colony centred on Monet and Boudin, a native of the town, began to be established around Honfleur, where the light has a special quality. Their work is commemorated in the Boudin Museum in the Rue L'Homme de Bois. The Ferme St Simeon, some 2 kilometres from the town, was the hotel in which many of these artists lived and is a splendid place to visit.

Whilst walking around the town don't miss the chemist's shop on the Rue des Logettes which advertises in large letters high on the wall, *Remèdes contre mal du mer.*

MOORINGS

Port de Plaisance.
FF60.00 per day.

RESTAURANTS

1 L'Absinthe:
10 Quai de la Quarantaine. (31) 89 39 00.
This restaurant is full of atmosphere, with small tables, candles and rough stone walls. The food is very good and there is a wide selection to suit all tastes. As its reputation grows so does its popularity so booking is very advisable.
Credit Cards: Amex, Carte Bleu, Diners.

2 Le Cheval Blanc:
2 Quai des Passagers. (31) 89 13 49.
Robert Samson's restaurant is a few metres away from the Lieutenance and is thought by some to be the best in the area.
Renovated in the style of Louis XIII, it has great atmosphere. The cooking is of the classic school and the food makes up for a slightly disdainful welcome. Don't let this get you down, it is meted out to everyone.

HARBOUR SERVICES (YACHTS)

General: Aubraye, 7 Rue de la Ville.

Mechanical Engineers:
Hue, Bassin Ouest, Quai Carnot.

SERVICES AVAILABLE

- ● Petrol
- ● Diesel
- ● Calor Gas
- ● Camping Gas
- ● Water
- ● Slipway
- ● Chandlery

HARBOUR SERVICES (PERSONAL)

Showers: Capitainerie.

3 **Post Office:**
Rue de la Republique.

Telephone: Capitainerie.

Yacht Clubs:
Club Nautique Honfleur.

CHEMISTS AND MEDICAL SERVICES

4 **Chemists:**
Pharmacie, Place Hamelin.

Medical: Hôpital, (31) 89 07 74

BANKS

5 **Crédit Agricole:**
Quai Sainte-Catherine.

COASTGUARD: (31) 89 06 02
POLICE: (31) 89 21 24

all at sea with your advertising?

The White Paper on Cost Effective Advertising

A portfolio presented to advertisers to illustrate successful marketing techniques.

WENSLEY BOWN, ADVERTISING & MARKETING.
CHESHAM, BUCKINGHAMSHIRE.

Our brochure can provide the solution

Wensley Bown, Advertising & Marketing
Island House, Moor Road, Chesham, Bucks. HP5 1NZ. Telephone: Chesham (0494) 775213.

DEAUVILLE/TROUVILLE

HARBOUR MASTER: (31) 88 56 16 or radio VHF Ch 9

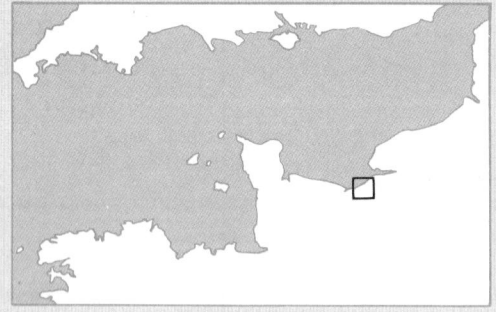

There is a world of difference between Deauville and Trouville, but those who see Trouville as the poor relation do this attractive working port a disservice for it possesses a charm and genuineness of its own.

Deauville was once one of the most fashionable resorts of Europe and for a few weeks each year it assumes this role even today. The popular season is during July and August, the high spot being the race meeting towards the end of August. The yacht harbour, Port Deauville, is a modern development, built like a 20th-century Venice with houses that have their own moorings. To the right, facing the town, runs the famous

Promenade des Planches, a wide walkway stretching the length of Deauville and filled with various amusements. Down here too is a new Olympic sized pool. The town caters for the wealthy; all the designer names of Paris can be found here and the prices are what you would expect – high.

Trouville lacks the broad promenades and the chic shops and restaurants but makes up for this with a character that is unspoilt by its glitzy neighbour. Walk along the Boulevard Moureaux which runs alongside the quay and take your pick of the many restaurants. Towards the casino on the left is the fish market which is usually interesting, and then of course there is the casino itself, a splendidly defiant memorial to a bygone era.

Although a busy working port Trouville does not lack for holiday visitors. It can be more complicated to enter than Port Deauville, and perhaps one solution is to moor at Port Deauville and enjoy the 15-minute walk into Trouville.

MOORINGS

Port de Plaisance, Deauville.
FF90.00 per day.   FF480.00 per week.

Port de Plaisance, Trouville.
FF64.00 per day.   FF322.00 per week.

RESTAURANTS

1 Le Ciro's:
Boulevard de la Mer. (31) 88 18 10.
If you want to eat in the most elaborate beach restaurant on the whole of the Channel coast seize the chance to visit this riviera-style restaurant near the new Olympic swimming pool.
It is the sort of place where being seen and seeing who is there and with whom is more important than the actual food and the size of the bill immaterial to the participation in the game. You will in addition enjoy a well-prepared meal in splendid surroundings and with a wonderful view over the beach. What a way to pass a few hours away on a warm summer's day.

2 Les Vapeurs:
160 Boulevard Fernand-Moureux, Trouville. (31) 88 15 24.
Very different to Le Ciro's, this is a frantic bistro situated close by the casino. It is something of an achievement that with all the activity the food is of the high standard that it is. The menu centres primarily on a variety of fish dishes not surprising as it is almost opposite the fish market. It is usually packed, but they seem to accommodate everyone even though you might have to wait a while. It is the kind of place that is only found in France and an experience not to be missed.

HARBOUR SERVICES (YACHTS)

General: Marina Ouest, Quai des Marchands, Deauville.

Mechanical Engineers:
Dellier, Deauville. (31) 88 62 62.

Electronic Engineers:
Manche Electronique, Deauville. (31) 88 63 07. Deauville.

SERVICES AVAILABLE

 Petrol   ● Water

● Diesel   ● Slipway

● Calor Gas   ● Chandlery

 Camping Gas

HARBOUR SERVICES (PERSONAL)

Showers: Port Deauville.

Post Office:
Boulevard Moureaux, Trouville.

Telephone: Port Deauville,

Laundry: Port Deauville

Yacht Clubs:
Deauville Yacht Club. (31) 88 38 19.

CHEMISTS AND MEDICAL SERVICES

Chemists:
Pharmacie, Boulevard Moureaux, Trouville.

Medical:
Hôpital, Deauville. (31) 88 14 00.

BANKS

Crédit Lyonnais:
60 rue du Leclerc

COASTGUARD: (31) 98 21 59
POLICE: (31) 88 13 07

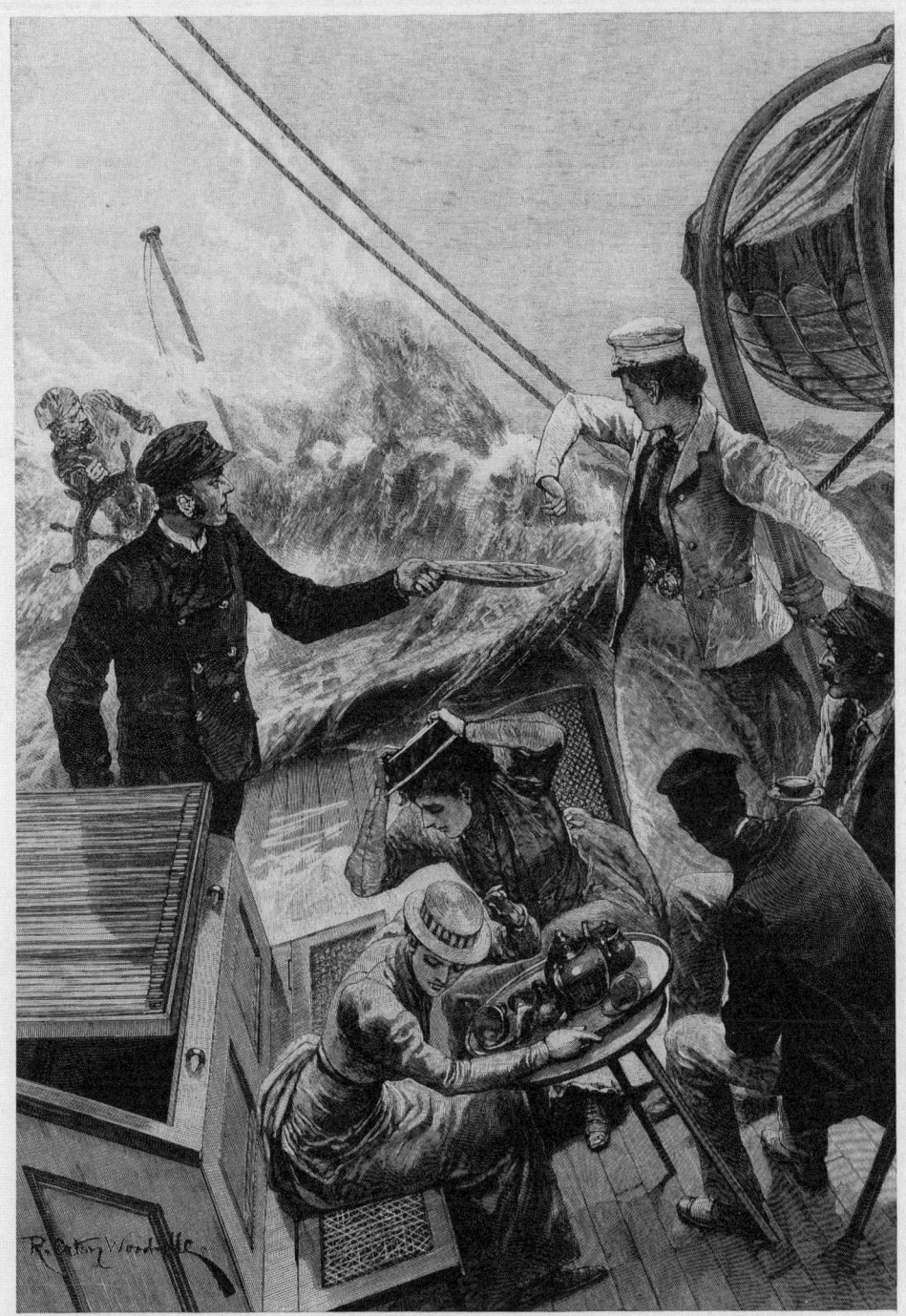

AFTERNOON TEA UNDER DIFFICULTIES.

OUISTREHAM

O uistreham Riva Bella is situated at the mouth of the Caen canal. Mooring is in a very pleasantly created Port de Plaisance surrounded by trees, but quite a walk from the town itself and with a slight feel of a motorway layby.

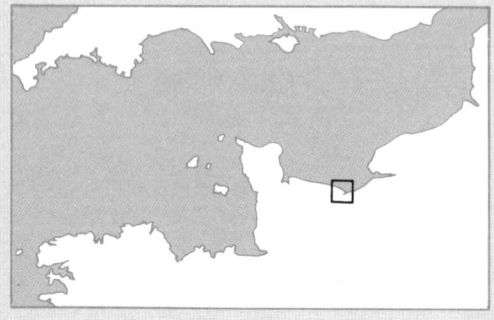

Ouistreham was the easternmost harbour in the Allied invasion of Europe in World War II and during the morning of 6 June 1944 the town was raised to the ground prior to the assault on the Normandy beaches. Today one blockhouse is all that remains from that fateful day. A museum commemorating the exploits of the 4th Anglo-French commando landing as well as the whole of D-Day is situated between Avenue Andry and Avenue Pasteur.

RESTAURANTS

La Broche d'Argent:
Place du Général de Gaulle.
(31) 97 15 24.

This restaurant in the Hotel de l'Univers has a pleasant terraced dining room looking across the square to the Port de Plaisance and it is not more than a stone's throw from the ferry terminal. A variety of *prix fixe* menus give a wide choice and since anywhere else involves a considerable walk you may be best advised to book here. Specialities centre on seafood.
Credit Cards: Amex, Diners, Visa.

MOORINGS

Port de Plaisance.
FF69.00 per day.   FF344.00 per week.

HARBOUR SERVICES (YACHTS)

General: Chantier du Maresquier, Serra-Marine, Port de Plaisance. (31) 96 30 76.

Mechanical Engineers: PL Marine. (31) 96 29 92.

Sailmakers: Normandie Voiles. (31) 97 06 29.

Boat Builders & Repairers: JPL Marine. (31) 96 29 92.

SERVICES AVAILABLE

- ● Petrol
- ● Diesel
- ● Calor Gas
- ● Camping Gas
- ● Water
- ● Slipway
- ● Chandlery

HARBOUR SERVICES (PERSONAL)

Showers: Port de Plaisance.

Post Office: Port de Plaisance.

Telephone: Port de Plaisance.

Laundry: Port de Plaisance.

Taxi & Cars: Falaize. (31) 97 14 09.

Yacht Clubs: Société des Régates de Caen-Ouistreham.

CHEMISTS AND MEDICAL SERVICES

Chemists: Pharmacie Herbert, 1 Place Général de Gaulle.

Medical: Dr Lhirondel, 76 Avenue de la Mer.

BANKS

Crédit Agricole: 45 Rue de la Mer.

COASTGUARD: (31) 97 14 43
POLICE: (31) 97 13 15

COURSEULLES

Courseulles is a small fishing port famous for its oysters, which are a significant element in its everyday life, and visiting yachtsmen may want to take the time to visit the farms and possibly seize the chance to enjoy a dozen, or more.

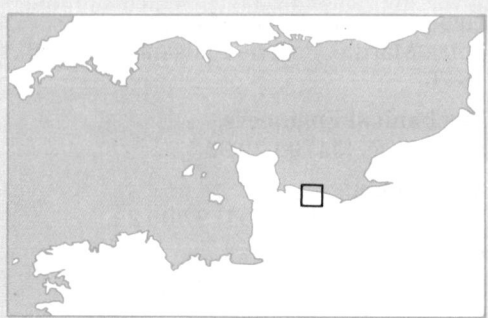

Like many of the ports along the Normandy beaches, Courseulles suffered severe damage during the Allied invasion of World War II; it was part of the Juno sector and was liberated by the Canadian troops.

There is a small harbour where mooring is possible, but care needs to be taken not to obstruct the fishing boats that sail from this port.

RESTAURANTS

Belle Aurore:
32 Rue Maréchal Foch. (31) 37 46 23. This charming hotel on the corner of the Quai Est overlooks the Port de Plaisance. A quietly elegant restaurant serves a variety of seafood to suit all tastes and because of the considerable oyster farming industry here, it is a must for oyster lovers.
Credit Cards: Amex, Diners, Visa.

HARBOUR SERVICES (YACHTS)

General: Postel et Cie, Quai Ouest.
Mechanical Engineers:
Serra. (31) 37 42 34.

MOORINGS

Port de Plaisance.
FF55.00 per day.

SERVICES AVAILABLE

● Petrol		● Water	
● Diesel		● Slipway	
● Calor Gas		● Chandlery	
● Camping Gas			

HARBOUR SERVICES (PERSONAL)

Showers: Port de Plaisance.

Post Office: Rue de la Mer.

Telephone: Capitainerie.

Laundry: Place du Marin.

Taxi & Cars: (31) 96 54 07.

Yacht Clubs:
Société des Régates Courseulles. (31) 37 47 42.

CHEMISTS AND MEDICAL SERVICES

Chemists:
Pharmacie, Rue de la Mer.

Medical:
Dr Lerosey, Place du Marche.

BANKS

BNP: 57 Rue de la Mer.

COASTGUARD: (31) 37 45 47
POLICE: (31) 37 46 75

PORT-EN-BESSIN

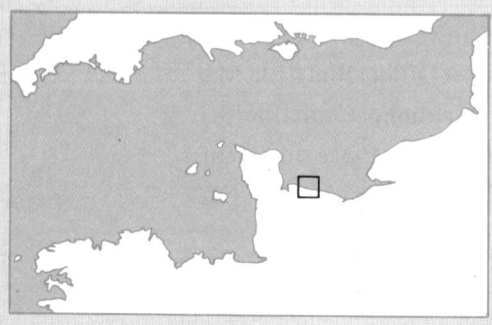

Port-En-Bessin is a small, quiet fishing town situated within sight of the Mulberry harbour off Arromanches. It is set in a cleft in the cliffs and the substantial breakwaters provide excellent shelter for those in the inner port. Yachts are welcome but only for a short stay. In the inner harbour you may have to moor alongside a fishing boat and be expected to cast off if the boat wants to leave, but for anyone wanting to visit the Normandy beaches, this is the most central of the ports. In heavy seas the entrance is dangerous and should be avoided. Also, the outer harbour dries out.

MOORINGS

Port de Plaisance.
FF45.00 per day.   FF264.00 per week.

RESTAURANTS

La Foncée:
12 Rue Lefournier. (31) 21 71 66.
This little restaurant tucked away up a side street just off the port has something of a farmhouse about it and its owner, Monsieur Genoux, prepares some really interesting dishes. Booking is very important.
Credit Cards: Amex, Carte Bleu.

La Marine:
Quai Letourneur. (31) 21 70 08.
There is little modern about this restaurant situated on the first floor of a forbidding hotel and entered by a staircase behind a bar on the ground floor where conversation tends to still when a stranger enters. However the food is genuine and the prices particularly reasonable. The view over the outer port is spectacular, particularly at sunset as the fishing boats return to port. It is not somewhere to go if you want atmosphere, but good if your party is self-contained.
Credit Cards: Carte Bleu, Diners.

HARBOUR SERVICES (YACHTS)

General: P.Hutrel, 5 Rue Maréchal-Lefournier.

Mechanical Engineers:
F. Digne, 8 Quai des Chantiers.

SERVICES AVAILABLE

●	Petrol	●	Water
●	Diesel	●	Slipway
●	Calor Gas	●	Chandlery
●	Camping Gas		

HARBOUR SERVICES (PERSONAL)

Showers: Port de Plaisance.

Telephone: Port de Plaisance.

Yacht Clubs:
Centre Nautique de Port-en-Bessin. (31) 21 79 02.

CHEMISTS AND MEDICAL SERVICES

Medical:
Hôpital, (31) 92 29 47.

COASTGUARD: (31) 21 71 52
POLICE: (31) 21 70 10

GRANDCAMP-MAISY

Grandcamp-Maissy is a small fishing port that today combines fishing with tourism and is developing its facilities for visitors. The small, quiet village has a certain appeal.

The yacht harbour is on the inner side of the harbour, leaving the outer area free for the small fishing fleet. There is an interesting fishmarket alongside.

MOORINGS

Port de Plaisance.
FF45.00 per day.   FF264.00 per week.

RESTAURANTS

La Marée:
Quai Cheron. (31) 22 60 55.
A seafood restaurant close to the port which is cheap, cheerful, busy and very French.
Credit Cards: Diners, Visa.

HARBOUR SERVICES (YACHTS)

General: Gailliot Marine, Le Port.

SERVICES AVAILABLE

- ● Petrol
- ● Diesel
- ● Calor Gas
- ● Camping Gas
- ● Water
- ■ Slipway
- ■ Chandlery

HARBOUR SERVICES (PERSONAL)

Showers: Port de Plaisance.
Post Office: Rue Aristide Briand.
Telephone: Port de Plaisance.
Taxi & Cars:
M and Mmme B. Flambard.

CHEMISTS AND MEDICAL SERVICES

Medical:
Doctor. (31) 22 60 50.

BANKS

Crédit Maritime: Quai Cheron.

POLICE: (31) 22 00 18

FISHING OFFSHORE.

CARENTAN

Carentan differs from almost all the other Channel **harbours** in that it is a centre for dairy produce and fishing plays

The Port de Plaisance is reached by sailing up a canal and is located about half a kilometre from the main part of the town.

The town is dominated by the Church of Notre-Dame which was built between the 12th and 15th centuries. It is known that there were settlements here as early as the 5th century and the rich soil has meant that agriculture has always played a major role in the local economy. The many surviving old buildings, some around the market square dating to the 15th century, make it difficult to imagine that Carentan was involved in the savage fighting that took place during the D-Day invasion, but a visit to the 101st Airborne Museum will testify to the horror of those days in early June 1944.

MOORINGS

Port de Plaisance.

RESTAURANTS

Auberge Normande:
17 Boulevard de Verdun. (33) 42 02 99.
Overlook the walk and make an effort to visit this delightful converted Normandy farmhouse. The only criticism is that it deserves a better position to the one it has, right by a main road. However, once you are in the little courtyard the noise of traffic abates and by the time you have entered the restaurant and been graciously shown to your table, you are only thinking of the pleasures to come. Gerard Bonnefoy who with his wife Anne-Marie run the Auberge, he in the kitchen whilst she runs the dining room, are well supported by a young team and everybody's aim seems to be to provide you with good food in a pleasant atmosphere. A place to treat yourself.
Credit Cards: Amex, Carte Bleu, Diners.

HARBOUR SERVICES (YACHTS)

General: G.A.M. Marine, Le Port.

Mechanical Engineers:
Hardy, 33 Rue 101 Air-Bonn.

SERVICES AVAILABLE

- ● Petrol
- ● Diesel
- ● Calor Gas
- ● Camping Gas
- ● Water
- ● Slipway
- ● Chandlery

HARBOUR SERVICES (PERSONAL)

Showers: Port de Plaisance.

Telephone: Port de Plaisance.

Taxi & Cars: (33) 42 04 55.

CHEMISTS AND MEDICAL SERVICES

Chemists:
Pharmacie Peron, Place de la Republique.

Medical:
Hôpital, 1 Avenue Qui-Qu'en-Grogne.

BANKS

Crédit Lyonnais:
2 Place Desplanques-Dumesnil.

COASTGUARD: (33) 52 72 13
POLICE: (33) 42 00 17

ST VAAST-LA-HOUGUE

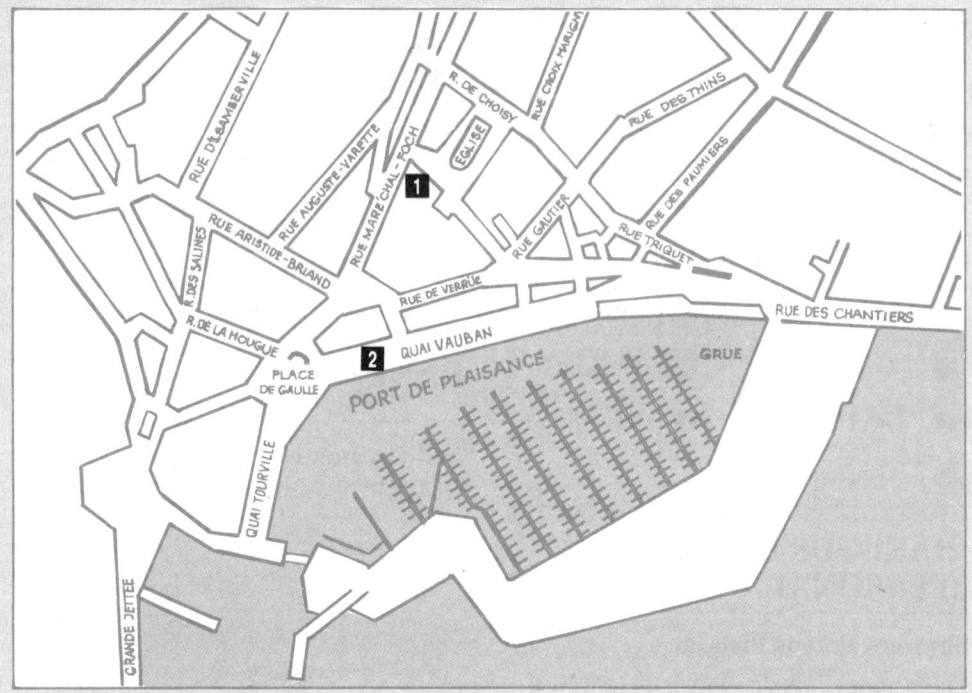

HARBOUR MASTER: (35) 97 01 30

St Vaast-La-Hougue is a pretty little fishing town with a considerable reputation for the cultivation of oysters. The Port de Plaisance is but a few years old but in a short time it has become very popular with yachtsmen, particularly English.

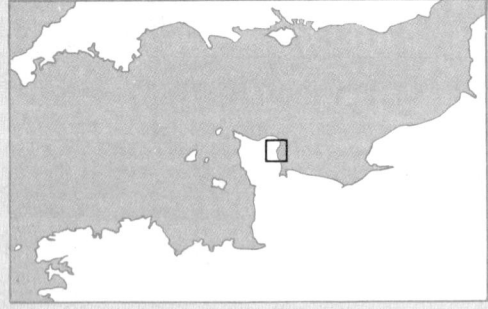

The harbour is sheltered by Tatihou Island, which has meant that for many centuries St Vaast has played an important role in the history of northern France. It was here that Edward III landed with his troops prior to the Battle of Crécy and in the 17th century Louis XIV assembled a fleet here to support James II in his attempt to regain the English throne. It was also during Louis XIV's reign that the military architect Vauban constructed the dyke that runs between St Vaast and Tatihou Island.

The small seamen's chapel, built in the 11th century, has a white painted cross to guide boats safely back to port. Today the yachts in the Port de Plaisance far outnumber the fishing boats, but despite this change in emphasis the port has not lost its charm. The numerous restaurants around it specialising in local oysters, and the oyster sheds where the freshly farmed oysters are sold direct to the customer, add to the ambiance and make a trip here a memorable experience.

As St Vaast is but 40 kilometres from Cherbourg it is well worth considering for a long weekend. Also, since it is close to Cherbourg airport, it can be used to swap crew or you may choose to leave the boat here in secure surroundings for a week or two.

MOORINGS

Port de Plaisance.
FF74.00 per day.   FF344.00 per week.

RESTAURANTS

1 Restaurant Fuchsias:
18 Rue Maréchal Foch. (33) 54 42 26. This restaurant has received rave reviews in most of the food guides but you may be disappointed, to judge from one experience: red wine placed on the table without any attempt to offer it for tasting, bottled water asked for three times before it arrived and the food placed on the table with all the care of a works canteen. Of course there is always the off night and this may have been it. Certainly the dining room is pleasant enough, the food itself good and the overall atmosphere promising. Credit Cards: Carte Bleu, Diners.

2 L'Escale:

9 Quai Vauban. (33) 54 42 60. This restaurant, under the direction of Jean-Yves Kuhn, specialises in seafood, notably local oysters and other shellfish, and is very conveniently located to the Port de Plaisance. Credit Cards: Access.

HARBOUR SERVICES (YACHTS)

General: G. Bernard. (33) 54 43 47.

Mechanical Engineers:
G. Gonraud. (33) 54 43 17.

SERVICES AVAILABLE

● Petrol	● Water	
● Diesel	● Slipway	
● Calor Gas	● Chandlery	
● Camping Gas		

ST VAAST-LA-HOUGUE Continued

HARBOUR SERVICES (PERSONAL)

Showers: Port de Plaisance.

Post Office: Rue Maréchal Foch.

Telephone: Port de Plaisance.

Laundry: Rue Triquet.

Yacht Clubs:
Cercle Nautique de la Hougue, Quai Albert-Paris. (33) 54 55 73.

CHEMISTS AND MEDICAL SERVICES

Medical:
Hôpital. (35) 97 00 11.

BANKS

Crédit Maritime:
Rue de Verrue.

COASTGUARD: (35) 97 05 27
POLICE: (35) 97 00 17

MERCHANTMAN UNDER SAIL.

BARFLEUR

Barfleur is a small harbour that dries out and is used by increasingly fewer fishing boats and more yachts. It is difficult to imagine that in the Middle Ages this was the most important port of Normandy, where William, Duke of Normandy, is said to have embarked on his ship *Le Mora* to invade England. The event is commemorated by a bronze plaque embedded in the rocks at the entrance to the port. What is more certain is that his principal navigation officer was Etienne Airard, a sailor from Barfleur.

The waters around Barfleur are notoriously tricky and the cause of many shipwrecks in the past. On the 25 November 1120 William Atheling, son of Henry I and the grandson of William the Conqueror, was sailing to England with his sister and 300 members of the Norman nobility when their ship *La Blanche Nef* struck the Quilleboeuf rock and sank, with the loss of all the passengers and crew. Today there is a lighthouse on the Pointe de Barfleur, 71 metres high and visible for nearly 60 kilometres, and races are held off the point.

Barfleur now has a population of under 1,000 and relies much on the visitors who arrive during the summer. Wandering around the quiet quayside it is difficult to imagine that on his way to the Crusades in 1194 Richard Coeur de Lion anchored his fleet of over 100 warships here.

MOORINGS

Port de Plaisance.
FF29.00 per day.

RESTAURANTS

Hôtel de Phare:
Rue St Thomas à Becket. (33) 54 02 07.
This small traditional inn just up the
High Street from the harbour is a
popular first or last night stop for ferry
passengers from Cherbourg and can get
quite full. It is unlikely that anyone will
leave feeling that they have had other
than good value for money.
Credit Cards: Access, Visa.

HARBOUR SERVICES (YACHTS)

Mechanical Engineers:
Bouly, 68 Rue St-Thomas.

SERVICES AVAILABLE

● Petrol		● Water
● Diesel		● Slipway
● Calor Gas		● Chandlery
● Camping Gas		

COASTGUARD: (33) 54 03 11

CHERBOURG

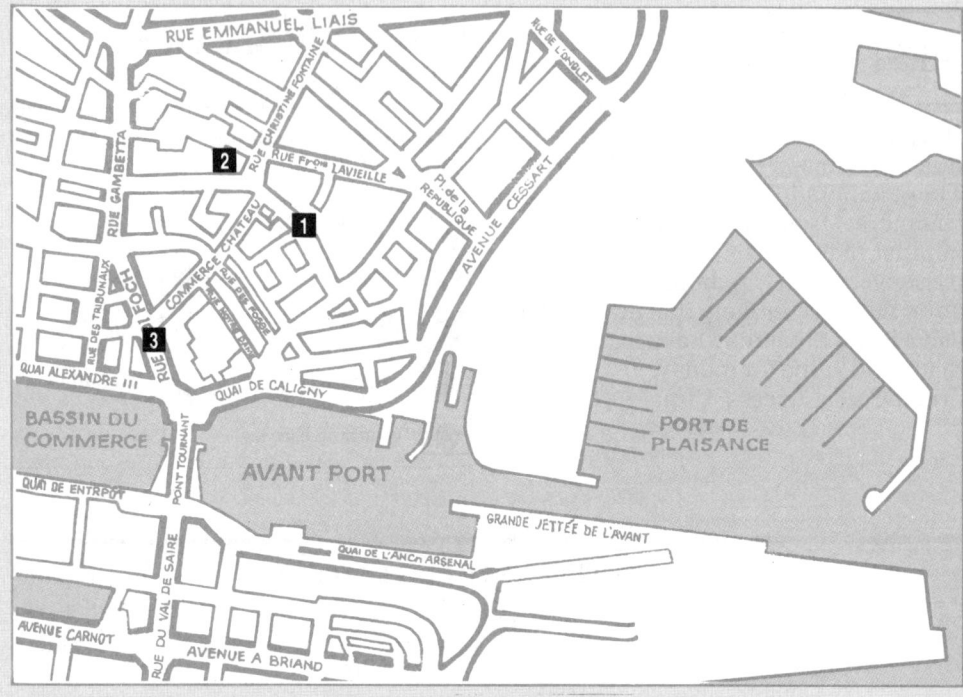

HARBOUR MASTER: (33) 53 75 16

Cherbourg is one of the busiest yacht harbours of northern France. Since it is available at all states of the tide it makes a useful starting point for those wishing to cruise the Normandy coastline to the east or Brittany and the Channel Islands to the west, and in the six months from May to September over 6,000 yachts visit the port, some 4,000 of them British. With all this traffic it is hardly surprising that the facilities are excellent and there is the added advantage of good

communications between Cherbourg and the UK by ferry and plane, and frequent flights to the Channel Islands.

Up to the mid-19th century Cherbourg was a major trading port and then became a significant naval base. During the great days of the transatlantic liners it was commonplace to see the *Normandie, France* and the two *Queens* moored up here and although, sadly, those days are over, there are still liners using the harbour and the QEII can sometimes be seen.

Cherbourg suffered considerable damage during the Second World War but its importance to the Allies as a supply port meant that it was rapidly repaired. It is worth visiting the Fort du Roule, an old German stronghold which is now a war museum and from which you get a panoramic view over Cherbourg.

From the Port de Plaisance it is a simple matter to walk into the town. Turn left on to the Avenue Cessart and walk up to Napoleon's statue, cross over into Place de la Republique and at the top take the Rue Lavieille, at the end of which you will arrive in the Rue Christine. From there you will find plenty of narrow streets with small restaurants, wide pedestrian walkways, markets and all the shops you could wish for.

Whilst Cherbourg is a large city and a major working port there are many advantages for the visiting yachtsman and a stopover here is not a bad way to start or finish your trip.

MOORINGS

Port de Plaisance.
FF77.00 per day.   FF398.00 per week.

RESTAURANTS

1 Le Plouc:
59 Rue au Blé. (33) 53 67 64.
Cherbourg possesses many restaurants where you can have a meal, enjoy it, and when asked about it later, you can never remember the name or quite where it was. Jacky Pain's restaurant close to the market is not one of these. Walking off the busy street into it is like entering a Normandy farmhouse. It is very comfortable even when full, which is most of the time. The service is attentive and its increasing popularity is testimony to the high standards it sets.
Credit Cards: Carte Bleu.

CHERBOURG Continued

HARBOUR SERVICES (YACHTS)

General: Cherbourg General Yachting, Le Port.

Mechanical Engineers:
Serelve. (33) 43 70 11.

SERVICES AVAILABLE

- ● Petrol
- ● Diesel
- ● Calor Gas
- ● Camping Gas
- ● Water
- ● Slipway
- ● Chandlery

HARBOUR SERVICES (PERSONAL)

Showers: Port de Plaisance.

Post Office:
Facility at Port de Plaisance.

Telephone: Port de Plaisance.

Laundry: Port de Plaisance.

Taxi & Cars:
Taxis de Cherbourg. (33) 53 70 70.

Yacht Clubs:
Yacht Club de Cherbourg, Port Chantereyne. (33) 94 28 05.

CHEMISTS AND MEDICAL SERVICES

2 **Chemists:**
Pharmacie, Rue Christine.

Medical: Hôpital. (33) 52 61 45.

BANKS

3 **Crédit Lyonnais:**
6 Rue du Maréchal-Foch.

POLICE: (33) 44 21 24

PIRATE SHIP ATTACKS MERCHANTMAN.

CARTERET

Carteret is a small harbour that dries out, lying some 22 kilometres east of Jersey. The entrance can be difficult in strong winds. As you come in there is a quay on the port side to which you can moor and further up you will come to the Port de Plaisance. Do not be deceived: this is really little more than a collection of privately owned buoys and at low water you will take to the mud. There is something rather attractive about this little port and if the tides are right it can be very pleasant to moor up to the quay and have lunch here.

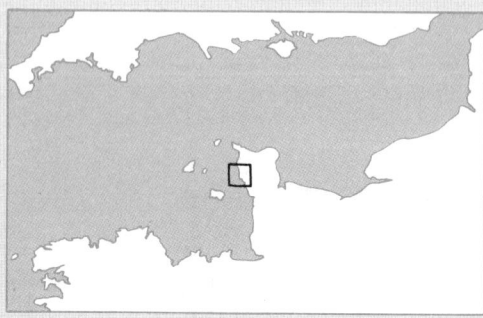

MOORINGS

Le Port.
FF28.00 per day.

BANKS

Crédit Mutuel: Place de l'Église.

VOLSPEC
The Volvo Penta Specialist

With our long and unrivalled reputation in the marine industry we realise the greatest pleasure for the Yachtsman is to be had on the water, not in the workshop. Should it be necessary, we have the expertise of an experienced and knowledgeable service team and we carry the largest stock of **Volvo Penta** spare parts in East Anglia. We would be pleased for you to drop in and see us at our well-appointed headquarters in Tollesbury to discuss your Volvo Penta requirements and with over 20 years experience we feel we are specialists in this field. Also as **Johnson** dealers and the Essex distributor for **GKN Aquadrive** we will certainly find many topics of conversation. Having dealt with us you'll soon realise our business is keeping you boating and happy.

We have a Mail/Telephone order service for UK and Export.
Call in and see us or give us a ring at

VOLSPEC LTD.

Woodrolfe Road, Tollesbury, Nr. Maldon
Essex, CM9 8SE
Telephone: (0621) 869756   Telex: 995078 VOLSPC

GRANVILLE

HARBOUR MASTER: (33) 50 20 06

Granville is a large town and very popular seaside resort, due in part to the vast expanse of beach that appears at low tide. The tide comes in at the rate of 62 metres a minute and it is quite interesting to watch and certainly something to watch out for.

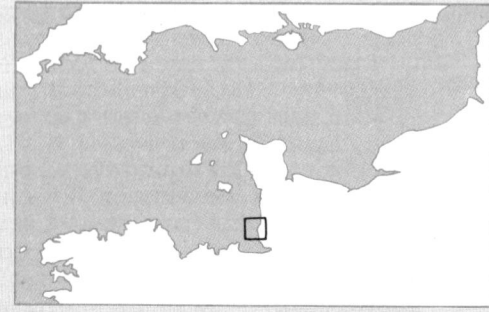

The town itself is in two very different halves. In the old town, which is approached over a drawbridge through the ramparts, time has stood still and unusually there has been no attempt to capitalise on its charm. What may come as something of a surprise is that Granville was founded by the English. In 1439, after an abortive attempt to capture Mont St Michel, the English force retired hurt to the rocky peninsula across the bay where they fortified the position. This was Granville's origin but the English did not last long. In 1442 knights from Mont St Michel under the command of d'Estouteville captured it in spite of the large ditch that the English had dug across the narrow isthmus, since known as the Tranchée aux Anglais.

The lower town, partly built on reclaimed land, is a busy commercial port and fishing fleet base, with a large Port de Plaisance on the sea side and bustling shops, bars and restaurants in the main part of the town just back from Boulevard Amiraux Granvillais.

Apart from the fact that Granville is an interesting and charming town, the view of Mont St Michel at dawn as you make passage from the Channel Islands or Les Chaussey or from St Malo must be one of the most beautiful sights of the world.

MOORINGS

Port de Plaisance.
FF86.00 per day.

RESTAURANTS

Le Phare:
11 Rue du Port. (33) 50 12 94.
You will find this restaurant by walking close to the end of the Rue du Port. There is a welcoming bar on the ground floor and the restaurant on the first floor looks out over the harbour. Anyone visiting Granville should try to make the time to come here as it is really a very pleasant experience. The young staff attend to their duties with quiet efficiency, leaving their customers to savour the food and admire the view. The emphasis is on seafood and it is very well prepared. Credit Cards: Amex, Diners, Visa.

La Potinerie:
19 Rue Georges-Clemenceau. (33) 50 17 31.
Situated on the other side of the town from the Port, this restaurant in a large hotel 'des Bains' opposite the casino – the sort of hotel where Monsieur Hulot might have stayed. The restaurant is a terraced room with some views over the sea and others over a carpark towards the casino. The food is better than the restaurant decor and comfort, whilst the service is efficient rather than friendly.

HARBOUR SERVICES (YACHTS)

General: Houry Nautic, Lecoulant Marine.

Mechanical Engineers: Lecoulant Marine.

SERVICES AVAILABLE

●	Petrol	●	Water
●	Diesel	●	Slipway
●	Calor Gas	●	Chandlery
●	Camping Gas		

HARBOUR SERVICES (PERSONAL)

Showers: Port de Plaisance.

Post Office: Rue Couraye.

Telephone: Port de Plaisance.

Yacht Clubs:
Yacht Club de Granville, Port de Herel. (33) 50 04 25.

CHEMISTS AND MEDICAL SERVICES

Medical: Hôpital. (33) 98 74 75.

BANKS

Crédit Lyonnais: 101 Rue Couraye.

COASTGUARD: (33) 50 20 06
POLICE: (33) 50 00 01

CANCALE

Cancale is a picturesque little port world-famous for its oysters and at low tide the oyster beds are visible as far as the eye can see towards Mont St Michel. It is estimated that 48 million Cancale oysters a year were consumed at the time of the First Empire. However, in the early part of the 20th century the oysters were smitten with a mysterious disease and the spat had to be imported from other oyster growing areas, mainly Belon. Today this is fortunately history and indigeneous spat are flourishing again.

Around the small harbour, which dries out, are a multitude of restaurants offering every conceivable style of oyster and many other predominantly fish dishes besides. The area around the port forms one part of the town, with the other part situated slightly above it.

However attractive the town may be, mooring here is problematical and a visit to Cancale is really only for a genuine oyster-lover. Anyone planning on spending some time at St Malo might consider taking the easy route and hiring a car.

RESTAURANTS

Restaurant de Bricourt:
1 Rue Duguesclin. (99) 89 64 76.
Oliver Roellinger, the son of a doctor
and trained as a chemical engineer, is
now one of the most highly regarded
young chefs of France. It may be
tempting to stay on the quayside and
eat in one of the many fine restaurants
that line it but if you steel yourself for a
long walk, 10 to 15 minutes, up the hill
to the centre of the town, your efforts
will be well rewarded. The restaurant is
set back in an imposing house and you
will be struck first by the feeling of
space and quiet, the thick carpet
soaking up the sound as the waiters
move around the tables. Whilst
deciding on your meal, it is possible to
take an aperitif in the large garden
behind the house, then into one of the
small dining rooms where the tables are
well spaced and beautifully set. The
food is quite outstanding and, if you
can, leave room for the sweets: even the
most die-hard non-dessert eaters may
be tempted to forswear their habits just
for this once as the creations that
emerge from the kitchen are simply out
of this world. You should leave feeling
privileged to have participated in an
experience that has little to do with
merely keeping body and soul together.
Booking is essential.
Credit Cards: Carte Bleu.

HARBOUR SERVICES (YACHTS)

General: Armand Nautisme. (99) 89 88
41.

Mechanical Engineers:
Garage Cancalais. (99) 89 88 41.

SERVICES AVAILABLE

☐	Petrol	⬛	Water
☐	Diesel	⬛	Slipway
⬛	Calor Gas	⬛	Chandlery
⬛	Camping Gas		

COASTGUARD: (99) 89 63 69
POLICE: (99) 89 60 21

ST MALO

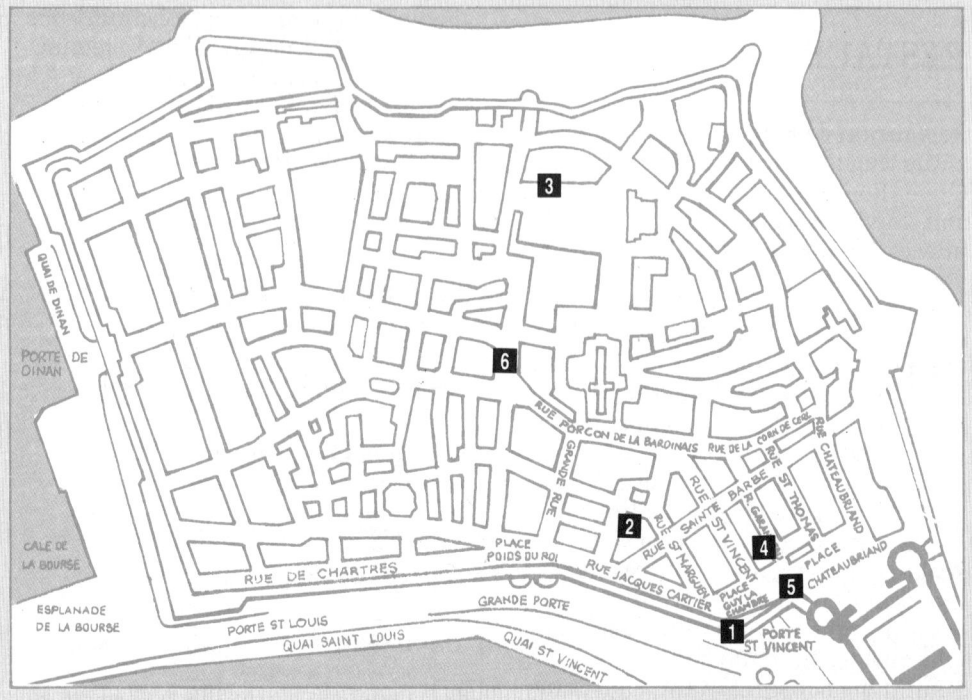

HARBOUR MASTER: (99) 81 62 86 VHF Ch 9

S t Malo is unique, a seaport with a remarkable history and great charm, and with very good facilities for yachtsmen. The problem is whether to moor at St Malo or St Servan. Mooring at St Malo involves waiting for the tide and then lock gates; St Servan has none of these problems but it is some way from St Malo and the large tidal falls make mooring to a pontoon a bumpy experience.

St Malo derives its name from a Welsh monk of the 6th century

who settled in nearby Aleth, now called St Servan. The population of Aleth moved to the rocky peninsula just to the west as a defensive measure and the town of St Malo came into being.

In those days it was cut off from the mainland at high tide, which helped to produce a fiercely independent breed of person whose wealth derived from the sea. *Ni Français, ni Bretons, Malouins suis.*

Famous natives of the town include Jacques Cartier, who discovered the St Lawrence River whilst seeking the North-West Passage in 1534. The resultant trade and the profits from cod fishing on the banks off Newfoundland ensured great prosperity for St Malo. In the 18th century the Malouin privateers Duguay-Trouin and Surcouf acquired enormous riches from their exploits on the high seas and carried special letters issued by the King permitting them to attack foreign shipping without being regarded as pirates. Even the writer Chateaubriand, born at St Malo in 1768, earned more through carrying arms than through his writing.

Walking around the ramparts of the town or along its narrow cobbled streets it is difficult to believe that St Malo is mostly new. German resistance in the last war was very dogged and during the first two weeks of August 1944 the Americans reduced the town to rubble: only the massive granite ramparts remained. But the spirit of independence lived on and the inhabitants set about rebuilding the town as it had been.

St Malo is one of the most visited towns of France and particularly during the summer the small streets are packed with holiday-makers. It is not the place to go if you are looking for peace and quiet but as one of the great maritime towns of the world a visit here will certainly linger in the memory.

MOORINGS

Bassin Vauban.
FF63.00 per day.

Les Sablons.
FF80.00 per day.

RESTAURANTS

1 La Duchesse Anne:
4 Place Chateaubriand. (99) 40 85 33. This restaurant is an institution in St Malo and has long been a favourite with visiting Englishmen. Inside the atmosphere is that of a traditional French bistro, but it also has tables outside where in summer you can watch the fun as well as enjoy the food.

Despite years of popularity, they have maintained their high standards, while many lesser places would have dropped standards and hiked up their prices long ago. Fish – the *choucroute de pecheur* is excellent – plays the major role, but there is something to suit every palate.

2 J-P Delaunay Restaurateur:
6 Rue Sainte Barbe. (99) 40 92 46. The name might seem a little pretentious but the restaurant most certainly is not and should satisfy any yachtsman wanting to try somewhere new but perplexed by the myriad of choices. Hidden away close to the ramparts, it is rather small and pleasantly decorated with enough paintings to do justice to the average museum. The menu offers a varied choice with, as usual, the slant towards fish.
Credit Cards: Amex, Carte Bleu, Diners.

HARBOUR SERVICES (YACHTS)

General: Sumalo Marine. (99) 82 33 44.

SERVICES AVAILABLE

- ● Petrol
- ● Diesel
- ● Calor Gas
- ● Camping Gas
- ● Water
- ● Slipway
- ● Chandlery

HARBOUR SERVICES (PERSONAL)

Showers: Port de Plaisance.

3 Post Office: Place Lemennais.

Telephone: Port de Plaisance.

Yacht Clubs:
Société Nautique Baie de Saint Malo, Quai du Bajoyer. (99) 40 84 42.

CHEMISTS AND MEDICAL SERVICES

4 Chemists:
Pharmacie, Rue St Vincent.

Medical: Hôpital. (99) 56 56 19.

BANKS

5 Société Générale:
2 Place du Pilori.

COASTGUARD: (99) 56 15 79
POLICE: (99) 81 52 30

HAULING IN THE CATCH.

DINARD

Towards the end of the last century a wealthy American, Mr Coppinger, visited a small fishing village on the other side of the Rance to St Malo and recognising the potential of the situation, invested in the development of Dinard. Up to the Second World War it was almost the exclusive playground of rich Americans and English, some of whom built the exotic mansions that dot the hillside.

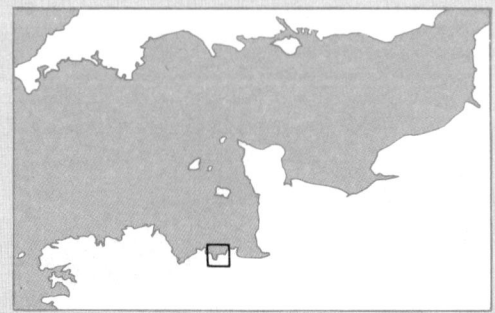

Dinard's days as one of the most fashionable resorts of Europe are over, but it still retains a popularity with the English. Mooring off the Yacht Club you will see the imposing facade of the Grand Hotel looking down over the mouth of the Rance towards St Malo. Walk down the Avenue Georges V to the Place J. Boutin and around to the Promenade des Allies and you will find the expanse of Plage de L'Ecluse with its large sea-filled swimming pool. Dominating the beach is the casino and the new Olympic-sized pool.

There has long been a great yachting rivalry between Dinard and St Malo. The most prestigious yacht races used to run to Dinard, the best known being the Cowes-Dinard race for the Edward VII trophy, St Malo has recently become the more significant racing centre. Dinard, however, remains a more genteel place at which to moor.

MOORINGS

Port de Plaisance.
FF57.00 per day.

RESTAURANTS

Altair:
18 Boulevard Feart. (99) 46 13 58.
If you want to eat in lively
surroundings by the sea on a hot sunny
day, this is not the place to go since the
hotel is in the middle of the town and
the building of a somewhat sombre
appearance. The restaurant is
traditional in decor and divided into
two parts on either side of the bar; if
you can, secure a table on the more
pleasant, right side. Either way, the
food is consistently good.
Credit Cards: Amex, Diners, Visa.

Hôtel de La Valée:
6 Avenue Georges V. (99) 46 94 00.
This imposing building by a small
beach with wonderful views across the
Rance estuary has a pleasant bar
renovated in Regency style and an airy
restaurant, a large outdoor terrace
serving food with much more
comfortable seating than usual. The
food is rather better than you might
expect to find in a holiday hotel, and
there are a number of *prix fixe* menus
to choose from. It gets very busy during
the season, particularly at lunchtime,
and if you want a table on the terrace
be early.

HARBOUR SERVICES (YACHTS)

General: Dinard Marine, Route du
Barrage.

SERVICES AVAILABLE

● Petrol	● Water	
● Diesel	● Slipway	
● Calor Gas	● Chandlery	
● Camping Gas		

CHEMISTS AND MEDICAL SERVICES

Medical: Hôpital. (99) 46 18 68.

COASTGUARD: (99) 46 66 15
POLICE: (99) 46 11 54

ST CAST

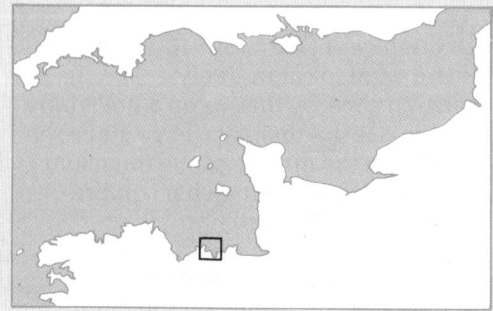

St Cast is not a much visited port and whilst the anchorage is good and the fundamental services available, the harbour is some way from the town centre and non-walkers are rather limited for choice.

Today St Cast has developed into a thriving holiday resort coupled with the neighbouring village Le Guildo and is known as St Cast-Le Guildo. The town falls into three areas: L'Isle, where the port is, Le Bourg and La Garde. If you walk from the harbour towards Le Bourg you will see a tall monument, which was erected to commemorate the French victory over the English at the battle of St Cast in 1758 and is surmounted by a leopard, for England, being trampled by a greyhound representing France. Local legend tells that the general commanding the French troops, the Duke of Aiguillon, directed the battle from a mill house, Moulin d'Anne, in the company of the miller's wife.' When the Attorney-General was told that the Duke and his men had covered themselves with glory, he replied 'and with flour as well'.

MOORINGS

Port de Plaisance.
FF57.00 per day.

RESTAURANTS

There is nowhere to suggest within easy reach of the port. The nearest restaurant of note can be found at the Plage de Pen-Guen, a few kilometres to the south.

Le Biniou:
Plage de Pen-Guen. (96) 41 94 53.
This is a perfectly placed restaurant, overlooking the beach. Jean-Claude Menard has enjoyed considerable success since he has been here, and has constructed a new dining room for over 50 guests.
The menu revolves around seafood and the consistency of the cooking and the care taken in the preparation make the travelling distance worth it.

HARBOUR SERVICES (YACHTS)

General: Jo Rouxel Marine. (96) 41 90 47.

SERVICES AVAILABLE

- ● Petrol
- ● Diesel
- ● Calor Gas
- ● Camping Gas
- ● Water
- ● Slipway
- ● Chandlery

HARBOUR SERVICES (PERSONAL)

Showers: Port de Plaisance.

Yacht Clubs:
Yacht Club de Saint Cast, Pointe de la Garde. (96) 41 91 77.

CHEMISTS AND MEDICAL SERVICES

Medical: Hôpital. (96) 39 27 60.

COASTGUARD: (96) 41 91 74
POLICE: (96) 41 81 84

ERQUY

The harbour here dries out completely and is always full of fishing boats, so its attraction for yachtsmen is hard to imagine unless it be the Coquille St-Jacques, for which Erquy is renowned.

The harbour is sheltered from winds from the north and east by the Cap d'Erquy and the surrounding area is blessed with some wonderful sandy beaches. Towns like Sables d'Or-les-Pins have sprung up to cater to holiday-makers who come to take advantage of these beaches sheltered by dunes and pine trees.

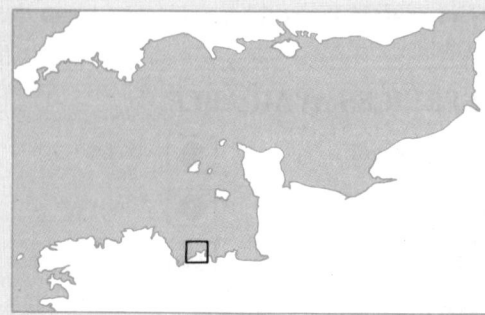

HARBOUR SERVICES (YACHTS)

General: Regina Plaisance, 15 Rue Foch.

Mechanical Engineers: Clérivet, 33 Rue Foch.

SERVICES AVAILABLE

● Petrol	● Water	
● Diesel	● Slipway	
● Calor Gas	● Chandlery	
● Camping Gas		

MOORINGS

Port de Plaisance. (30′ Yacht)
FF27.00 per day.   FF136.00 per week.

RESTAURANTS

L'Escurial:
Boulevard de la Mer. (96) 72 31 56.
If you like scallops, you will be more than at home in this unprepossessing restaurant overlooking the harbour. Since the fishermen of Erquy are famous for catching scallops, there is a real possibility that the best land up here.
Credit Cards: Amex, Carte Bleu.

HARBOUR SERVICES (PERSONAL)

Showers: Port de Plaisance.
Telephone: Port de Plaisance.
Yacht Clubs:
Cercle de la Voile, Le Port. (96) 72 32 40.

BANKS

Société Générale:
24 Rue du Maréchal-Foch.

COASTGUARD: (96) 72 30 13

RETURN OF THE FISHING FLEET.

BINIC

Binic has the largest Port de Plaisance in the Bay of St Brieuc. In earlier times it was an important cod fishing port and the first fishermen to catch cod off Newfoundland are said to have come from here. Today the wide beaches draw holiday-makers in the summer and tourism has become the main commercial activity. It is quite a small place, with one long quayside street on which everything happens.

RESTAURANTS

There are places to eat but no restaurants that particularly deserve a mention.

MOORINGS

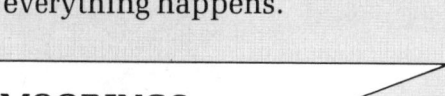

Club Nautique.
FF52.00 per day.

HARBOUR SERVICES (YACHTS)

General: Jean Bart Marine, Quai Jean Bart.

Mechanical Engineers: Binic Nautique, Route de St Brieuc.

THE CAPTAIN THROWING THE BAIT.

ST QUAY-PORTRIEUX

St Quay-Portrieux is another of the places along this stretch of coast where the traditional activity of fishing has given way to tourism, although there is still some fishing, mainly for shellfish. You might not see any 'Kiss me quick' hats at St Quay-Portrieux but you may well have a horrible feeling that one will appear around the next corner.

A considerable marina project is presently under way which, on completion, will dramatically change the face of this port and its interest to yachtsmen.

MOORINGS

Port de Plaisance.
FF36.00 per day.   FF133.00 per week.

RESTAURANTS

Ker Moor:
13 Rue du Président-Le-Sénécal.
A pleasant walk from the site of the new marina along the coastline towards the Pointe de St-Quay will bring you to Ker Moor, high on the hillside overlooking L'Ilot du Fort. If told that the interior had been designed by a film producer it would be no surprise. The concept is a garden with gilded wrought-iron bowers of roses surrounding the tables. The views are stunning, and given that you might suspect you are paying for atmosphere rather than culinary skills, the food is surprisingly good and the service friendly. Altogether an experience.
Credit Cards: Amex, Carte Bleu, Diners.

HARBOUR SERVICES (YACHTS)

General: Cras. (96) 70 57 83.

SERVICES AVAILABLE

☐ Petrol	⬛ Water
☐ Diesel	☐ Slipway
⬛ Calor Gas	⬛ Chandlery
⬛ Camping Gas	

BANKS

Société Générale:
2 Quai de la Republique.

COASTGUARD: (96) 70 56 62

PAIMPOL

Paimpol is a prosperous holiday town with an attractive square, plenty of bars and restaurants, and a well-equipped Port de Plaisance. Once this was a major fishing port but fishing has now almost ceased and the memories of the men who fished the Icelandic seas are confined to Pierre Loti's novel *Pêcheur d'Islande* and the Maritime Museum on the Quai Pierre-Loti.

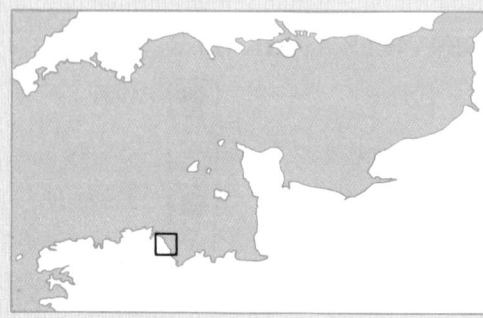

MOORINGS

Port de Plaisance.
FF46.00 per day.

RESTAURANTS

Repaire de Kerroc'h:
29 Quai Morand. (96) 20 50 13. Conveniently placed for the Port de Plaisance, this late 18th-century-granite pension has a very attractive Louis XVI-style dining room. The usual variety of prix fixe menus means that there is something for everybody.

HARBOUR SERVICES (YACHTS)

General: Comptoir Nautique Paimpolais. (96) 20 88 58.

Mechanical Engineers: Scaviner, Quai Kernoa.

SERVICES AVAILABLE

- ● Petrol
- ● Diesel
- ● Calor Gas
- ● Camping Gas
- ● Water
- ● Slipway
- ● Chandlery

HARBOUR SERVICES (PERSONAL)

Showers: Port de Plaisance.
Post Office: Avenue Général de Gaulle.
Telephone: Port de Plaisance.

CHEMISTS AND MEDICAL SERVICES

Chemists:
Pharmacie, Avenue Général de Gaulle.

Medical: Hôpital. (96) 20 86 02.

BANKS

Société Générale:
6 Place de la Republique.

COASTGUARD: (96) 20 88 09
POLICE: (96) 20 80 17

LOBSTER FISHING.

ILE DE BREHAT

To call Ile de Bréhat a harbour would not be accurate; rather it is a cruising area with some anchorages. For yachtsmen these waters are particularly challenging and rewarding. Given the right conditions the water is blue and clear, the sun shows up the pink of the granite rocks, and you will find it hard to imagine a better place to be. The island itself is very picturesque. It is about 3 kilometres long and 1½ kilometres wide at its broadest, and considering its size and its proximity to the mainland has a remarkably individual climate and vegetation. It rains less and is warmer than the mainland, and palm trees, fig trees and wonderful wild flowers grow freely. Cars are forbidden and for those not prepared to walk, a taxi service is offered by the local farmers, who will carry you in a trailer hitched up to a tractor. Bréhat is in fact two islands joined by the Pont ar Prat, which was built in the 18th century by Vauban. The southerly island is the more cultivated, whilst the northern part is much more wild and rugged. Of the two villages, Port Clos is little more than a hotel and a couple of cottages, and it is the centrally located Le Bourg which is the main 'town'.

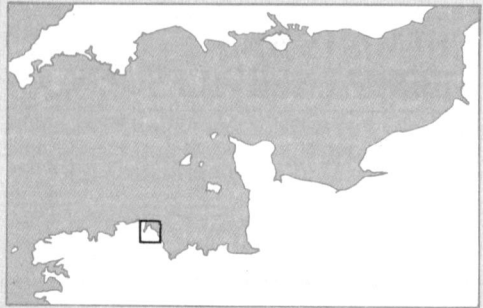

Walking to the northernmost point takes you to the Phare du Paon where there are wonderful coastal views. Swinging back towards Le Bourg you see the other lighthouse on the island, Rosedo, and crossing over the Pont ar Prat there is St Michel's Chapel on the west.

RESTAURANTS

La Vieille Auberge:
Le Bourg. (96) 20 00 24.
This quite delightful, simple inn in the middle of the 'town', near the main square with a few shops and a couple of bars, is entered through a very small courtyard, with the glass-fronted dining room on the left. The food is simple, the service attentive and friendly, and the atmosphere and surroundings idyllic.

HOMEWARD BOUND.

LÉZARDRIEUX

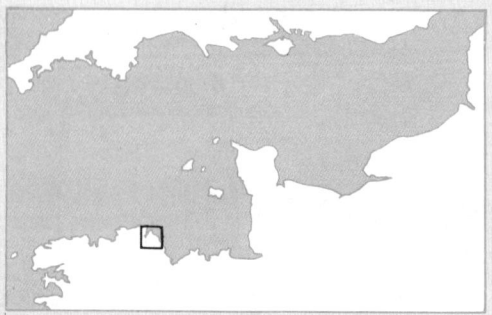

Lézardrieux on the Trieux River is a delightful place to visit, but some care has to be taken mooring in the river as the currents are strong. Most yachtsmen head for the Port de Plaisance, which has every facility you could want and saves you the walk up the hill to the dreamy little town. However, the walk is well worth the effort since the quiet town, particularly its main square, is charming, and there are a few bars and restaurants to refresh you on the way down.

It is possible to sail up river another 10 kilometres to the town of Pontrieux, a trip which can be an interesting and sometimes exciting diversion.

MOORINGS

Port de Plaisance.
FF58.00 per day.

RESTAURANTS

Relais Brenner:
Pont de Lézardrieux. (96) 20 11 05. This is a quite magnificent hotel superbly situated overlooking the Trieux and if you think that hyperbole wait till you have eaten. When asked if it were possible to moor a dinghy at the bottom of the grounds, which slope down to the estuary, the answer was, 'Yes, but we usually send the car to the Port de Plaisance'. The dining room is quietly luxurious in an understated way and the food of a particularly high standard. As for the view from the dining room, well see for yourself.

HARBOUR SERVICES (YACHTS)

General: Trieux Marine, Le Port.

Mechanical Engineers:
Ruffloc'h, Le Port.

SERVICES AVAILABLE

- ● Petrol
- ● Diesel
- ● Calor Gas
- ● Camping Gas
- ● Water
- ● Slipway
- ● Chandlery

HARBOUR SERVICES (PERSONAL)

Showers: Port de Plaisance.

Telephone: Port de Plaisance.

COASTGUARD: (96) 20 00 66

TRÉGUIER

Tréguier, situated on a junction of two rivers, the Jaudy and Guindy, is one of the most pleasant towns on the Channel. The Port de Plaisance is very well equipped and leaves you wanting for nothing. About 200 metres away in the Place Général de Gaulle are a few restaurants and a bar.

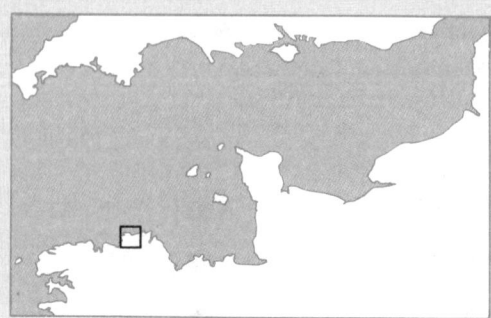

You have to walk up a fairly steep hill to get to the town centre, which is dominated by the Cathedral of St Tugdual, named after the monk who converted the town to Christianity in the 6th century. The Cathedral, one of the finest examples of Gothic architecture in northern France, was built between 1339 and 1468 and the town was a bishopric until the revolution. There are many interesting tales connected with the Cathedral. Yves Helori, who was born in nearby Minihy, became a lawyer and churchman, and such was his reputation as a righter of wrongs that he was canonized in 1348 only 45 years after his death. St Yves became the patron saint of lawyers and Brittany; Duke Jean V of Brittany held him in such regard that he asked to be buried as close as possible to him. On 19 May, the feast day of St Yves, there is a procession from the Cathedral to the little 15th-century church at Minihy.

In front of the Cathedral there is a statue to Ernest Renan, a great theological philosopher of the 19th century. Today the house where he was born is a museum. Around the main square are plenty of shops one of which is a rather splendid patisserie and coffee house.

MOORINGS

Port de Plaisance.
FF59.00 per day.

RESTAURANTS

The Hôtel de L'Estuaire:
Place Général de Gaulle. (96) 92 30 25.
The main advantage of this hotel is that
it is within some 200 metres of the Port
de Plaisance and hence saves you the
walk up the hill to the town. The
first-floor restaurant offers some
splendid views over the river and there
are a number of reasonable *prix fixe*
menus.

Au petit Savoyard:
17 Rue le Peltier. (96) 92 43 04.
The proprietors here are from the
south-east and some dishes are more
familiar in the ski-resorts there. A good
walk will stir the appetite and there are
plenty of little bars around the main
square to keep you going. A simple,
friendly, rustic bistro, particularly
recommended for those looking for a
change from sea food.

HARBOUR SERVICES (YACHTS)

General: Marina Sports, Quai de
Treguier.

Mechanical Engineers:
Prigent. (96) 92 43 52.

SERVICES AVAILABLE

●	Petrol	●	Water
●	Diesel	●	Slipway
●	Calor Gas	●	Chandlery
●	Camping Gas		

HARBOUR SERVICES (PERSONAL)

Showers: Port de Plaisance.

Post Office: Rue St André.

Telephone: Port de Plaisance.

CHEMISTS AND MEDICAL SERVICES

Medical: Hôpital. (96) 92 30 72.

COASTGUARD: (96) 23 23 04
POLICE: (96) 92 30 38

PERROS-GUIREC

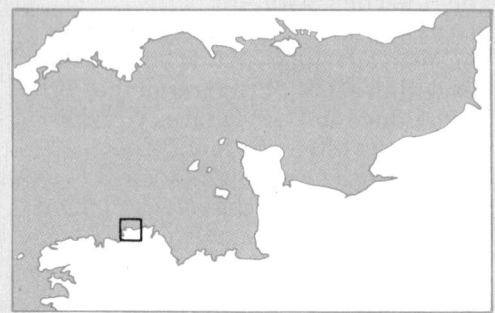

If the peace of Lézardrieux and the restrained air of Tréguier are not what you want, then Perros-Guirec should fit the bill. The Port de Plaisance is bordered by a road that runs beside the harbour and the landward side is full of modern hotels, apartment blocks, souvenir shops and all the signs of a big holiday centre. In the evening there are discotheques and generally all the fun of the fair.

Its popularity is due in part to its two beaches, Trestraou and Trestringel, which are north-facing and quite a little walk away. The older part of the town along with the Casino overlooks these beaches. The modern area is around the harbour and most accessible.

The pontoons all have names and the facilities are well sign-posted, except for the showers where an arrow sends you off in one direction and another sends you back again with no sign of a shower block anywhere. They are in the Capitainerie on the other side of the road.

RESTAURANTS

For those not wanting the walk there are many restaurants around the Port de Plaisance, all readily visible.

Les Sept-Iles:
53 Boulevard Clemenceau.
(96) 23 22 94.
This restaurant is in the Hotel Les Feux des Iles, grandly situated in a park overlooking the bay. The *prix fixe* menus are surprisingly reasonable for a restaurant of this type, if chosen wisely. Credit Cards: Carte Bleu, Diners.

HARBOUR SERVICES (YACHTS)

General: Loc' Amor. (96) 23 05 08.

SERVICES AVAILABLE

- ● Petrol
- ● Diesel
- ● Calor Gas
- ● Camping Gas
- ● Water
- ● Slipway
- ● Chandlery

HARBOUR SERVICES (PERSONAL)

Showers: Port de Plaisance.

Telephone: Port de Plaisance.

CHEMISTS AND MEDICAL SERVICES

Chemists: Opposite the pontoons.

BANKS

Société Générale:
4 Rue de la Poste.

COASTGUARD: (96) 23 20 16
POLICE: (96) 23 20 17

MORLAIX

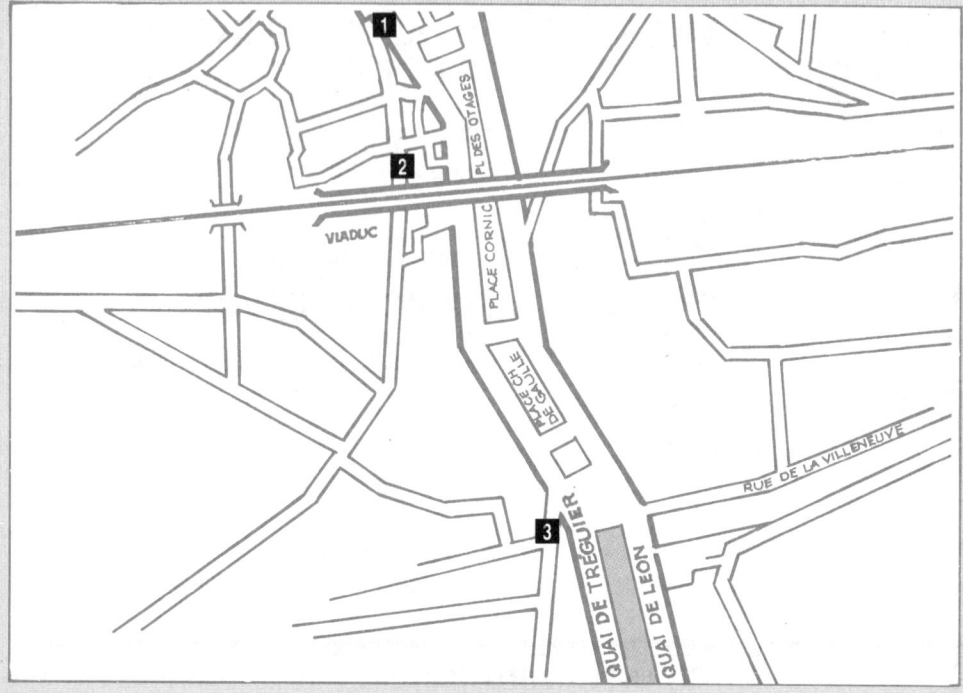

HARBOUR MASTER: (98) 62 13 14 or radio VHF Ch 9

Sheltered in a deep valley some 11 kilometres from the sea, Morlaix is dominated by a huge viaduct, about 60 metres high, which was built over 100 years ago to carry the railway line from Paris to Brest.

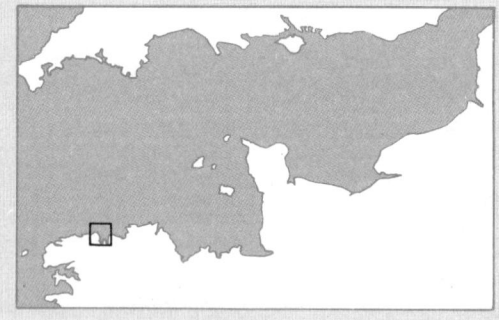

The moorings are fairly central, though to walk to Place des Otages, just the other side of the viaduct, where the town becomes a little busy, takes about 10 minutes. Morlaix is not too far from Roscoff and the cross-Channel ferries, and yachtsmen who wish to leave their boat for any length of time will find as secure a mooring here as anywhere.

The town motto, *'S'ils te mordent, mords-les'*, if they bite you, bite them, stems from a fracas with the English in 1522, when as a result of a raid against Bristol led by Jean de Coetanlem, the English attacked Morlaix. According to legend, most of the people were away at a festival at Guingamp and Noyal-Pontivy, the English ransacked the town, in the process discovering a warehouse full of wine. On their return, the Bretons not only found their town severely damaged but the perpetrators so drunk that they were quickly able to avenge the attack by putting the English to the sword. The coat of arms of Morlaix depicts a leopard confronted by a lion, with the town's motto, and was created during the celebrations that that followed.

MOORINGS

Port de Plaisance.
FF40.00 per day.   FF280.00 per week.

RESTAURANTS

1 L'Europe:
1 Rue Aiguillon. (98) 62 11 99.
A number of young chefs in France are returning, after *nouvelle cuisine*, to a more traditional style of cooking based rather strictly on local produce. It is known as '*cuisine de terroir*' and Patrick Jeffroy is one of its leading exponents. His skill has led to L'Europe becoming one of the great restaurants of northern France. The sombre dining room, due to be redecorated, does not do justice to the cooking, but for anyone seriously interested in food, a visit to see if they are witnessing the arrival of a new Bocuse is a must.

2 La Marée Bleue:
3 Rampe St Mélaine. (98) 63 24 21.
Just under the viaduct and up a small street on the left, this traditional French town restaurant is efficiently run by Monsieur and Madame Coquart. The place is comfortable, the decor cheery, the food above average and the service friendly.

MORLAIX Continued

HARBOUR SERVICES (YACHTS)

General: Société Morlaisienne de la Mer. (98) 62 19 21.

Mechanical Engineers:
Société Morlaisienne de la Mer. (98) 62 19 21.

SERVICES AVAILABLE

- ● Petrol
- ● Diesel
- ● Calor Gas
- ● Camping Gas
- ● Water
- ● Slipway
- ● Chandlery

HARBOUR SERVICES (PERSONAL)

Showers: Port de Plaisance.

Post Office: Rue de Brest.

Telephone: Port de Plaisance.

Yacht Clubs:
Yacht Club de Morlaix, Quai de Tréguier. (98) 62 08 51.

CHEMISTS AND MEDICAL SERVICES

Medical: Hôpital. (98) 88 40 22.

BANKS

3 **Crédit Mutuel de Bretagne:** Quai de Tréguier.

COASTGUARD: (98) 89 31 31
POLICE: (98) 88 58 13

ROSCOFF

There is a Purbeck feel to this ferry port which is blessed with a mild climate due to the Gulf Stream and attracts visitors as a health resort. Apart from the ferry business, the port's main activity is the export of vegetables, particularly onions. Roscoff also has an important marine biology centre. The problem for yachtsmen is that the harbour dries out, but if the tides are right this historical town makes an interesting break in a trip.

Fortunately the association with England is much happier today than in the past. Roscoff was burnt to the ground by the English in 1387 and some years later there was a great naval battle off Cap St-Matthieu when the French had their revenge. Mary Queen of Scots landed here in 1548 on her way to celebrate her engagement to the Dauphin of France when she was just five years old and according to legend stayed in the house near the town's old Church. One of the towers on the old ramparts is still known as Mary Stuart tower.

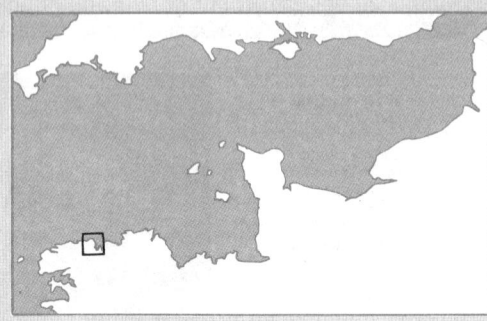

MOORINGS

Port de Plaisance.
FF40.00 per day.   FF200.00 per week.

RESTAURANTS

The Bellevue:
Rue Jeanne D'Arc. (98) 61 23 38.
In a town where the staple diet appears to consist of crêpes, it makes a pleasant change to walk along the seafront towards the ferry terminal to this imposing hotel. Situated on the corner of the bay overlooking the sea it provides respectable food with the added advantage of L'Albatros, its own in-house pub to visit before or after your meal.
Credit cards: Carte Bleu.

HARBOUR SERVICES (YACHTS)

General: C.N. de Primel. (98) 72 30 06.

SERVICES AVAILABLE

- ● Petrol
- ● Diesel
- ● Calor Gas
- ● Camping Gas
- ● Water
- ● Slipway
- ● Chandlery

HARBOUR SERVICES (PERSONAL)

Showers: Port de Plaisance.
Post Office: Rue Gambetta.
Telephone: Port de Plaisance.
Taxi & Cars: (98) 69 70 69

CHEMISTS AND MEDICAL SERVICES

Chemists:
Pharmacie, Amiral Réveillère.
Medical: Hôpital. (98) 88 40 22.

BANKS

Crédit Mutuel: Rue Louis Pasteur.

COASTGUARD: (98) 69 71 14
POLICE: (98) 69 00 48

L'ABER-WRAC'H

The similarity between the Breton and Welsh languages is shown by the name Aber, meaning mouth. Aberavon, Aberystwyth are two Welsh examples and the three Abers, L'Aber-Wrac'h, L'Aber-Benoit and L'Aber-Ilut their Breton counterparts. Of these three L'Aber-Wrac'h is the most significant from a yachtsman's point of view, offering a sheltered anchorage accessible at all states of the tide. Also it provides a good port to await the right tide before going through the Chenal du Four and southwards to the Bay of Biscay. Not regarded by many as more than a staging post, as the area is bleak and windswept, it none the less is admirably suited for this role. The yacht club provides most services and offers a warm welcome to visitors.

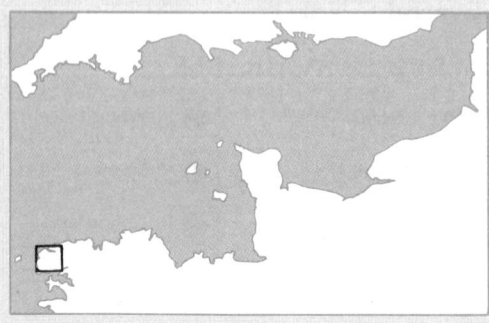

HARBOUR SERVICES (YACHTS)

General: Chantier Naval, Sainte-Antoine.

Mechanical Engineers: Mer'Aber. (98) 04 75 81.

SERVICES AVAILABLE

●	Petrol	●	Water
●	Diesel	●	Slipway
●	Calor Gas	●	Chandlery
●	Camping Gas		

MOORINGS

Port de Plaisance.
FF72.00 per day.   FF432.00 per week.

HARBOUR SERVICES (PERSONAL)

Showers: Port de Plaisance.

Telephone: Port de Plaisance.

Yacht Clubs:
Yacht Club des Abers, L'Aber-Wrac'h.
(98) 04 92 60

CHEMISTS AND MEDICAL SERVICES

Medical:
Hôpital (Brest). (98) 46 11 33.

COASTGUARD: (98) 80 50 50
POLICE: (98) 04 00 18

RACING TOWARDS THE CHANNEL.

BREST, MOULIN BLANC

HARBOUR MASTER: (98) 02 20 02 or radio VHF Ch 9

Mooring in the Port de Plaisance at Le Moulin Blanc is rather like participating in a boat show. If there is a problem vaguely connected with a yacht, there is almost certainly someone here who can fix it. The port is some kilometres from the centre of the city of Brest, but there are plenty of restaurants and bars on site to enable you to stay put and not have to worry about finding taxis to and from the town.

Because of its sheltered situation, Brest has always been an important port. It was frequently under attack from the English but it was Colbert during the 17th century who made it into one of the foremost naval ports of France. During the last war it was developed by the Germans as a major submarine base and was bombed to ruins by the Allies. Brest today is an imposing, modern city of some quarter of a million inhabitants, with naval dockyards that may be visited by anyone of French nationality and also a substantial commercial port.

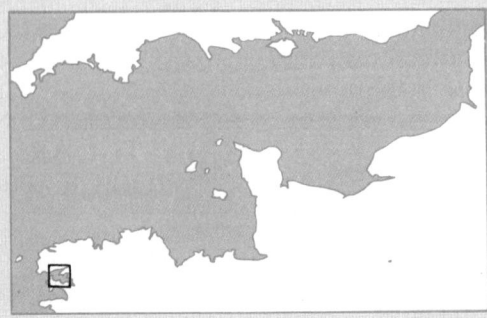

If you are planning a cruise to southern Brittany and beyond, there are many more attractive harbours, but the facilities are excellent and yachtsmen breaking their passage to the south will be hard put to find a better equipped port than this.

MOORINGS

Port de Plaisance.
FF66.00 per day.

RESTAURANTS

Moulin Blanc is sufficiently far from the main part of Brest to deter all but the most eager. The Port de Plaisance has a variety of bars and restaurants, but none that is outstanding enough to list.

HARBOUR SERVICES (YACHTS)

General: Service Plaisance, Port Moulin-Blanc.

Mechanical Engineers:
Navi-Ouest, Port Moulin-Blanc.

SERVICES AVAILABLE

- ● Petrol
- ● Diesel
- ● Calor Gas
- ● Camping Gas
- ● Water
- ● Slipway
- ● Chandlery

HARBOUR SERVICES (PERSONAL)

Showers: Port de Plaisance.

Post Office: Facilities at Port de Plaisance.

Telephone: Port de Plaisance.

Laundry: Port de Plaisance.

CHEMISTS AND MEDICAL SERVICES

Medical: Hôpital. (98) 46 11 33.

BANKS

Société Générale:
72 Rue de Siam.

COASTGUARD: (98) 89 63 16
POLICE: (98) 22 83 90

THE CHANNEL ISLANDS

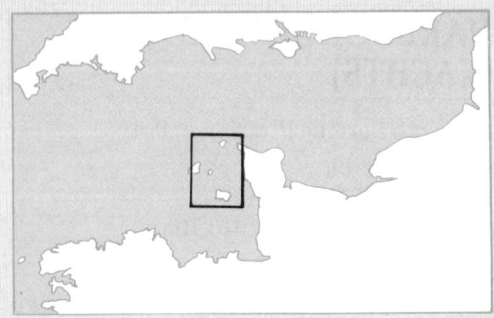

Most yachtsmen will visit these islands at some time or another for their beauty and interest. They present a unique way of life far removed from that found on either the English or French mainlands, and enjoy a status within the Commonwealth peculiar to themselves. They have been fiercely loyal to the British Crown since William of Normandy, to whom they belonged, conquered England in 1066. His heirs have maintained a direct control over the Islands ever since and the style of government is based on Norman law to this day.

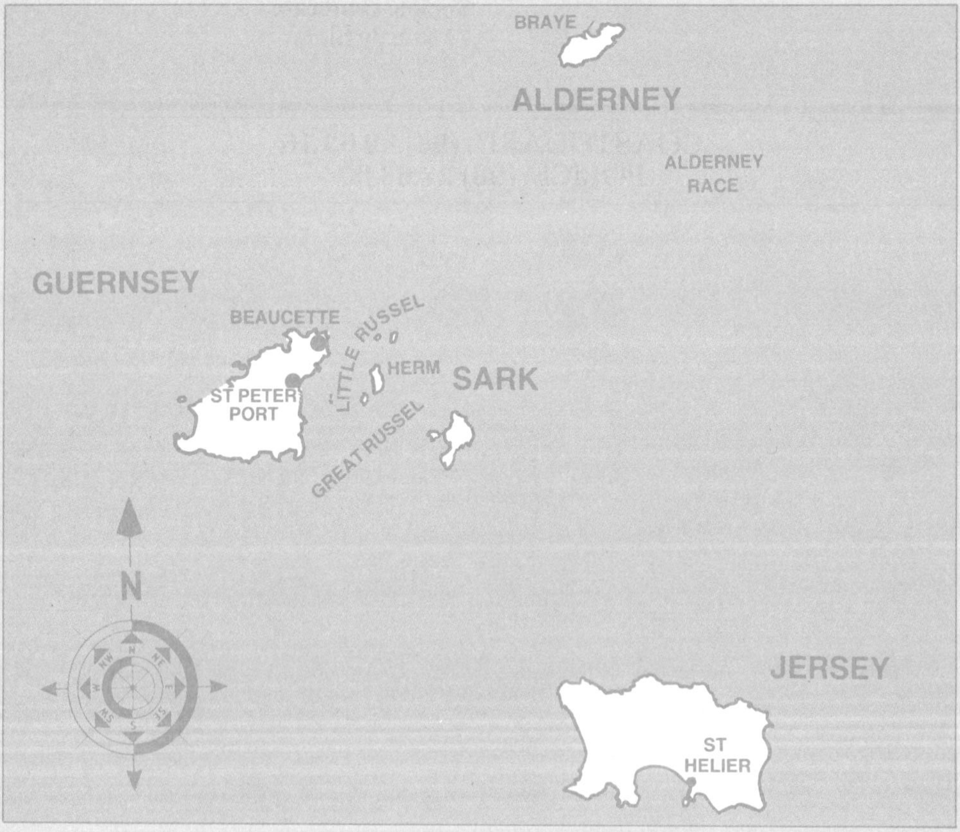

BRAYE

ALDERNEY

ALDERNEY
RACE

GUERNSEY

BEAUCETTE

LITTLE RUSSEL

HERM

SARK

ST PETER
PORT

GREAT RUSSEL

N

JERSEY

ST
HELIER

QUEEN VICTORIA'S VISIT TO GUERNSEY 1846.

JERSEY

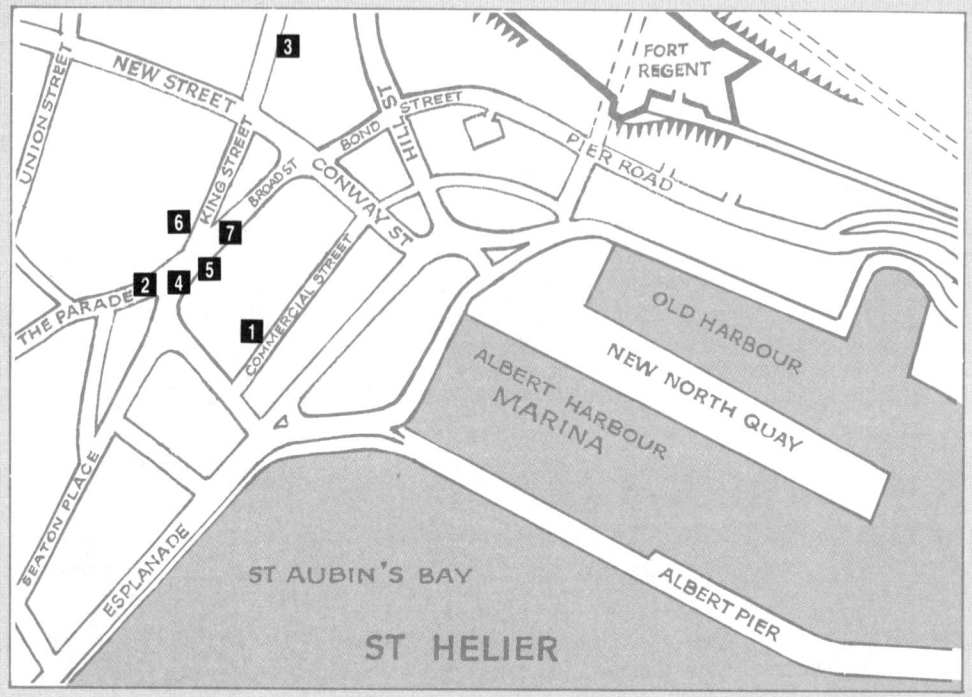

HARBOUR MASTER: (0534) 34451

The harbour front belies the rest of Jersey's capital of St Helier. Cranes and old warehouses line the quayside as reminders of the days when all the vegetable and flower exports were packed at the harbour. Today the farmers pack on site and the redundant warehouses are finding new lives as offices. But the harbour is still drab and it is only when you have walked into the town that St Helier comes into its own.

Providing tax-free goods for visitors is one of the major sources of revenue and employment, and the town has the feel of a modern shopping centre. There are places of great attractiveness like Royal Square and the Victorian market and evidence of a longer history in Elizabeth Castle, which was built on the orders of Queen Elizabeth I and was the home of Sir Walter Raleigh when he was Governor of Jersey. Overlooking the whole town is Fort Regent, which has now been converted

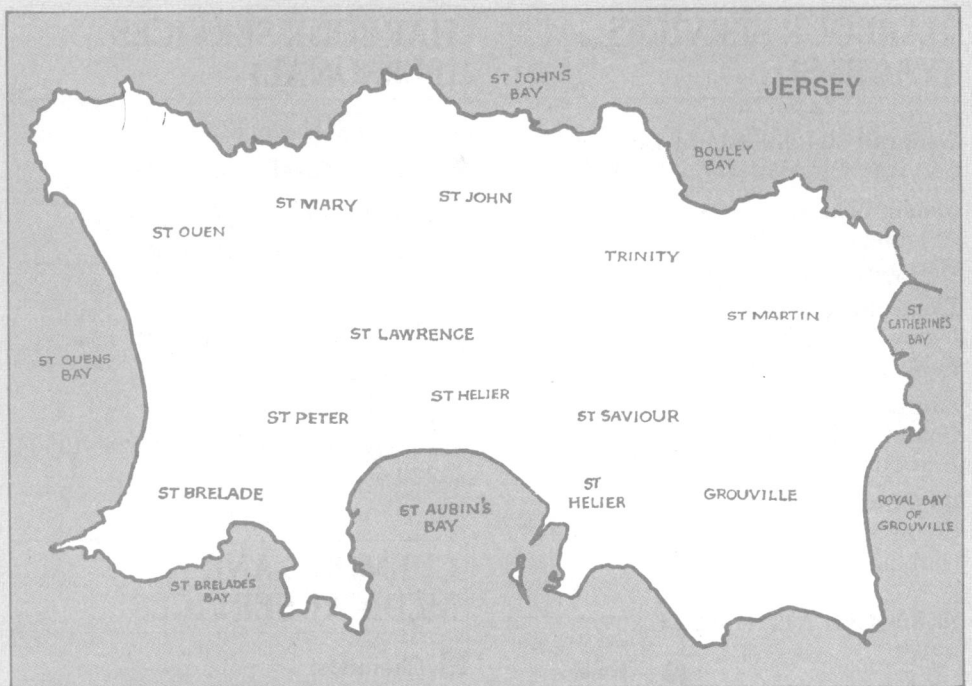

into a vast conference and leisure centre. Just behind the port you will find the Jersey Museum with a marvellous recreation of a Victorian pharmacy and a room devoted to Lillie Langtry, who was born on the island. However, you cannot get the true feel of Jersey just from a visit to St Helier and if there is one place where a hire car would justify itself, it is here.

MOORINGS

St Helier Marina.
(0534) 79549
£7.00 per day.   £49.00 per week.

RESTAURANTS

1 **La Bastille:**
Commercial Street.
Plateau des fruits de mer washed down with a bottle of Muscadet can be many people's idea of heaven and since this is the speciality of the house, be a devil and treat yourself. There is also an extensive general menu for those who do not care for fish. Informal and very convenient to the port.
Credit Cards: Access, Amex, Diners, Visa.

HARBOUR SERVICES (YACHTS)

General: Channel Island Yacht Services, Old Harbour. (0534) 42071.

Mechanical Engineers: Channel Island Yacht Services, Old Harbour.

Electronic Engineers: Jersey Marine Electronics, Unit 2, La Folie. (0534) 21603.

Sailmakers: Channel Island Yacht Services, Old Harbour.

Boat Builders & Repairers: Channel Island Yacht Services, Old Harbour.

SERVICES AVAILABLE

● Petrol		● Water	
● Diesel		● Slipway	
● Calor Gas		● Chandlery	
● Camping Gas			

HARBOUR SERVICES (PERSONAL)

Showers: St Helier Marina.

2 Post Office: Broad Street.

Telephone: St Helier Marina.

Laundry: Enquire at Marina.

Taxi & Cars:
Taxi Rank, Broad Street (0534) 23001.
Tower Cabs (0534) 75431.
Yellow Cabs (0534) 73500.

Yacht Clubs:
St Helier Yacht Club, South Pier. (0534) 32229.

CHEMISTS AND MEDICAL SERVICES

3 Chemists:
Boots. Queen Street.

Medical:
Jersey General Hospital, Gloucester Street. (0534) 71000.

BANKS

4 Barclays: Library Place.

5 Lloyds: Broad Street.

6 Midland: Broad Street.

7 National Westminster: Broad Street.

COASTGUARD: (0534) 34451
POLICE: (0534) 7551

MONT ORGUEIL CASTLE IN THE 19TH CENTURY.

ALDERNEY

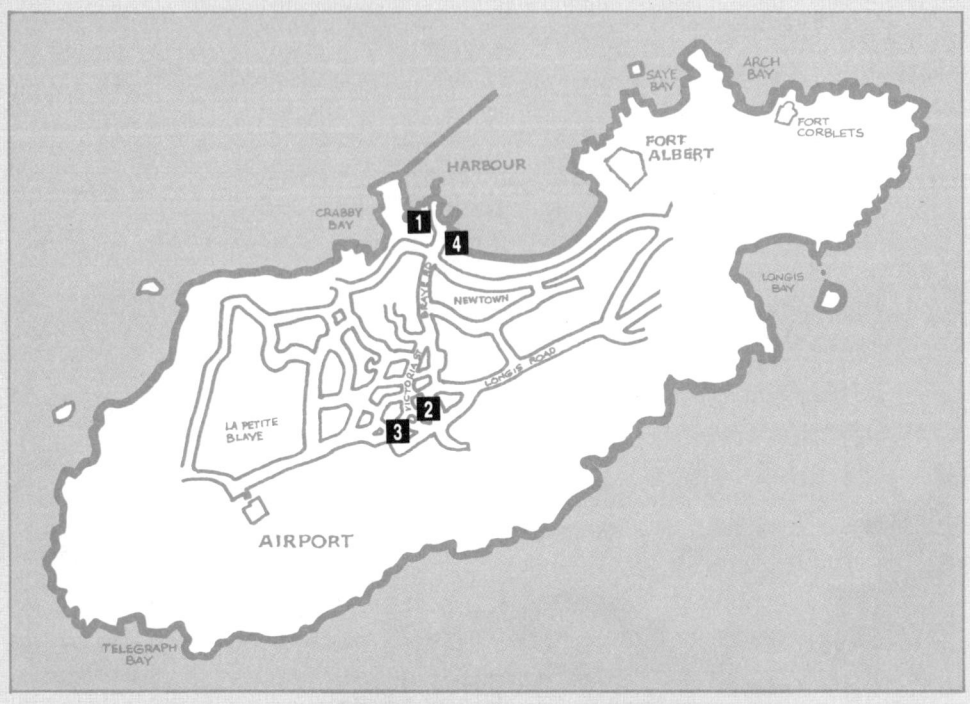

HARBOUR MASTER: (048 182) 2620 or radio VHF 12/74

The most noticeable feature of Alderney's Braye harbour is the massive breakwater that runs north-east from the north side of Braye. This ugly edifice was built to provide shelter from the north, and it succeeds in part, but the harbour is still very exposed to north-easterlies. Mooring is offshore but there is a water taxi to take you to and fro. During the season the harbour is very busy, but there are good facilities available and little chance of not securing a mooring unless the weather prevents access. Leaving the harbour to visit Brittany or the other islands takes you through some of the most dangerous waters in the Channel, the Swinge to the north and the Alderney Race to the east. Great care needs to be taken in both cases.

Another Braye landmark is Fort Albert. This fort, built by the Victorians and then strengthened by the Germans during the occupation in World War II, lies on the eastern side of Braye harbour between Rosselle and Bibette points. It has been allowed to fall into ruin but remains a potent reminder of the scale of fortifications built on the islands: some of the German batteries have walls four metres thick. Destroying such forts represents a formidable task, which explains why there are so many about.

There are a few restaurants and pubs at Braye but otherwise you need to go to the town of St Anne, three-quarters of a mile away up a long, winding and fairly steep hill. Most of the shops and commercial activity are centered in Victoria Street, a charming cobbled road lined with small, brightly painted cottages.

MOORINGS

Harbour Master, Braye Harbour.
(048 182) 2620 VHF Ch 12/74
£4.00 per day.   £24.00 per week.

RESTAURANTS

1 The First and Last:
Braye Harbour. (048 182) 3162.
As its name suggests, this small restaurant is the first you come to once ashore. The upstairs restaurant has views across the whole harbour, whilst downstairs there is a cosy little bar. Very friendly and particularly welcoming to yachtsmen, it has an atmosphere like that of an informal cocktail party and it does not take long to find yourself in conversation with other crews, no doubt telling you where you went wrong coming in and how much more difficult their passage was than yours. The food is fresh, fish local and a speciality of the house, and it is good value for money. Definitely worth a visit, but as usual with the good places, booking is advisable.
Credit Cards: Access, Amex, Diners, Visa.

2 Nellie Gray's:
Victoria Street, St Anne. (048 182) 3333.
By the time you have walked up to this restaurant you will be fully justified in forgetting any thoughts of diets and indulging yourselves in the fine food provided here: large servings of steak and fish; guacomole as a starter maybe. The menu is interesting and the surroundings in this cottage-style restaurant attractively turn-of-the-century. It is very comfortable, with an attractive bar where you can sit and ponder the menu.

ALDERNEY Continued

PUBS

3 The Coronation Inn:
High Street, St Anne.
This is a small pub situated in the High Street and almost on the junction with Victoria Street. Real ale in a friendly atmosphere.

4 The Moorings Hotel:
Braye Harbour.
Just 60 or so metres up from the harbour, this hotel has an interesting conservatory bar with views over the beach and bay. Food is available, with a barbecue in the summer and a large terrace for open-air drinking in good weather.

HARBOUR SERVICES (YACHTS)

General: Mainbrayce Marine Services, Inner Harbour, Braye. (048 182) 2772 VHF Ch 37.

Mechanical Engineers: Mainbrayce.

Electronic Engineers: Mainbrayce.

Sailmakers: Mainbrayce.

Boat Builders & Repairers: Mainbrayce.

SERVICES AVAILABLE

- ● Petrol
- ● Diesel
- ● Calor Gas
- ● Camping Gas
- ● Water
- ● Slipway
- ● Chandlery

HARBOUR SERVICES (PERSONAL)

Showers: Near harbour, opposite First and Last restaurant.

Post Office: Victoria Street, St Anne.

Telephone: Adjacent to First and Last restaurant.

Laundry: In shower block.

Taxi & Cars:
Town Taxis. (048 182) 2658.

THE FOUNDING OF A HARBOUR OF REFUGE AT ALDERNEY 1847.

LE PORT DE GUERNSEY 1862.

GUERNSEY

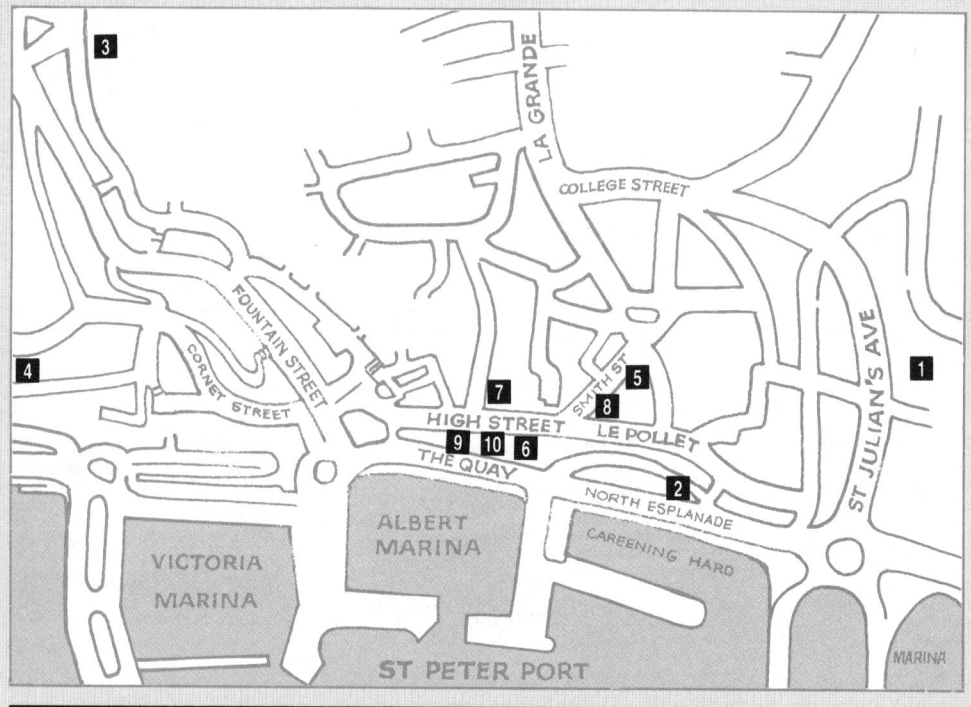

HARBOUR MASTER: (0481) 20229

Not as remote as Alderney or as obviously beckoning as Jersey, Guernsey is a very popular port of call for yachtsmen. There are two harbours on the island, St Peter Port and Beaucette. St Peter Port is Guernsey's capital and the marina now occupies part of the commercial port, but there are extensive building works taking place and during 1988 the North Beach Marina will be opened. Whilst there are many moorings available for visitors, they are in great demand and it is not unknown for the harbour to be full, a situation which should change with the opening of North Beach.

A great advantage to the harbour at St Peter Port is its proximity to the town, a hilly place with small cobbled streets full of beautifully laid out shops which give the whole town an air of a village Bond Street. There are many very good restaurants, mostly specialising in fish and all easily accessible from the harbour. The town is hard work to walk around but well worth

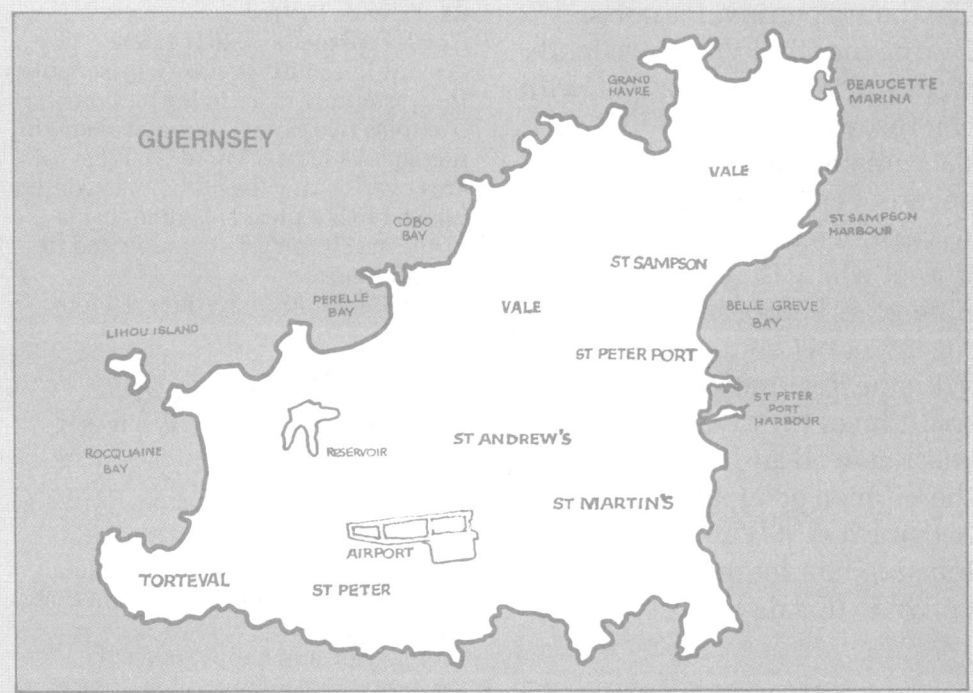

the effort. The market between Fountain Street and Market Street is a must. Stalls with fish, meat, poultry, cheese, bread, vegetables, stand side by side in this grand Victorian building, whilst at the High Street end there is a mass of florists. Past the market, walk up Mill Street with its boutiques or walk down the High Street with all its duty-free shops. There is something for everyone here and it is little wonder it is so popular.

Beaucette is on the northern tip of the island and although it has a natural feel, it was in fact a quarry and the narrow entrance was blasted through by engineers. The facilities are self-contained and extremely good so any yachtsman wanting to moor here need not worry about it being several miles from St Peter Port.

Evidence of settlements on Guernsey exist from over 5,000 years ago. As with all the Channel Islands, the real development started in the Middle Ages and inevitably was centred on the sea. Piracy and smuggling were rampant and the proximity of the French coast meant frequent skirmishes with ships from the Brittany and

GUERNSEY Continued

Cherbourg peninsular ports. During the Civil War the islands were split in their loyalties, with Guernsey supporting Parliament. The royalist governor and troops loyal to him were driven back to Castle Cornet where they held out for nine years before surrendering to the forces of Cromwell in 1651. With the Restoration, the tradition of loyalty to the crown was renewed and except during the German occupation in the Second World War it has remained under the British crown to this day.

MOORINGS

Harbour Master.
(0481) 20229
£8.00 per day.   £56.00 per week.

RESTAURANTS

1 La Frégate:
Les Côtils. (0481) 24624.
A splendidly appointed country house hotel with a magnificent restaurant, La Frégate overlooks the harbour and is a haven for anyone looking for refinement and style. Quiet, courteous service supplements a well-thought-out menu and well-prepared food. Jackets and ties are required and booking is essential.
Credit Cards: Access, Amex, Diners, Visa.

2 Friends Bistro:
North Esplanade. (0481) 21503.
Cheerful, friendly and very reasonable, this restaurant close to the harbour occupies two floors of what was an old merchant's house. There is a large bar area overlooking the harbour so waiting for a table is a pleasure when this is necessary. It can get very crowded in the summer.
Credit Cards: Access, Amex, Diners, Visa.

3 La Récolte:
Mansell Street. (0481) 22640.
It may seem a longish walk but as it takes you past the market and up Mill Street it is one worth taking. Remember too, that it is downhill on the way back. The small wood-panelled bistro has something of a farm kitchen air about it. There is a good wine list, a menu that changes according to market availability, and happy, relaxed service, which all make this a place where you are sure to enjoy a pleasant lunch or dinner. It can get very busy, so it is worth booking.
Credit Cards: Access, Amex, Diners, Visa.

4 Whistler's Bistro:
Lower Hauteville. (0481) 25809.
Their card says 'Tell only your real friends', and perhaps they are right for this is certainly a rather special place, combining informality and good food. There is a large grill behind the bar for steaks and the like and, as with most Island restaurants, fish is prominent. Add a well-represented wine list and what more can you want? It is very close to the harbour, asssuming you can find and, more to the point, survive the steep flight of steps that leads up to it. Look for the steps in an alley off South Esplanade. Evenings only.
Credit Cards: Access, Amex, Diners, Visa.

HARBOUR SERVICES (YACHTS)

General: Boatworks + Ltd, Castle Emplacement..(0481) 26071.

Mechanical Engineers:
Boatworks + Ltd, Castle Emplacement.

Electronic Engineers:
Boatworks + Ltd, Castle Emplacement.

Sailmakers:
David Bowker, Castle Emplacement.

Boat Builders & Repairers:
Boatworks + Ltd, Castle Emplacement.

SERVICES AVAILABLE

- ● Petrol
- ● Diesel
- ● Calor Gas
- ● Camping Gas
- ● Water
- ● Slipway
- ● Chandlery

HARBOUR SERVICES (PERSONAL)

Showers: Marina.

5 **Post Office:** Smith Street.

Telephone: Marina.

Laundry: Tudor House Shopping Centre.

Taxi & Cars:
Church Square. (0481) 24818.

Yacht Clubs:
Guernsey Yacht Club, Castle Emplacement. (0481) 25342.

CHEMISTS AND MEDICAL SERVICES

6 **Chemists:**
Boots. High Street.

Medical:
Princess Elizabeth, St Martins. (0481) 25241.

BANKS

7 **Barclays:** 6-8 High Street.

8 **Lloyds:** Smith Street.

9 **Midland:** High Street.

10 **National Westminster:**
35 High Street.

COASTGUARD: (0481) 20085
POLICE: (0481) 25111

SARK

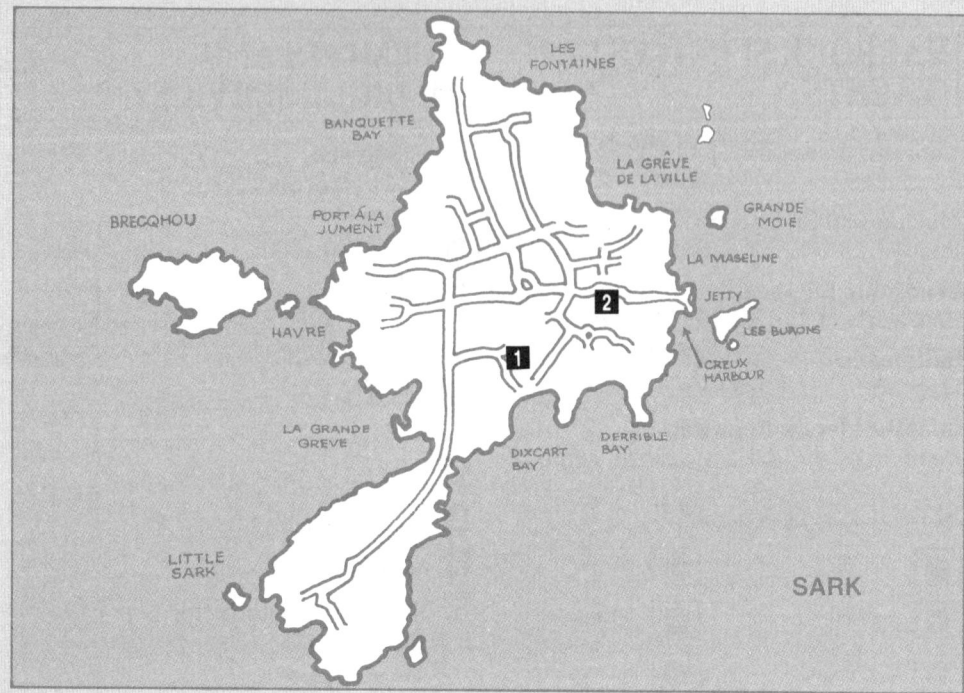

For some this is the most picturesque of all the Channel Islands not only because of its natural beauty, but also due to the romance to be found by visiting a feudal island in the twentieth century.

The yachtsman has a number of choices where he may anchor, the two harbours of Maseline and Creux on the eastern side of the island provide anchorages.

Maseline does not dry but can be uncomfortable and you may not anchor when the harbour is being used by passenger ships or when it is unattended. Creux, while much more attractive, does dry and is very small but if you can cope it is most people's favourite. Around the island there are several bays where you may anchor; notably La Grande Greve and Havre Gosselin on the west side of the island and Dixcart Bay and Derrible Bay on the east.

After a turbulent history, when it was, for a time, a pirate stronghold, Sark became virtually uninhabited. In the mid-sixteenth century Queen Elizabeth 1 granted Helier de

Carteret permission to colonise the island. This he duly did and introduced the form of government that is essentially in force today. The Seigneur, who is today Mr Michael Beaumont, meets with parliament,known locally as the Chief Pleas, in the school house and is comprised of the tenants of Sark's forty farmsteads. The meetings, that take place whenever it is felt necessary, are presided over by the Seneschal, the judge. Nearby is the island's tiny prison, not often inhabited today as all serious cases are sent for trial in Guernsey.

There are a few tractors on the island, but cars are forbidden as are planes. There are few facilities as such on the island, but those who come prepared, fueled and watered, will not be disappointed.

RESTAURANTS

1 **The Dixcart Hotel:**
If you like lobster then this old hotel, overlooking the Dixcart valley, will be a place to remember. If you are anchored in Dixcart Bay the walk up to the hotel will take about ten minutes. Yachtsmen are welcomed at the Hotel and sometimes, when convenient, patrons may find they are given the opportunity of using one of the Hotel's bathrooms.

PUBS

2 **The Bel Air:**
Top of Harbour Hill.
If the walk up from the harbour is not a good enough reason to try this pub, then maybe the fact that it is the first you come across from Creux will be.

ISLES OF SCILLY

The only recognised harbour in the Scillies is Hugh Town on St Mary's but, given the right weather conditions, there are many sheltered moorings between the islands where yachtsmen can anchor if the conditions are favourable. However, it cannot be stressed enough that these waters are extremely difficult and that only those with considerable experience should consider visiting the Scilly Isles. There is a warm welcome for visiting yachtsmen and you can be assured of every assistance from the local community providing you have some understanding of the problems they face day to day.

The scarcity of water is the most outstanding of these. St Mary's depends on a well drilled through granite for its daily supply. Car washing is forbidden during summer months and some of the toilets have two flush systems fitted, a half flush and a full flush, in order to conserve water. A yachtsman who comes in and wants to wash his hull down is likely to get short shrift. Water is charged at 2p a gallon, which is the cost price. Fuel too is expensive when compared to mainland England and France, but it should be remembered that all fuel has to be shipped to the Islands. The *Scillonian*, the ship that plies between the Scillies and Penzance, is a genuine lifeline and its importance to the inhabitants cannot be overemphasised. If a visiting yachtsman wants to take on fuel or water, check with the Harbour Master so that this can be done at a time when the *Scillonian* is not due in. The visitor who appreciates the local circumstances will find a visit to these islands well worthwhile.

Originally the Scilly Isles were one land mass but as the sea took its toll so the islands were formed, and by the early Middle Ages they existed much as we know them today. They are made up of over 100 islands, although most of these are little more than rock outcrops. Of the thirteen islands of some size, five are inhabited, the largest of

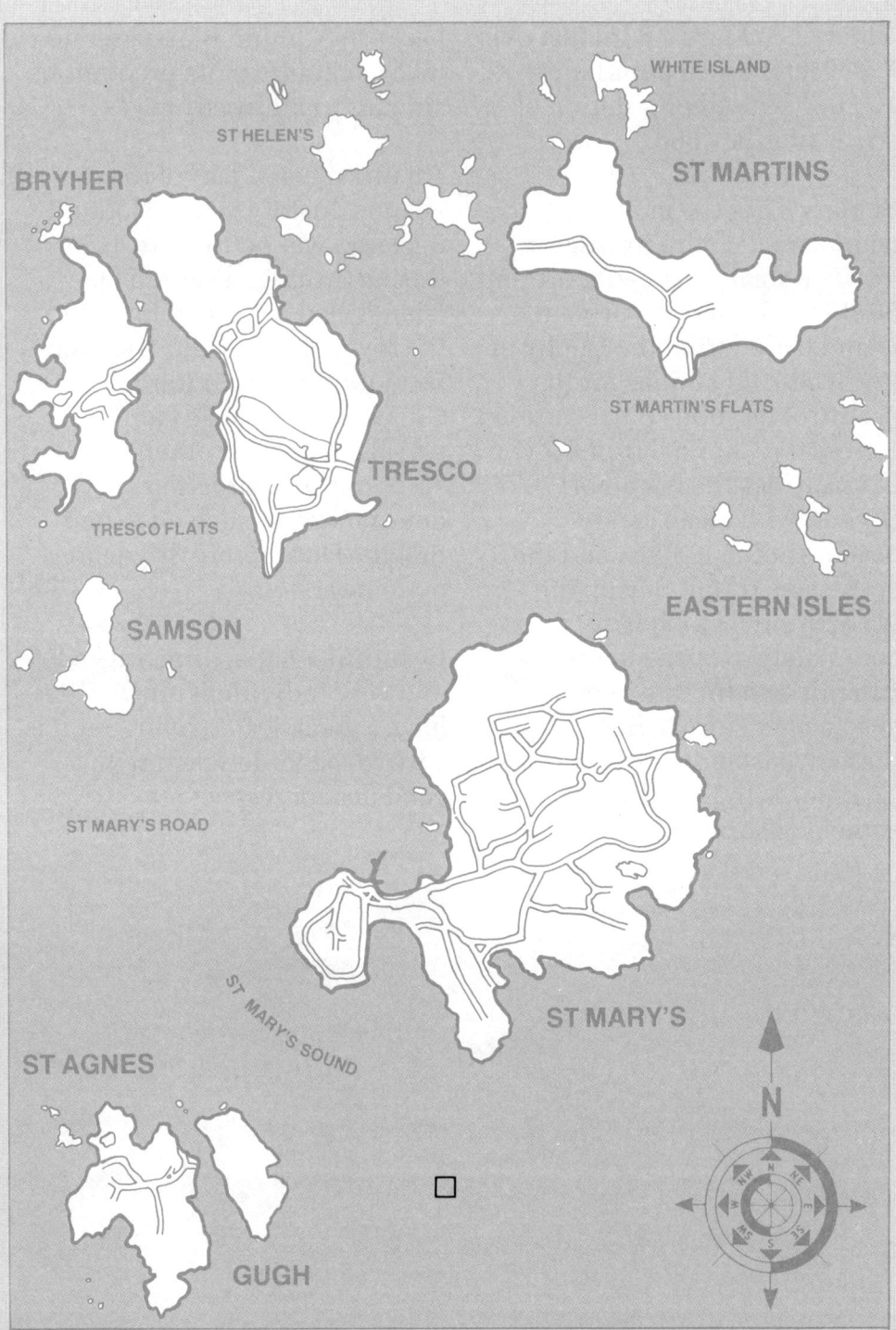

WHITE ISLAND

ST HELEN'S

BRYHER

ST MARTINS

ST MARTIN'S FLATS

TRESCO

TRESCO FLATS

SAMSON

EASTERN ISLES

ST MARY'S ROAD

ST MARY'S SOUND

ST MARY'S

ST AGNES

N

GUGH

which is St Mary's with just over 1,500 acres and a population of 1,450. The total population of the islands is 1,860.

St Mary's has the main commercial centre in Hugh Town, a small town with around 20 shops. Tresco is a private island leased from the Duchy of Cornwall and famous for the beauty of its subtropical gardens. Across the Channel from New Grimsby lies the Island of Bryher, with clean sandy beaches at Rushy Bay, and the aptly named Hell Bay on the western side which is completely exposed to the Atlantic and the site of many spectacular storms. Between these two islands is the Tresco Channel with Hangman's Island at the northern end, so called because Admiral Blake used to take advantage of its precipitous sides as a gallows drop.

An unexpected part of the islands' history is that Holland declared war on them in 1651 during Cromwell's era. The islands had remained loyal to the royalist cause and were the headquarters of Sir John Grenville, who led a band of privateers against other shipping. The situation deteriorated to such an extent that the Dutch were driven to extreme action.

Beautiful, challenging, rugged and very individual, the Scillies have a great deal to offer, but it is a trip to be undertaken with a good deal of respect.

TOWN AND HARBOUR OF ST MARY'S.

ST. MARY'S

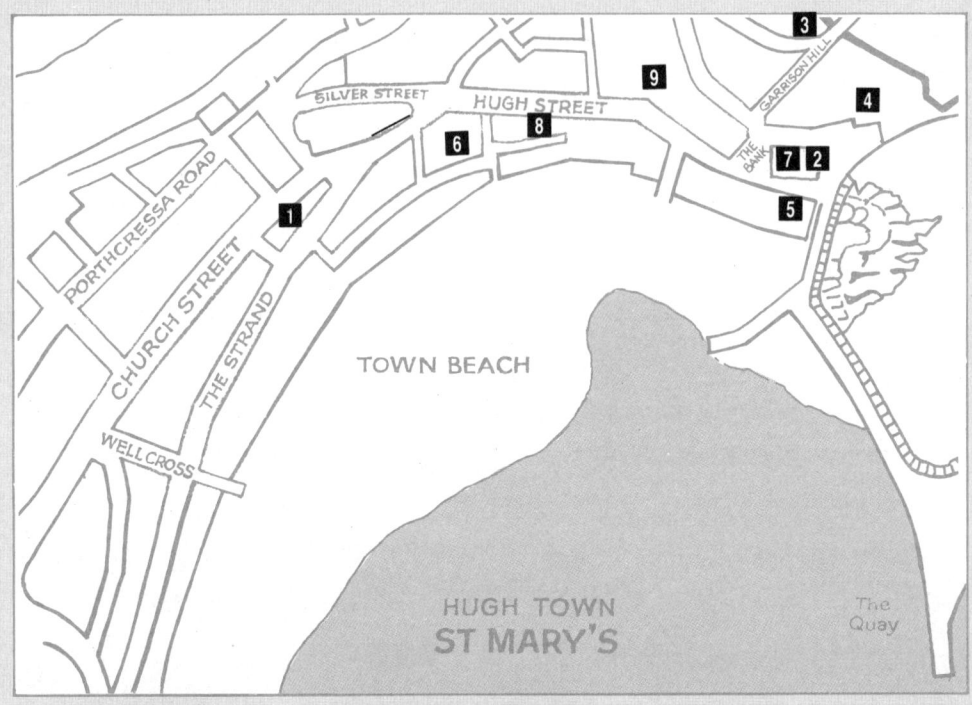

HARBOUR MASTER: (0720) 22768 or radio VHF 16/14

St. Mary's is the largest of the islands and the commercial centre. Many visitors to the Scilly Isles move quickly to the other islands and do not take the time to explore this very attractive island. It has a coastline of nine miles, which makes it possible to walk around in a day, but most people settle for a rather less energetic programme and take several of the well known walks over a longer period.

The Garrison Walk can well start and finish at The Mermaid. Walking, from there up Garrison Hill and through the Garrison Gate takes you past Star Castle. This was built on the orders of Queen Elizabeth 1 after the Spanish Armada and was completed in 1594. It became a hotel in 1933 and the first luncheon guest was the Duke of Windsor, then Prince of Wales. Continuing along the footpath takes you around the Steval Point Battery, along to the Woolpack Point Battery and on past the Morning Point Battery.

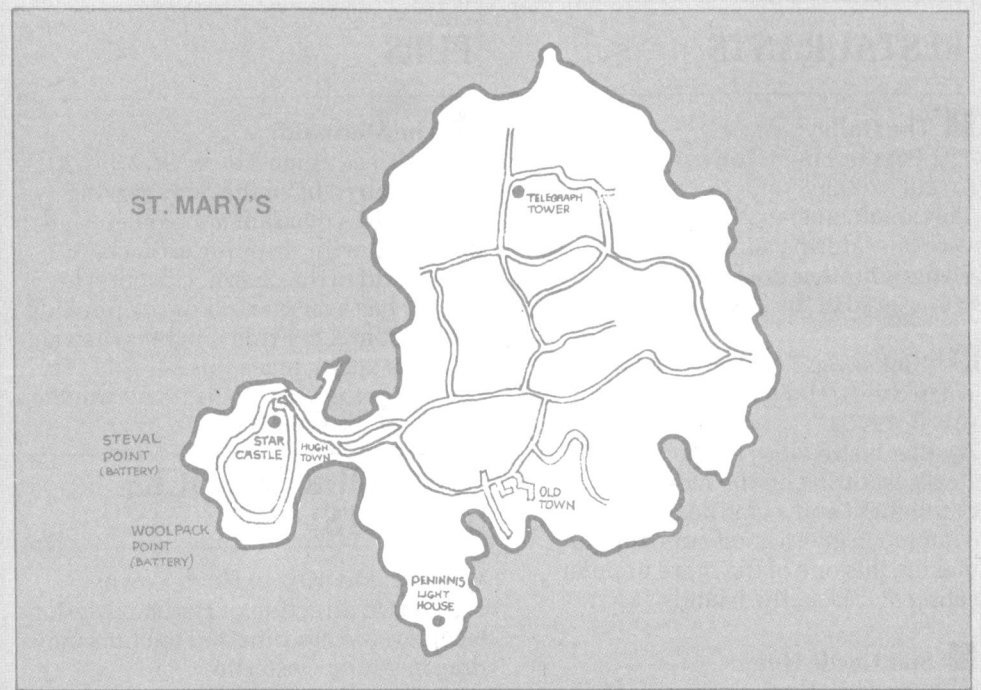

These fortifications were built at the turn of the century. The lane then passes the offices of The Duchy of Cornwall and the island residence of the Prince of Wales, before bringing you back to Garrison Gate.

Another pleasant walk is from Hugh Town and up past St. Mary's Church to Peninnis Head. While the major landmark is the light-house, the rock formations that are found at The Head are quite fascinating and some have been given names like Monk's Cowl, Big Jolly Rock and The Witches Head.

Hugh Town itself becomes very busy during the summer season but provides all the basic facilities a yachtsman may require.

MOORINGS

Hugh Town Harbour.
(0720) 22768
£4.00 per day.   £28.00 per week.

RESTAURANTS

1 The Galley:
The Parade, Hugh Town, St. Mary's.
(0720) 22602.
This small, upstairs fish restaurant gets
very busy during summer months. The
owner's brother is a fisherman so you
are assured of the best.

2 Pilot's Gig:
Hugh Street, Hugh Town, St. Mary's.
(0720) 22654.
A cellar bistro close to the quay with
steaks featuring on the menu.
Candlelight and a granite paved floor
combine to give a good atmosphere,
making this one of the more popular
eating places on the islands.

3 Star Castle Hotel:
Garrison Hill, Hugh Town, St. Mary's.
(0720) 22317.
The original Castle was built during the
reign of Queen Elizabeth I and stands at
the top of the hill overlooking the
islands. It is a must if only for the view
but fortunately you will also receive a
warm welcome from Mr and Mrs
Reynolds, good if simple food in a
delightful dining room and the
opportunity of a pre- or post-meal drink
in the Dungeon Bar.

4 Tregarthens Hotel:
Garrison Hill, Hugh Town, St. Mary's.
(0720) 22540.
The spacious dining room here has
excellent views over the harbour and
towards St Martin's. The service is very
friendly in a slightly formal way and
the food is straightforward, no-
nonsense fare. There is also the
possibility of having a snack lunch in
the bar.

PUBS

5 The Mermaid:
Hugh Street, Hugh Town, St. Mary's.
A fine pub right by the quay serving
real ales in a pleasant atmosphere and
decorated with shipping artifacts
which add to the charm. Upstairs the
Gig bar has a large window overlooking
the harbour. On Friday nights when gig
racing is taking place this bar gets very
full and is the place to be if you want to
be part of the scene.

HARBOUR SERVICES (YACHTS)

General: Mooring in Hugh Town
Harbour at direction of Harbour Master.
No quayside mooring and anchors may
drag in strong westerlies.

Mechanical Engineers:
Scilly Island Steamship Co Chandlery,
The Strand.

Electronic Engineers:
Southard Engineering, The Quay.
(0720) 22539.

Boat Builders & Repairers:
Tom Chudleigh. (0720) 22505.

SERVICES AVAILABLE

●	Petrol	●	Water
●	Diesel	●	Slipway
●	Calor Gas	●	Chandlery
●	Camping Gas		

HARBOUR SERVICES (PERSONAL)

Showers: Behind Harbour Master's office.

6 **Post Office:** Hugh Street.

Telephone: By Harbour Office.

Laundry: W. Hall. (0720) 22894.

Taxi & Cars: W. Hall. (0720) 22894.

Yacht Clubs:
Isles of Scilly Yacht Club, The Quay. (0720) 22352.

CHEMISTS AND MEDICAL SERVICES

7 **Chemists:**
R. Douglas. The Bank and Hugh Street.

Medical: Hospital, (0720) 22392

BANKS

8 **Barclays:** Hugh Street.

9 **Lloyds:** Hugh Street.

COASTGUARD: (0326) 317575
POLICE: (0720) 22444

HUGH TOWN – ST MARY'S.

TRESCO

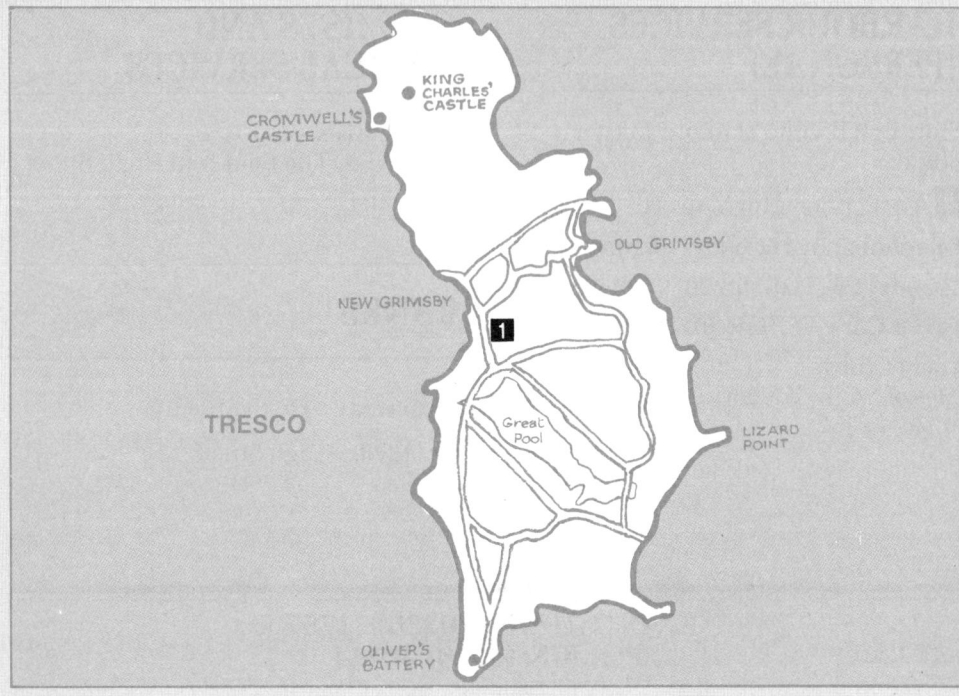

This island is renowned for the sub-tropical gardens that surround the Abbey house. These gardens were started by Augustus Smith in the middle of the nineteenth century and have been lovingly maintained ever since. They cover an area of some twelve acres on the southern part of the island. Tresco is a private island, leased from the Duchy of Cornwall to the Dorrien-Smith family, and there is a landing charge. In the unlikely event that a visiting yachtsman should have a dog on board it must be kept on a lead while ashore.

On the much wilder northern part of the island there are the ruins of Cromwell's castle built in 1651 as King Charles' castle, situated on a hill above it, was unable to provide the protection thought necessary at the time. Yachtsman usually anchor in an area between the quay and Cromwell's Castle and care must be taken to ensure that the access to the quay is left clear for local craft.

PUBS

1 **The New Inn:**
Between New Grimsby and Dolphin Town, Tresco.
As well as bar snacks, there is a restaurant specialising in locally caught seafood.

ST. MARTINS

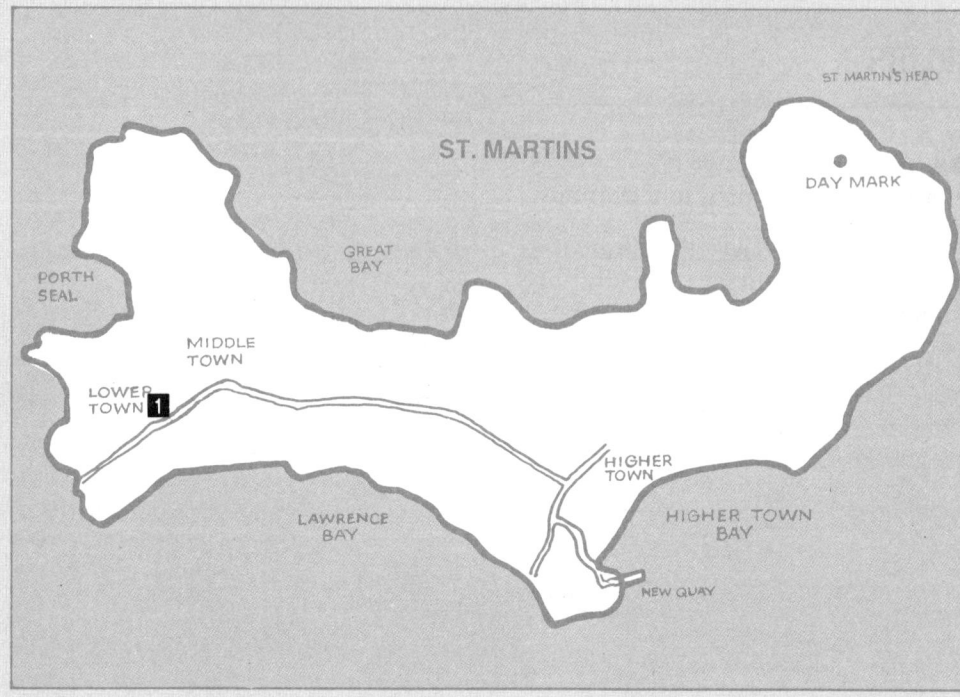

This island is really a two mile stretch of granite, the northern side battered by the weather and the southern part sloping gently to the sea. This is where the island's population of 81 derive their livelihood as the light, sandy soil is excellent for the cultivation of flowers. Conversely the qualities that are so ideal for growing plants are also responsible for much of the damage that they sometimes suffer as the wind can drive the soil among the crop destroying all in its path.

Yachtsmen will probably anchor in the shelter of Cruther's Hill, the energetic can walk up to Higher Town and then to St Martin's Head where on a clear day the Seven Stones reef can be seen some seven miles to the north-east, or they may go to Great Bay where on a sunny day the expanse of clear, white sand and blue, blue sea will make anyone forget the Mediterranean, if only for as long as it takes to feel the chill of the water.

The less hardy will probably make their way to the Seven Stones Inn in Lower Town.

PUBS

1 Seven Stones Inn:
St. Martin's.
A large barn-like pub close to Lower
Town which is very much part of the
social life of the island.

BRYHER

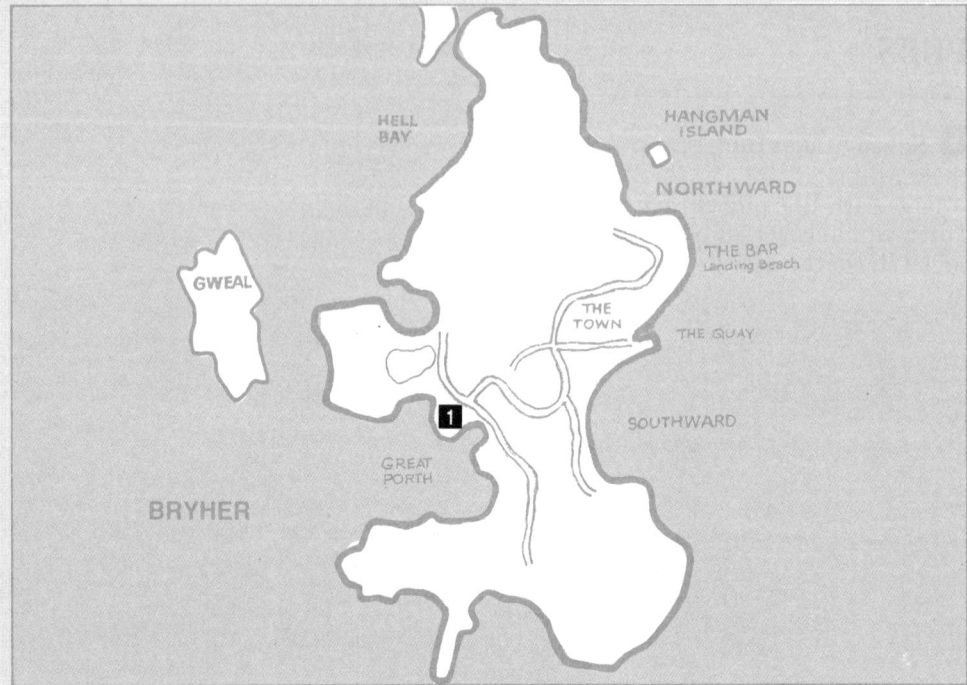

A ny yachtsman anchored in Tresco Channel should take the opportunity of visiting this wild island and take the walk up to Watch Hill. It was from this point that the inhabitants used to look out for ships in distress or for those wanting a pilot to guide them through the western approaches and it provides a wonderful panoramic view over the Scillies.

The cultivation of flowers in the lower, sheltered parts, is, with tourism the prime activity of the islands 63 inhabitants.

PUBS

1 **Hell Bay Hotel:**
Bryher.
A few minutes walk from the quay towards Gweal Hill, this hotel is open all day, and serves Bar snacks. The restaurant is open in the evening.

ST. AGNES AND GUGH

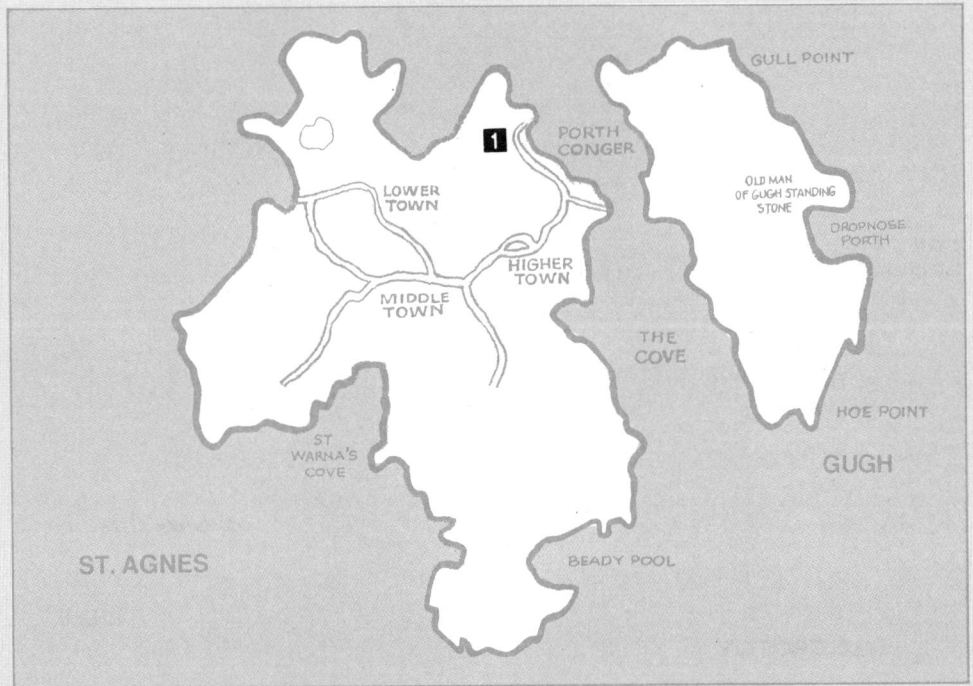

The two islands provide a good sheltered anchorage except when the wind is from the west. Care should be taken when approaching Porth Conger as there are two rocks, The Cow and The Calf, which guard the entrance. There is also a sand spit that runs between the islands separating Porth Conger and The Cove and is not visible at high water.

Like most of the other islands, horticulture is the mainstay of the economy, a far cry from the days when the inhabitants were notorious wreckers.

PUBS

1 Turks Head Inn:
St. Agnes.
A small pub where bar food is available. Reached through Higher Town to the north by Porth Conger.

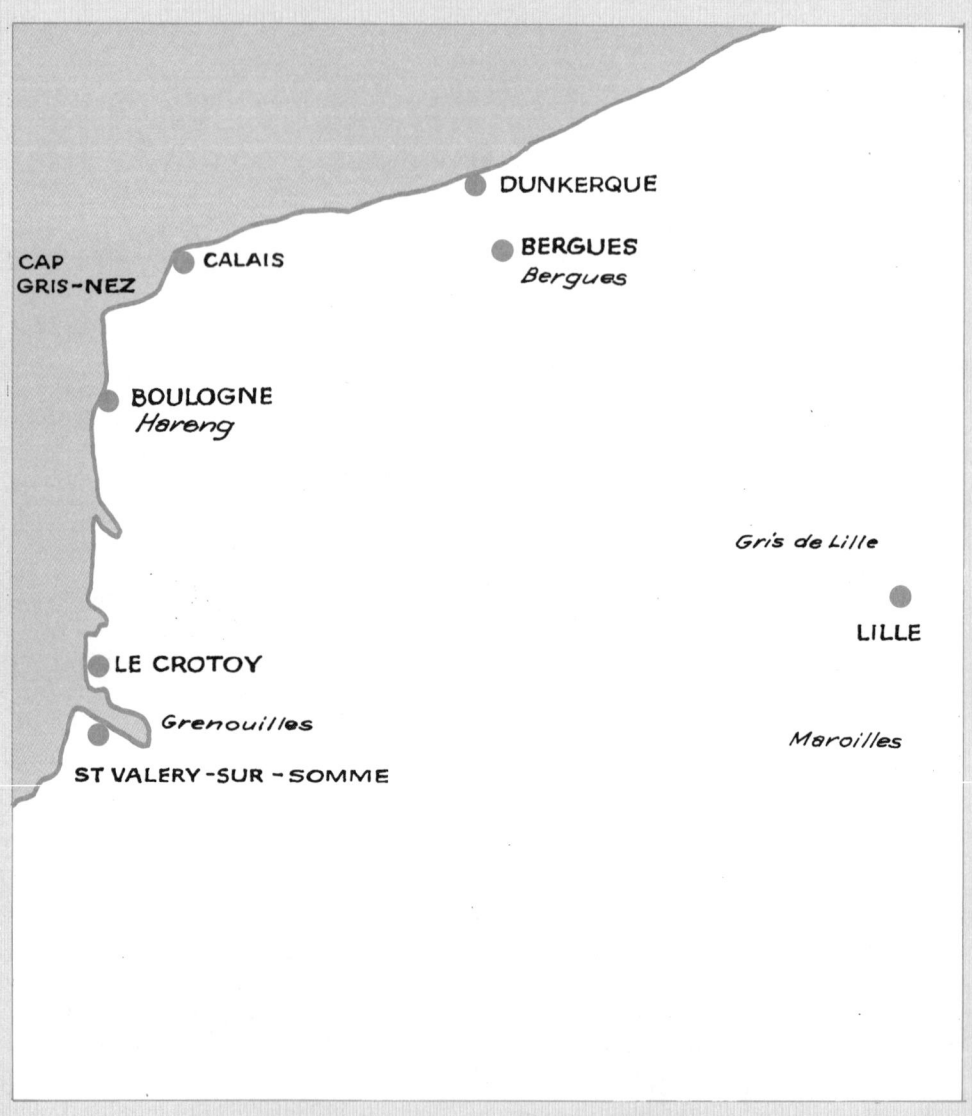

CAP
GRIS-NEZ

CALAIS

DUNKERQUE

BERGUES
Bergues

BOULOGNE
Hareng

Gris de Lille

LILLE

LE CROTOY

Grenouilles

Maroilles

ST VALERY -SUR - SOMME

NORD, PAS-DE-CALAIS and SOMME

The flat, dull, northern plains of France have over the centuries played ghoulish host to the armies of the world. As a consequence, regional tradition, folklore and style have all been affected. The armies that billeted themselves in the towns, villages and fields of this area had to be fed and watered, and it is not surprising that this is reflected in the kitchen. Soldiers are not renowned for drinking wine and it is no coincidence that this area produces the finest beer of France. Cattle, which require plenty of space, are difficult to rear on a battlefield, so pork, lamb and game play important roles in the cooking of this region and where there is the sea, fish will generally feature strongly.

Specialities of the region include:

Andouille or *Andouillette* A strong tasting layered sausage made from pig's intestines. *Andouille* is larger than *Andouillette* and is often served cold. Not a dish for the squeamish or faint-hearted.
Boudin blanc, noir. This is a fine textured sausage. *Boudin noir* is like black pudding. *Boudin blanc* is similar to the Weisswurst of Munich and should be prepared and eaten on the same day. The best *Boudin blanc* are highly prized and sought-after and can be quite expensive.
Carbonnade A beef casserole cooked in beer with vegetables, notably potatoes and onions. Quite the thing after a long sail.
Chaudrée The north's answer to Bouillabaisse. Sea-water fish stewed in a stock with potatoes. Sometimes mussels and conger eel are included.
Cheese: Bergues a sharp, tangy, round cheese cured in beer comes from the village of Bergues near Dunkerque. *Gris de Lille*, a strong cheese, cured in brine or beer, that gets noticed by the next table. *Maroille*, made in the same way as *Gris de Lille*, but softer and less salty. This is the best known cheese from this area.
Drinks: Beer. Genièvre, a gin type drink taken neat. Just the answer on a cold evening.
Grenouilles The Somme estuary is a breeding ground for frogs and as well as finding them served plain, they will sometimes turn up in a soup or casserole.
Hareng herring Very popular along this part of the coast. Often served smoked or pickled and much improved with a glass of cold *Genièvre*.
Hochepot If you are lucky and find the genuine article it will consist of oxtail, a pig's head and a variety of vegetables as well as other odd bits of meat. The result is a warming and filling stew.
Tripée Pig's offal cooked in white wine and vegetables.
Waterzoï A stew, generally of fish or chicken of Belgian origin.

FOOD AND WINE OF NORTHER

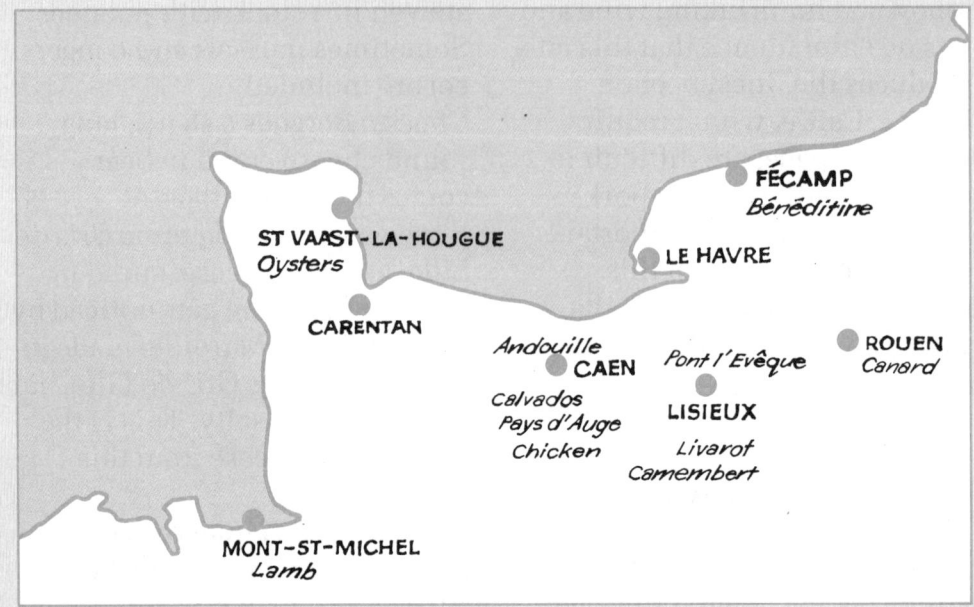

FÉCAMP
Bénédictine

ST VAAST-LA-HOUGUE
Oysters

LE HAVRE

CARENTAN

Andouille
CAEN

Pont l'Evêque

ROUEN
Canard

Calvados
Pays d'Auge
Chicken

LISIEUX

Livarot
Camembert

MONT-ST-MICHEL
Lamb

NORMANDY

The origins of Normandy cuisine are to be found in Scandinavia. When this region was invaded by the Vikings they introduced dairy farming to the area. Over the years the distinctive brown and white Normandy cow evolved and from this breed comes the milk that makes Normandy dairy produce famous the world over. The moderate climate together with the soil is ideal for growing apples, which in turn has affected the cuisine as the farmers tended to rear animals that could exist in orchards without damaging the trees. Pigs and poultry particularly ducks, were favoured especially as pigs could feed off the windfalls in the autumn.

Normandy's considerable coastline provides the last strand in the Norman cuisine – not only fish and shell-fish, but also the lambs that graze on the salt marshes around Mont-St-Michel.

Normandy cuisine is rich and varied. Many dishes are cooked in cream, calvados or cider and in many instances a combination of all three. If, during a meal, you need a pause try un trou Normand. This is a small glass of calvados served between courses to clear the palate and revitalise the system.

Regional Specialities include:

Andouillette de Vire This sausage from the town of Vire is regarded by some as the best that money can buy, a view hotly disputed by the inhabitants of nearby Caen.

Barbue Cauchoise Brill cooked in cider and cream and particularly pleasant when accompanied with a glass of cider.

Canard/Caneton Rouen has long been famous for the quality and taste of it's duck. There is not one particular style of cooking, it may be served with apple, cherries or orange, but the question is the breed of the duck, for it is this that gives the distinctive gamey taste that is synonymous with ducks from the Rouen region.

Cheese Bondon A soft barrel-shaped cheese from Bray should be available at the harbours between Dieppe and Le Havre in particular as it is very local.

Camembert Contrary to popular belief this cheese is not at it's best when running off the table. The whole cheese should be of the same firmness and it can be eaten young. If you are offered *Camembert fermier* don't let the opportunity pass by, as this is made from unpasteurised milk which gives it a more rounded taste. *Livarot*, a round cheese with an orange rind and a strong smell that belies its curiously delicate flavour. *Pont l'Evêque*, another quite mild cheese with an orange rind, but this is rectangular in shape.

Drinks Bénédictine The famous brandy based liqueur made by the monks in Fécamp. *Calvados*, distilled apple brandy, aged in oak casks. Look for *AC Calvados du Pays d'Auge*. VSOP will mean that it has aged for at least four years in the barrel. Extra or Napoleon means at least five years in the barrel. *Cidre* Cider, very easy to find and well worth trying. Most of it will be still, but you can ask for *cidre bouché*, which comes in a champagne style bottle and is very lively.

Marmite A sea fish stew often made with cider as an alternative to white wine.

Poulet Vallée d'Auge Chicken cooked in cider, calvados and cream; ideally the chicken are free-range.

Sole The restaurants of Normandy will serve sole in just about every way imaginable.

Tripes à la mode de Caen Ox tripe prepared with vegetables and calvados. The very best is cooked with the addition of a cow's heel.

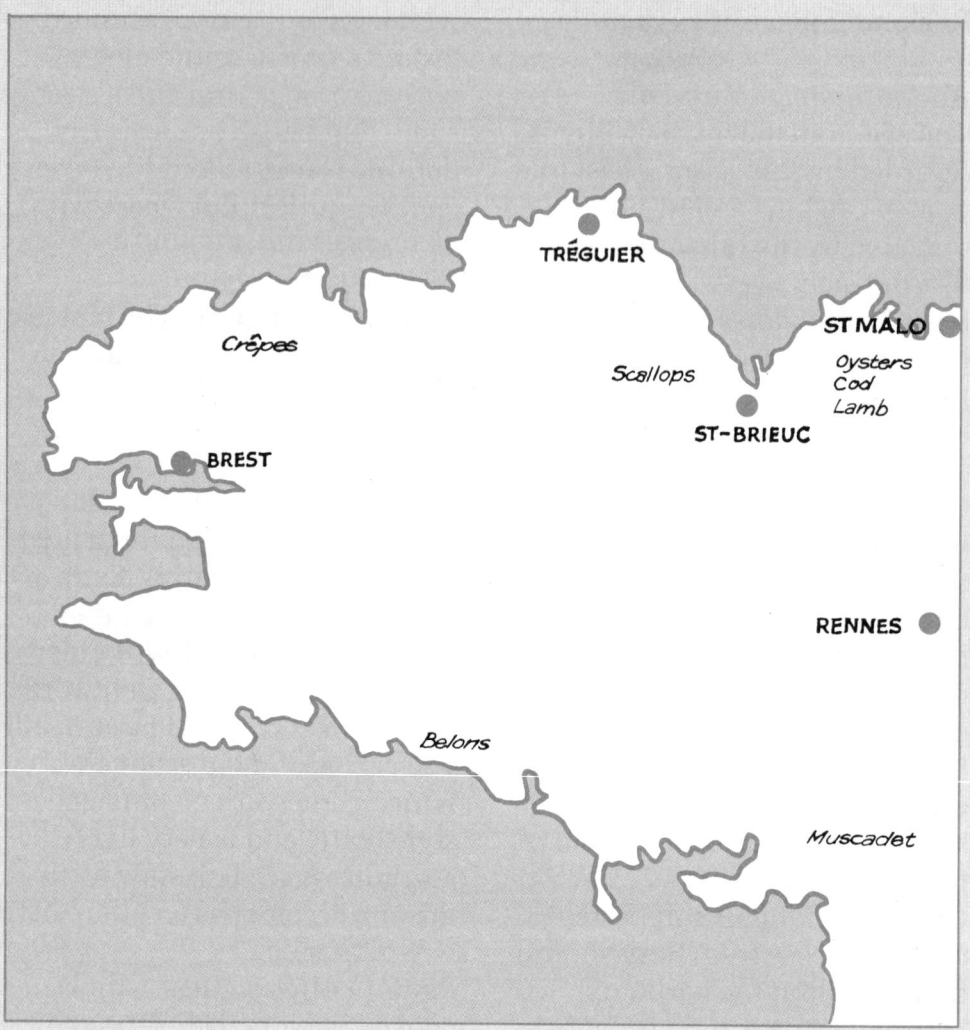

TRÉGUIER

ST MALO

Crêpes

Scallops

Oysters
Cod
Lamb

ST-BRIEUC

BREST

RENNES

Belons

Muscadet

BRITTANY.

The cuisine of this area has been determined by the wild, rugged landscape to the north-west, the fertile inland plains and the coastline that extends for some two thousand miles and that is washed by the Gulf Stream.

The Bretons have always been a fiercely independent people and have over the years maintained their own language. This independence or stubbornness has meant that until recently this was one of the poorest regions of France. The farmers today have changed all that and are responsible for providing France with her greatest supplies of pigs, eggs, poultry and vegetables. However it is from the poor past rather than the prosperous present that the style of Breton cookery is to be found. The classic example is the *Galette*. This bread textured biscuit is made from wheat and was used to give substance to a meal in the same way as rice is used in the Far East. Today there is no need for that but the *Galette* is now an established part of Breton cuisine.

Specialities of the region include:

Cabillaud Cod, which for generations the fishermen of this region have sailed to the banks off Newfoundland to catch.

Cheese Port-Salut, a mild semi-soft cheese with an orange rind, the best known of the *St-Paulin* cheeses.

Cotriade A fish soup originally made for the fishermen with the left-overs from their catch, a good one will have a wide selection of fish in it with potatoes, herbs and vinegar. The latter gives the soup a strong flavour that can overpower accompanying wine.

Crêpes Wafer thin pancakes served with a variety of fillings, generally sweet.

Drinks Cidre. Muscadet, a dry, white wine made from the muscadet grape. This was introduced to this region from Burgundy. The wine is very light, low in alcohol and best drunk when young. Over sixty million bottles are produced annually and amongst these there is a great deal of mediocre wine. The best comes from the departement de Sèvre-et-Maine and is "sur lie". This means that it has been bottled direct from the cask. Particularly good are the wines from around the villages of Clisson and Vallet.

Galette A type of bread or biscuit that is used in conjunction with savoury fillings.

Gigot d'Agneau Leg of lamb which should have the distinctive taste of sheep that grazed on the salt-fields. Usually served with beans and tomatoes.

Huîtres Oysters are farmed on many parts of the French Coast, but some of the finest are generally recognised to come from this region. *Belons* from the mouth of the River Belon in southern Brittany are particularly sought after. Cancale is well known as a major producer of *Portugaises* or *Huîtres Creuses*.

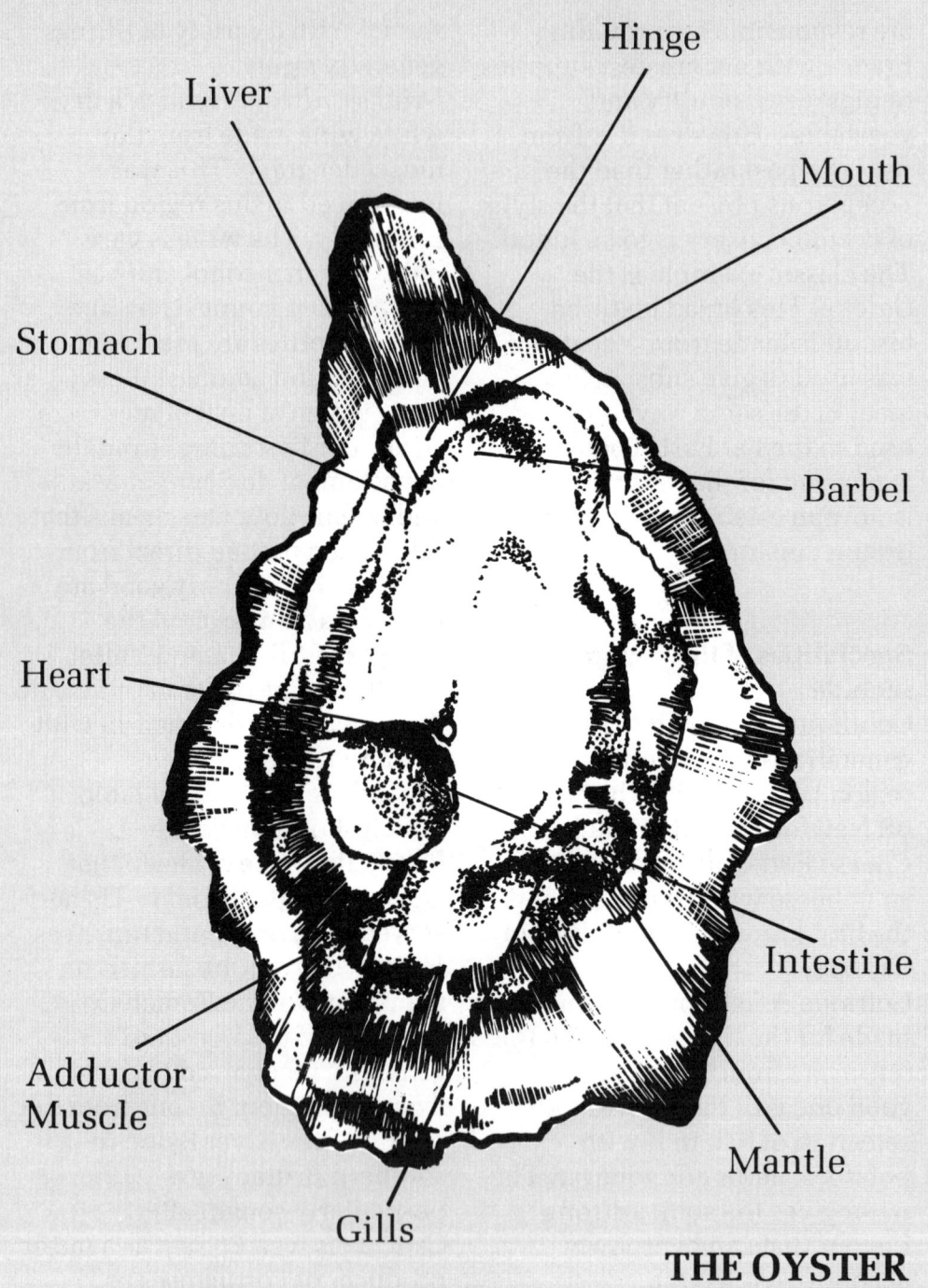

Hinge

Mouth

Liver

Stomach

Barbel

Heart

Intestine

Adductor
Muscle

Mantle

Gills

THE OYSTER

The oyster is a fascinating mollusc. It has been regarded as a gourmet's delight since the time of the Roman Empire and there is evidence that they were also a prized delicacy in the time of the Pharaohs.

It consists largely of water but is also very strong in vitamins, which may be the reason that it has long been thought of as an aphrodisiac.

The farming of oysters is a long-drawn-out business. The oyster is a hermaphrodite. When the female cells mature it will lay up to 3,000,000 eggs, of which only a small proportion do not fall prey to other fish. The spat will develop over a period of weeks before forming a shell and sinking to the sea floor where they attach themselves to rocks. Farmers reproduce these conditions by providing materials to which the oyster can attach itself. The oyster takes some four years to mature. During this time it feeds on small organisms that exist in the sea through drinking up to 25 litres of water a day. The mature oysters are removed from the bed and put into basins where they are fully fattened before finally being placed in final cleansing basins to remove any impurities.

Once farmed the oysters are graded according to size:

No.0 = 90g
No.1 = 75g
No.2 = 60g
No.3 = 50g
No.4 = 40g

These gradings are what you will find on certain menus. *Claires* and *fines de claires* refer to oysters that have been through a specific fattening process.

Lobster There is a continuing discussion whether *hommard à l'armoricaine* or *hommard à l'américaine* is the correct description for this well-known style of preparation. Under either heading it will be fiendishly expensive and it must be questionable if a fresh lobster needs to be cooked with tomatoes, oil, garlic and eau de vie.

Scallops A mollusc, much prized like the oyster for its special delicate flavour. Unlike the oyster they are not served raw and are often served baked with butter and breadcrumbs – *Coquille St Jacques* A hermaphrodite like the oyster, the orange centre is the female part, the white surround the male.

GLOSSARY OF MENU TERMS

A

Abatis (Abattis) poultry giblets

Abats offal

Ablette freshwater fish

Abricots apricots

Acarne sea-bream

Acidulé (e) acid

Affiné (e) refined

Africaine (à l') African style: with aubergines, tomatoes, cèpes

Agneau lamb

Agneau de pré-salé lamb fed on salt marshes

Agnelet young lamb

Agnès Sorel thin strips of mushroom, chicken and tongue

Aiglefin haddock

Aigre-doux sweet-sour

Aiguillettes thin slices

Ail garlic

Aile wing

Aileron winglet

Aïoli mayonnaise, garlic, olive oil

Airelles cranberries

Albert white cream sauce, mustard, vinegar

Albuféra béchamel sauce, sweet peppers

Alénois watercress-flavoured

Algues seaweed

Aligot purée of potatoes, Tomme cheese, cream, garlic, butter

Allemande velouté sauce with egg yolks

Allemande (à l') German style: with sauerkraut and sausages

Allumettes puff pastry strips

Alose shad

Alouette lark

Alouette de mer sandpiper

Aloyau sirloin of beef

Alsacienne (à l') Alsace style: with sauerkraut, sausage and sometimes foie gras

Amandes almonds

Amandine almond-flavoured

Amer bitter

Américaine (à l')

Armoricaine (à la) sauce with dry white wine, cognac, tomatoes, shallots

Amourettes ox or calf marrow

Amusettes appetisers

Ananas pineapple

Anchoïade anchovy crusts

Anchois anchovy

Ancienne (à l') in the 'old style'

Andalouse (à l') Andalusian style: tomatoes, sweet red peppers, rice

Andouille cold smoked sausage

Andouillette chitterling (tripe) sausage

Aneth dill

Ange angel

Angevine (à l') Anjou style: with dry white wine, cream, mushrooms, onions

Anglaise (à l') plain boiled

Anguilles eels

Anis aniseed

Arachides peanuts

Araignée de mer spider crab

Ardennaise (à l') Ardenne style: with juniper berries

Argenteuil asparagus flavoured (usually soup)

Arlésienne stuffed tomatoes á la provençale, eggplant, rice

Armoricaine see Américaine

Aromates aromatic – either spicy or fragrant

Artichaut artichoke

Asperges asparagus

Assiette- (de) plate (of)

Aubergine aubergine, eggplant

Aulx (plural of ail) garlic

Aumonière pancake

Aurore (à l') pink sauce, tomato flavoured

Auvergnate (à l') Auvergne style: with cabbage, sausage and bacon

Avelines hazelnuts

Avocat avocado pear

B

Baba au rhum sponge with rum syrup

Baguette long bread loaf

Baies berries

Baigné bathed or lying in

Ballotine boned and stuffed poultry or meat in a roll

Banane banana

Bar sea-bass

Barbarie Barbary duck

Barbeau barbel

Barbue brill

Barigoule (à la) brown-sauce with artichokes and mushrooms

Baron de lapereau baron of young rabbit

Barquette boat-shaped pastry

Basilic basil

Basquaise (à la) Basque style: Bayonne ham, rice and peppers

Bâtarde butter sauce, egg yolks

Baudroie monkfish, anglerfish

Bavaroise bavarois mould, usually of custard, flavoured with fruit or chocolate. Can describe other dishes – particularly shellfish

Bavette skirt of beef

Béarnaise thick sauce with egg yolks, shallots, butter, white wine and tarragon vinegar

Béatilles (Malin de) sweetbreads, livers, kidneys, cocks' combs

Beaugency *Béarnaise* sauce, artichokes, tomatoes, marrow

Bécasse woodcock

Bécassine snipe

Béchamel creamy white sauce

Beignets fritters

Belons flat-shelled oysters

Bercy sauce with white wine and shallots

Berrichone *Bordelaise* sauce

Betterave beetroot

Beuchelle à la Tourangelle kidneys, sweetbreads, morels, truffles, cream

Beurre butter

Beurre blanc sauce with butter, shallots, wine vinegar and sometimes dry white wine.

Beurre noir sauce with browned butter, vinegar, parsley

Bifteck steak

Bigarade (à la) orange sauce

Bigarreau type of cherry

Bigorneaux winkles

Billy By mussel soup

Biscuit à la cuiller sponge finger

Bisque shellfish soup

Blanc (de volaille) white breast (of chicken): can describe white fish fillet or white vegetables

Blanchailles whitebait

Blanquette white stew

Blettes Swiss chard

Blinis small, thick pancakes

Boeuf à la mode beef braised in red wine

Boeuf Stroganoff beef, sour cream, onions, mushrooms

Bombe ice cream

Bonne femme (à la) white wine sauce, shallots, mushrooms

Bonne femme (à la) potato, leek, carrot soup

Bordelais (e) (à la) Bordeaux style: brown sauce with shallots, red wine and beef bone marrow

Bouchée mouthfull size (either a tart or *vol-au-vent*)

Boudin sausage-shaped pudding

Boudin blanc white coloured – pork and sometimes chicken

Boudin noir black pudding

Bouillabaisse Mediterranean fish stew and soup – see Côte d'Azur

Bouillon broth, light consommé

Boulangère sauce of onions, potatoes

Boulette small ball of fish or meat

Bouquet prawn

Bourdaloue hot poached fruit

Bourdelot whole apple pastry

Bourgeoise (à la) sauce of carrots, onions, diced bacon

GLOSSARY OF MENU TERMS

Bourguignonne (à la) Burgundy style: red wine, onions, bacon, mushrooms

Bourride creamy fish soup with *aïoli*

Braisé braised

Brandade de morue salt cod

Bréjaude cabbage and bacon soup

Brème bream

Brési thin slices dried beef

Bretonne sauce with celery, leeks, beans, mushrooms

Brioche sweet yeast bread roll

Broche (à la) spit roasted

Brochet pike

Brochette (de) meat or fish on a skewer

Brouet broth

Brouillade stewed in oil

Brouillés scrambled

Broutard young goat

Brugnon nectarine

Brûlé toasted

Brunoise diced vegetables

Bruxelloise sauce with asparagus, butter, eggs

Bugnes sweet pastry fritters

C

Cabillaud cod

Caen (à la mode de) cooked in Calvados and white wine

Café coffee

Cagouilles snails

Caille (Caillette) quail

Calmars inkfish, squid

Campagne country style

Canapé a base, usually bread

Canard duck

Canard à la presse (Rouennaie) duck breast cooked in blood of carcass, red wine and brandy

Canard sauvage wild duck

Caneton (canette) duckling

Cannelle cinnamon

Capilotade small bits or pieces

Capoum scorpion fish

Caprice *whim* (desserts)

Capucine nasturtium

Carbonnade braised beef in beer, onions and bacon

Cardinal *béchamel* sauce, lobster, cream, red peppers

Cardons large celery-like vegetable

Caroline chicken consommé

Carpe carp

Carré d'agneau lamb chops from best end of neck

Carré de porc pork cutlets from best end of neck

Carré de veau veal chops from best end of neck

Carrelet flounder, plaice

Carvi caraway seeds

Casse-croûte snack

Cassis blackcurrants

Cassolette small pan

Cassoulet casserole of beans, pork or goose or duck

Céleri celery

Céleri-rave celeriac

Cèpes fine, delicate mushrooms

Cerfeuil chervil

Cerises (noires) cherries (black)

Cerneaux walnuts

Cervelas pork garlic sausages

Cervelle brains

Champignons (des bois) mushrooms (from the woods)

Chanterelles apricot-coloured mushrooms

Chantilly whipped cream, sugar

Chapon capon

Chapon de mer *rascasse* or scorpion fish

Charcuterie cold cut meats

Charcutière sauce with onions, white wine, gherkins

Charlotte sweet of sponge fingers, cream, etc.

Charolais (Charollais) beef

Chartreuse a mould form

Chasse hunting (season)

Chasseur sauce with white wine, mushrooms, shallots

Châtaignes chestnuts

Châteaubriand thick fillet steak

Châtelaine garnish with artichoke hearts, tomatoes, potatoes

Chaud (e) hot

Chaudrée fish stew

Chausson pastry turnover with various fillings

Chemise (en) pastry covering

Chevreuil roe-deer

Chicon chicory

Chicorée curly endive

Chiffonnade thinly-cut

Chinoise (à la) Chinese style: with bean sprouts and soy sauce

Chiperones see *calmars*

Choisy braised lettuce, sautéed potatoes

Choron *Béarnaise* sauce with tomato

Chou (vert) cabbage

Choucroute sauerkraut pepper-corns, boiled ham, potatoes, Strasbourg sausages

Chou-fleur cauliflower

Chou-pommé white-heart cabbage

Chou rouge red cabbage

Choux (au fromage) puffs (cheese)

Choux de Bruxelles Brussels sprouts

Ciboules spring onions

Ciboulettes chives

Cidre cider

Citron lemon

Citron vert lime

Civet stew

Civet de lièvre jugged hare

Clafoutis tart (usually cherries)

Claires oysters

Clamart with petits pois

Clouté (de) studded with

Cochon pig

Cochonnailles pork products

Cocotte (en) cooking pot

Coeur (de) heart (of)

Coffret (en) in a *small box*

Coing quince

Colbert (à la) fish, dipped in milk, egg and breadcrumbs

Colin hake

Colvert wild duck

Compote stewed or preserved fruit

Concassée coarsely chopped

Concombres cucumbers

Condé creamed rice and fruit

Confit (e) preserved or candied

Confiture jam

Confiture d'oranges marmalade

Congre conger eel

Consommé clear soup

Contrefilet sirloin, usually tied for roasting

Copeaux literally *shavings*

Coq (au vin) chicken in red wine sauce (or name of wine)

Coque (à la) soft-boiled – or served in shell

Coquelet young cockerel

Coques cockles

Coquillages shellfish

Coquilles St.-Jacques scallops

Corail (de) coral (of)

Coriandre coriander

Cornichons gherkins

Côte d'agneau lamb chop

Côte de boeuf side of beef

Côte de veau veal chop

Côtelette chop

Cou (d'oie) neck (of goose)

Coulibiac hot salmon *tourte*

Coulis (de) thick sauce (of)

Coupe ice cream dessert

Courge pumpkin

Courgettes baby marrows

Couronne circle or ring

Court-bouillon aromatic poaching liquid

Crabe crab

Crapaudine (à la) grilled game bird with backbone removed

Crécy with carrots and rice

Crème cream

Crème (à la) served with cream or cooked in cream sauce

Crème à l'anglaise light custard sauce

Crème brûlée same, less sugar and cream and with praline

Crème pâtissière custard filling

Crème plombières custard filling: egg whites, fresh fruit flavouring

Crêpe thin pancake

Crêpes Suzette sweet pancakes with orange liqueur sauce

Crépinette (de) wrapping (of)

Cresson watercress

Cressonière purée of potatoes, watercress

Crêtes cockscombs

GLOSSARY OF MENU TERMS

Creuse long, thick-shelled oyster

Crevettes grises shrimps

Crevettes roses prawns

Cromesquis croquettes

Croque Monsieur toasted cheese or ham sandwich

Croquette see *boulette*

Croustade small pastry mould with various fillings

Croûte (en) pastry crust (in a)

Croûtons bread (toast or fried)

Cru raw

Crudités raw vegetables

Crustacés shellfish

Cuillère soft (cut with spoon)

Cuisses (de) legs (of)

Cuissot (de) haunch (of)

Cuit cooked

Cul haunch or rear

Culotte rump (usually steak)

Cultivateur soup of chopped vegetables

D

Dariole basket-shaped pastry

Darne slice or steak

Dattes dates

Daube stew (various types)

Daurade sea-bream

Dégustation tasting

Délice delight

Demi-glace basic brown sauce

Demi-sel lightly salted

Diable seasoned with mustard

Diane (à la) peppered cream sauce

Dieppoise (à la) Dieppe style: white, wine, cream, mussels, shrimps

Dijonnaise (à la) with mustard sauce

Dijonnaise (à la belle) blackcurrant sauce

Dinde young hen turkey

Dindon turkey

Dindonneau young turkey

Dodine (de canard) cold stuffed duck

Dorade dorado

Doria with cucumbers

Douceurs desserts

Doux (douce) sweet

Du Barry cauliflower soup

Duxelles chopped mushrooms, shallots and cream

E

Echalotes shallots

Echine spare ribs

Echiquier *checkered* fashion

Ecrevisses freshwater crayfish

Ecuelle bowl or basin

Effiloché (e) frayed, thinly sliced

Emincé thinly sliced

Encornets cuttlefish

Endive chicory

Entrecôte entrecôte, rib steak

Entremets sweets

Epaule shoulder

Eperlan smelt

Epices spices

Epinards spinach

Epis de maïs sweetcorn

Escabèche fish (or poultry) marinated in *court-bouillon* – cold

Escalope thinly cut (meat or fish)

Escargots snails

Espadon swordfish

Estouffade stew with onions, herbs, mushrooms, red or white wine (perhaps garlic)

Estragon tarragon flavoured

Etrilles crabs

Etuvé (e) cooked in little water or in ingredient's own juice

Exocet flying fish

F

Façon cooked in a described way

Faisan (e) pheasant

Farci (e) stuffed

Farine flour

Faux-filet sirloin steak

Favorite garnish *foie gras*, truffles

Favouilles spider crabs

Fenouil fennel

Féra freshwater lake fish

Ferme (fermier) farm (farmer)

Fermière mixture of onions, carrots, turnips, celery etc.

Feuille de vigne vine leaf

Feuilleté light flaky pastry

Fèves broad beans

Ficelle (à la) tied in a string

Ficelles thin loaves of bread

Figues figs

Filet fillet

Financière (à la) Madeira sauce with truffles

Fines herbes mixture of parsley, chives, tarragon, etc

Flageolets kidney beans

Flamande (à la) Flemish style

Flambé flamed

Flamiche puff pastry tart

Flan tart

Flétan halibut

Fleur flower

Fleurons puff pastry crescents

Florentine with spinach

Foie liver

Foie gras goose liver

Foies blonds de volaille chicken liver mousse

Foin (dans le) cooked in hay

Fond (base) basic stock

Fondant see *boulette*: a bon-bon

Fonds d'artichauts artichoke hearts

Fondue (de fromage) melted (cheese with wine)

Forestière with bacon and mushrooms

Four (au) baked in oven

Fourré stuffed

Frais, fraiche fresh or cool

Fraises strawberries

Fraises des bois wild strawberries

Framboises raspberries

Française (à la) mashed potato filled with mixed vegetables

Frangipane almond custard filling

Frappé frozen or ice cold

Friandises sweets – *petits fours*

Fricadelles minced meat balls

Fricandeau sliced topside veal

Fricassée braised in sauce or butter, egg yolks and cream

Frisé (e) curly

Frit fried

Frites chips

Fritot fritter

Frittons see *grattons*

Friture small fried fish

Frivolles fritters

Froid cold

Fromage cheese

Fromage de tête brawn

Fruit de la passion passion fruit

Fruits confits crystallised fruit

Fruits de mer seafood

Fumé smoked

Fumet fish stock

G

Galantine cooked meat, fish or vegetables in jelly – served cold

Galette pastry, pancake or cake

Galimafrée (de) stew (of)

Gambas big prawns

Garbure (Garbue) vegetable soup

Gardons small roach

Garni (e) with vegetables

Garniture garnish

Gâteau cake

Gâtinaise (à la) with honey

Gaufre waffle

Gayettes faggots

Gelée aspic jelly

Géline chicken

Genièvre juniper

Génoise rich sponge cake

Germiny sorrel and cream soup

Gésier gizzard

Gibelotte see *fricassée*

Gibier game

Gigot (de) leg (of lamb) – can describe other things

Gigue (de) shank (of)

Gingembre ginger

Girofle clove

Girolles apricot-coloured fungi

Glacé iced. Crystallised. Glazed

Glace ice cream

GLOSSARY OF MENU TERMS

Godard see *financière (à la)*

Gougère round-shaped, egg and cheese *chou* pastry

Goujonnettes (de) small fried pieces (of)

Goujons gudgeon

Gourmandises sweetmeats – can describe *fruits de mer*

Gousse (de) pod or husk (of)

Graine (de capucine) seed (nasturtium)

Graisse fat

Graisserons duck and goose fat scratchings

Grand Veneur sauce with vegetables, wine vinegar, redcurrant jelly and cream

Granité water ice

Gratin browned

Gratin Dauphinois potato dish with cream, cheese, garlic

Gratin Savoyard potato dish with cheese and butter

Gratiné top of sauced dish browned with butter, cheese, etc.

Grattons pork scratchings

Gravettes oysters

Grecque (à la) cooked vegetables served cold

Grenade pomegranate

Grenadin thick veal escalope

Grenouilles frogs

Grillade grilled meat

Grillé (e) grilled

Griottes bitter red cherries

Grisets mushrooms

Grive thrush

Grondin gurnard, red gurnet

Gros sel coarse rock or sea salt

Groseilles gooseberries

Groseilles noires blackcurrants

Groseilles rouges recurrants

Gruyère hard, mild cheese

Gyromitres fungi

H

Habit vert *dressed in green*

Hachis minced or chopped-up.

Hareng herring

Hareng fumé kippered

Hareng salé bloater

Haricot (de) stew (of)

Haricots beans

Haricots blancs white beans (dried)

Haricots rouges kidney beans

Haricots verts green beans or French beans

Hochepot thick stew

Hollandaise sauce with butter, egg yolk, lemon juice

Homard lobster

Hongroise (à la) Hungarian style: sauce with tomato, paprika

Hors d'oeuvre appetisers

Huile oil

Huîtres oysters

Hure (de) head (of). Brawn. Jellied

I

Ile flottante unmoulded soufflé of beaten egg white and sugar

Imam bayeldi aubergine with rice, onions and sautéed tomatoes

Impératrice (à la) desserts with candied fruits soaked in *kirsch*

Indienne (à l') Indian style: with curry powder

Italienne (à l') Italian style: artichokes, mushrooms, pasta

J

Jambon ham

Jambonneau knuckle of pork

Jambonnette (de) boned and stuffed (knuckle of ham or poultry)

Jardinière diced fresh vegetables

Jarret de veau stew of shin of veal

Jarretons cooked pork knuckles

Jésus de Morteau – smoked Jura pork sausage

Joinville *velouté* sauce with cream, crayfish tails, truffles

Joue (de) cheek (of)

Judru cured pork sausage

Julienne thinly-cut vegetables. See *lingue*

Jus juice

L

Lait milk

Laitance soft roe

Laitue lettuce

Lamproie eel-like fish

Langouste spiny lobster or crawfish

Langoustines Dublin Bay prawns

Langue tongue

Languedocienne (à la) mushrooms, tomatoes, parsley garnish

Lapereau young rabbit

Lapin rabbit

Lapin de garenne wild rabbit

Lard bacon

Lard de poitrine fat belly of pork

Lardons strips of bacon

Lavaret freshwater lake fish

Lèche thin slice

Léger (ère) light

Légumes vegetables

Lieu fish – like cod

Lièvre hare

Limande lemon sole

Limon lime

Lingue ling – cod family

Lit bed

Livèche lovage (like celery)

Longe loin

Lotte (barbot) burbot – like eel

Lotte de mer monkfish, anglerfish

Lou magret see *magret*

Loup de mer sea-bass

Lyonnaise (à la) Lyonnaise style: sauce with wine, onions, vinegar

M

Macédoine diced fruit or veg'

Madeleines tiny sponge cakes

Madère sauce *demi-glace*, Madeira

Magret (de canard) breast (of duck)

Maigre fish – like sea-bass

Maillot carrots, turnips, onions, peas and beans

Maïs maize flour

Maison (de) of the restaurant

Maître d'hôtel sauce with butter, parsley, lemon

Maltaise (sauce) orange-flavoured hollandaise sauce

Manchons see *goujonnettes*

Mandarine tangerine

Mangetout peas and pods

Mangues mangoes

Manière (de) style (of)

Maquereaux mackerel

Maraîchère (à la) market-gardener style: *velouté* sauce with vegetables

Marais marsh or market-garden

Marbré (e) marbled

Marc pure spirit

Marcassin young wild boar

Marché market

Marchand de vin sauce with red wine, chopped shallots

Marée fresh seafood

Marengo tomatoes, mushrooms, olive oil, white wine, garlic, herbs

Marennes (blanches) oysters, flat shelled

Marennes (vertes) green shells

Mareyeur fishmonger

Marinade – mariné(e) pickled

Marinière see *moules*

Marjolaine marjoram

Marjolaine almond and hazelnut meringue with chocolate cream and praline

Marmite stewpot

Marquise (de) water ice (of)

Marrons chestnuts

Matelote (d'anguilles) fresh-water fish stew (or of eels)

Mauviette lark

Médaillon (de) round piece (of)

Mélange mixture or blend

Melba (à la) poached peach, with vanilla ice cream, raspberry sauce

Ménagère (à la) housewife style: onions, potatoes, peas, turnips, carrots

Menthe mint

Mer sea

Merlan whiting (in Provence – hake)

Merle blackbird

GLOSSARY OF MENU TERMS

Mérou grouper (sea fish)

Merveilles hot, sugared fritters

Mesclum mixture of salad leaves

Meunière (à la) sauce with butter, parsley, lemon (sometimes oil)

Meurette red wine sauce

Miel honey

Mignardises *petits fours*

Mignon (de) small round piece

Mignonette coarsely ground white pepper

Milanaise (à la) Milan style: dipped in breadcrumbs, egg, cheese

Mijoté (e) cooked slowly in water

Millassou sweet maize flour flan

Mille-feuilles *1001* thin layers of pastry

Mimosa chopped hard-boiled egg

Mique stew of dumplings

Mirabeau anchovies, olives

Mirabelles golden plums

Mirepoix cubes of carrots, onion, ham

Miroton (de) slices (of)

Mitonée (de) soup (of)

Mode (á la) in the manner of

Moelle beef marrow

Mojettes see Poitou-Charentes

Moka coffee

Montagne (de) from mountains

Montmorency with cherries

Morilles edible, dark brown, *honeycombed* fungi

Mornay cheese sauce

Morue cod

Mostèle (Gâteau de) cod mousse

Mouclade mussel stew

Moules mussels

Moules marinière mussels cooked in white wine and shallots

Mousse cold, light, finely-minced ingredients with cream and egg whites

Mousseline hollandaise sauce with whipped cream

Mousserons edible fungi

Moutarde mustard

Mouton mutton

Mulet grey mullet

Mûres mulberries

Muscade nutmeg

Museau muzzle

Myrtilles bilberries. Blueberries

N

Nage (à la) *court-bouillon:* aromatic poaching liquid

Nantua sauce for fish with crayfish, white wine, tomatoes

Nature plain

Navarin stew, usually lamb

Navets turnips

Nègre literally *negro*

Newburg sauce with lobster brandy, cream and Madeira

Nid nest

Nivernaise (à la) Nevers style: carrots and onions

Noisette sauce of lightly browned butter

Noisettes (de) round pieces (of)

Noix nuts

Noix (de veau) topside of leg (veal)

Normande (à la) Normandy style: fish sauce with mussels, shrimps, mushrooms, eggs and cream

Nouilles noodles

Nouveau (nouvelle) new or young

Noyau sweet liqueur from crushed stones (usually cherries)

O

Œufs à la coque soft-boiled eggs

Œufs à la neige see *île flottante*

Œufs à la poêle fried eggs

Œufs brouillés scrambled eggs

Œufs durs hard-boiled eggs

Œufs moulés poached eggs

Oie goose

Oignon onion

Oison rôti roast gosling

Omble chevalier freshwater char: looks like large salmon trout

Ombre grayling

Ombrine see *maigre* – fish

Onglet flank of beef

Oreilles (de porc) ears (pigs')

Orléannaise (à l') Orléans style: chicory and potatoes

Orly dipped in butter, fried and served with tomato sauce

Orties nettles

Ortolan wheatear (thrush family)

Os bone

Oseille sorrel

Ouillat see Southwest

Oursins sea-urchins

P

Pailletté (de) spangled (with)

Paillettes pastry straws

Pain bread

Pain doré bread soaked in milk and eggs and fried

Paleron shoulder

Palmier (cœurs de) palm hearts

Palombe wood pigeon

Palomête see *maigre* – fish

Palourdes clams

Pamplemousse grapefruit

Panaché mixed

Panade flour or bread paste

Panais parsnip

Pané (e) breadcrumbed

Panier basket

Pannequets like *crêpes*, smaller and thicker

Paon peacock

Papillote (en) cooked in oiled paper (or foil)

Paquets (en) in parcels

Parfait (de) *perfect*

Parisienne (à la) leeks, potatoes

Parmentier potatoes

Pascade sweet or savory pancake

Pascaline (de) *quenelle (of)*

Passe-pierres seaweed

Pastèque watermelon

Pastis (sauce au) aniseed based

Pâté minced meats (of various types) baked. Usually served cold

Pâte pastry, dough or batter

Pâte à choux cream puff pastry

Pâte brisée short crust pastry

Pâté en croûte baked in pastry crust

Pâtes (fraîches) fresh pasta

Pâtés (petits) à Provençale anchovy and ham turnovers

Pâtisserie pastry

Pâtisson custard marrow

Patte *claw, foot, leg*

Paupiettes thin slices of meat or fish – used to wrap fillings

Pavé (de) thick slice (of)

Paysan (ne) (à la) country style

Peau (de) skin (of)

Pêche peach

Pêcheur *fisherman*

Perche perch

Perdreau partridge

Périgourdine (à la) sauce Périgueux and goose liver

Périgueux sauce with truffles, Madeira

Persil parsley

Persillade mixture chopped parsley, garlic

Petite marmite strong consommé with toast and cheese

Petits fours miniature cakes, biscuits, sweets

Petits gris small snails

Petits pois tiny peas

Pétoncle small scallop

Pets de nonne small soufflé fritters

Pieds de porc pig trotters

Pigeonneau young pigeon

Pignons pine nuts

Pilau rice dish

Pilou drumstick

Piments doux sweet peppers

Pintade (pintadeau) guinea-fowl (young guinea-fowl)

Piperade omelette or scrambled eggs with tomatoes, peppers, onions, sometimes ham

Piquante (sauce) sharp-tasting sauce with shallots, capers, wine

Piqué larded

Pissenlits dandelion leaves

Pistaches green pistachio nuts

GLOSSARY OF MENU TERMS

Pistil de safran saffron (*pistil* from autumn-flowering crocus)

Pistou see Côte d'Azur

Plateau (de) plate (of)

Pleurotes mushrooms

Plie franche plaice

Plombières sweet with vanilla ice cream, *kirsch*, candied fruit, and *crème chantilly*

Pluches sprigs

Pluvier plover

Poché (e)-Pochade poached

Pochouse freshwater fish stew with white wine

Poêlé fried

Poire pear

Poireaux leeks

Pois peas

Poisson fish

Poitrine breast

Poitrine fumée smoked bacon

Poitrine salée unsmoked bacon

Poivrade a peppery sauce with wine vinegar, cooked vegetables

Poivre noir black pepper

Poivre rose red pepper

Poivre vert green peppercorns

Poivrons sweet peppers

Pojarsky minced meat or fish – cutlet shaped and fried

Polenta boiled maize flour

Polonaise Polish style: with buttered, breadcrumbs, parsley, hard-boiled eggs

Pommade thick, smooth paste

Pommes apples

Pommes de terre potatoes

  à l'anglaise boiled

  allumettes thin and fried

  boulangère sliced with onions

  château roast

  dauphine croquettes

  duchesse mashed with egg yolk

  en l'air hollow potato puffs

  frites fried chips

  gratinées browned with cheese

  Lyonnaise sautéed with onions

  vapeur boiled

Pomponnette savoury pastry

Porc (carré de) loin of pork

Porc (côte de) pork chop

Porcelet suckling pig

Porto (au) port

Portugaise (à la) Portuguese style: fried onions and tomatoes

Portugaises oysters with long, deep shells

Potage thick soup

Pot-au-crème dessert – usually chocolate or coffee

Pot-au-feu clear meat broth served with the meat

Potée heavy soup of cabbage, beans etc.

Pouchouse see *pochouse*

Poularde large hen

Poulet chicken

Poulet à la broche spit-roasted chicken

Poulet Basquaise chicken with tomatoes and peppers

Poulet de Bresse corn-fed, white flesh chicken

Poulet de grain grain-fed chicken

Poulette young chicken

Poulpe octopus

Pounti small, egg-based, savoury soufflé with bacon or prunes

Poussin small baby chicken

Poutargue grey mullet roe

Praires small clams

Pralines caramelised almonds

Praslin caramalised

Primeurs young vegetables

Princesse velouté sauce, asparagus tips and truffles

Printanière (e) (à la) garnish of diced vegetables

Produits (de) products (of)

Profiteroles choux pastry, custard filled puffs

Provençale (à la) Provençal style: with tomatoes, garlic, olive oil, etc.

Pruneaux prunes

Prunes plums

Purée mashed

Q

Quenelles light dumplings of fish or pultry

Quetsches small, purple plums

Queue de boeuf oxtail

Queues tails

Quiche (Lorraine) open flan of cheese, ham or bacon

R

Râble de lièvre (lapin) saddle of hare (rabbit)

Raclette scrapings from specially-made and heated cheese

Radis radish

Ragoût stew, usually meat, but can describe other ingredients

Raie (bouclée) skate (type of)

Raifort horseradish

Raisins grapes

Ramequin see *cocotte* (en)

Ramier wood pigeon

Rapé (e) grated or shredded

Rascasse scorpion fish

Ratafia brandy and unfermented Champagne. Almond biscuits

Ratatouille aubergines, onions, courgettes, garlic, red peppers and tomatoes in olive oil

Raves (root) turnips, radishes, etc.

Ravigote sauce with onions, herbs, mushrooms, wine vinegar

Ravioles ravioli

Régence sauce with wine, truffles, mushrooms

Reine chicken and cream

Reines-Claude greengages

Reinette type of apple

Réjane chicken consommé with shredded eggs

Rémoulade sauce of mayonnaise, mustard, capers, herbs, anchovy

Rillettes (d'oie) potted pork (goose)

Rillons small cubes of fat pork

Ris d'agneau lamb sweetbreads

Ris de veau veal sweetbreads

Rissettes small sweetbreads

Rivière river

Riz rice

Riz à l'impératrice cold rice pudding

Robert sauce *demi-glace*, white wine, onions, vinegar, mustard

Rocambole like a shallot

Rognonnade veal and kidneys

Rognons kidneys

Romarin rosemary

Rossini see *tournedos*

Rôti roast

Rouelle (de) round piece or slice

Rouget red mullet

Rouget barbet red mullet

Rouille orange-coloured sauce with peppers, garlic and saffron

Roulade (de) roll (of)

Roulée (s) rolled (usually *crêpes*)

Roux flour, butter base for sauces

Royans fresh sardines

Rutabaga swede

S

Sabayon sauce of egg yolks, wine

Sablés shortbread

Safran saffron (see *pistil de*)

Sagou sago

St-Germain with peas

St-Hubert sauce *poivrade*, bacon and cooked chestnuts

St-Jacques (coquilles) scallops

St-Pierre John Dory

Saisons (suivant) depending on the season of the year

Salade Niçoise tomatoes, beans, potatoes, black olives, anchovy, lettuce, olive oil, perhaps tuna

Salade panachée mixed salad

Salade verte green salad

Salé *salted*

Salicornes marsh samphire

Salmigondis hotchpotch

Salmis red wine sauce

GLOSSARY OF MENU TERMS

Salpicon meat or fish and diced vegetables in sauce

Salsifis salisfy

Sanciau thick sweet or savoury pancake

Sandre freshwater fish, like perch

Sang blood

Sanglier wild boar

Santé potatoes and sorrel

Sarcelle teal

Sarriette (poivre d'âne) savory, bitter herb

Saucisse freshly-made sausage

Saucission large, dry sausage

Saucission cervelas saveloys

Sauge sage

Saumon blanc hake

Saumon salmon

Saumon fumé smoked salmon

Sauté browned in butter, oil or fat

Sauvage wild

Savarin see *baba au rhum*

Savoyarde with Gruyère cheese

Scarole endive

Scipion cuttlefish

Seiches squid

Sel salt (see *gros sel*)

Selle saddle

Selon grosseur (S.G.) according to size

Serpolet wild thyme

Sévigné garnished with mushrooms, roast potatoes, lettuce

Smitane sauce with sour cream, onions, white wine

Soissons with white beans

Sole à la Dieppoise sole fillets, mussels, shrimps, wine, cream

Sole Cardinale poached fillets of sole, cream sauce

Sole Dugléré sole with tomatoes, onions, shallots, butter

Sole Marguery sole with mussels, prawns, white wine

Sole Walewska *mornay* sauce, truffles and prawns

Sorbet water ice

Soubise onions sauce

Soufflé (e) beaten egg whites, baked (with sweet or savoury ingredients)

Soupière soup tureen

Soupion small inkfish

Sourdons cockles

Souvaroff a game bird with *foie gras* and truffles

Spaghettis (de) thin strips (of)

Spoom frothy water ice

Strasbourgeoise (à la) Strasbourg style: *foie gras, choucroute*, bacon

Sucre sugar

Suppions small cuttlefish

Suprême sweet white sauce

Suprême boneless breast of poultry – can also describe a fillet of fish

T

Talleyrand truffles, cheese, *foie gras*

Tanche tench

Tapé (e) dried

Tartare raw minced beef

Tartare (sauce) sauce with mayonnaise, onions, capers, herbs

Tarte open flan

Tarte Tatin *upside down* apple tart

Terrine baked minced meat or fish, served cold

Tête de veau vinaigrette calf's head *vinaigrette*

Thé tea

Thermidor grilled lobster with browned *béchamel* sauce

Thon tunny fish

Thym thyme

Tiède mild or lukewarm

Tilleul lime blossom

Timbale mould in which contents are steamed

Tomates tomatoes

Topinambours Jerusalem artichokes

Torte sweet-filled flan

Tortue turtle

Tortue sauce with various herbs, tomatoes, Madeira

Toulousaine (à la) Toulouse style: truffles, *foie gras*, sweetbreads, kidneys

Tournedos fillet steak (small end)

Tournedos chasseur with shallots, mushrooms, tomatoes

Tournedos Dauphinoise with creamed mushrooms, croûtons

Tournedos Rossini with goose liver, truffles, port, croûtons

Tourte (Tourtière) covered savoury tart

Tourteaux large crabs

Tranche slice

Tranches de bœuf steaks

Tripes à la mode de Caen tripe stew

Tripettes small tripe

Trompettes de la mort fungi

Trou water ice

Truffée with truffles

Truffes truffles – black, exotic tubers

Truite trout

Truite (au bleu) trout poached in water and vinegar – turns blue

Truite saumonée salmon trout

Tuiles tiles (thin almond slices)

Turbot (turbotin) turbot

V

Vacherin ice cream, meringue, cream

Valenciennes (à la) rice, red peppers, onions, tomatoes, white wine

Vallée d'Auge sauce with Calvados and cream

Vapeur (à la) steamed

Veau veal

Veau à la Viennoise (escalope de) slice of veal with chopped egg

Veau Milanaise (escalope de) with marcaroni, tomatoes, ham, mushrooms

Veau pané (escalope de) thin slice of veal in flour, eggs and bread-crumbs

Velouté white sauce with *bouillon* and white roux

Velouté de volaille thick chicken soup

Venaison venison

Ventre belly or breast

Vernis clams

Véronique grapes, wine, cream

Verte green mayonnaise with chervil, spinach, tarragon

Vert-pré thinly-sliced chips, *maître d'hôtel* butter, watercress

Verveine verbena

Vessie (en) cooked in a pig's bladder – usually chicken

Viande meat

Vichy glazed carrots

Vichyssoise creamy potato, leek soup – served cold

Vierge (sauce) olive oil sauce

Vierge literally *virgin*

Vigneron wine-grower

Vinaigre (de) wine vinegar or vinegar of named fruit

Vinaigre de Jerez sherry vinegar

Vinaigrette (à la) French dressing with wine vinegar, oil etc

Volaille poultry

Vol au vent puff pastry case

X

Xérès (vinaigre de) sherry (vinegar)

Y

Yaourt yoghourt

Z

Zeste (d'orange) rubbing from (orange skin)

If you come across any terms not in the glossary asking for the constituent parts to be written down; translate them using these pages. Example: sauce gribiche three of the ingredients you'll recognise – mayonnaise, capers and herbs. The other ingredients of oeufs durs (hachis) and cornichons can be translated easily.

1. TYPES OF BOAT

Bateau citerne	Tanker
Bateau de course-croisière	Ocean racer
Bateau de croisière	Cruiser
Bateau mixte	Motor sailer
Bateau de pêche	Fishing boat
Bateau pilote	Pilot boat
Bateau de sauvetage	Life-boat
Canot, dinghy	Dinghy
Cotre	Cutter
Croiseur à moteur	Motor cruiser
Géolette	Schooner
Ketch	Ketch
Navire de commerce	Merchant vessel
Remorqueur	Tug
Sloop	Sloop
Vedette	Launch
Yacht	Yacht

2. EQUIPMENT, SAILS

Ancre	Anchor
Artimon	Mizzen
Balancine	Topping lift
Bastaque	Backstay
Barres de flèche	Crosstrees
Beaupré	Bowsprit
Bôme	Boom
Bordure	Foot
Cabestan	Capstan
Cadène	Chain plate
Chute	Leech
Cordage	Rope
Cosse	Thimble
Drisse	Halyard
Drosses	Steering wires
Ecoute	Sheet
Ecoute de grand-voile	Main Sheet
Ecoute de misaine	Fore sheet
Envergure	Luff
Epissure	Splicing, splice

Etai avant	Forestay
Femelot	Pintle
Foc	Jib
Garcette	Reef Point
Génois	Genoa
Grand-mât	Main mast
Grand-voile	Main sail
Guindant	Luff
Hauban	Shroud
Manille	Shackle
Mât	Mast
Nœud	Knot
Point d'amure	Tack
Point d'écoute	Clew
Point de drisse	Head
Poulie	Block
Ridoir	Turnbuckle
Spinnaker	Spinnaker
Taquet	Cleat
Trinquette	Staysail
Voile	Sail
Voile d'étai	Mizzen staysail
Voile d'étai d'artimon	Mizzen staysail

3. PARTS OF A BOAT

Arrière à tableau	Transom stern
Balcon arrière	Pushpit
Balcon avant	Pulpit
Barre	Tiller
Barrot	Beam
Bordage	Planking
Bouchain, fonds	Bilges
Cabine	Cabin
Cale	Bilges
Carène	Bottom
Carlingue	Keelson
Chaumard	Fairlead
Chandelier	Stanchion
Cloison	Bulkhead
Cockpit	Cockpit
Coque	Hull
Corne de brume	Foghorn
Couchette	Bunk
Défense	Fender
Ecoutille	Hatch

Etambot	Sternpost
Etrave	Stern
Filière	Lifeline
Gaffe	Boathook
Gouvernail	Rudder
Grue	Derrick, crane
Hélice	Propeller, screw
Instructions nautiques	Sailing directions, pilot
Ligne de flottaison	Waterline, boot topping
Longueur hors-tout	Length overall
Pavois	Bulwark
Plancher	Cabin sole
Plat-bord	Gunwale
Pont	Deck
Poste avant	Foc'sle
Poupe	Stern
Puits à chaine	Chain locker
Quille	Keel
Roue	Wheel
Roue de gouvernail	Steering wheel
Soute à voiles	Sail locker
Tangon de spi	Spinnaker boom
Toilette	Lavatory, head
Timonerie	Wheelhouse
Tirant d'eau	Draught
Varangue	Floor

4. ENGINE

Alternateur	Alternator
Arbre d'hélice	Propeller shaft
Batterie	Battery
Bielle	Connecting rod
Bobine d'allumage	Ignition coil
Boîte de vitesse/ Inverseur	Gearbox
Boulon	Bolt
Courroie de transmission	Drive belt
Culasse	Cylinder head
Démarreur	Starter motor
Dynamo	Generator
Eau distillée	Distilled water
Eau douce, potable	Fresh water
Ecrou	Nut
Embrayage	Clutch
Filtre à combustible	Fuel filter
Graisse	Grease
Huile	Oil
Hélice	Propeller
Injecteur	Atomiser, injecter
Liquide hydraulique	Hydraulic fluid
Moteur à essence	Petrol engine
Moteur diesel	Diesel engine
Pompe d'injection	Diesel fuel pump
Pompe à eau	Water pump
Pompe de cale	Bilge pump
Poupe	Stern
Réservoir à combustible	Fuel tank
Tuyau	Hose

5. NAVIGATION

Alignement	Leading line
Bâbord	Port side
Balise	Beacon
Bouée	Buoy
Cap, route	Course
Carte marine	Chart
Chenal	Channel
Compas	Compass
Compas de relèvement	Hand bearing compass
Déclinaison	Variation
Degré	Degree
Déviation	Deviation
Echo sondeur	Echo sounder
En arrière	Astern
En avant	Ahead
Est	East
Feux	Lights
Haut-fond	Shoal
Ile	Island
Jumelles	Binoculars
Latitude	Latitude
Loch enregistreur	Patent log
Longitude	Longitude

Mouillage	Anchorage
Nord	North
Ouest	West
Par le travers	Abeam
Poste réçepteur	Radio receiver
Profondeur	Depth
Promontoire	Headland
Radiogonomètre	Radio direction finder
Récif	Reef
Remous	Overfalls
Rochers	Rocks
Sud	South
Table â cartes	Chart table
Tribord	Starboard
Vase	Mud

6. TIDES

Amplitude	Range
Basse mer	Low Water
Courant	Tidal stream
Dérive	Drift
Echoué	Aground
Marée descendante	Ebb
Marée montante	Flood
Morte eau	Neap (tides)
Pleine mer	High water
Porter	Set
Profondeur	Depth
Vitesse	Rate
Vive eau, grande marée	Spring (tides)
Zéro des cartes	Chart datum

7. RADIO

Fréquence	Frequency
Heures d'émission	Operating time
Indicatif	Call sign
Radiophare	Radio beacon
Radio-téléphone	Radio telephone
Station d'émission	Radio station

8. PORTS

Accostage interdit	Mooring prohibited
Agent du service de l'immigration	Immigration officer
Bac	Ferry
Bassin	Harbour
Bassin pour yachts	Yacht harbour
Bitte d'amarrage	Mooring bitts
Bouée	Buoy
Bureau de douane	Customs office
Bureau du capitaine	Harbour master's office
Canal	Canal
Capitaine de port	Harbour master
Défense de mouiller	Anchoring prohibited
Ecluse	Lock
Escalier du quai	Harbour steps
Point d'accostage	Mooring place
Pont basculant	Lifting bridge
Pont mobile	Movable bridge
Pont tournant	Swing bridge
Port de pêche	Fishing harbour
Zone interdite	Prohibited area

9. SHIP'S SUPPLIES

Beurre	Butter
Confiture	Jam
Eau douce	Fresh water
Fromage	Cheese
Fruits	Fruit
Jambon	Ham
Lait	Milk
Légumes	Vegetables
Moutarde	Mustard
Œufs	Eggs
Pain	Bread
Poisson	Fish
Poivre	Pepper
Sel	Salt
Viande	Meat
Vinaigre	Vinegar

ETEOROLOGICAL TERMS Cont

10. METEOROLOGICAL TERMS

Accalmie	Lull
Agité	Moderate
Amélioration	Improvement
Anticyclone	Anticyclone
Augmentation	Increasing
Aujourd'hui	Today
Averse	Shower
Avis	Warning
Avis de coup de vent	Gale warning
Basse pression	Low pressure
Beau, clair	Fine, fair
Belle (mer)	Smooth
Brise	Breeze
Brise de mer	Sea breeze
Brise de terre	Land breeze
Brouillard	Fog
Bruine	Drizzle
Brume	Mist
Calme	Calm
Carte	Chart
Coup de vent	Gale
Courant	Current
Couvert	Overcast
Demain	Tomorrow
Dépression (bas)	Depression (low)
Direction	Direction
Dorsale	Ridge
En baisse	Falling
En hausse	Rising
Eclaircie	Bright interval
Echelle de Beaufort	Beaufort scale
En formation	Building
Etat de la mer	State of sea
Force du vent	Wind force
Fort	Strong
Forte	Rough
Fort coup de vent	Strong gale
Frais	Fresh
Fréquent	Frequent
Front	Front
Front chaud	Warm front
Front froid	Cold front
Grain	Squall
Grand frais	Near gale
Grêle	Hail
Houle	Swell
Instable	Unstable
Léger	Light
Mauvais temps	Foul weather
Mer	Sea
Modéré	Moderate
Moyen	Moyen
Neige et pluie	Sleet
Nœuds	Knots
Nuage	Cloud
Nuageux	Cloudy
Orage	Thunderstorm
Ouragan	Hurricane
Perturbation	Disturbance
Pluie	Rain
Précipitation	Precipitation
Pression	Pressure
Prévision	Forecast
Probabilité	Probability
	Chances of
Profond	Deep
Rafale	Gust
Région	Area
Sans nuages	Cloudless
Situation générale	General synopsis
Stationnaire	Stationary
Tempête	Storm
Temps (heure)	Time
Temps qu'il fait	Weather
Variable	Variable
Vent frais	Strong breeze
Zone	Area
Zone de haute pression	High pressure

RADIO BEACONS

Name	Position		Identification		Freq.	Range
	Lat.	Long.	Letter	Morse		
Round Island Lt	49°58′	06°19′	RR	·—· ·—·	308	150nm
Lizard Lt	49°57′	05°12′	LZ	·—·· ——··	298.8	70nm
Penzance Heliport	50°07′	05°31′	PH	·——· ····	333	15nm
Penlee Point	50°19′	04°11′	PE	·——· ·	298.8	50nm
Plymouth	50°25′	04°06′	PY	·——· —·——	396.5	10nm
Start Point	50°13′	03°38′	SP	··· ·——·	298.8	70nm
Berry Head	50°23′	03°29′	BHD	—··· ···· —··	318	25nm
Exeter	50°45′	03°17′	EX	· —··—	337	15nm
Portland Bill	50°30′	02°27′	PB	·——· —····	291.9	50nm
Poole Harbour	50°40′	01°56′	PO	·——· ———	303.4	10nm
Bournemouth/Hurn	50°48′	01°43′	HRN	···· ·—· —·	322	15nm
Fawley/Hythe	50°51′	01°23′	FAW	·——· ·— ·——	394	40nm
St Catherine's Pt Lt	50°34′	01°17′	CP	—·—· ·—·.	291.9	50nm
Bembridge	50°40′	01°05′	IW	·· ·——	276.5	15nm
Lee-on-Solent	50°53′	01°06′	LS	·—·· ···	407	10nm
Chichester Bar Bn	50°45′	00°56′	CH	—·—· ····	303.4	10nm
Goodwood	50°51′	00°45′	GWC	——· ·——·—·	370	25nm
Shoreham	50°49′	00°17′	SHM	··· ···· ——	332	10nm
Brighton Marina	50°48′	00°05′	BM	—··· ——	303.4	10nm
Newhaven	50°46′	00°03′	NH	—· ····	303.4	10nm
Royal Sovereign Lt	50°43′	00°26′	RY	·—· —·——	310.3	50nm
Lydd	50°58′	00°57′	LYX	·—·· —·—— —··—	397	15nm
Dungeness Lt	50°54′	00°58′	DU	—·· ··—	310.3	30nm

Name	Position		Identification		Freq.	Range
	Lat.	Long.	Letter	Morse		
East Goodwin Lt V	51°13′	01°36′	GW	——· ·——	305.7	30nm
North Foreland Lt	51°22′	01°26′	NF	—· ··—·	301.1	50nm
Falls Lt	51°18′	01°48′	FS	··—· ···	305.7	50nm
Calais/Dunkerque	50°59′	02°03′	MK	—— —·—	275	15nm
Dunkerque Lanby	51°03′	01°51′	DK	—·· —·—	294.2	10nm
Saint Inglevert	50°53′	01°44′	ING	·· —· ——·	387.5	50nm
Calais Main	50°58′	01°51′	CS	—·—· ···	305.7	20nm
Boulogne	50°44′	01°35′			289.6	5nm
Cap d'Alprech Lt	50°41′	01°33′	PH	·——· ····	310.3	50nm
Bassurelle Lt V	50°32′	00°57′	UL	··— ·—··	310.3	50nm
Le Touquet/Paris Plage	50°32′	01°35′	LT	·—·· —	358	20nm
Eu/Le Tréport	50°04′	01°25′	EU	· ··—	330	20nm
Pte d'Ailly Lt	49°55′	00°57′	AL	·— ·—··	310.3	50nm
Cap d'Antifer Lt	49°41′	00°10′	TI	— ··	291.9	50nm
Le Havre/Octeville	49°35′	00°11′	LHO	·—·· ···· ———	346	15nm
Le Havre Lanby	49°31′	00°09′	LH	·—·· ····	291.9	30nm
Pte de Ver Lt	49°20′	00°31′	ER	·—· ·—·	291.9	20nm
Cherbourg	49°38′	01°22′	MP	—— ·——·	373	
Port en Bessin Rear Lt	49°21′	00°45′	BS	—··· ···	313.5	5nm
Pte de Barfleur Lt	49°41′	01°15′	FG	··—· ——·	291.9	70nm
Cherbourg W Fort Lt	49°40′	01°38′	RB	·—· —···	312.6	20nm
Granville	48°55′	01°28′	GV	——· ···—	321	25nm

RADIO BEACONS

| Name | Position | | Identification | | Freq. | Range |
	Lat.	Long.	Letter	Morse		
Le Grand Jardin Lt	48°40′	02°04′	GJ	— — · · — — —	294.2	10nm
Cap Fréhel Lt	48°41′	02°19′	FÉ	· · — · · · — · ·	305.7	20nm
St Brieuc	48°34′	02°46′	SB	· · · — · · ·	353.5	35nm
Roches-Douvres Lt	49°06′	02°48′	RD	· — · — · ·	298.8	70nm
Rosédo Lt, Ile Bréhat	48°51′	03°00′	DO	— · · — — —	294.2	10nm
Lannion	48°43′	03°18′	LN	· — · · — ·	345.5	50nm
Roscoff	48°43′	03°57′	BC	— · · · — · — ·	287.3	10nm
Landivisiau	48°32′	04°08′	LDV	· — · · — · · · · · —	324	60nm
Lle Vierge Lt	48°38′	04°34′	VG	· · · — — — ·	298.8	70nm
Ouessant SW	48°31′	05°49′	SW	· · · · — —	294.2	10nm
Pte de Créac'h Lt	48°27′	05°07′	CA	— · — · · —	308	100nm
Pte St Mathieu Lt	48°19′	04°46′	SM	· · · — —	289.6	20nm
Lanvéoc, Poulmic	48°17′	04°26′	BST	— · · · · · · —	316	80nm
Ile de Sein NW Lt	48°02′	04°52′	SN	· · · — ·	303.4	70nm
Channel Lt V	49°54′	02°53′	CR	— · — · · — ·	287.3	10nm
Casquets Lt	49°43′	02°22′	QS	— — · — · · ·	298.8	50nm
Alderney	49°42′	02°11′	ALD	· — · — · · — · ·	383	50nm
St Peter Port	49°27′	02°31′	GY	— — · — · — —	285	10nm
Guernsey	49°26′	02°38′	GUR	— — · · · — · — ·	361	30nm
La Corbière	49°10′	02°14′	CB	— · — · — · · ·	305.7	20nm
St Helier Harbour	49°10′	02°07′	EC	· — · — ·	287.3	10nm
Jersey East	49°13′	02°02′	JEY	· — — — · — · —	367	75nm
Jersey West	49°12′	02°13′	JW	· — — — · — —	329	25nm

TIDAL STREAM ATLAS

T his atlas that has been reproduced from British Admiralty Charts and from Hydrographic Publications with the permission of the Controller of H.M. Stationary Office and the Hydrographer of the Navy.

On these charts the direction of tide is indicated by the direction of the arrows. The strength of tide is shown by the size of arrow.

The figures alongside the arrows indicate the tidal rate for mean, neap and spring tides and are shown as one tenth of a knot. i.e. 13.23 equals a mean neap rate of 1.3 knots and a mean spring rate of 2.3 knots.

TIDAL STREAM ATLAS

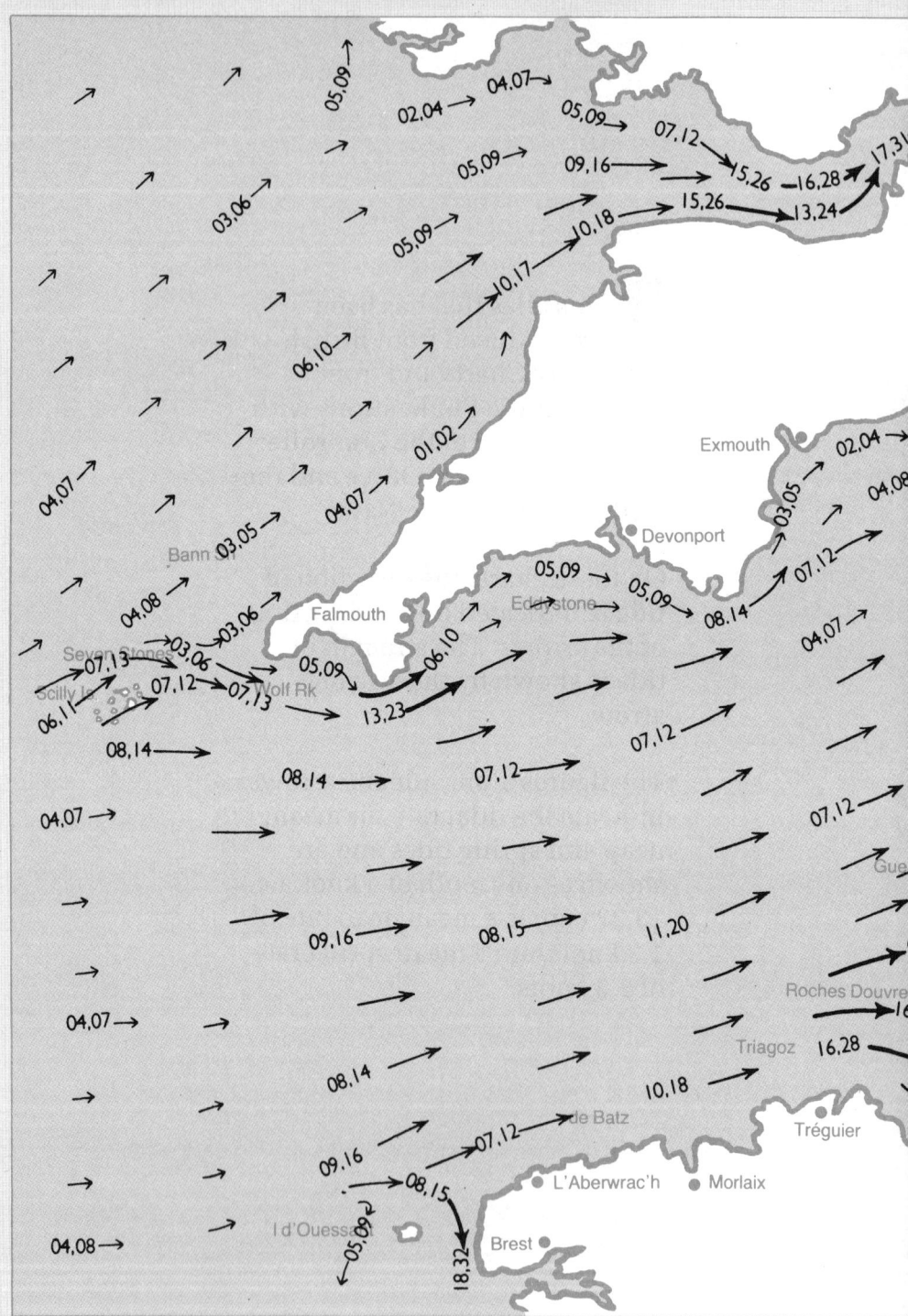

6 HOURS BEFORE HIGH WATER DOVER

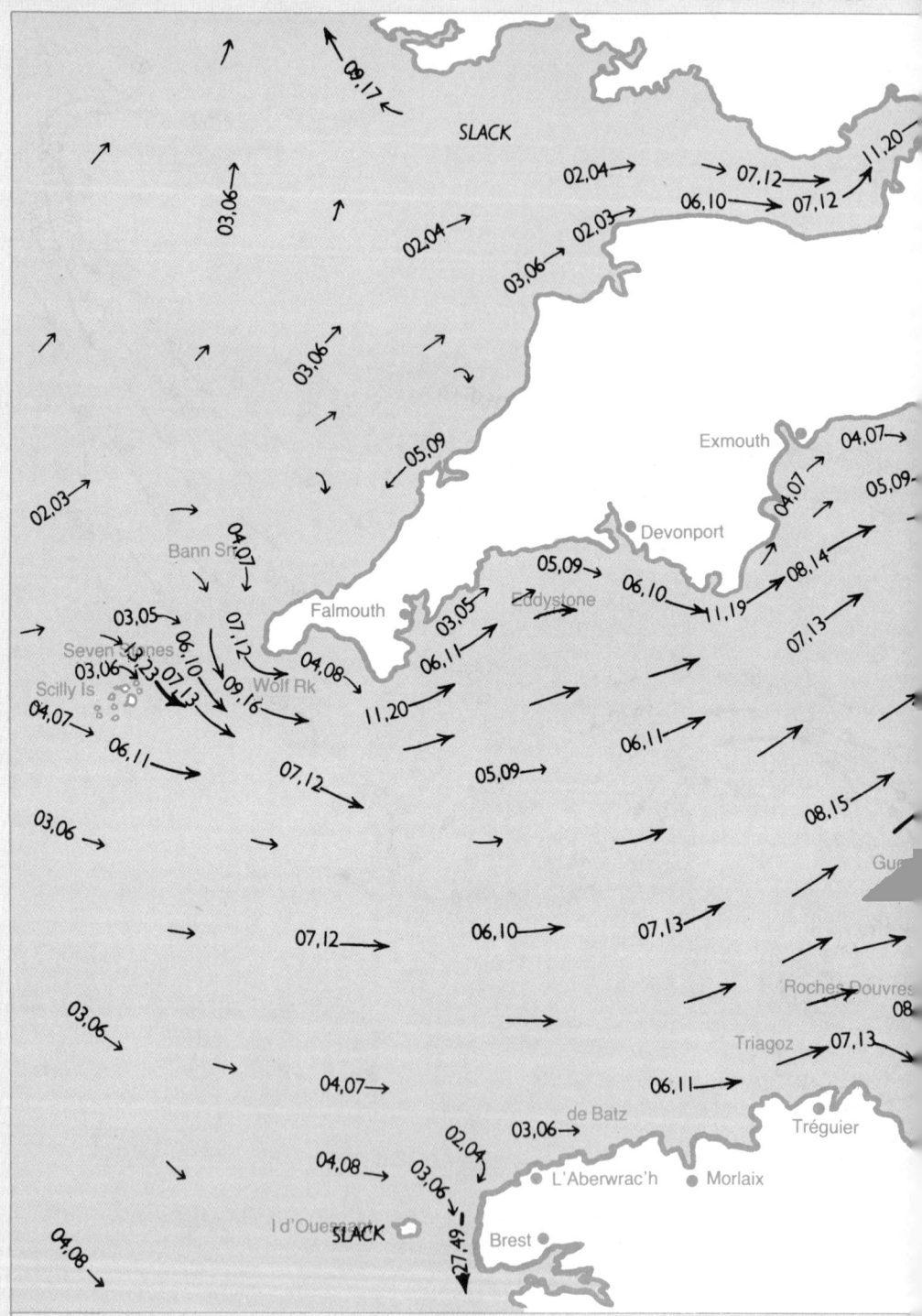

5 HOURS BEFORE HIGH WATER DOVER

SLACK

SLACK SLACK 02,03

SLACK

06,10

4,26

12,21 3,23

Dover 06,10 17,30

12,21 14,25 18,32

05,09 08,14 10,17 Bo..ne

Southampton 08,15 11,..

Portsmouth Shoreham 06,10 09,16

Littlehampton Newhaven

Poole ..b Tr 08,15→ Royal Sovereign 03,05→

14,25 10,17 13,24 01,02

2,22 09,17 13,23 15,27 06,11→ Bassurelle

11,20 07,12→ 02,03

13,24 11,19→ 09,16→ 02,03 SLACK

14,26 05,09 02,03

16,28 02,03→ Dieppe

0,36 18,32 30,53 12,21→ 02,03

28,50 11,19 09,17→ 08,15 Le Havre

Cherbourg 04,08→ 07,12→ 10,18→

..Heller

04,07

04,07→

04,08→ 07,12 08,15

06,10

..→ 04,08→

04,08→

St Malo

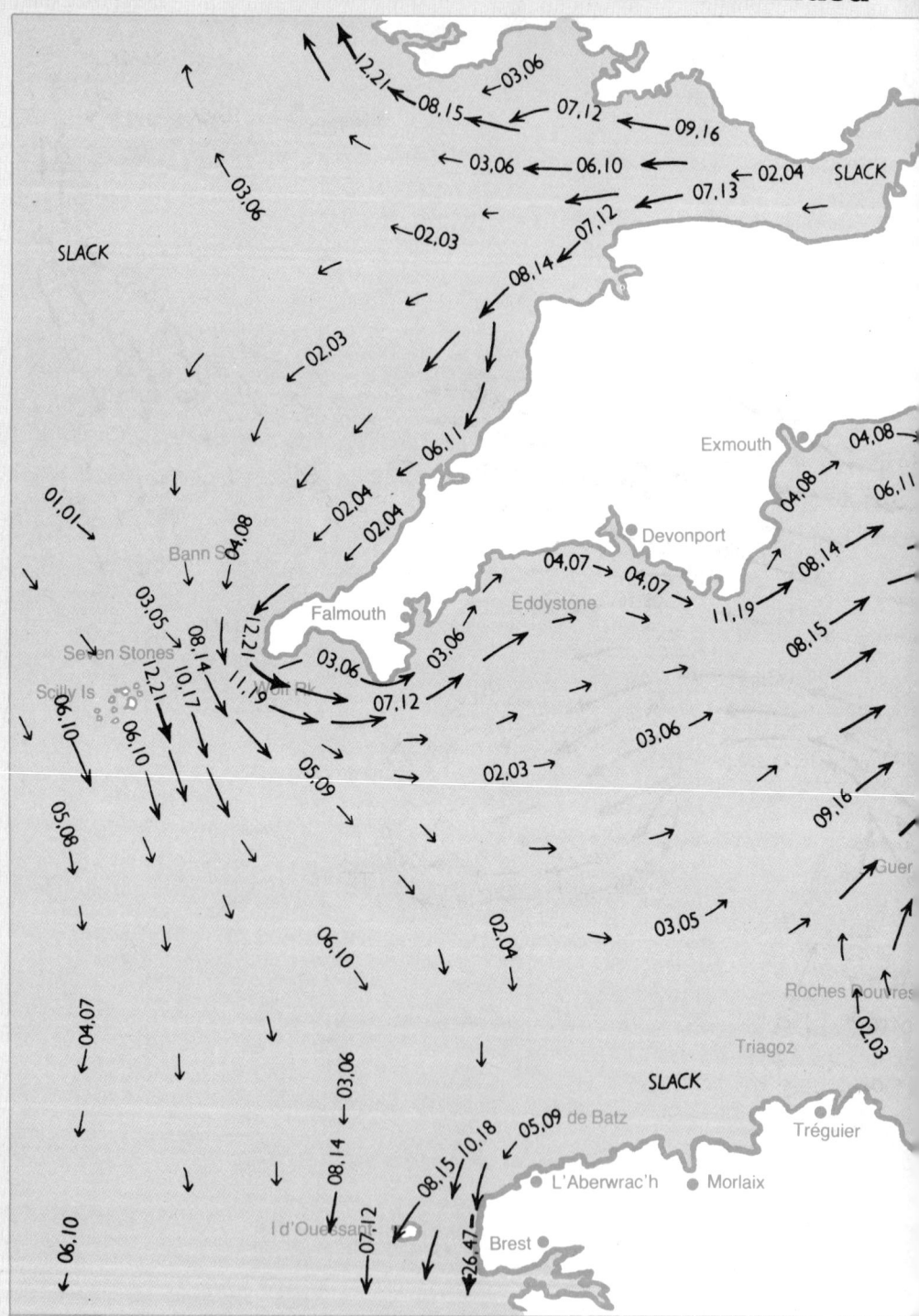

4 HOURS BEFORE HIGH WATER DOVER

04,08← ←04,08←←07,12
←04,07 —10,18
←04,08 08,14
16,29
12,21 7,31

Dover

06,11
02,04 10,1←
05,09 07,13 12,21
21,37
Boulogne
06,10

06,11
Basqurelle
04,07
04,07
04,07
SLACK

06,10 →

Dieppe

Southampton
Portsmouth
Littlehampton
Shoreham
Newhaven

Poole

15,26
12,22 12,21 13,24 09,16 → 11,19
15,21 18,32 11,20 Nab 16,29 Royal Sovereign
16,28 16,28 13,23 → 11,19
07,12 →
20,35 → 17,30
15,27 →
23,41
21,38 11,20 → 10,18 →
02,03 29,51 09,16 →
42,75 20,36 12,21 →
11,19 06,11 →
Cherbourg 07,12 → 07,13 → 09,17 → 07,12 → Le Havre
11,19 11,19 →

12,21
13,23
14,26 Selller
05,09 ← 11,20
←05,09 ↑
26 ← 02,03 05,09 ←
←04,07 SLACK
St Malo

COURSE BELOW HIGH WATER DOVER

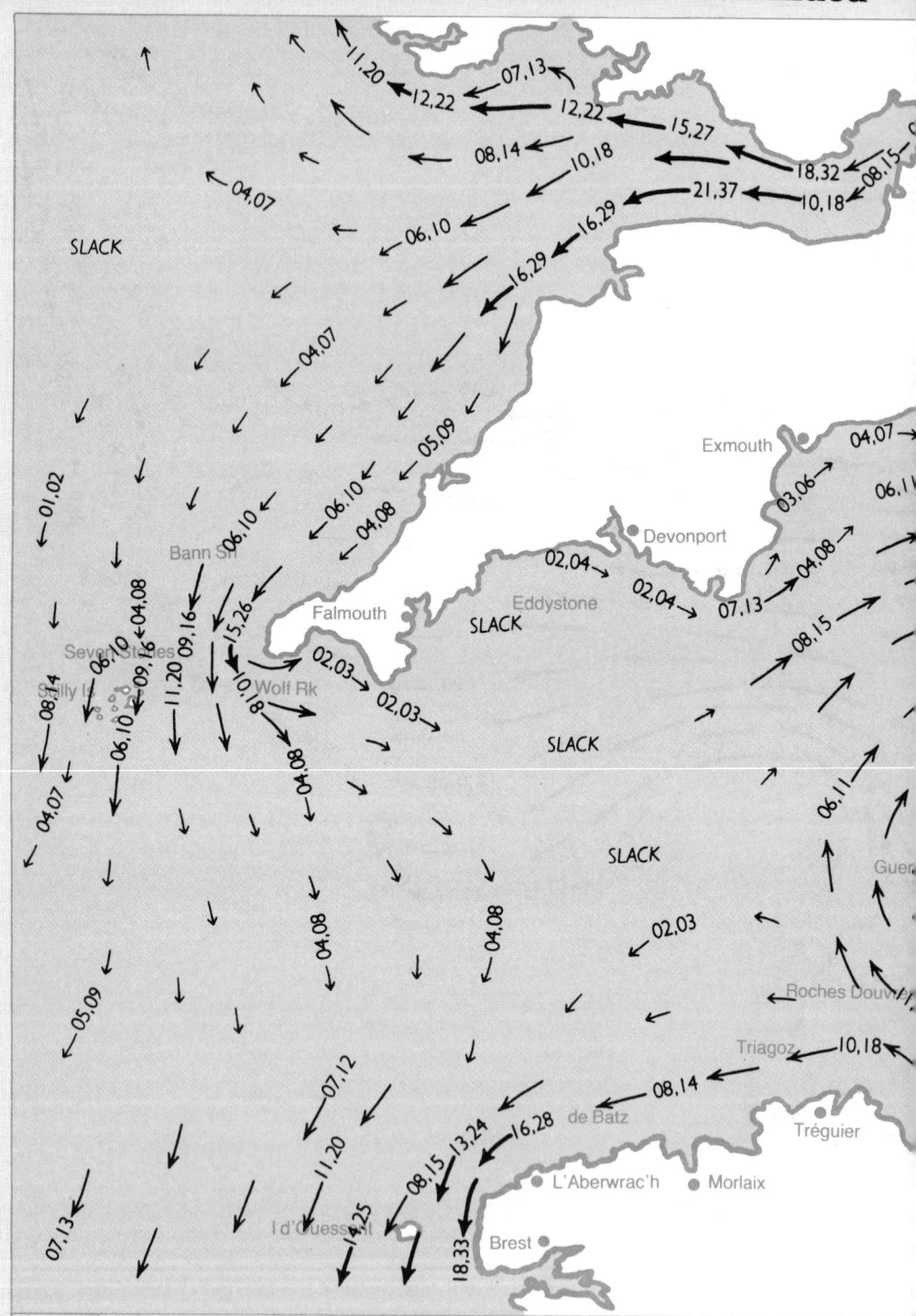

3 HOURS BEFORE HIGH WATER DOVER

Poole
Southampton
Portsmouth
Littlehampton
Shoreham
Newhaven
Dover
Boulogne

11,19
04,08
10,17
07,12
06,10
10,17
15,26
11,19
8,32
14,26
05,09
08,15
05,09
15,27
02,04
07,12

SLACK

13,23
11,19
08,15
13,23
08,15
Tab Tr
15,26
Royal Sovereign
04,08
1,19
11,20
17,31
15,27
13,23
Bassurelle
06,10
03,06
13,23
15,26
14,25
15,26
11,19
20,35
18,32
19,34
11,20
10,17

23,42
18,33
13,24
15,26
Dieppe
10,18,10
13,24
21,38
10,17
10,18
13,23
39,70
09,16
07,12
08,15
Cherbourg
06,11
07,12
06,11
07,12
Le Havre

19,34
10,18
07,13
St Helier
11,20
12,21
09,16
9,17
06,10
04,07
07,12

St Malo

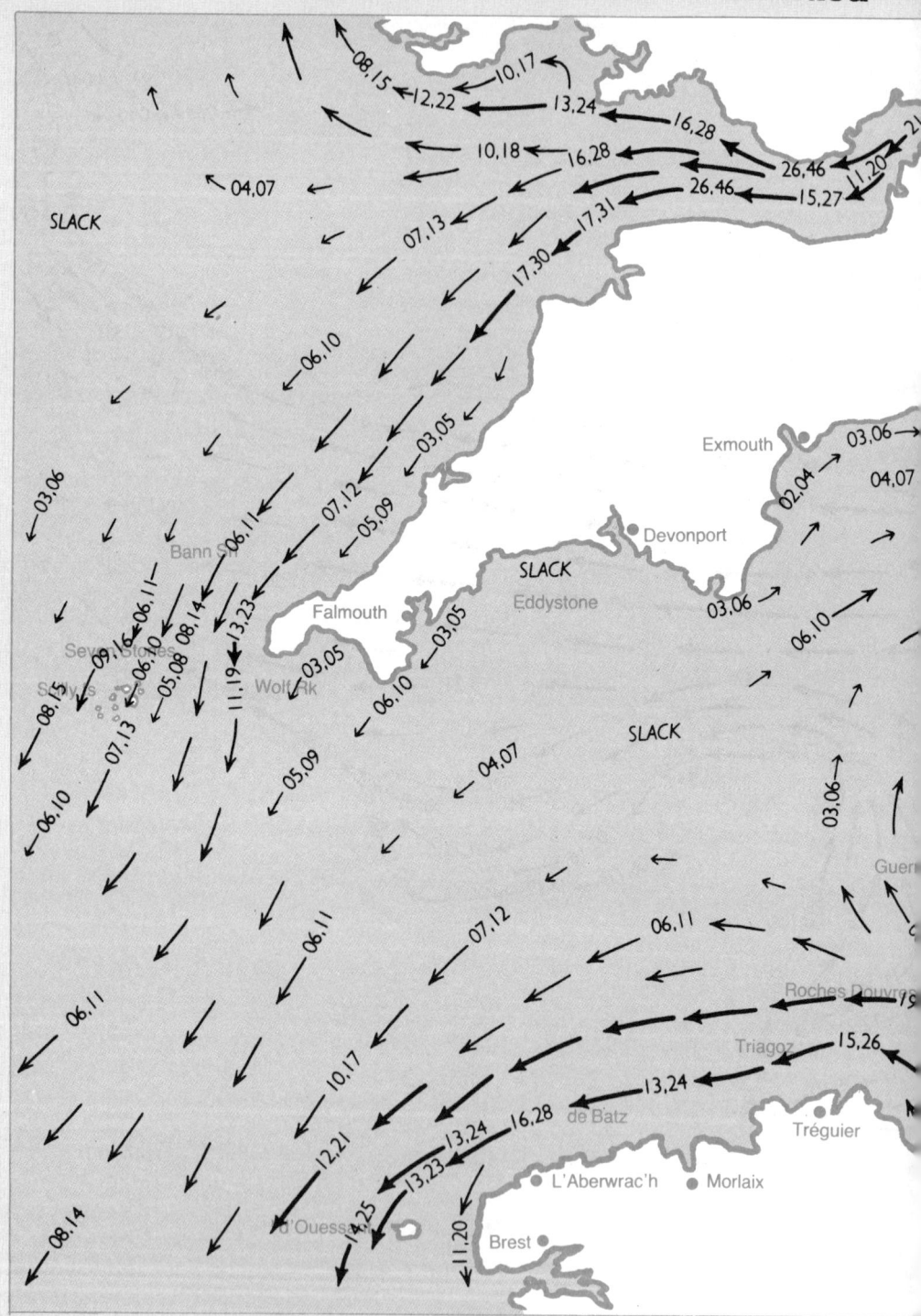

2 HOURS BEFORE HIGH WATER DOVER

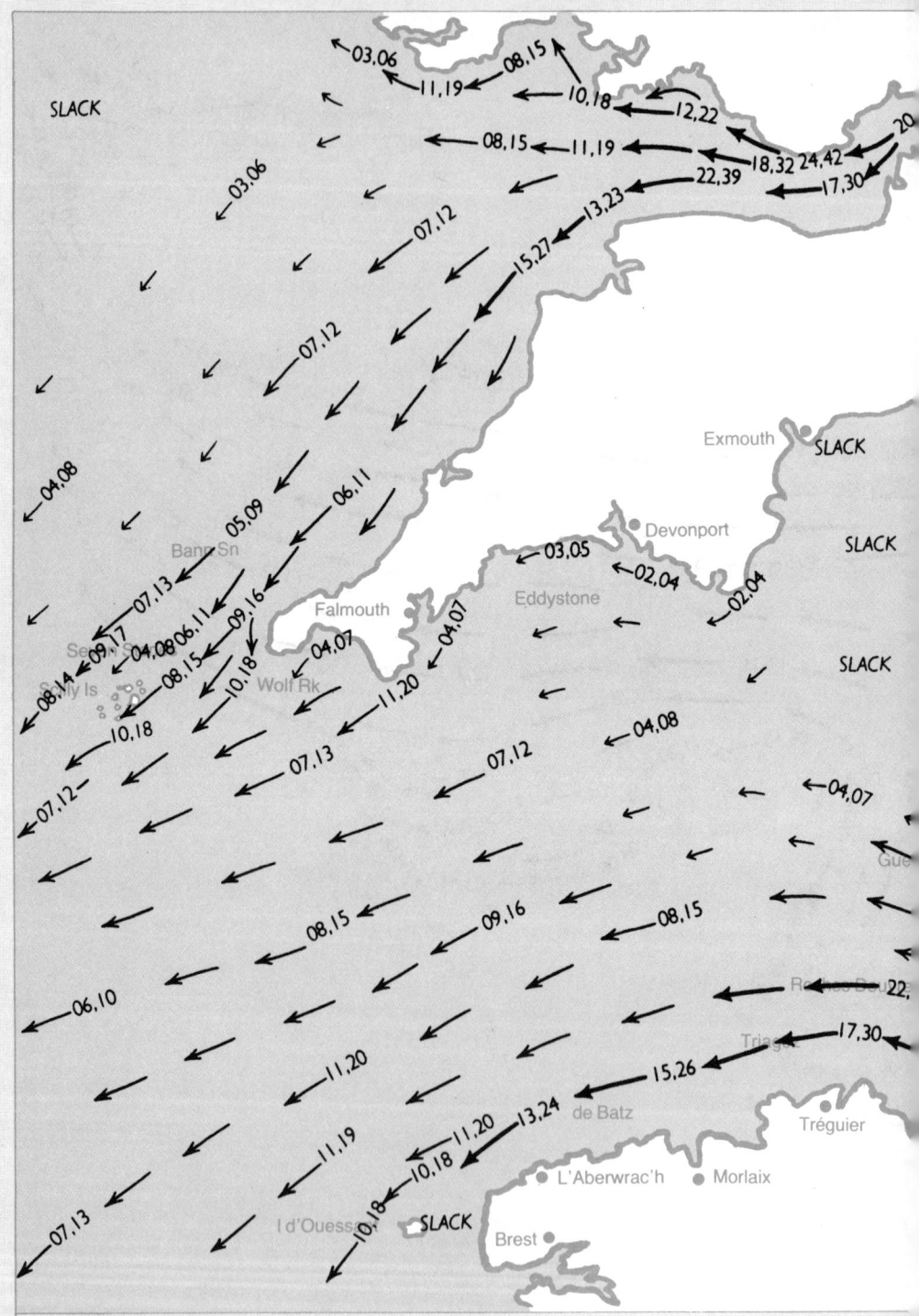

1 HOUR BEFORE HIGH WATER DOVER

Southampton

Portsmouth

Shoreham

Littlehampton

Newhaven

Poole

Dover

SLACK

03,06

02,04

04,08

07,12

06,10

06,10

08,16

Boulogne

SLACK

Royal Sovereign

Bassurelle

Dieppe

Le Havre

Cherbourg

SLACK

SLACK

SLACK

SLACK

St Helier

SLACK

St Malo

09,17

06,10

10,18

08,14

09,16

08,15

03,06

04,08

04,08

07,13

07,13

04,08

07,13

08,15

08,14

08,15

08,15

08,15

07,12

09,16

11,19

09,16

07,13

05,09

09,16

08,14

04,08

06,10

06,10

06,10

07,12

02,04

04,08

03,06

03,06

03,06

05,09

04,07

02,04

03,05

03,05

03,06

03,05

08,14

SLACK

SLACK

06,10

16,28

16,28

15,27

10,18

04,07

07,12

03,05

18

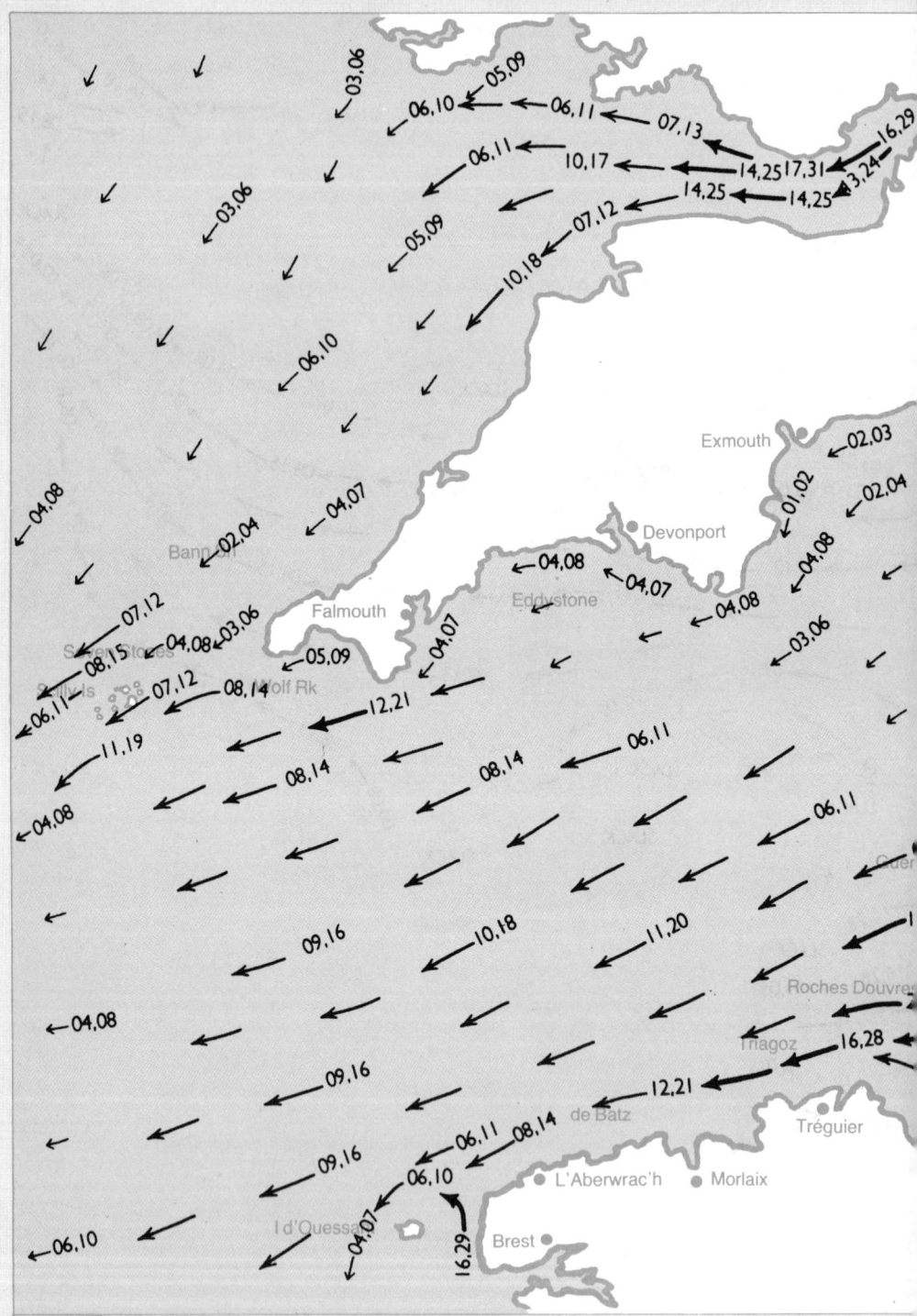

HIGH WATER DOVER

SLACK

07,12 ← 03,05

07,13 → 09,16 ← 08,15 — 09,16

13,24

12,21

07,13

Dover

07,12

08,15 → 11,19

15,26

07,13 → 08,14 → 16,28

04,07 → 08,15 09,17

Southampton

Portsmouth

Shoreham

Littlehampton

Newhaven

← 04,07

SLACK

01,02 →

Boulogne

08,14

Poole

08,15

Royal Sovereign

06,10 → 08,14

04,07 ← 08,15

05,09 ← 03,06

← 08,14

Nab

03,06 ← 06,10

Bassurelle

09,16

10

← 03,05

← 04,07

← 04,08

02,04 →

04,08 →

03,06 →

SLACK

02,04

03,06 →

03,06

← 02,04

← 03,05

03,05 →

Dieppe

14,25

06,11 ← 13,23

02,03 →

05,09

Cherbourg

← 06,10

02,04 →

03,06

03,05 ← 04,07

Le Havre

← 01,02 ← 06,10

11,19 SLACK

St Helier

2,22 ← 06,11

13,24

23 ←

09,16 06,11

← 05,09

St Malo

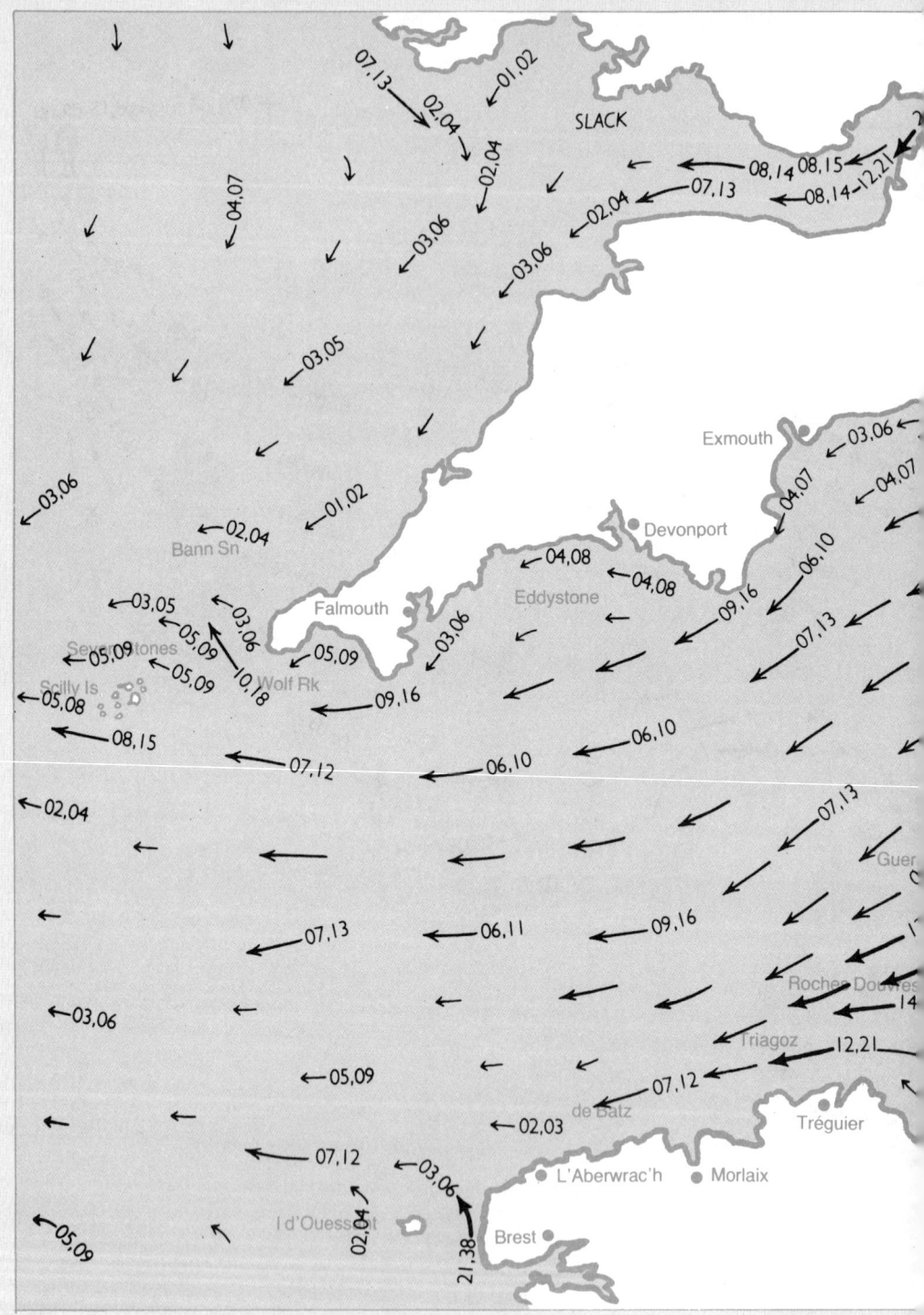

1 HOUR AFTER HIGH WATER DOVER

SLACK 07.13

SLACK

←03.05

Dover

13.23

17.30

13.24

07.13

17.30

11.19

13.23

03.05→11.19

06.11

08.14

22.39

Boulogne

11.20

Southampton

Portsmouth

Shoreham

Littlehampton

Newhaven

08.14

04.08

06.11

Poole

←10.18

07.12

←04.08

SLACK

←11.19

Royal Sovereign

Bassurelle

9

12.21←11.20

←08.15

13.24

←11.19

09.17

12.21

13.24

SLACK

←11.19

13.24

13.24

←04.08

←04.08

02.03

←13.23

09.16

SLACK

←04.08

13.24

06.11

←04.07

SLACK

Dieppe

.30

13.24

12.21

17.30

15.27

26.47

11.20←03.06

←04.07

←11.19

Cherbourg

08.14

09.16←06.10

Le Havre

←04.07

←03.05

←03.06

09.16

Helier

04.07

08.15

←03.05

7.12

.18

←06.10

06.11

13

SLACK

St Malo

2 HOURS AFTER HIGH WATER DOVER

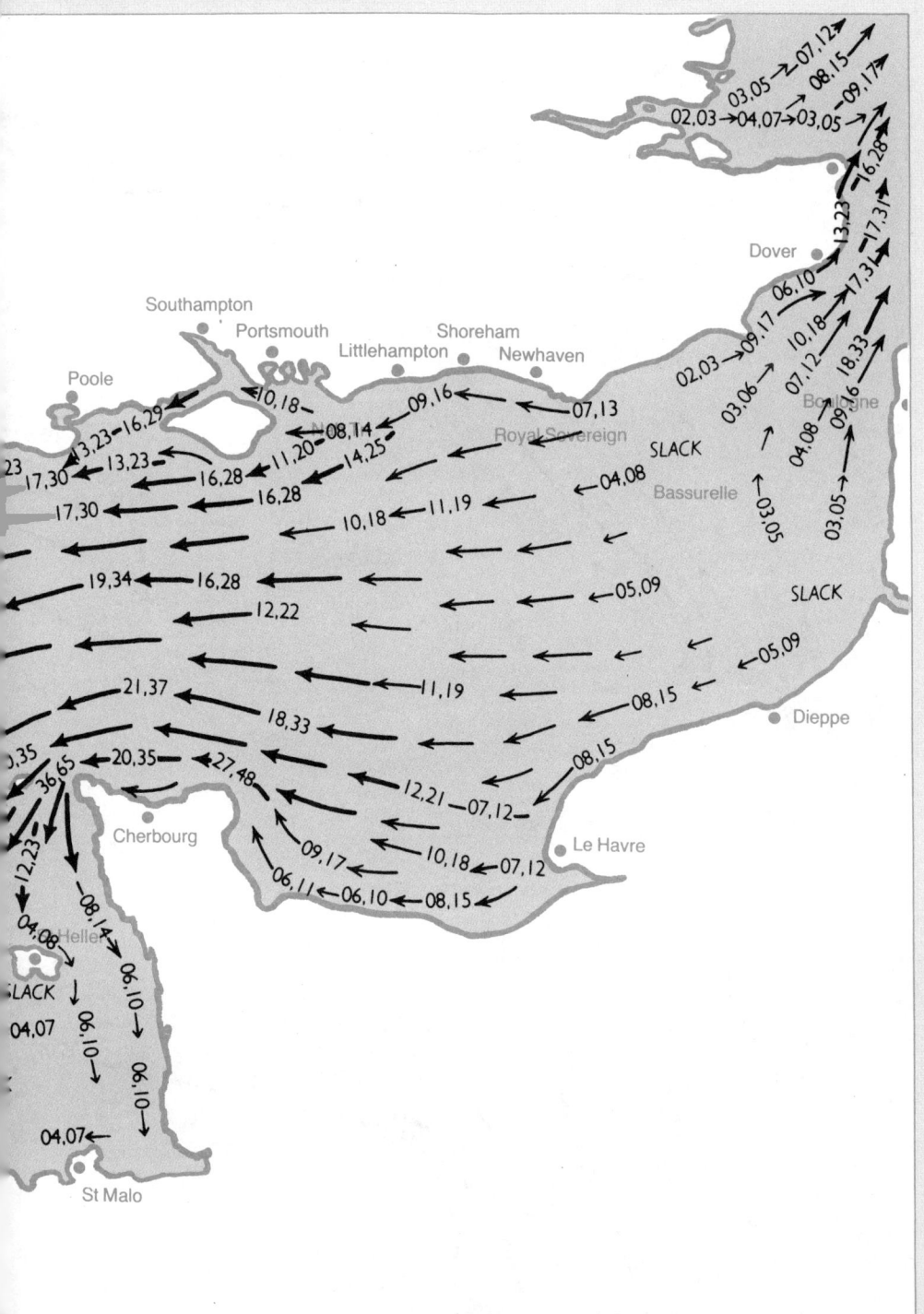

TIDAL STREAM ATLAS Continued

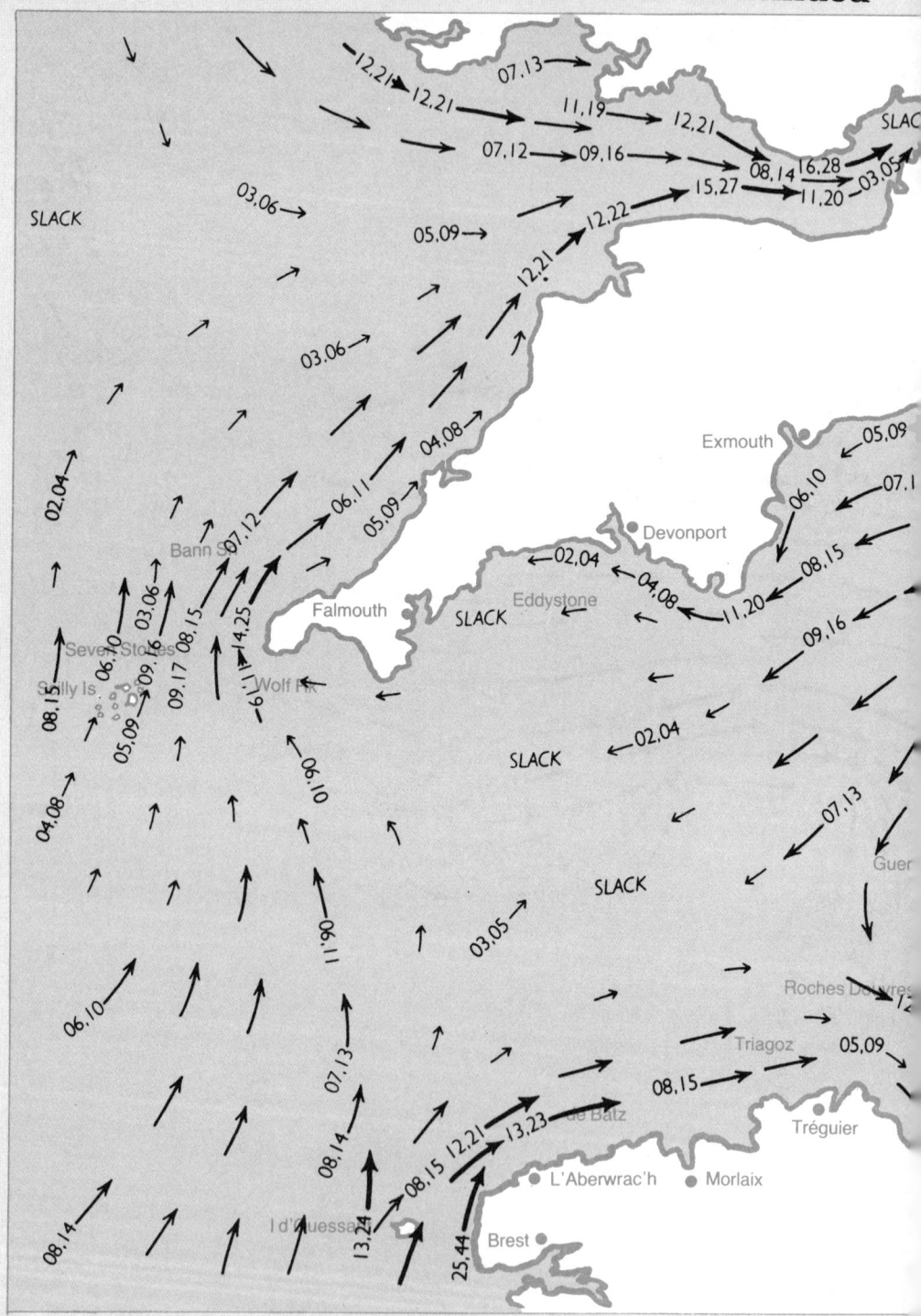

3 HOURS AFTER HIGH WATER DOVER

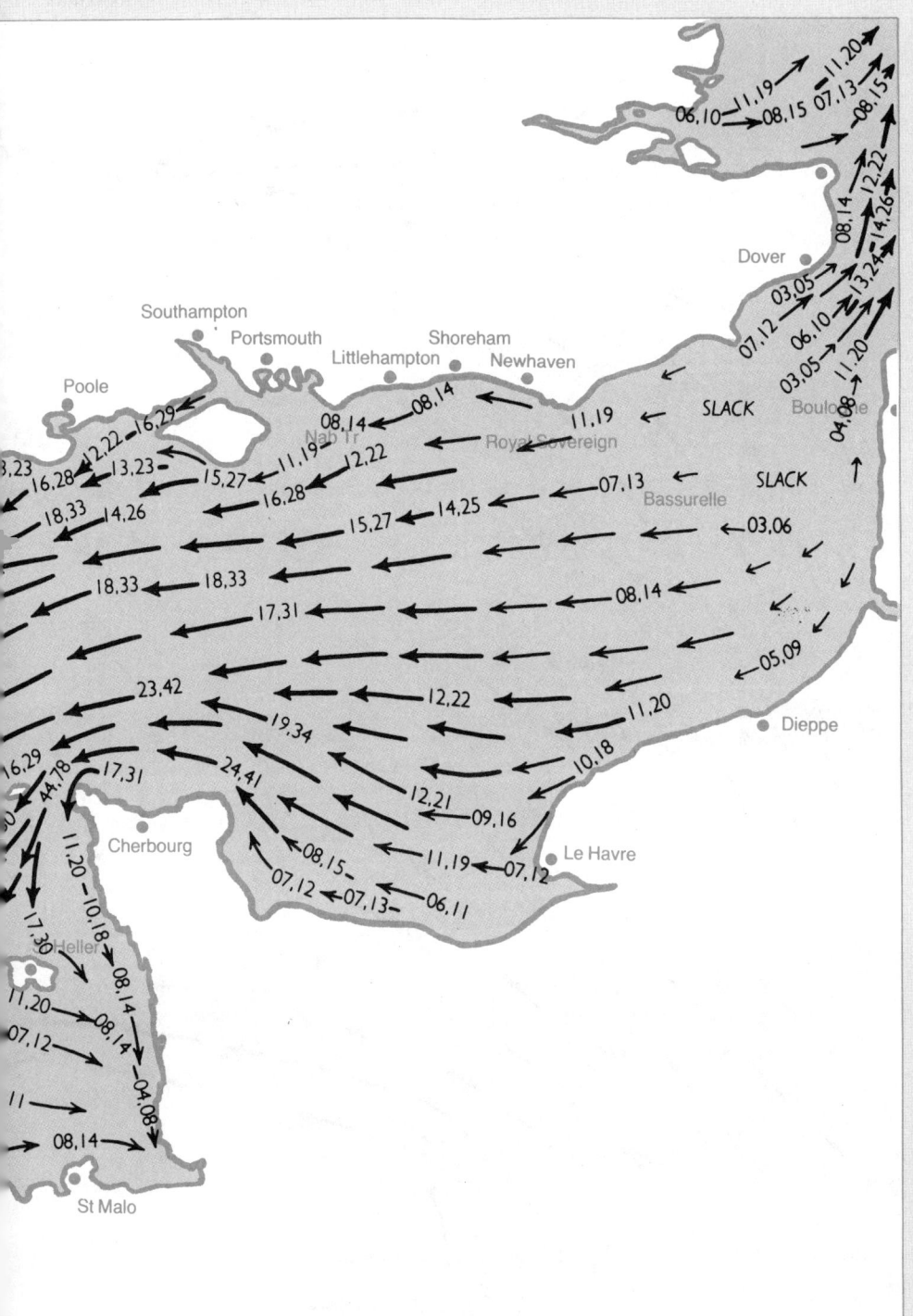

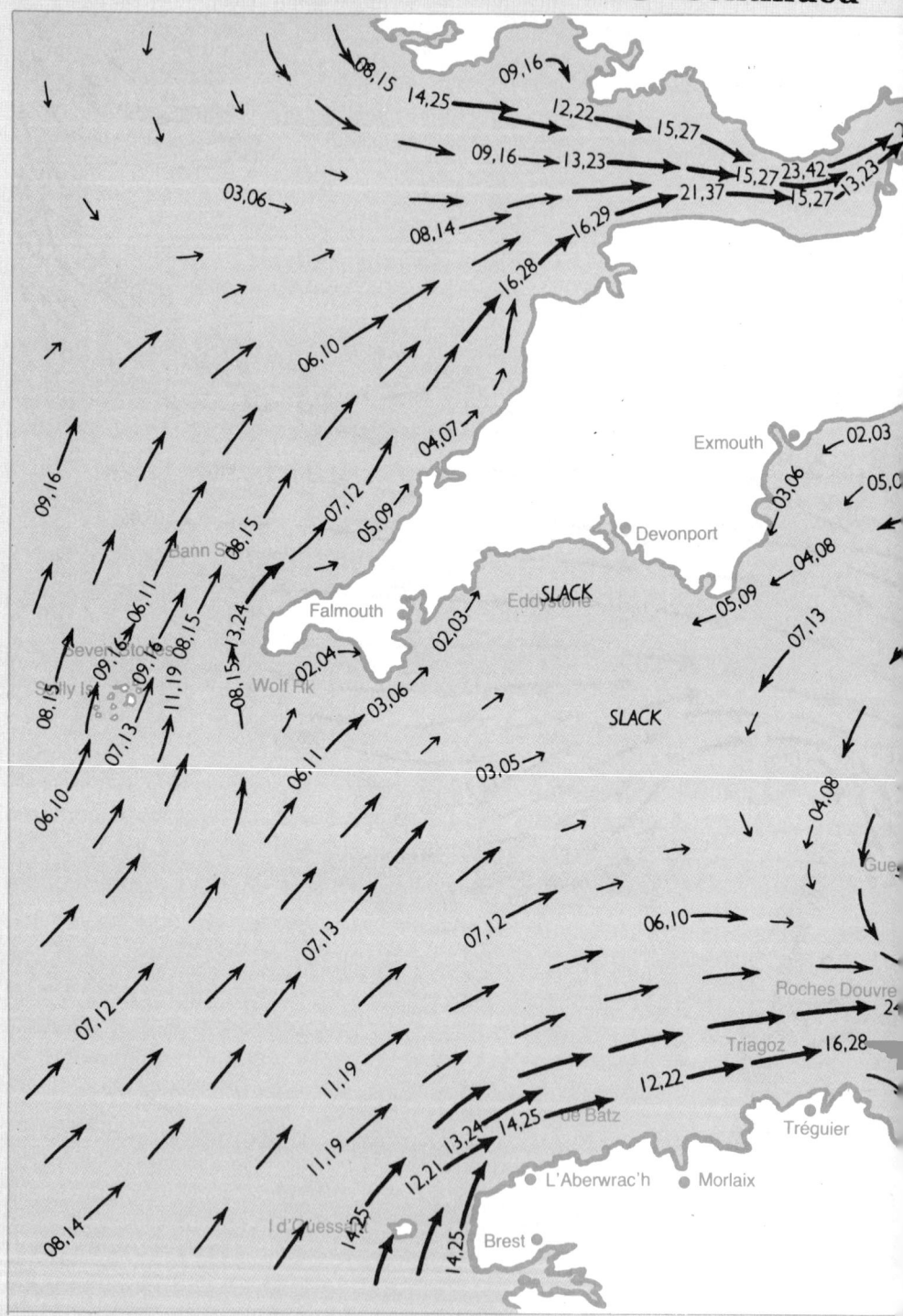

4 HOURS AFTER HIGH WATER DOVER

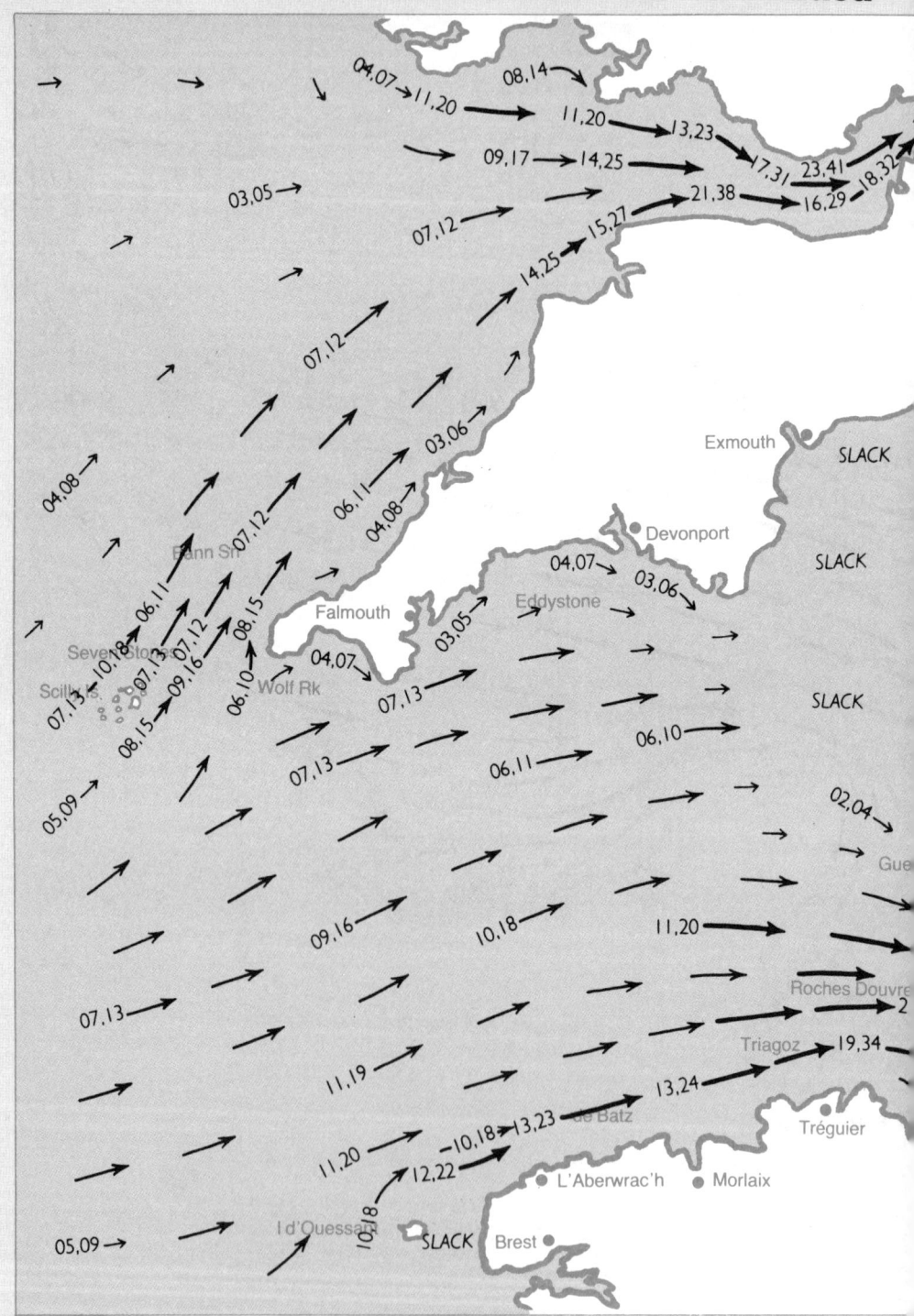

04,07→11,20   08,14
11,20   13,23
09,17→14,25   17,31   23,41   18,32
21,38   16,29
03,05→
07,12   15,27
14,25
07,12
03,06
06,11   03,06
04,08→
Exmouth   SLACK
04,08→
Devonport   SLACK
Fann St.07,12
04,07   03,06
Seven Stones   06,11   08,15
Falmouth   Eddystone→
Scilly Is.   10,18   07,12   07,12   03,05
07,13 Is.   09,16   04,07→   SLACK
06,10   Wolf Rk.   07,13→
08,15   06,10→
05,09→   07,13→   06,11→   02,04→
Gue
07,13→   11,20
09,16→   10,18→   Roches Douvre
2
Triagoz   19,34
07,13→   13,24
11,19   de Batz
11,20→ →10,18→13,23   Tréguier
12,22   L'Aberwrac'h   Morlaix
05,09→   I d'Ouessant   SLACK   Brest

5 HOURS AFTER HIGH WATER DOVER

Southampton

Portsmouth

Shoreham

Littlehampton   Newhaven

Poole

Dover   SLACK

SLACK

SLACK

02.04

02.04

05.09   04.08

04.07

03.05

03.06

Boulogne

Bassurelle

09.16 – 10.17   09.16

08.15   08.14

08.15

03,06

04,08

03,05   03,05   03,05

03,06

04,07

03,06

04,07   05,09   Crab Tr   04,07   Royal Sovereign   09,17   05,09   05,09

07,13   06,10   05,09   09,16   05,09

04,08   05,09   07,12

08,15   09,16   09,16   09,16   07,12

16,29   09,17

12,22   09,16   07,12

08,14   10,18   Dieppe

03,05   03,06   05,09   09,16

06,10   08,15   06,11   Le Havre

Cherbourg   04,08   SLACK

09,17   08,15   04,07   03,06

24   23,41

St Helier   08,14   03,05

19,34

22,40   11,19

13,24   09,17

13,23

St Malo

6 HOURS AFTER HIGH WATER DOVER

CHANNEL DISTANCE CHARTS

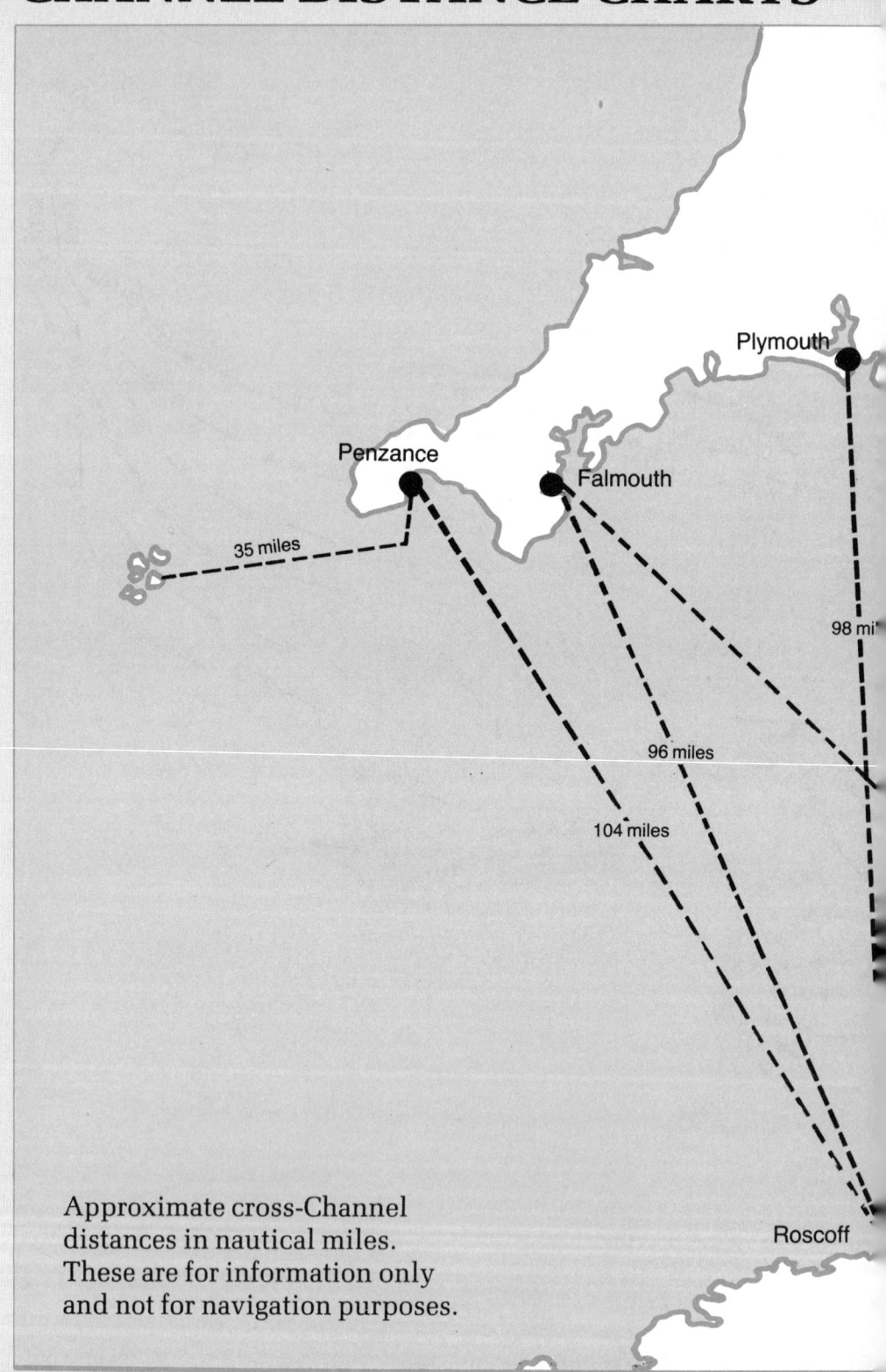

Penzance

35 miles

Falmouth

Plymouth

98 mi*

96 miles

104 miles

Roscoff

Approximate cross-Channel
distances in nautical miles.
These are for information only
and not for navigation purposes.

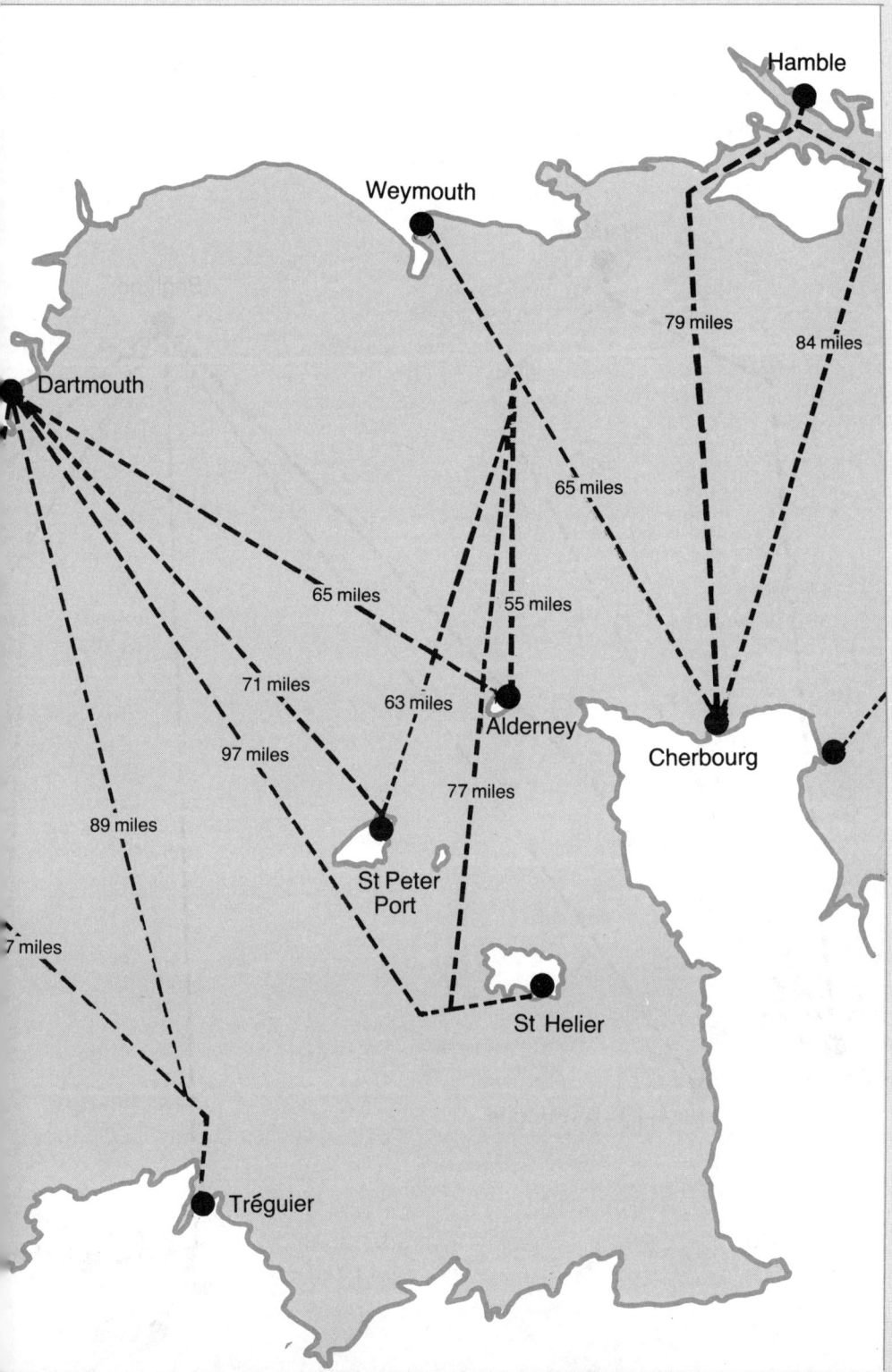

Hamble

Weymouth

79 miles

84 miles

Dartmouth

65 miles

65 miles

55 miles

71 miles

63 miles

Alderney

97 miles

Cherbourg

77 miles

89 miles

St Peter
Port

7 miles

St Helier

Tréguier

CHANNEL DISTANCE CHARTS

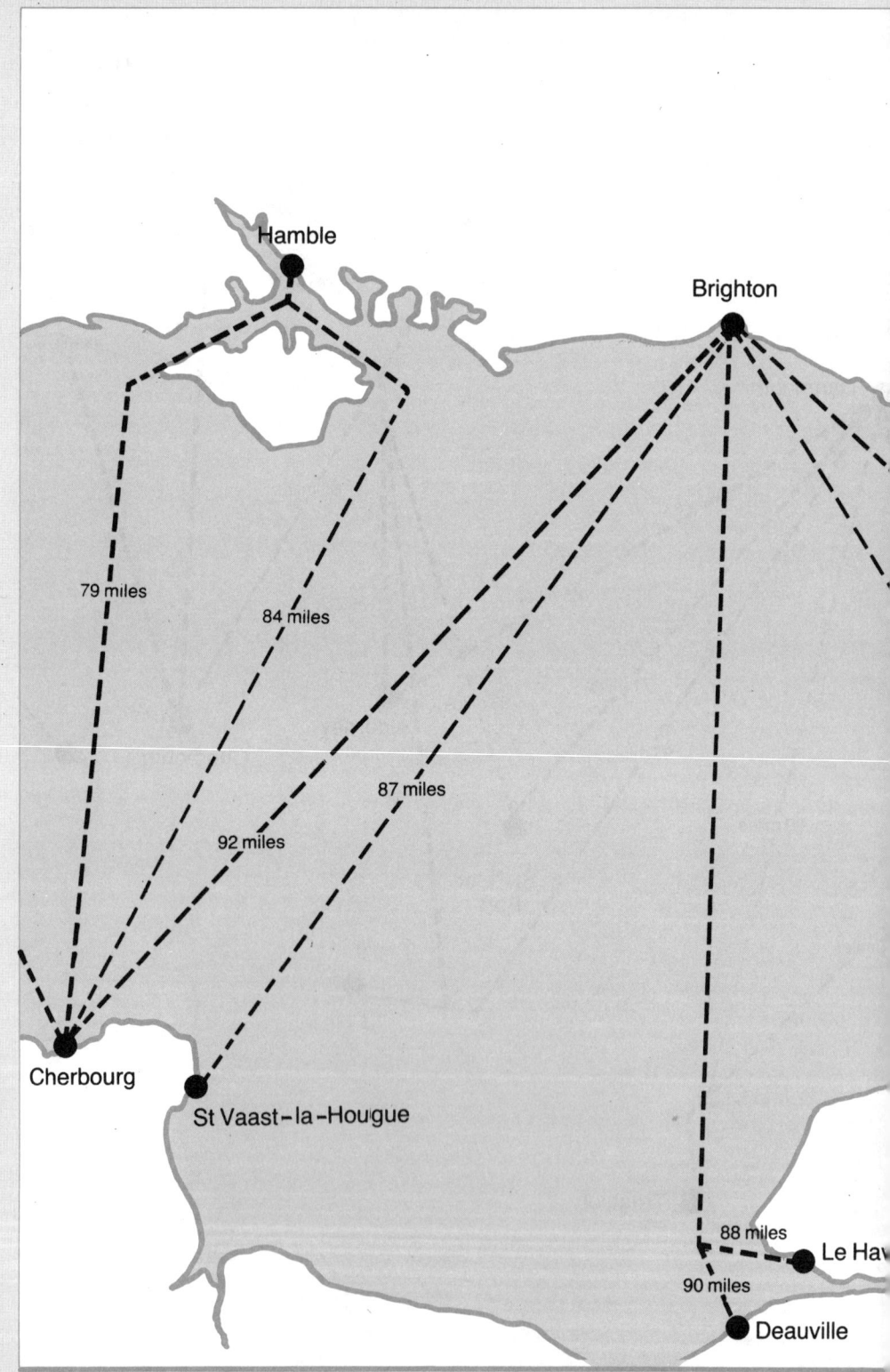

Hamble

Brighton

79 miles

84 miles

87 miles

92 miles

Cherbourg

St Vaast-la-Hougue

88 miles

Le Hav

90 miles

Deauville

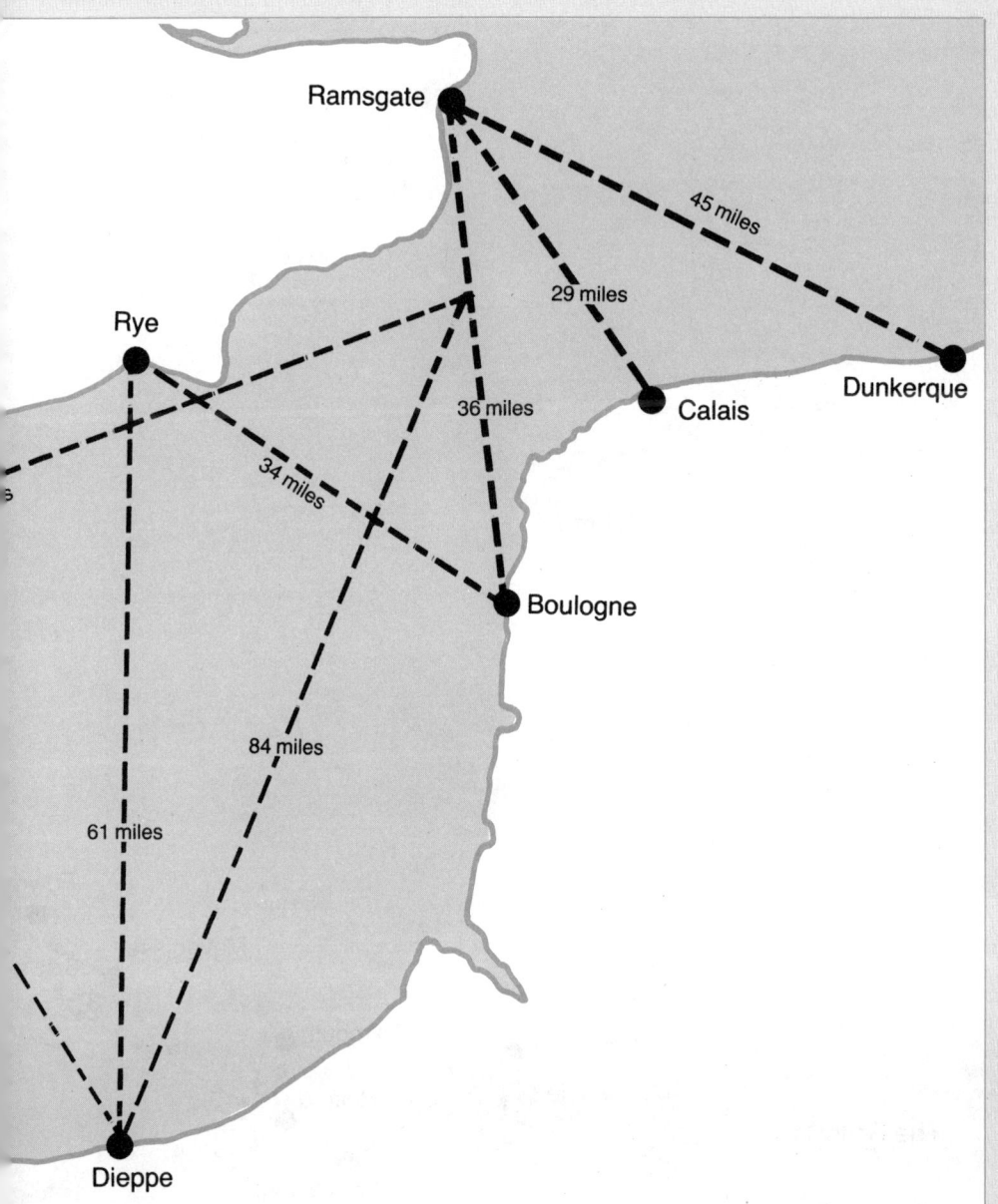

Ramsgate

45 miles

29 miles

Dunkerque

Rye

36 miles

Calais

34 miles

Boulogne

84 miles

61 miles

Dieppe

Approximate cross-Channel
distances in nautical miles.
These are for information only
and not for navigation purposes.

CHANNEL DISTANCE CHARTS

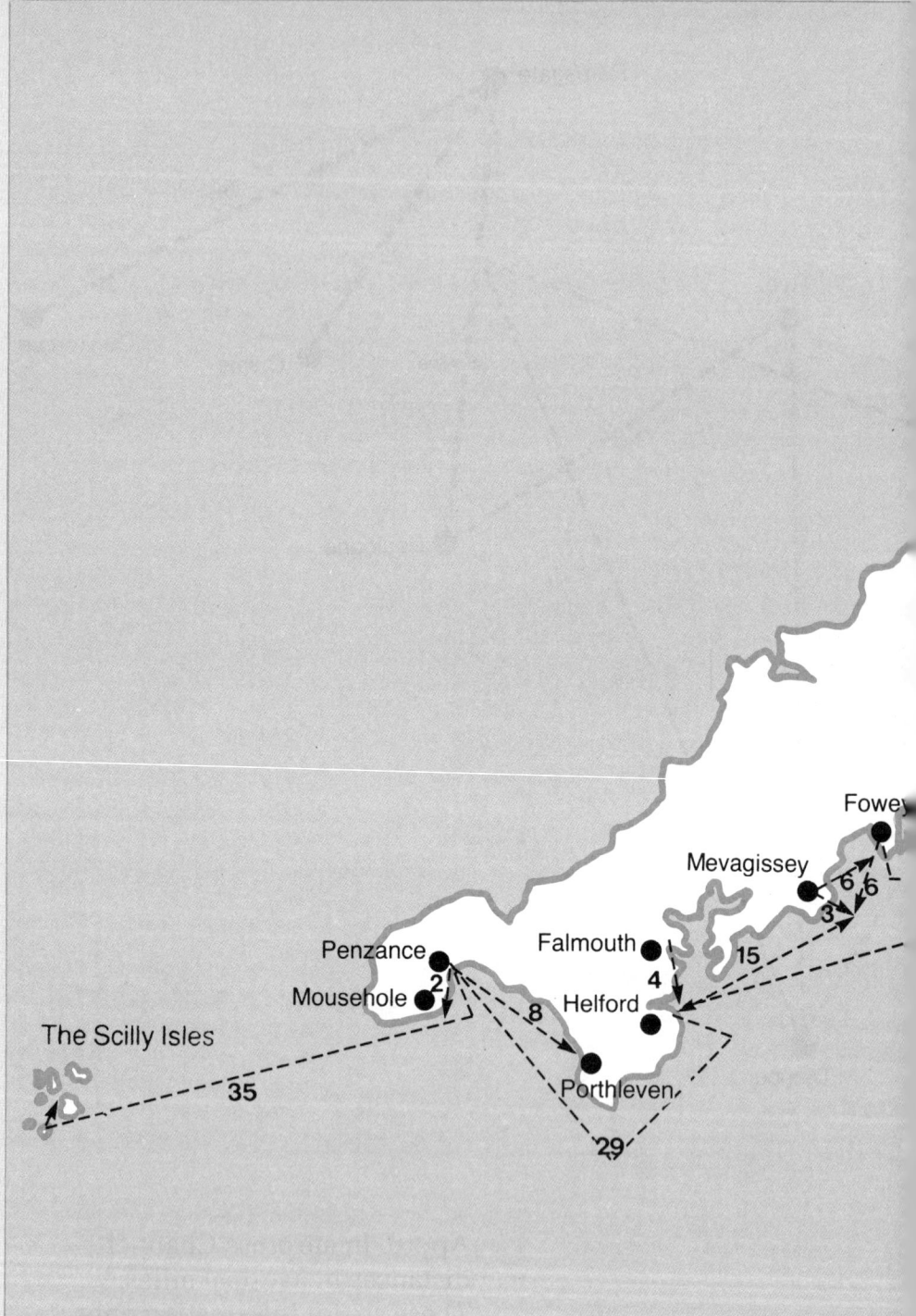

The Scilly Isles

Penzance

Mousehole

35

8

Porthleven

29

Helford

Falmouth

4

15

Mevagissey

3

6 6

Fowey

2

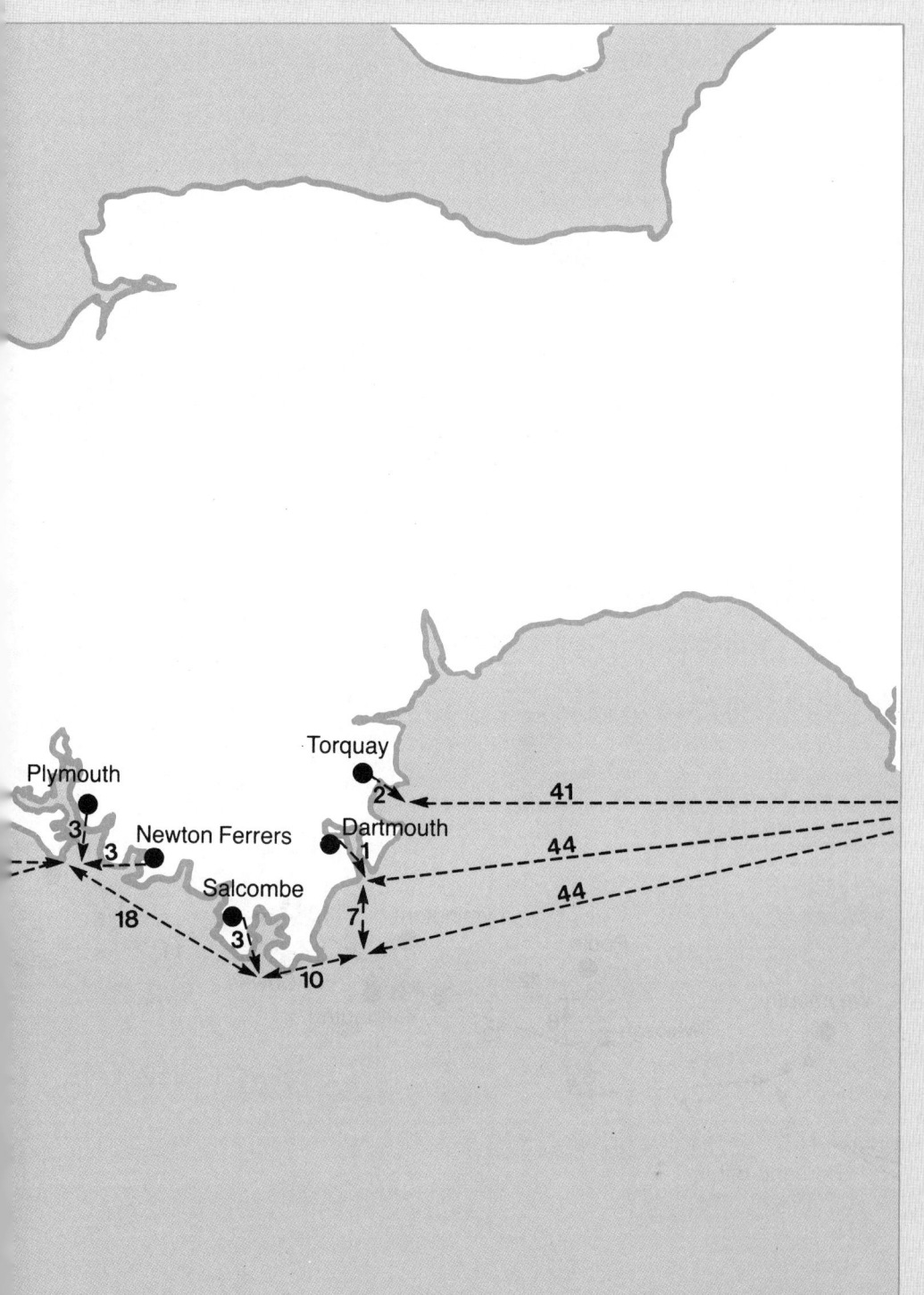

Torquay

Plymouth

Newton Ferrers

Dartmouth

Salcombe

41

44

44

3

3

18

3

10

7

1

2

Distances indicated
are in nautical miles.

CHANNEL DISTANCE CHARTS

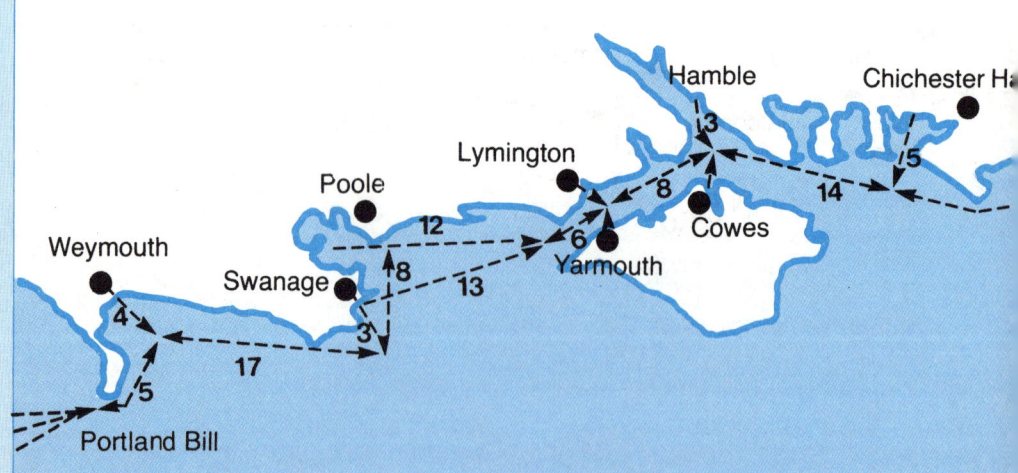

Hamble

Chichester Ha

Lymington

13

Poole

8

14

5

Cowes

Weymouth

12

6

Yarmouth

Swanage

8

13

4

3

17

5

Portland Bill

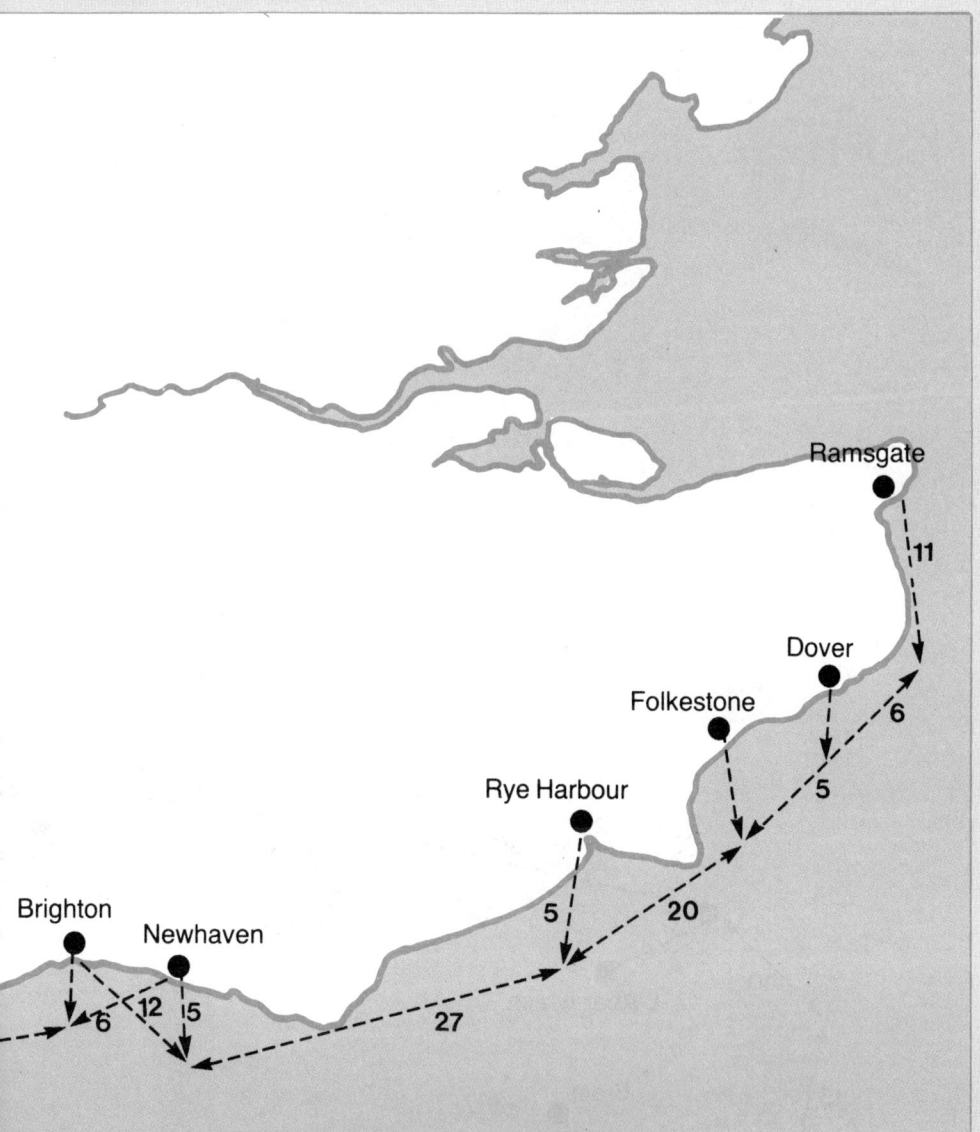

Ramsgate

11

Dover

Folkestone

6

5

Rye Harbour

5

20

Brighton

Newhaven

6 12 5

27

Distances indicated
are in nautical miles.

CHANNEL DISTANCE CHARTS

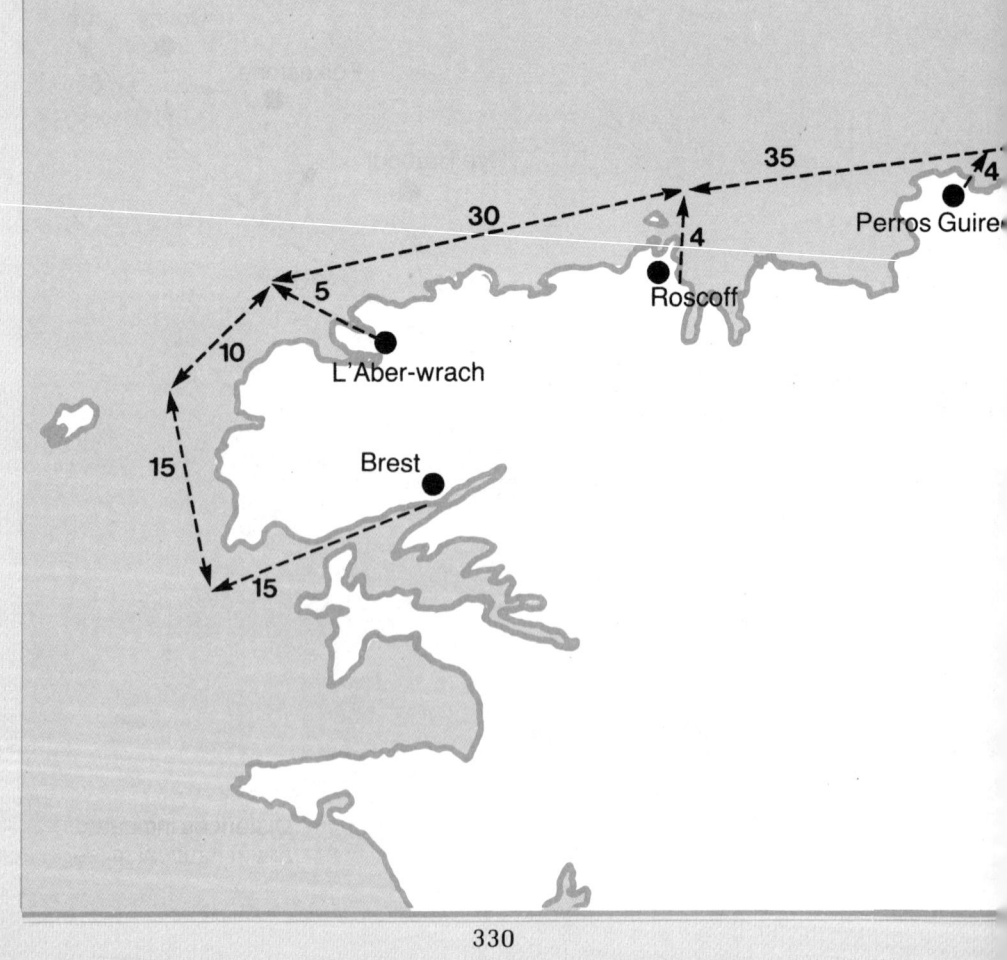

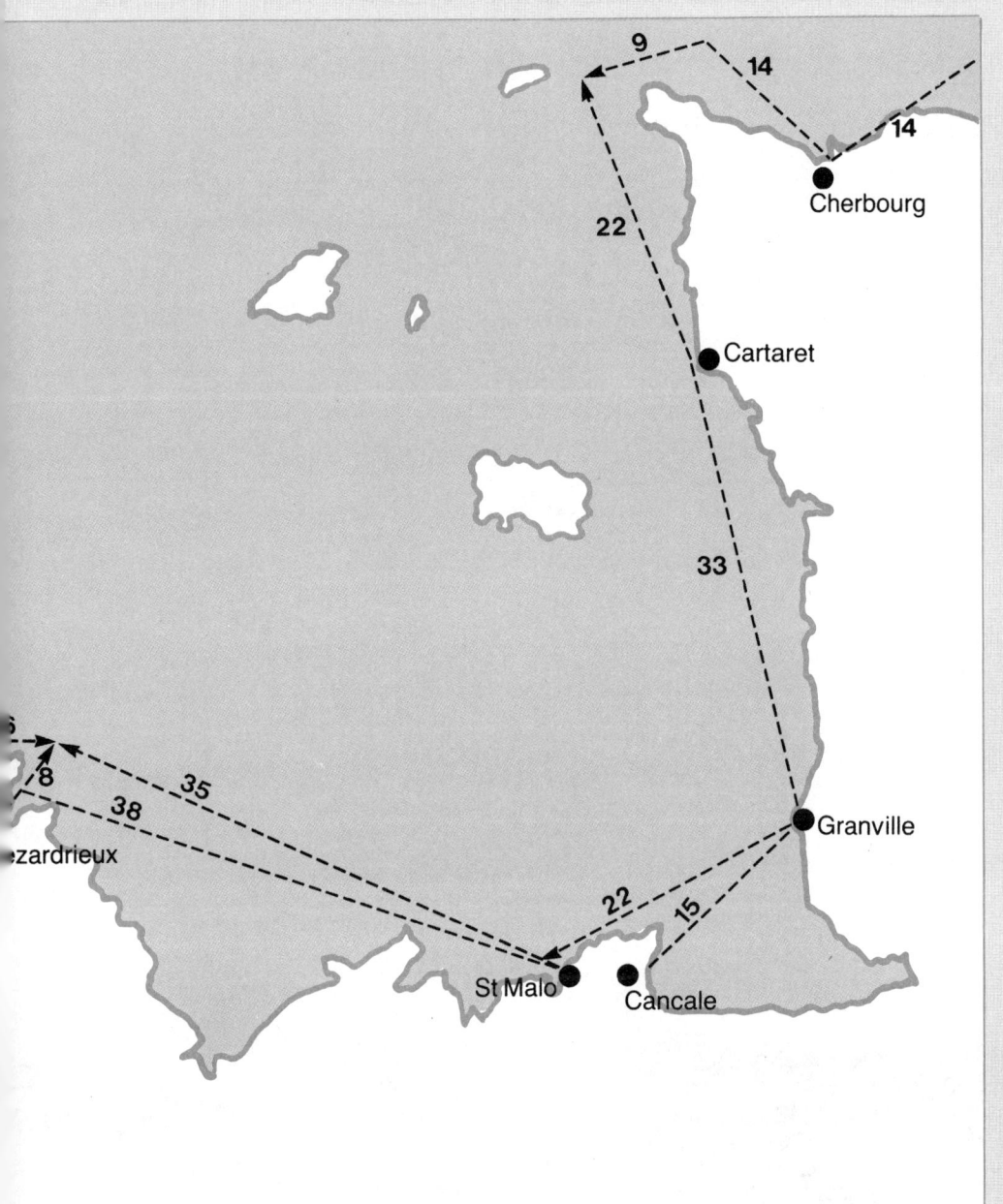

9

14

14

Cherbourg

22

Cartaret

33

8

35

38

ezardrieux

Granville

22

15

St Malo

Cancale

Distances indicated
are in nautical miles.

CHANNEL DISTANCE CHARTS

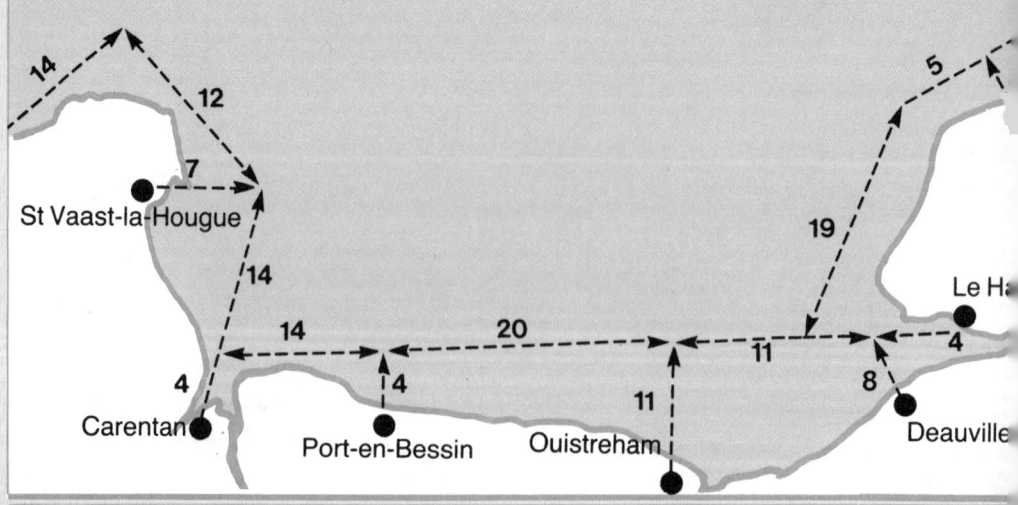

14

12

7

St Vaast-la-Hougue

14

14

20

11

5

19

4

8

11

11

Le H

Carentan

4

Port-en-Bessin

4

Ouistreham

Deauville

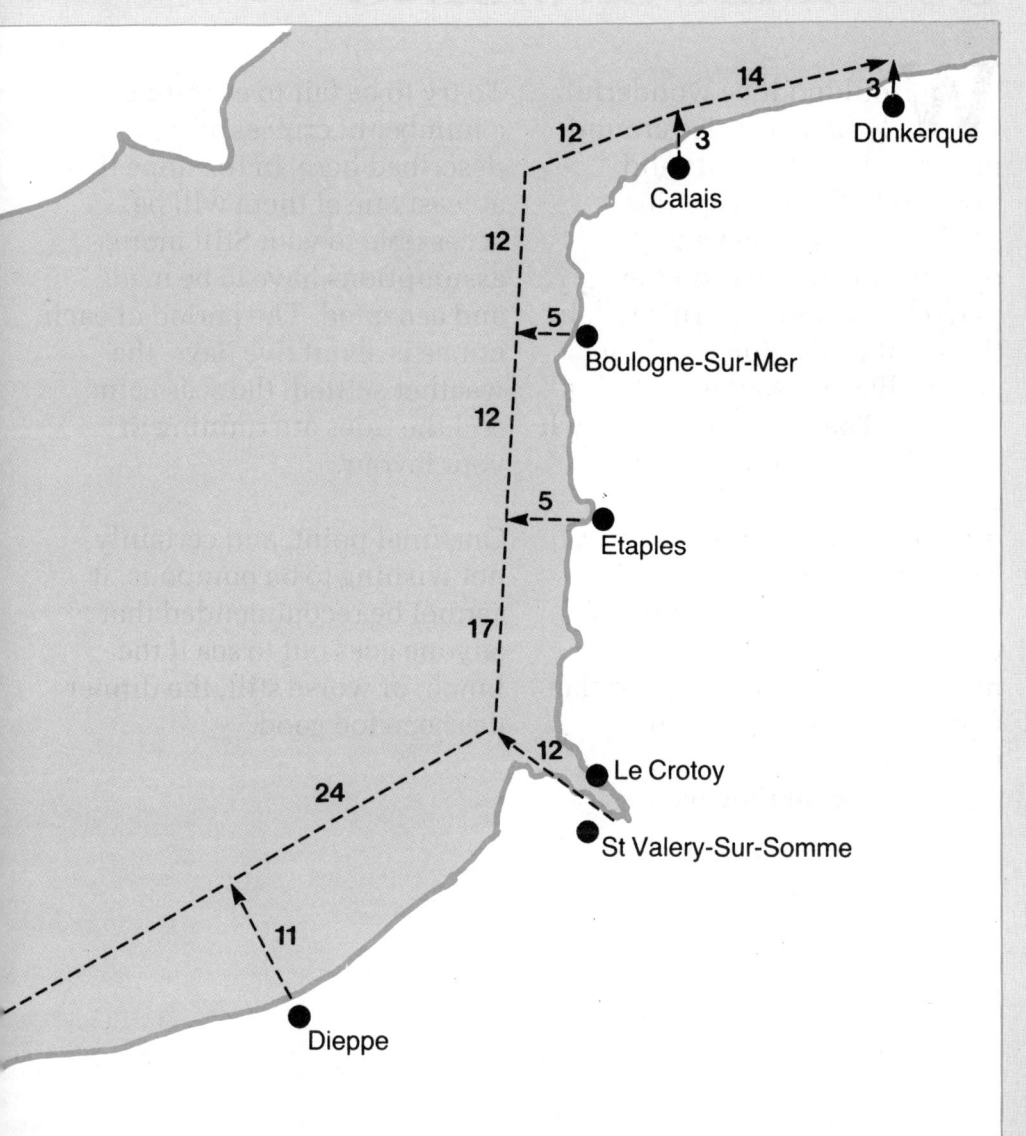

14

12

3
Dunkerque

3
Calais

12

5
Boulogne-Sur-Mer

12

5
Etaples

17

12
Le Crotoy

St Valery-Sur-Somme

24

11

Dieppe

Distances indicated
are in nautical miles.

GOURMET CRUISING

Wouldn't it be wonderful to plan a cruise around memorable restaurants and pubs? While preparing this guide there has been every opportunity to muse on the perfect gastronomic cruise . . . in the event perfection is seldom achievable and so it is with this concept. The best place for lunch is maybe to be found on the Channel Islands and that for dinner a twelve-hour sail away. Inevitably there must be a compromise. Also, it would be unfair to leave readers, who for no fault of their own beyond that of mooring their boat in the wrong place, drooling at the thought of what they were missing.

To try to be fair to everyone, a number of cruises are described here, in the hope that at least one of them will be accessible to you. Still more assumptions have to be made and accepted. The period of each cruise is about five days, the weather settled, the seas calm and the tides are running in your favour.

One final point, and certainly not wishing to be pompous, it cannot be recommended that anyone goes out to sea if the lunch, or worse still, the dinner has been too good.

Cruise 1
FALMOUTH – FOWEY – PLYMOUTH – HELFORD RIVER – FALMOUTH

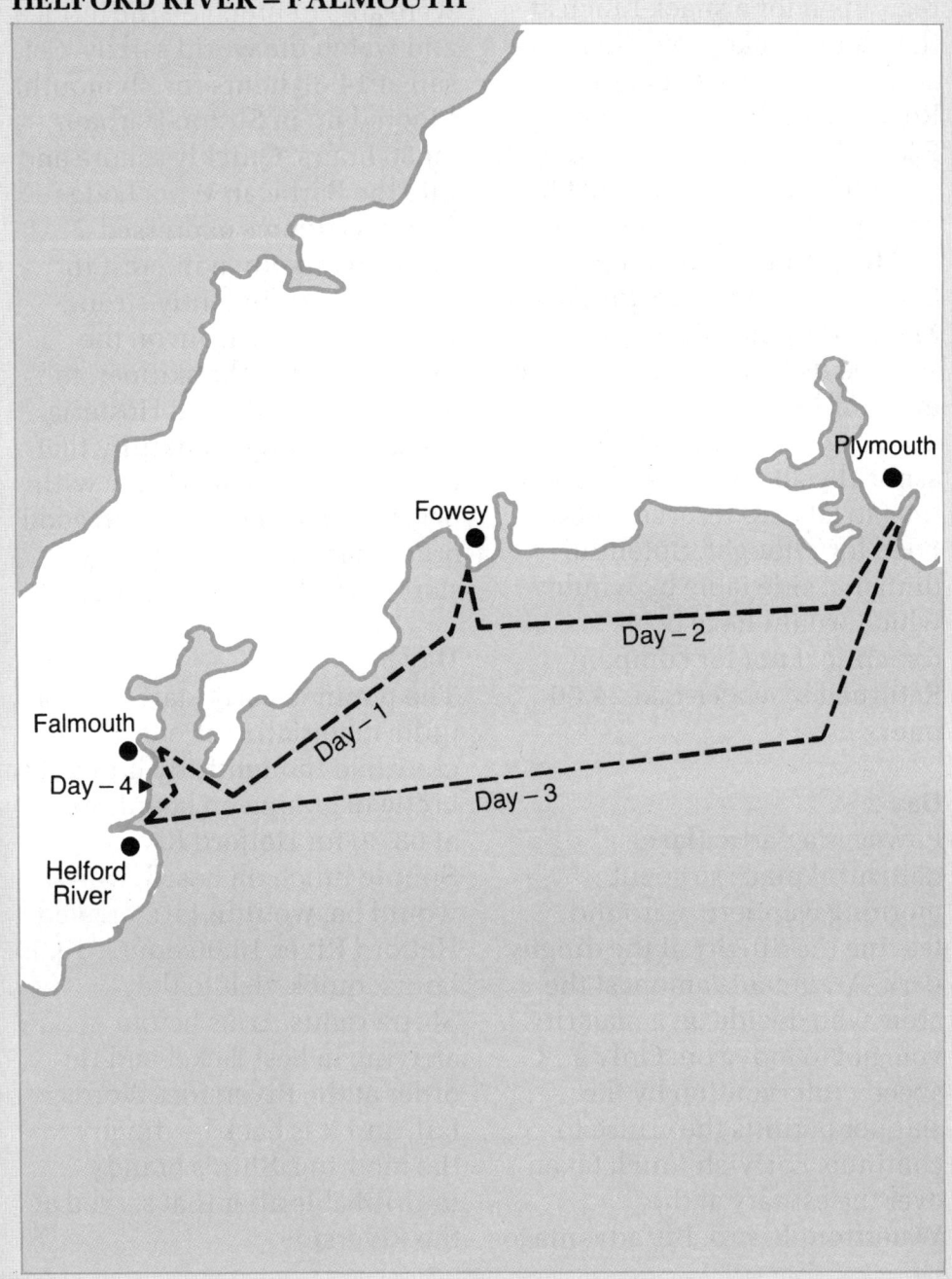

GOURMET CRUISING

Day 1

The crew enjoyed a leisurely morning in Falmouth and regrouped for a snack lunch at the Chain Locker. Weather sunny and views over Carrick Roads splendid. All agreed that E.T.D should be 13.15. Williams realised at last moment that he had forgotten washing kit and had to go into town to replace. Set sail at 14.00 hours for Fowey. Met by Harbour Master who showed us to a mooring. On the mooring by 19.00 hours. Called up the water-taxi and were ashore by 20.15 hours in good time to take up reserved table at Food for Thought. Splendid dinner at side table by window which would have been romantic if not for company. Returned by water-taxi 24.00 hours.

Day 2

Fowey is a particularly delightful place so spent morning wandering around, leaving the dinghy at the dinghy park. Arguments amongst the crew who decide on a majority vote not to move on. Only a speedy intervention by the skipper permits the cruise to continue. Earlyish lunch taken over the estuary at the Waterfront Bistro. Big advantage that they have a dinghy park. Weather warm and sunny so were able to lunch on the terrace and watch the world sail by. Set sail at 14.30 hours for Plymouth. Moored up in Sutton Harbour 19.30 hours. Quickly ashore and into the Barbican Wine Lodge where Williams expressed a hitherto unknown interest in jazz. Were sufficiently strong-willed to leave, again on the intervention of the skipper, to take up reservation at Hosteria Romana, noting thankfully that the Italians eat late. Heavy with pasta, returned on board in good order ready to make an early start the following morning.

Day 3

The planned early start did not quite materialise as one of the crew had thoughtfully brought a bottle of grappa on board, so left at 08.30 for Helford River. Simple lunch on board, well it would be, wouldn't it? Arrived Helford River 18.00 hours. 19.00 hours: quick visit to the Shipwrights Arms before arriving in best jacket and tie order at the Riverside. Words fail, and it is back by dinghy to the mooring. Ship's brandy undrinkable after that served at the Riverside.

Day 4
10.00 hours: leisurely start for
trip to Restronguet Pool. Arrived
13.00 hours and anchored in
Pool before setting off by dinghy
to the Pandora Inn for lunch.
Many others with the same idea
and were forced to abandon
ideas of a simple snack and opt
for a table in the restaurant, still
most enjoyable. Back to the boat
14.45 hours and returned to
mooring at Falmouth 16.00
hours. Decided to drive back the
following morning and called to
see if table available at Sea Food
Bar. Were relieved that one still
was since by now all crew
smitten with hunger pains.
Williams surprised that the crew
can actually fit in this tiny
restaurant. Excellent meal and
crew retired relatively early at
23.00 hours.

GOURMET CRUISING

Cruise 2
HAMBLE – YARMOUTH – SALCOMBE –

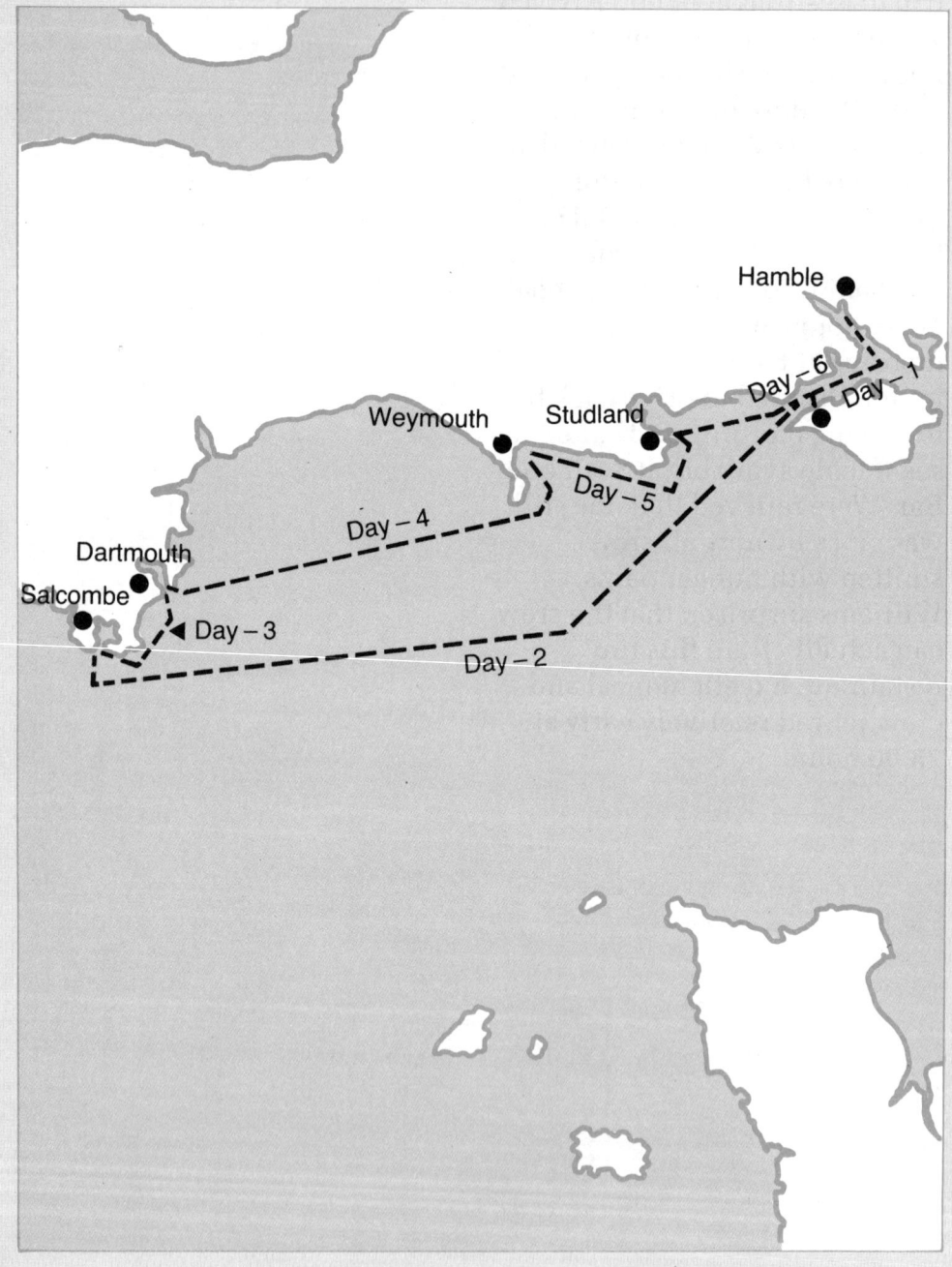

Day 1

10.00 hours: depart Hamble for Yarmouth. Racing off Cowes required more attention from crew than had bargained for. Numerous protests but at last were through fleet. Avoiding action needed due to departure of ferry from Yarmouth which caught crew flat-footed or maybe, as it was now after 12.00 hours, it may be more charitable to say they were all below searching for the beer. Williams, it transpired, had left it in the boot of his car. With much help from the Harbour Master moored up at 12.30 hours. Arguments amongst the crew as to who was to inflate dinghy to take party up to Puffins Fisheries to purchase lobsters for lunch. Only after their departure was it realised that the other shore party had no way of getting ashore to obtain provisions of wine. Williams had left this with the beer in the boot of his car. Shore party took water-taxi to the jetty and obtained wine. Then went to the George as the realisation dawned that the lobster party were rowing up the Yar against the tide. Returned to boat at 14.00 hours. Lobster party already on board and fine meal had by all. Departed 19.00 hours for night sail to Salcombe.

Day 2

Usual arguments about Portland race. Skipper intervened and it was left a good five miles to starboard. Past Portland 02.00 hours. Start Point looking majestically sinister on the bow at dawn. Williams convinced that it was Berry Head. Fortunately he was not navigating. Start Point turns out to be Berry Head after all and Williams is instantly appointed navigator. 11.00 hours: round Start Point and into the Salcombe estuary at 13.00 hours. Very friendly Harbour Master shows us to a buoy. 13.30 hours: moored up. Dinghy inflated and it is off to join the crowds on the terrace of the Ferry Inn. 16.30 hours: crew set off for the Yacht Club to enjoy a well-earned shower. Rendez-vous at 19.00 hours at the Victoria for some of their magnificent draught Bass. Great difficulty in persuading Williams that his promotion to navigator does not entitle him to be bought beer all night. Repair to Dusters 21.00 hours. Most of the crew have been coming here for years and it never disappoints. Funny looking around and noticing that most of the clientele are trying desperately hard to look like sailors. Crew ignored, as they

GOURMET CRUISING

certainly do not. 23.30 hours: pick up dinghy at Whitestrand and return to boat.

Day 3

Crew rather slow off the mark but land at Whitestrand 09.45. All troop up to Yacht Club to make use of facilities. No hurry this morning. Some of the crew have breakfast at a crêperie near Whitestrand. Skipper and others return to boat which is now sandwiched amongst four other yachts. Skipper starts arguing that lunch should be taken ashore rather than having Williams' wine, pâté and cheese on the run. Consensus amongst those present was that skipper frightened of making a fool of himself in front of other yachtsmen and the wellie brigade on the terrace of the Ferry. Crew absolutely correct. 11.55 hours: skipper and party return ashore and break news re lunch to others. 11.56 hours: after a great deal of persuading, crew join wellie brigade at the Ferry. Skipper spends lunch sitting on the terrace wall willing yachts to move. No problem as there is a long wait for expensive crab sandwiches. 15.00 hours: skipper extracts boat masterfully. 17.00 hours: round Start Point and heading for the Mew stone. 18.45 hours: moor up at Dart Marina. Showered in hotel. Some of crew arranged to meet at the Dartmouth Arms, others went to the Old Country House. 20.30 hours: crew met at the Carved Angel. A difficult choice as some of the crew wanted to try Bistro 33. Skipper prevailed. Meal, wine, service quite outstanding. 23.00 hours: return to boat. Williams has acquired a rather superior Hine which crew tuck into.

Day 4

07.00 hours: leave Mew stone to port and head off towards the Bill. 12.30: crew delighted that skipper persuaded them to lunch ashore yesterday as nobody had thought about lunch. Williams' picnic gratefully received. 15.00 hours: decide to go inside of race and put into Weymouth. Crew argue about how close you can go to the Bill but passage uneventful. 16.45 hours: moored up south side of harbour just opposite the Yacht Club. Crew delighted as most, if not too, convenient to the King's Arms. 20.15 hours: across the bridge and into the Sea Cow. Dinner spent discussing plans for rest of cruise as no one mad to go straight back to Hamble. 23.00 hours: all crew on board. A record.

Day 5

07.00 hours: depart Weymouth. 07.45 hours: Williams, remembering time serving Queen and Country, checks Radio Solent to ensure boat does not become a target for some new recruit to Her Majesty's Royal Artillery. 11.00 hours: left Peveril Point well to port and are crossing Swanage Bay. 12.00 hours: round Old Harry to be greeted by a forest of masts. Find space to drop anchor and persuade crew to inflate dinghy. 13.05: hours arrive at Bankes Arms collect beer and order food. Sit on grass and talk about life. 13.06 hours: subject changes to cricket. 14.35 hours: crew in heated discussion as to whether Ian Botham or Imran Khan world's greatest all rounder. 15.15 hours: returned to boat upped anchor and set sail for Poole. 16.00 hours: past the chain ferry and moored up at Poole Harbour Yacht Club. Crew ashore to shower and look at other boats. Skipper to chandlery. 19.00 hours: crew assembled in yacht club bar and voted narrowly to call a taxi and dine in Poole. 20.00 hours: arrived at Poole Quay. Tried to secure table at Mansion House and failed. Got last table at Corkers and sat in their bar and ordered dinner. Everyone except Williams orders fish. He has steak and creates a terrible fuss when rest of party won't allow him to have a bottle of Brouilly all to himself. Back to boat 24.00 hours. Crew relented regarding Williams' Brouilly and he is now endeavouring to sing sea-shanties. Skipper steps in firmly as others are asleep and does not want to be anti-social.

Day 6

02.30 hours: crew woken by crew on nearby boat singing sea-shanties. Williams forbidden to join them. 08.15: depart for the Hamble. Uneventful sail and arrive at mooring 15.45 hours. Crew vote to return early the following morning and invite skipper for dinner at Beths. 23.30 hours: after a splendid dinner skipper handed the bill as rest of crew have forgotten their Amex cards.

GOURMET CRUISING

Cruise 3
LYMINGTON – ALDERNEY – ST MALO – LÉZARDRIEUX – GUERNSEY – LYMINGTON

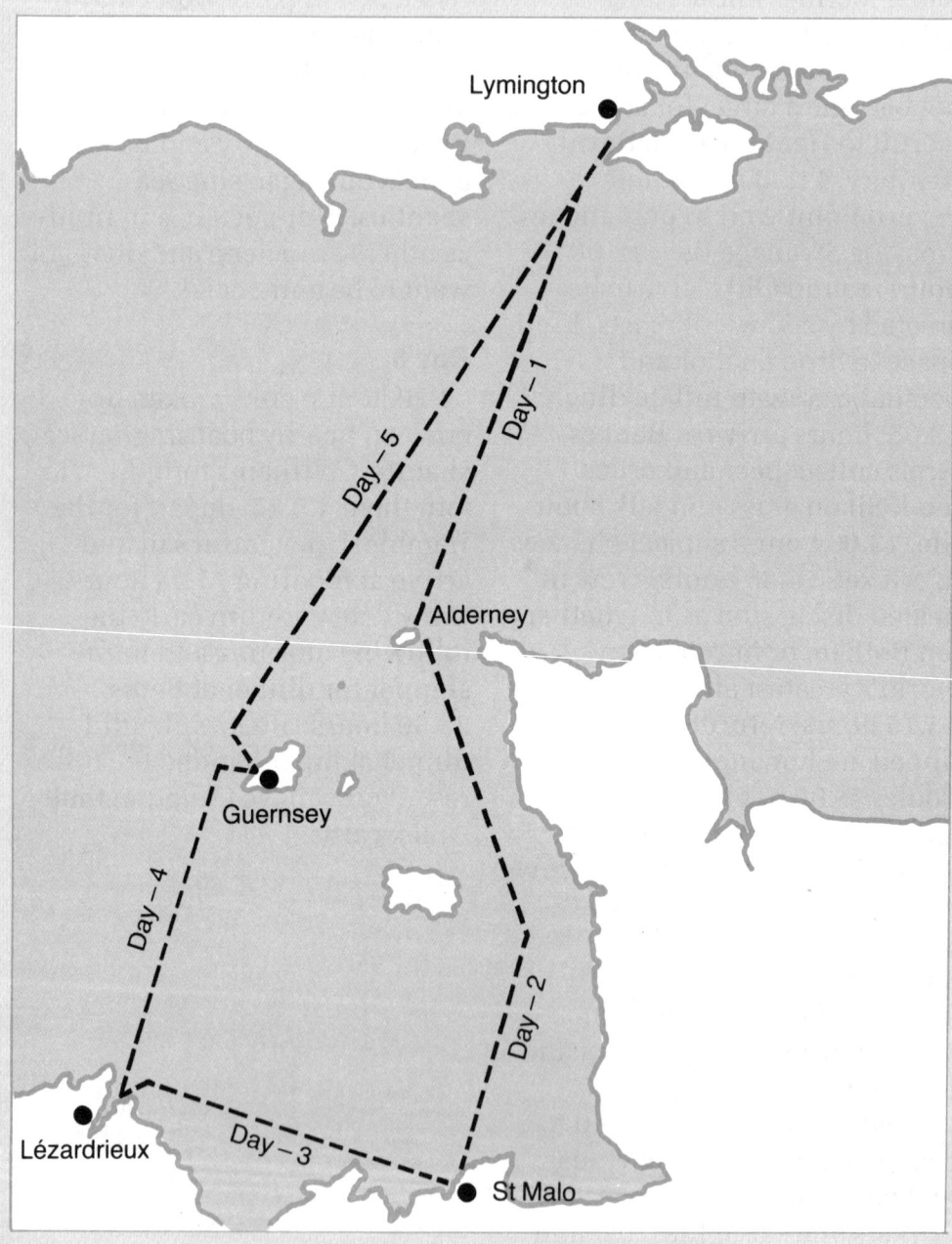

Day 1

Left Lymington 08.00 hours. The successful motor-trader on his first voyage surprises everyone by offering to make coffee. Rounded the Needles 09.00 hours. Crew all struggle into foul-weather gear. Reminded Williams that his golfing waterproofs are really not suitable. The successful motor-trader puts everyone to shame by appearing on deck looking immaculate and ready for anything the Southern Ocean might throw at him. Williams very disgruntled and retires to chart-table muttering. 12.00 hours: crew on full alert as the shipping lanes are coming up. 13.00 hours: lunch courtesy of the skipper's wife. A rather splendid steak, kidney and oyster pie. Weather fair and forecast good so skipper permits the uncorking of a bottle of Fleurie to accompany the pie. 16.00 hours: Alderney sighted on the bow. 18.15 hours: turned into Braye harbour and dropped anchor in the lee of the harbour wall. 19.00 hours: Williams calls up Mainbrayce on R/t to get a lift ashore in their water-taxi. Crew all highly amused when boatman suggests whoever had called him attends the R/t course he is running that evening.

Williams starts muttering again. Into the First and Last. Tremendous welcome and staff have some difficulty in getting crew to sit down for dinner. Celebrations continue after dinner. Boatman in no rush to take crew back to boat. 23.45: all back on board.

Day 2

08.00 hours: depart Braye Harbour and set off through the race to St Malo. The race is fortunately very friendly and strong tides put boat well on her way. 16.30 hours: wait for lock doors to gain entry to Port de Plaisance at St Malo. Beautiful mooring underneath the ramparts of St Malo. All except the successful motor-trader agree it would be much better if the busy main road did not run alongside two sides of the Port. After showers crew quickly into the town. Crew reassemble in the Place Guy la Chambre 19.30 hours. After a pleasant drink sitting outside in the square crew move towards La Duchesse Anne for dinner. The successful motor-trader states that as he is enjoying himself so much he proposes buying some champagne. Williams starts muttering about flash somebody

GOURMET CRUISING

or something which seemed most ungracious particularly as he seems perfectly prepared to enjoy a few glasses of it. Fortunately table was reserved outside and after dinner crew were able to enjoy a succession of street entertainers. Williams had to be restrained from giving a rendition of 'Rule Britannia'. 23.15 hours: crew decide to walk around the ramparts. The successful motor-trader has joined an adjacent table and is extolling the virtues of the new BMW 7 series to wealthy-looking British skipper. 24.00 hours: crew finished tour of the ramparts and see the successful motor-trader shaking hands with the wealthy-looking skipper. Williams points out that there is an empty bottle of champagne in front of them.

Day 3
09.00 hours: through the lock and sails set en route for Lézardrieux. 13.00 hours: wonderful lunch of pâté and cheese purchased the previous evening from a variety of delicatessens in St Malo. 16.00 hours: arrive at the mouth of the River Trieux. 17.00 hours: moored up at Lézardrieux. Williams reports the heads not functioning. Skipper decides to

draw lots to determine which member of crew should try to effect repairs. Skipper draws short straw and rest of crew depart for the clubhouse. Skipper establishes nothing wrong with heads and on going on deck is invited onto neighbouring boat for drinks. 19.30 hours: crew return and are dismayed to find skipper nursing a monstrous pink gin and evidently none the worse for what they clearly hoped was going to be a singularly unpleasant experience. 20.15 hours: car arrives from the Relais Brenner to take crew up to their restaurant for dinner. Dinner quite outstanding. The successful motor-trader votes his lobster as good as anything he has ever eaten. 23.45 hours: crew return to boat.

Day 4
10.00 hours: leave mooring after leisurely breakfast near the Port. Some small difficulty in declining offer to crew of pink gin from skipper of neighbouring boat. Tremendous sail, the successful motor-trader at the helm for the first time. Williams appears on deck with two life-lines on. 13.00 hours: lunch on board. 17.00 hours: arrive St Peter Port. Crew ashore for

showers. Williams has never been to Guernsey before and marvels at the charm of the town. The successful motor-trader seems to know the place very well indeed but declines to explain why. Decide to have dinner at Whistler's Bistro. Some of the crew want to spend more time looking around and the skipper experiences a little trouble trying to explain how to get there. The trick is to find the right flight of steps. 20.45: crew all assembled at the Bistro. Very busy but fortunately skipper had presence of mind to book. The table is to the left of the door which enables crew to glance at everyone who enters. Three gentlemen in dark suits come in, the successful motor-trader promptly leaps to his feet and with cries of 'What a surprise' and with a 'please excuse me for a minute' he is off to their table. 23.00 hours: set to depart, the successful motor-trader is still in deep conversation with his acquaintances. Williams starts muttering about the two bottles of empty champagne on the table. 23.45 hours: return to boat.

Day 5
Skipper up early to go to the market and spends lavishly on items for lunch. 08.45: leave St Peter Port. 13.00 hours: in the shipping lanes visibility clear. Skipper decides to delay lunch. 13.30 hours: crew take lunch in shifts. Oysters and crab receive much praise as does the cheese. 16.55 hours: St Catherine's well in view. 18.30 hours: round the Needles. 19.45 hours: return to mooring. Argument breaks out regarding customs formalities. Have been flying the yellow flag since entering the Solent. Majority of crew all for calling a taxi and heading into town. Argument resolved on arrival of two customs officers. 20.15 hours: customs officers seem to be taking their task very seriously which is causing an air of disquiet to come over the crew as a table has been reserved at New Flounders for dinner at 20.30 hours and nobody has bought a thing anyway. 20.45: customs officers now gone and crew pile into a waiting taxi. 21.00 hours: arrive at restaurant and to everyone's relief find the table still free. Williams buys champagne for the crew to celebrate the purchase of a new 7 series BMW.

GOURMET CRUISING

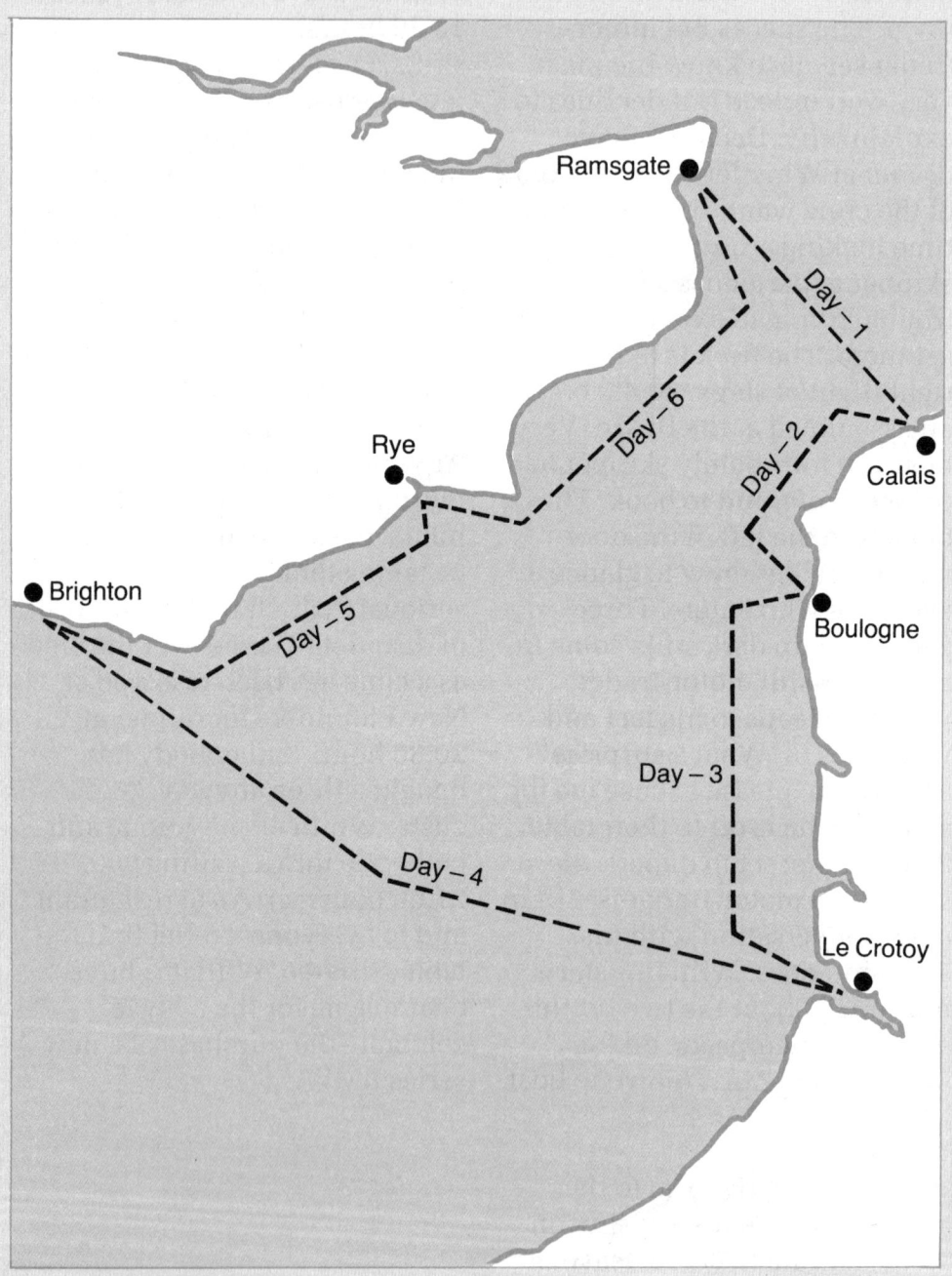

Day 1

10.00 hours: crew complete. All said how easy the journey down had been. Took note of the next Sally Line sailing and left mooring soon after the ferry at 10.45 hours. Easy crossing to Calais. Wind coming from the north-west. Lunch taken in the cockpit by all the crew as there is plenty of shipping about and the more eyes the better. A hovercraft passes us about 200 metres to port. The successful motor-trader suggests that Williams, who had been delayed by an early morning meeting in the City and is joining us in Calais, was probably on board. 17.00 hours: off Calais, motor started and the sails taken down and stowed. Skipper requests that fenders put out both sides. 17.20 hours: enter outer harbour and find luck on our side as the lock gates to the Port de Plaisance are open. 17.45 hours: moored up and crew disembark for the facilities at the clubhouse. No sign of Williams. 19.30 hours: discussion among crew as to whether to take a taxi to the Hôtel des Dunes at Blériot Plage or to walk. The successful motor-trader wants to walk as it is a nice evening and argues that the exercise will improve the appetite. Generally agreed to walk and some fifteen minutes later arrive at the hotel. Williams, who had made the dinner reservation by phone the week before, was not in the corner of the bar where we expected to find him and indeed nobody at the hotel had seen him. The bar is rather on the small side and fortunately no one else is using it. The successful motor-trader is delighted that while the restaurant is busy we appear to be the only English. The last time he had a meal here there was a party of very noisy people from the City who apparently spent most of lunch braying about their Porsches and it seems that none drove a BMW. 20.30 hours: decide to order. Vast plâteau de fruits de mer washed down with Pouilly Fumé followed by grilled sole and cheese. Crew all looking very satisfied. Coffee and *fines* arrive with Williams who totters in through the door. The successful motor-trader notes that the meeting must have been very profitable. Williams, by way of a riposte, suggests that the only way we were able to navigate to Calais was by following the ferry. 23.15: hours call for a taxi, some of the crew decide to walk back and the

GOURMET CRUISING

others order more coffee and *fines*. 24.00 hours: crew all back on board.

Day 2
08.30 hours: crew, with the exception of Williams, walk into the Place des Armes for coffee and croissants. The successful motor-trader suggests that lunch is left to him and sets off purposefully in the direction of the maison du fromage. 11.30 hours: leave Calais for Boulogne. Lunch, taken off Cap Gris- Nez and consisting of a variety of cheese aided and abetted by three bottles of Morgon, voted magnificent by the whole crew with Williams abstaining on the grounds that he had introduced the successful motor-trader to the shop in the first place and therefore the credit was really his. Arrive off Boulogne 15.45 hours and decide to spend an hour or so practising sail changes. This was followed by a man overboard drill. 18.00 hours: enter Boulogne harbour and moor up by the Quai Chanzy. Agree to meet at La Matelote at 20.15 hours, giving everybody time to smarten up particularly as the susccessful motor-trader has been talking about calling in at the casino which is almost opposite the restaurant. Williams starts muttering something about 'typical of the breed'. After a splendid meal where the crew surprisingly all chose the pâté de langoustines au beurre rosé and then half opted for turbot and the other half sweetbreads. 22.30 hours: the skipper and the successful motor-trader decide to take coffee and a digestif across at the casino. Skipper mentions that Prince Charles would have a field day addressing the RIBA if this building was ever to be copied and built in England. 23.45: hours the skipper is by now a dejected and rather wretched looking specimen having to be consoled over his losses by the successful motor-trader who is buying magnums of champagne to celebrate his winnings. The successful motor-trader stakes the skipper a 100-franc chip on the understanding that he not the skipper places the bet. Low and behold 29 comes up and good as his word the successful motor-trader passes 3,500 francs to the bemused skipper, suggesting as he did so that he tips the table 100 francs.

Day 3
01.30 hours: the champagne is finished and the skipper and the

successful motor-trader return to the mooring. Williams, who is playing bridge with the rest of the crew, seems somehow not too pleased that the gambling party had actually won and retires muttering.

Day 3
09.00 hours: crew split up and go their various ways for breakfast. Skipper impresses crew on need to reassemble at 10.30 hours as he wants to make Le Crotoy at high water which is at 19.20 hours and have the best part of three hours of tide before it turns. The successful motor-trader warmed by his triumph with lunch and on the tables offers to shop for lunch. Williams mutters something about 'I better go with him in case...'. 10.30 hours: much to the surprise of the skipper the crew are all back and the boat leaves according to schedule. 13.15 hours: a good mornings sail has put the boat a few miles over halfway to Le Crotoy and the crew take lunch. Another fine achievement, this time it is made up of various cold meats, pâté, baguettes and Brouilly to help it all on its way. 16.45 hours: off the mouth of the Somme and with a rising tide and Williams navigating have no trouble in reaching the little marina at Le Crotoy. 22.00 hours: the main reason for the trip is at hand as the crew reverently enter Chez Mado. The table was, as requested by Williams when he made the reservation, by the window in the conservatory-style front of the hotel. The views over the estuary were magnificent and the the crew decided on Kir while debating the menu. The successful motor-trader was in seldom seen state of indecision: Moules Mado, almost a legend among those who know this hotel, or oysters. After much wavering he chose the moules. The sole was universally praised and the Sancerre did not let anyone down. 23.30 hours: crew returned to the boat discussing the potential of a return visit.

Day 4
08.00 hours: depart Le Crotoy and with tide make good mileage out of the Somme estuary. Crew debate necessity of returning to Ramsgate in one run and the successful motor-trader fouls the water by stating that the Flushing Inn at Rye is having one of their gourmet evenings and that his office had on the off chance made a provisional reservation. Crew sorely tempted

GOURMET CRUISING

and eventually succumb. Flushed with success, the successful motor-trader then proposes a visit to Brighton Marina which is unanimously accepted. Williams sets course for Brighton and gives an ETA of 19.00 hours. The successful motor-trader promptly organises a raffle amongst the crew and draws ETA 18.00 hours. Immediately requests the helm and orders the genny down and the spinnaker up. Williams refuses to navigate. Skipper tries to intervene and is told by the successful motor-trader to prepare lunch 'for a change'. Lunch voted worst of the trip by the crew and there is muted talk about making the successful motor-trader skipper for the next trip. Skipper is forced to remind the crew that it is after all his boat. The successful motor-trader counters by saying that he is thinking of purchasing one for himself and most of the crew with the exception of Williams seem to think that to be a very good idea. Skipper suddenly realises how lonely life at the top can be, particularly as the concept of cruising with Williams as the only crew is hard to take on board. 18.00 hours arrive Brighton Marina.

The successful motor-trader wins the sweepstake. Williams commences muttering about 'you cannot trust these people'. The skipper calls up the Harbour Master and is advised that there is a mooring available alongside the visitor's pontoons. 18.30 hours: Customs Officers arrive and on observing the assembled crew equally quickly depart. 19.00 hours: crew ashore to make use of the excellent facilities. Williams surprised at the scale of the works taking place. Crew decide to take a taxi into the town to wander around The Lanes for a while before returning to Kemptown for dinner at La Marinade. Over dinner the successful motor-trader drops another bombshell. Tomorrow, he announces, there is racing at Brighton and a friend of his is saddling a certain winner in the 2.30. It takes all the skipper's power of command to explain to the crew that there is no way they can be at Brighton Races and sail to Rye for dinner. Fortunately a compromise is reached whereby the crew will all back the horse, the successful motor-trader will R/T his bookmaker and departure is set for 09.00 hours.

Day 5

09.00 hours: much to the skipper's surprise the crew cast off and set sail for Rye. 17.00 hours: off Rye Harbour and Williams calls up the Harbourmaster to enquire if there is a mooring, advised that there was one available on the piles. Williams also enquires the name of the winner in the 2.30 at Brighton and crew break into cheers on learning that the successful motor-trader's friend had saddled the winner at 9–1. 18.00 hours: safely moored. Crew discuss the best course of action as Rye Harbour is quite a distance from Rye town itself. Williams suggests taking the dinghy but skipper agrees with those who feel that a 2-mile run in the dinghy late at night on a falling tide will be asking for trouble. The successful motor-trader has never been to Rye before and wants to have a look around so he and two other crew take a taxi early. 20.00 hours: skipper and rest of crew take a taxi to the Flushing Inn. Memorable evening; theme was Provence. Williams now delighted that there is no dinghy to take back. 23.45 hours: crew take taxis back to Rye Harbour. The successful motor-trader has enjoyed himself so much that he offers to make coffee.

Day 6

01.15 hours: Crew retire. 09.30 hours: after a leisurely breakfast depart Rye Harbour. 17.00 hours: arrive Ramsgate. Some of crew make a hasty departure including Williams who has another early meeting in the City. The skipper and the successful motor-trader decide to leave early the following day and plan on an early meal at the nearby Crab and Oyster bar. 22.00 hours: back on board after a very adequate supper.

INTRODUCTION TO COMMENTS

Every care has gone into the preparation of this guide, however situations do change, restaurants are sold, pubs refurbished and new facilities come on stream. The purpose of these last few pages is to give you the opportunity to comment on the facilities listed, make suggestions and provide us with information that hopefully will make the next edition even better.

While you are very welcome to comment on any aspect of the guide, we are particularly interested in restaurants where your experience in any way differs from ours, and also restaurants you like and feel deserving of a mention in the guide.

Robin Knox-Johnston will judge the reports received and the entry that in his opinion is the one we must include in the next guide will win its author a bottle of Champagne Mumm.

YOUR COMMENTS

NAME

ADDRESS

POST CODE

NAME OF YACHT

SAILING FROM

SAILING TO

NAME OF HARBOUR

DATE VISITED

COMMENTS
(if restaurant please describe dishes and wines selected and give an indication of cost).

YOUR COMMENTS cont.

Please send to:

WHITE'S GUIDES LTD.
Island House, Moor Road,
Chesham, Bucks HP5 1NZ.

YOUR COMMENTS

NAME

ADDRESS

POST CODE

NAME OF YACHT

SAILING FROM

SAILING TO

NAME OF HARBOUR

DATE VISITED

COMMENTS
(if restaurant please describe dishes and wines selected and give an indication of cost).

YOUR COMMENTS cont.

Please send to:

WHITE'S GUIDES LTD.
Island House, Moor Road,
Chesham, Bucks HP5 1NZ.

YOUR COMMENTS

NAME

ADDRESS

POST CODE

NAME OF YACHT

SAILING FROM

SAILING TO

NAME OF HARBOUR

DATE VISITED

COMMENTS
(if restaurant please describe dishes and wines selected and give an indication of cost).

YOUR COMMENTS cont.

Please send to:

WHITE'S GUIDES LTD.
Island House, Moor Road,
Chesham, Bucks HP5 1NZ.

YOUR COMMENTS

NAME

ADDRESS

POST CODE

NAME OF YACHT

SAILING FROM

SAILING TO

NAME OF HARBOUR

DATE VISITED

COMMENTS
(if restaurant please describe dishes and wines selected and give an indication of cost).

YOUR COMMENTS cont.

Please send to:

WHITE'S GUIDES LTD.
Island House, Moor Road,
Chesham, Bucks HP5 1NZ.

YOUR COMMENTS

NAME

ADDRESS

POST CODE

NAME OF YACHT

SAILING FROM

SAILING TO

NAME OF HARBOUR

DATE VISITED

COMMENTS
(if restaurant please describe dishes and wines selected and give an indication of cost).

YOUR COMMENTS cont.

Please send to:

WHITE'S GUIDES LTD.
Island House, Moor Road,
Chesham, Bucks HP5 1NZ.

YOUR COMMENTS

NAME

ADDRESS

POST CODE

NAME OF YACHT

SAILING FROM

SAILING TO

NAME OF HARBOUR

DATE VISITED

COMMENTS
(if restaurant please describe dishes and wines selected and give an indication of cost).

YOUR COMMENTS cont.

Please send to:

WHITE'S GUIDES LTD.
Island House, Moor Road,
Chesham, Bucks HP5 1NZ.

YOUR COMMENTS

NAME

ADDRESS

POST CODE

NAME OF YACHT

SAILING FROM

SAILING TO

NAME OF HARBOUR

DATE VISITED

COMMENTS
(if restaurant please describe dishes and wines selected and give an indication of cost).

YOUR COMMENTS cont.

Please send to:

WHITE'S GUIDES LTD.
Island House, Moor Road,
Chesham, Bucks HP5 1NZ.

YOUR COMMENTS

NAME

ADDRESS

POST CODE

NAME OF YACHT

SAILING FROM

SAILING TO

NAME OF HARBOUR

DATE VISITED

COMMENTS
(if restaurant please describe dishes and wines selected and give an indication of cost).

YOUR COMMENTS cont.

Please send to:

WHITE'S GUIDES LTD.
Island House, Moor Road,
Chesham, Bucks HP5 1NZ.

YOUR COMMENTS

NAME

ADDRESS

POST CODE

NAME OF YACHT

SAILING FROM

SAILING TO

NAME OF HARBOUR

DATE VISITED

COMMENTS
(if restaurant please describe dishes and wines selected and give an indication of cost).

YOUR COMMENTS cont.

Please send to:

WHITE'S GUIDES LTD.
Island House, Moor Road,
Chesham, Bucks HP5 1NZ.

YOUR COMMENTS

NAME

ADDRESS

POST CODE

NAME OF YACHT

SAILING FROM

SAILING TO

NAME OF HARBOUR

DATE VISITED

COMMENTS
(if restaurant please describe dishes and wines selected and give an indication of cost).

YOUR COMMENTS cont.

Please send to:

WHITE'S GUIDES LTD.
Island House, Moor Road,
Chesham, Bucks HP5 1NZ.

YOUR COMMENTS

NAME

ADDRESS

POST CODE

NAME OF YACHT

SAILING FROM

SAILING TO

NAME OF HARBOUR

DATE VISITED

COMMENTS
(if restaurant please describe dishes and wines selected and give an indication of cost).

YOUR COMMENTS cont.

Please send to:

WHITE'S GUIDES LTD.
Island House, Moor Road,
Chesham, Bucks HP5 1NZ.

YOUR COMMENTS

NAME

ADDRESS

POST CODE

NAME OF YACHT

SAILING FROM

SAILING TO

NAME OF HARBOUR

DATE VISITED

COMMENTS
(if restaurant please describe dishes and wines selected and give an indication of cost).

YOUR COMMENTS cont.

Please send to:

WHITE'S GUIDES LTD.
Island House, Moor Road,
Chesham, Bucks HP5 1NZ.

GENERAL INDEX

A

Agamemnon 94
Alabaster Coast 156
Alderney 242-45, 294,
    322-23, 342-45
    Race 242
Ancasta Marine 96
Arromanches 180
Arun Yacht Club 112

B

Barfleur 190-92
Bart, Jean 138
Bassin Vauban 203
Bassurelle Light V 293
Bay of St Brieuc 212
Bayards Cove 55
Beaucette 246, 247
Beaulieu Palace House 94
Beaulieu River 94-95
Beaumont, Michael 251
Belon, River 271
Bembridge 292
Bergues 267
Berry Head 292, 339
Bibette Point 242-43
Binic 212
Birdham 106
    Pool 106
Blake, Admiral 254
La Blanche Nef 190
Blériot Plage 143, 347
Bosham 106
Boudin, Eugène 169
Boudin Museum 169
Boulogne 146-48, 293,
    324-25, 332-33, 346-51
Bounty 29

Bournemouth 292
Bray 269
Braye Harbour 242, 243,
    343
Bresle, River 156
Brest 234-35, 330-31
Brighton 113, 114-17,
    324-25, 328-29, 346-51
    Marina 116, 292
Britannia Royal Naval
    College 54-55
Brittany 270-73
Brixham 58-60
    Yacht Club 59
Broadstairs 132
Bryher 254, 264
Bucklers Hard 94
    Yacht Harbour 94
Bursledon 102-103
Byron, Lord 112

C

Caen 269
Canal 176
Calais 142-44, 293, 324-25,
    332-33, 346-51
    Main 293
Camper & Nicholson
    Marina 104
Cancale 200-201, 271,
    330-31
Canche, River 150
Cap d'Alprech Light 293
Cap d'Antifer Light 293
Cap d'Erquy 210
Cap Fréhel Light 294
Cap Gris Nez 146, 348
Cap St-Matthieu 230
Carentan 184-85, 332-33
Carrick Roads 24, 28, 336
Carteret 196, 330-31

Carteret, Helier de 250-51
Cartier, Jacques 203
Casquets Light 294
Channel Distance Charts
    322-33
The Channel Islands
    236-51
Channel Light V 294
Chateaubriand 203
Chenal du Four 232
Cherbourg 187, 192-94,
    293, 322-23, 324-25,
    330-31
    W Fort Light 293
Chichester 106-107, 328-29
Chichester, Sir Francis 44
Chichester Bar Beacon 292
Chichester Yacht Basin,
    Birdham 106
Christchurch 84-85
Clisson 271
Club Nautique, Binic 212
Cobbs Quay 81
Courseulles 178-79
Cowes 96-97, 328-29, 339
    to Dinard race 206
Creux Harbour 250

D

Dart, River 54, 55
Dart Harbour and
    Navigation Authority 55
Dart Marina 55, 340
Darthaven Marina 55
Dartmouth 54-57, 322-23,
    326-27, 338-41
Deauville 172-74, 324-25,
    332-33
Derrible Bay 250
Devonport 44
Dickens, Charles 104, 126

GENERAL INDEX Continued

L

L'Aber-Wrac'h 232-33, 330-31
La Corbière 294
La Grande Greve 250
Landivisiau 294
Langtry, Lillie 239
Lannion 294
Lanvéoc 294
Le Bourg 218
Le Crotoy 152-53, 332-33, 346-51
Le Guildo 208
Le Havre 156,166-67, 269, 293, 332-33
   Lanby 293
Le Touquet 150-51, 293
Le Tréport 156-57, 293
Lee-on-Solent 292
Lézardrieux 220-21, 330-31, 342-45
Littlehampton 112-13
Lizard Light 292
Lle Vierge Light 294
Looe 42-43
Loti, Pierre 216
Lower Town 262
Lulworth Cove 74-75
Lydd 292
Lyme Regis 68-69
Lymington 86-88, 90, 328-29, 342-45
   Marina 87
   Yacht Haven 87

M

Marazion 19
Margate 132
Mary Rose 104

Maseline Harbour 250
Mayflower 44, 45
Mayflower Marina 45
Meeching 118
Melcombe Regis 70
Meteorological Glossary 288-91
Mevagissey 34-35, 326-27
Mew Stone 340
Minihy 222
Monet, Claude 169
Monmouth, Duke of 68
Mont Orgueil Castle 241
Mont St Michel 198, 200
Moody Marina, Swanwick 102
Morlaix 226-28
Moulin Blanc 234-35
Mousehole 12-13, 326-27
Mulberry Harbour 180
Mylor 28-29

N

Nautical Glossary 288-91
Needles 85, 90, 343, 345
Nelson, Admiral Horatio 94, 102, 104
New Grimsby 254
New Romney 122
Newhaven 118-20, 292, 328-29
   Marina 119
Newlyn 12, 14-15
Newton Ferrers 48-49, 326-27
Nord 266-67
Normandy 268-69
North Foreland Light 293
Northney Marina 108

O

Ocean Village Marina 99
Octeville 293
Old Harry 341
Ouessant SW 294
Ouistreham 176-77, 332-33
Ouse, River 118

P

Paimpol 216-17
Pandora, HMS 28-29
Paris Plage 293
Pas-de-Calais 266-67
Peninnis Head 257
Penlee Point 292
Penryn River 28
Penzance 16-19, 322-23, 326-27
   Heliport 292
Perros-Guirec 224-25, 330-31
Peveril Point 341
Plage de Pen-Guen 208
Plymouth 44-47, 292, 326-27, 335-37
Pointe d'Ailly Light 293
Pointe de Barfleur 190
   Light 293
Pointe de Créac'h Light 294
Pointe de Ver Light 293
Pointe St Mathieu Light 294
Polperro 40-41
Polruan 37, 38
Pont ar Prat 218
Pontrieux 220
Poole 80-83, 328-29, 341
Poole Harbour 292
   Yacht Club, 81, 341

GENERAL INDEX Continued

PUBS AND RESTAURANTS